CALIFORNIA
The Golden Shore by the Sundown Sea

W.H. HUTCHINSON

REVISED EDITION

Star

PUBLISHING COMPANY

Star

PUBLISHING COMPANY
P.O. BOX 68
BELMONT, CALIFORNIA 94002

Typesetting – M. Anderson
Graphics – Douglas Hurd

Copyright © 1984 by W.H. Hutchinson

First Edition Copyright © 1980 by W.H. Hutchinson

Printed in the United States of America

ISBN: 0-89863-02-075-4 (Paperback)
0-89863-02-076-2 (Hardcover)

TABLE OF CONTENTS

AIDS TO UNDERSTANDING

For

Michael Harrison
Un caballero muy valiente

ACKNOWLEDGEMENTS

Many individuals over many years have sought to sharpen the pot metal of my perceptions concerning California. In this regard, I have especial obligations to Professors Clarence F. McIntosh, California State University, Chico, and Gerald T. White, University of California, Irvine.

It is seemly to express my indebtedness to the work of Professors L. T. Wallace and B. Delworth Gardner, University of California, Davis-Berkeley, and to that of the late John E. Skinner, California Department of Fish and Game. Dorothy Mortensen and Ross Wurm, Modesto and Henry Schacht, San Francisco, enabled me to cope with California agriculture, while William "Bill" Rintoul, Bakersfield and Gabrielle Hall, San Francisco, provided needed information on the state's petroleum industry. Frank A. Hall, Stockton; Jacqueline and JoEllen Hall, Chico, and Mary Alice Hubbard, Sacramento, did research chores that aided my under-standings of various topics. Congressman Harold T. "Bizz" Johnson and State Senator Ray Johnson and their staffs helped a lame dog over several high stiles, so to speak. Frederick Waterhouse, Delta Steamship Lines, and Charles Regal, Matson Navigation Co. brought me up to date on developments offshore since I "swallowed the anchor" many years ago.

In illustrative matters I was helped most generously by Suzanne Gallup, The Bancroft Library; Mark Fox, Calif. Historical Society, Los Angeles; Elaine Gilleran, History Room, Wells Fargo Bank, San Francisco; Isabel Roper, Louisiana-Pacific Corp., Portland, Or.; Robert A. Weinstein, Los Angeles; Karl Kortum, National Maritime Museum at San Francisco; Kenneth I. Pettit and the staff of the California Room, State Library, Sacramento; and Ronald J. Fahl, Forest History Society, Santa Cruz. Gordon S. Metroka prepared the maps and neither he nor any of those named above are responsible for the errors of omission, commission and interpretation that may appear hereinafter.

Retirement from full time teaching provided the time to make this book, while my red-haired friend of forty years made it possible.

W. H. Hutchinson
Professor Emeritus of History

California State University, Chico
January 30, 1984

CHAPTER ONE

MYTHIC ISLAND, STATE OF MIND

"On the right hand of the Indies . . . very close to the Earthly Paradise" was the geographical location of the mythical island of California created by Garci Ordonez de Montalvo in his romantic confection, *Las Sergas de Esplandian*, published in Seville about 1510.

At this time, Cortes had not conquered Mexico, nor had anyone in Europe any accurate idea of what lay north, south or west beyond unnamed Cape Horn. Thus Senor Montalvo had no geographical basis from which to extract the name "California," and inasmuch as the setting of his romance was in the eastern Mediterranean countries, the name had no derivation that can be traced to the state which now bears it.

Montalvo peopled his island with black Amazons, ruled by a Queen Calafia. He studded it with griffins, creatures which were half-eagle, half-lion; and he filled it to overflowing with pearls, and precious metals, and all the wonders that an impecunious soldier-turned-author could imagine. In the light of subsequent historical developments, Montalvo was a much better prophet than novelist.

The name "California" was given by Cortes and his men to the

California as an island, from a map of North America by Henricus Hondius, 1642.
— *Courtesy The Bancroft Library*

land that lay to the west of Mexico across the Gulf of California (Sea of Cortes), or what we know today as Baja California. In the wake of the first Spanish voyages up the unknown coast from Mexico, the name became applied to all of Spain's territorial claims from Cape Lan Lucas (Baja) into the shrouding Alaskan mists. After Spain's settlement at San Diego, the name was split into "Alta California" and "Baja California" to reflect the two administrative provinces of Spain into which the original California was divided.

Under the Mexican regime, the name "Alta California" encompassed generally the land mass between the Continental Divide and the Pacific Ocean between 42° north latitude — the state's present northern boundary — and Mexico proper. Thus, it included the present states of California, Nevada, Utah and Arizona, plus parts of Wyoming, Colorado, and New Mexico. With the foregoing in mind, it should be remembered that hereafter the name "California" refers only to the present area of the state, unless specifically noted otherwise.

California today totals 158,693 square miles or 101,563,500 acres, making it the third largest state in the nation. Its smallest county in area is San Francisco while its largest county, San Bernardino, is equal to the combined areas of New Hampshire, Vermont, and Rhode Island. Its geographical diversity spans ten degrees of latitude, and its coastline meanders along the Pacific seaboard for 1,264 miles, a distance equal to that covered along the Atlantic Coast by the twelve states from the rock-bound shores of Maine to the peanut farms of Georgia. The 100-mile stretch of this coast from Pt. Ano Nuevo north to Bodega Bay may well be the major shark-attack zone in the world and such attacks have increased greatly since 1974. This expanse of coastline facilitated smuggling during the Hispanic period and eased the task of rum-running during Prohibition. It has great potential, as well, for California's future. The Coastal Zone Conservation Commission protects, some say over-protects, against developmental damage to this asset through its power to overrule the zoning laws of local governments.

Within this land mass, the population virtually has doubled every twenty years since the first federal census of 1850, which lacked population figures for its major urban center, San Francisco, due to destruction by fire. A state-conducted census in 1852, showing a population of 264,435 may be regarded as the first accurate tally of humanity in the American period. The state's population on July 1, 1982 was 24,000,000$^{\pm}$, making it the most populous state in the nation, and the Department of Finance projects a population of about 27,905,000 in the year 1990. Alpine County has the lowest population today, 1,100, which represents a 60% increase since 1970, while Los Angeles County is the largest with more than 7,477,657. It and its satellite counties expect to increase by more than 3,000,000 by 2000. The state growth since 1850 has been caused by the second largest *voluntary* migration in the history of all mankind, being exceeded only by the sustained emigration from Europe to the United States between 1815-1914. Even today, with procreation outstripping immigration as the source of the state's growth, more than one-third of its residents have been born elsewhere. This dramatic demonstration of the basic American freedom of personal mobility is continued within the state, especially in its urban centers where, in Richard G. Lillard's pungent phrase, "spinsters move as often as call girls."

California Street, April 18, 1906. — *Photo by W.E. Worden*
— Courtesy History Room, Wells Fargo Bank

This mass movement of people to California has come about because of a fundamental human characteristic. So long as there is, or people think that there is, greater personal opportunity elsewhere, there will be a movement towards that greater opportunity, and this human movement is as inevitable as water seeking its own level. It has been said of the United States that for the first time in mankind's recorded history, a huge population is concerned not with the problem of wresting a bare living from their environment but with the problem of deciding what kind of a life they want to live. If this be true of the nation as a whole, it is aggravated and accentuated in California, which has the strongest economy in the nation in terms of people working, their income level, and their general living standards. California has an annual gross product exceeding *two hundred billions* of dollars, which places it among the *top ten business nations of the world*. This makes it understandable why recent governors at times have acted as though they were the head of a truly sovereign nation and regarded Washington, D.C. as if it were the capital of a misguided and backward foreign country. In this they reflect the notion of an independent Pacific Republic which has flickered in and out of California's consciousness since the Gold Rush.

California's remarkable ability to sustain an ever-accelerating growth since 1849 has been made possible through technological utilization of a most bounteous natural resource base. The various segments of this base have been developed in a sequence, which gives an illusion of design to what was more likely historical happenstance. As a result California's growth has been a chain reaction in which factors acting upon one another do not break sharply into clean compartments but interweave and interact. Until the turn of the century at least, this interaction gave California a self-generating and self-contained accumulation of surplus capital that made it unnecessary to seek outside financing for the state's continuing development and growth. In and of itself, this factor separated California from the rest of the trans-Missouri states and laid substantial foundations to support the "state of mind" that is an integral part of the state's inheritance from the past.

California always has been deficient in the major components of the Industrial Age — coal and iron. Even today, the huge Fontana steel mill depends upon coal imported from New Mexico. Too, California is as yet lacking in the wonder element of the twentieth century — uranium. Had she had those things, the imaginary riches of Senor Montalvo's mythical island would seem even more pallid by comparison than they do.

California's climate, even when it becomes unusual enough to be classed as *weather*, has been of incalculable direct and indirect value to the state's sustained growth. From immigrants to irrigation, from citrus fruits to cinema, from astronomical observatories to space-age hardware, climate has been inseparable from growth, and water is the key to California's future.

In John W. Caughey's words, "Gold is the Cornerstone" of California's growth. It provided the initial thrust of human energy that overcame a millennia-long inertia, and it vitally affected our national history as well.

Agriculture may seem inseparable from the climate. But its role as a bulwark of the state's commerce and industry, coupled with the saga of its transition from post-Gold Rush days to the present, warrant its separation from the climate that has made it possible.

California's timber stands gave the state a self-contained supply of basic building material that was vital to the Gold Rush and to initial urban development. Forests today yield tremendous returns from the chemical utilization of wood fibers, and the state's timberlands — private, state, and federal — are vital to watershed protection and recreational facilities.

The "black gold" of petroleum gave California a self-contained basic energy source that was expanded immeasurably by the utilization of natural gas. It was particularly important to the industrial growth of Southern

A Sierra stream on its way to the Great Valley it brings to productive life.
— *Courtesy Pacific Gas & Electric Co.*

California, which lacked the hydro-electric energy of Northern California; and this growth was vital to that section's rise to dominance in the state's affairs today.

The state was blessed with one of the world's few major sources of quicksilver, a matter of great importance to the early mining phases. The state also is secure in a tremendous supply of cement and silicates, while clays, and borates, and building aggregates, and rare earth compounds augment its arsenal of industrial minerals, including "kitty litter."

Silver, too, belongs in the California roster of resources because of the Comstock Lode. While physically within the political boundaries of Nevada, the Comstock belonged economically to California for its productive life, and it gave the state a renewed source of surplus investment capital as the impact of the Gold Rush waned. Economic control of the Comstock had political overtones of such magnitude that it was said for many years that California was the one state possessed of four United States Senators, two of whom just happened to maintain their residences in Nevada, converting it to the largest "rotten borough" known to history.

The major resources may be categorized simply as white gold, yellow gold, green gold, and black gold, with the Comstock weaving a silver thread among their twisting strands. These treasures were present for millions of years before the technological level of the mid-nineteenth century began to unlock them. They were created by the slow evolving of the California landscape — a landscape whose features strongly affect contemporary life in the state. The story of California begins with the formation of its physical features.

Steam from Sonoma County's geysers is used to generate electricity for the conurbation north of San Francisco Bay.   — *Courtesy Pacific Gas & Electric Co.*

In this age of supersonic intrusions upon our nearest galactic neighbors and of preoccupation with the superficial in our daily lives, we take the landforms around us for granted or, far worse, for annoyances. Our short-term successes in tinkering with our physical environment have given us the dangerous belief that we control Nature. Yet for all our technological triumphs, California remains firmly influenced by certain physical factors which we have ameliorated but which we do not as yet control and are not likely to in man's foreseeable future.

Perhaps 60,000,000 years ago, what is now the Sierra Nevada consisted of a corrugation of troughs and basins between elevated ridges, whose tops had been so badly eroded that they were almost inconspicuous. The Pacific Ocean lapped against the western base of this massif, and the ridge crests were so low that they did not squeeze dry the moisture-laden prevailing westerly winds as they swept inland in the immemorial pattern that still governs California's rainfall. Thus, oceanic moisture was carried several hundred miles inland, permitting luxuriant vegetation in what are now the arid

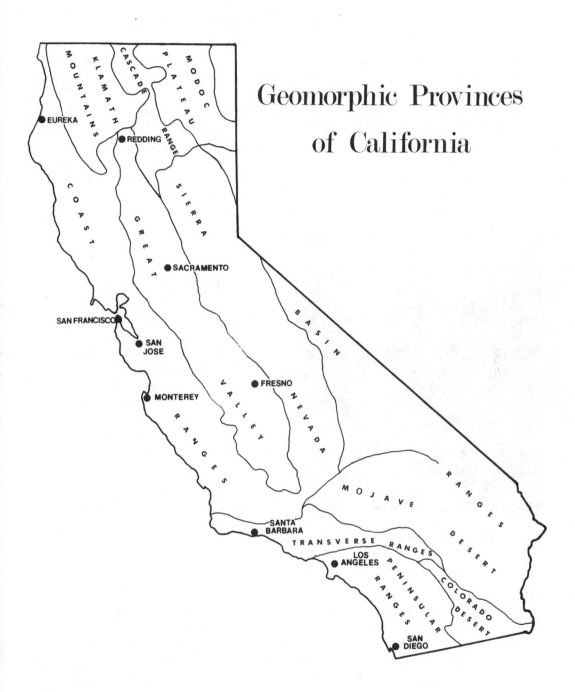

Geomorphic Provinces of California

EUREKA

REDDING

SACRAMENTO

SAN FRANCISCO

SAN JOSE

MONTEREY

FRESNO

SANTA BARBARA

LOS ANGELES

SAN DIEGO

KLAMATH MOUNTAINS

CASCADE RANGE

MODOC PLATEAU

COAST

GREAT

SIERRA

VALLEY

RANGES

BASIN

NEVADA

MOJAVE

RANGES

DESERT

TRANSVERSE RANGES

PENINSULAR

RANGES

COLORADO

DESERT

lands of Nevada. In the Diablo Range, above the western San Joaquin Valley, the remains of a giant sea lizard, twenty-five feet long, have been found; as well as a dog-sized horse and fragments of a duck-billed dinosaur.

During Miocene time, perhaps 16,000,000 years past, the Sierra Nevada was upthrust enough, say to two thousand feet, that it cut off the moisture-laden winds moving inland (the "rain shadow" effect) and began the transition of the Great Basin into aridity. In early Pleistocene time, say 1,500,000 years past, very marked earth movements took place, which created Lake Tahoe, the third deepest lake in North America, only Crater Lake in Oregon and Great Slave Lake in Canada being deeper. About 800,000 years ago, the "Range of Light" assumed the basic shape it has today. Among other dramatic charms, it offers the most magnificent example of "fault block" mountains in the nation, as seen vividly from Owens Valley, and another example of "fault block" construction is the Warner Range in Modoc County.

San Francisco's Union Street in 1906. The bountiful land is also earthquake country.
— *The Bancroft Library*

Geologic convulsions still continue, with some 5,000 earth shocks occurring yearly. These seldom are heeded by ordinary people until some major ripple along the earth's crust compels a smashed-crockery awareness. Since 1900 almost 4,000 *tremblors* registering higher than 4.0 on the Richter scale have been charted on the map of California. The clusters of epicenters start in the coastal waters off Eureka and range down to El Centro in the Imperial Valley. Linking them like a run in pantyhose is the San Andreas Fault, which acts almost as the spinal column for the other major faults — Hayward, Garlock, San Jacinto. The comparatively recent science of plate tectonics explains the existence of these faults as the movement of gigantic land masses called "plates."

The Pacific Plate that affects California is continuously being formed out of the earth's core at a rift in the ocean floor south of Baja California. This plate carries little dry land, except a sliver of both Baja California and our state, and this plate grinds slowly northwards along the line of the San Andreas fault, which marks the western edge of the North American Plate. The great San Francisco earth quake of 1906 occurred when the two plates, which had been held together by friction overlong, suddenly slipped and moved as much as twenty feet past one another in a flash of time, to cause

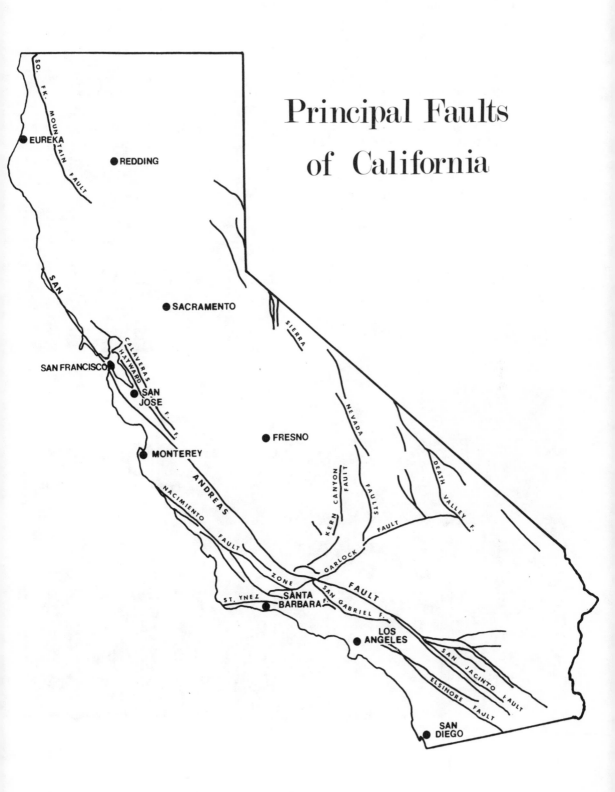

Principal Faults
of California

SO. FK. MOUNTAIN FAULT

● EUREKA

● REDDING

SAN

● SACRAMENTO

SIERRA

CALAVERAS
HAYWARD
SAN FRANCISCO ●

● SAN
JOSE

F.

F.

NEVADA

● FRESNO

● MONTEREY

ANDREAS

NACIMIENTO FAULT

KERN CANYON FAULT

FAULTS

DEATH VALLEY F.

FAULT

GARLOCK

ZONE

FAULT

ST. YNEZ

SANTA
BARBARA F.

SAN GABRIEL F.

● LOS
ANGELES

SAN JACINTO FAULT

ELSINORE FAULT

● SAN
DIEGO

the worst municipal disaster in our history. Geologic time is hard for impatient humans to appreciate, but the movement of the Pacific Plate will bring Los Angeles, which is on it, abreast of San Francisco, which is on the North American Plate, in about ten million years. In about fifty million years, California west of the San Andreas Fault will secede from the state and head for Alaska. The movement of the earth is charted continuously in Hollister, which literally is wired for earthquake study, and the slippage there is about one-half inch per year. Whenever the instruments show an increase in this rate, scientists anticipate a shock of some magnitude as the tensions between the plates are released.

Looking down Post Street. Crocker Building on right.   *— Photo by W.E. Warden*
— Courtesy History Room, Wells Fargo Bank

The author experienced the 1933 temblor that disintegrated buildings in Compton.
— Courtesy The Bancroft Library

Volcanism was prevalent in latter Pleistocene time, the period in which we live today, and the geysers of Sonoma and Lake Counties are a legacy from this fiery period. The geothermal potential of the geysers already has been tapped for their natural dry steam, which is used to generate enough electricity for a city of 900,000, which would require 10,000,000 barrels of oil to replace. Additional construction by Pacific Gas & Electric Company, the Northern California Power Agency, and the state Department of Water Resources will add more than 500 Mew of electricity for a saving of another 5,500,000 barrels of oil. Such oil savings are a matter of great importance in these oil-dominated days and will do much to reduce the nation's unfavorable balance of foreign trade which stems largely from oil imports. Inasmuch as we use Mew to stand for megawatt, it seems proper to define a megawatt as "A measure of power of one million *watts*, which is equal to one million *volts* driving one million *amperes* of current, or enough to meet the energy needs of 500 households." Additional geothermal generation of electricity is under construction at Heber in the Imperial Valley. This project involves pumping hot brine up from 2,000 to 10,000 feet below the surface and then "flashing" it into steam with which to generate electricity. This plan when finished will supply enough "juice" for a city of 45,000 at a saving of 556,000 barrels of oil per year. The City of Susanville, Lassen County, also has plans to use hot, sub-surface water for its municipal buildings and local residences which already have formed a Mutual Energy District. Very optimistic projections suggest that geothermal energy in its several forms could provide 25% of the state's total energy needs within the foreseeable future.

Mt. Lassen "blows its top" in 1914. — *Courtesy Dr. Norris Bleyhl.*

A spiritually refreshing legacy from volcanism is the jumbled mountain mass known to the Maidu tribelets as *the-long-high-mountain-that-was-broken-off*, which we know as Lassen Peak. Until Mt. St. Helens erupted in Washington on March 27, 1980, it was the most recently active volcano in the forty-eight contiguous states. The vast lava flows of northeastern California, including the Lava Beds National Monument, where Kientepoos (Captain Jack) and his Modoc band made their last stand, bear witness to its activity down the tiered millennia of time. On the east side of the Sierra, the Mammoth Lakes lie inside the huge caldera called Long Valley, which was created some 700,000 years ago by a volcanic eruption perhaps more powerful than any the earth has witnessed since.

Lassen is the southernmost peak of the Cascade Range, not the northernmost peak of the Sierra Nevada, and its neighbor in the Cascade chain is Mount Shasta, which at 14,161 feet above sea level, is only 335 feet lower than Mount Whitney. "Lonely as God and white as a winter moon," wrote Joaquin Miller, "Mount Shasta starts up sudden and solitary from the heart of the great black forests of Northern California." Both Lassen Peak and Mount Shasta are reminders of California's place in the "Pacific Ring of Fire," that vast, horseshoe-shaped arc that extends from New Zealand to Japan and thence to Alaska, whence it stretches down the length of the Pacific Coast to Cape Horn.

Pleistocene time has been dubbed "one of the most remarkable interludes in earth's history," and it includes another remarkable shaper of the California landscape in the glacial stages it encompassed. Basically, there were four glacial and interglacial stages, perhaps but three in California, and they began about one million years before the present. Our primary concern here is the last glacial stage, which began about 100,000 years ago and which had two main periods: the first one being its culmination and arrest about 55,000 years ago, and the second being the start of the last main ice retreat, about 30,000 years later.

Between these periods, the level of the world's seas was reduced as much as 300 feet; there was a land bridge, probably, across the Bering Strait between Asia and North America, and San Francisco Bay virtually was a dry lake. Also between these periods, Southern California had truly different flora and fauna than have been known in historic time. The bones of extinct animals that then roamed along today's Los Angeles' Wilshire Boulevard have been recovered from the La Brea Tar Pits. Other specimens of similar animals — the dire wolf and giant jaguar among them — have been retrieved from a "dig" near Maricopa and have been dated as belonging almost 14,000 years before the present. The present physical features of Yosemite Valley and of King's Canyon are results of the forces of the last glacial movement. The grandeur of these natural features so captivated "John of the Mountains" Muir that he became the primary force in persuading Congress to establish Yosemite National Park and in organizing the Sierra Club (1892) to be the

The cathedral-columned redwoods give meaning to the saying that "The groves were God's first temples." — *Gabriel Moulin, courtesy Forest History Society*

watchdog over the environment of the whole Sierra Nevada chain.

Parenthetically, it should be noted that there has been a substantial warming of the earth's surface since 1970. This is due to increasing the carbon dioxide in the earth's atmosphere which traps the heat waves from the earth to create a "greenhouse" effect. It has been customary to lay the blame for this effect upon the fossil-fuels burning of an industralized civilization. Irrespective of cause, should this warming trend melt the present Greenland and Antarctic ice sheets the level of the world's seas would be raised perhaps 100 feet, thus embarrassing much of coastal California.

For added emphasis on the glacial epochs, it also should be noted that during the glacial stage of 325,000–225,000 years past, Death Valley contained a lake *90 miles in length and at least 600 feet deep*, while Mono Lake, now threatened with destruction by Los Angele's thirst for water, was about 900 feet deep during this period. The contrast with today's conditions east of the High Sierra, especially in Death Valley, dramatizes the changes wrought by geologic time and forces.

As a result of Pleistocene happenings, California today is separated by geologists and geographers into distinct geomorphic provinces. (See map, p. 7) For reference purposes, these provinces are tabulated as: Sierra Nevada, Basin Ranges, Mojave Desert, Colorado Desert, Modoc Plateau, Cascade Range, Klamath Mountains, Great Valley, Coast Ranges, and Transverse Ranges. In many respects, the Sierra Nevada province is the key to California's past, present, and future.

Extending some 430 miles as California's eastern wall, and ranging from forty to eighty miles in width, the Sierra Nevada held the gold of the Mother Lode, the *Veta Madre* of the Spaniards. It held, and still holds, most of the state's vast resources of coniferous timber — the "West Sierra Pine Forest" — and is said by professional foresters to be one of the world's most favored timber-growing regions, especially in its northern reaches on the west side of the range. More important than gold or timber or recreation, the vital water-catchment section of the Sierra Nevada in normal seasons receives between 30 and 40 feet of snowfall, with more

Johnsville, a hopeful mining camp in Plumas County, endures a Sierra winter, ca. 1890.
— Courtesy The Bancroft Library

than 60 feet in peak years and a record fall of 70 feet 4 inches recorded at the hamlet of Tamarack.

These peak years occur approximately every forty-two years, with rough fourteen-year intermediate swings within this span. The last peak snowfall year was the winter of 1951-52, when the streamliner *City of San Francisco* was marooned on Donner Pass for three days; an intermediate peak season occurred in 1966-67, and another one in 1981-82. The value of this snowpack to agriculture in the Great Valley and to hydroelectric power generation goes without saying, and the value of the snowpack to the ever-increasing water needs of Los Angeles and all of urban California is illustrated directly by the Oroville Dam and the whole California Water Plan. This aspect of the Sierra Nevada's importance is one that cannot be over-emphasized, especially to those who have no other knowledge of water than that it is a substance to get out of a faucet by turning the handle. This importance was dramatized by a recent two-year drought, which made obvious the necessity of additional storage capacity for winter run-off that otherwise would be wasted.

In the Great Valley, which is comprised of the San Joaquin and Sacramento valleys, the Sutter Buttes near Marysville make a distinct contrast to the valley floor. A volcanic mass rising some 2,100 feet above the surrounding farmlands, the Buttes are often called "a miniature mountain range," which they are not. They mark roughly the northern limits of what was, when the Spaniards first came, one of the continent's great wintering grounds for migratory waterfowl. From the Buttes to below Stockton to Carquinez Strait, the land was a veritable marsh during most of every winter; and early fur trappers, including the organized brigades of the Hudson's Bay Company, found sanctuary at the Buttes when life became too water-logged elsewhere. (Federal wildlife refuges in this region today provide a haven for millions of migratory ducks, geese, and similar sky-farers.) In this same Hispanic period, Tulare Lake in the upper (southern) San Joaquin Valley was an immense body of water resulting from the flow of the Kern River. Down the years, it has been reclaimed for agricultural purposes, but in the unusually wet spring of 1967 and again in 1983, even the best of man's restraining devices could not prevent the flooding of thousands of acres of this old lake bed.

The basic forces of creation gave California certain natural barriers that contributed to its long isolation. They consisted of the arid expanse between the Rocky Mountains and the Sierra Nevada; the formidable barrier of the Sierra Nevada itself; the desert wastes stretching from San Gorgonio and Cajon passes to the Colorado River and onwards into Sonora, Mexico; and the adverse winds and currents off-shore that hindered sea exploration and sea transportation northward from Mexico. These same forces, which include the terrestrial sweep of Pacific winds and currents, still shape one of California's greatest assets — its climate.

In common with Chile, parts of southern Africa and southern Australia, as well as countries ringing the Mediterranean, much of California enjoys the dry-summer, subtropical conditions that are popularly called a

The Shoshone called it "The-Place-of-Ground-On-Fire" — Death Valley.

— *Courtesy of The Bancroft Library*

"Mediterranean-type" climate. While this classification has four major sub-types within the state, we are here concerned only with the basic Mediterranean climate that affects the area containing the bulk of the state's population.

Mediterranean climates occur between 30° and 40° of latitude, either south or north, and their basic characteristics are mild winters and dry summers, with a high percentage of sunny days the year round. They are distinct among the world's climates for their winter rainy season, and California's political boundaries encompass the *only region in North America* of summer drought and winter rainfall. Because evaporation losses naturally are less during the winter season, these winter rains and snows are more lastingly beneficial than equal amounts in climates where precipitation occurs throughout the year.

The first requirement for this climate is the presence of a large body of water to windward, with its consequent cool, high-barometric-pressure area in summer. The Pacific High in summer generally dominates the ocean between California and Hawaii, extending well to northwards of the latitude of San Francisco. It acts as a buffer, shunting middle latitude storms toward the Pole. In winter, the ocean to our west becomes warmer than the land; the Pacific High weakens and retreats southward toward the equator, and the storm track moves south, bringing the winter rains and snows upon which California's life depends. The general effect of California's latitudinal length is to reduce average annual precipitation amounts from north to south along the coast: Crescent City receives 74 inches annually and San Francisco but 22 inches, while Los Angeles receives 11 inches and San Diego only 9 inches.

Air movements develop around the Pacific High and, under the influence of the earth's rotation, circulate in a clockwise direction in the Northern Hemisphere. Flowing in the same direction day after day after day, the air currents that directly affect California — the so-called "trade winds" and "prevailing westerlies" — set ocean currents in motion parallel to the air currents. While this mass movement of air and water is almost beyond individual comprehension, it may be approached in two ways: the air movements enabled the Japanese to launch explosive-laden balloons across the Pacific during WW II, one of which landed near Bly, Oregon, killing a woman and five children on a picnic outing. Another example occurred in 1981, when the helium-filled balloon *Golden Eagle V* lifted off from Japan and crash landed on the California coast less than four days later. Her crew walked away from the wreckage. The mass movement of water can be grasped by realizing that what we call the "California Current" is known in Japan as the *kurashio*, or Black Current, as it makes its way clockwise around the Pacific Ocean above the Equator. Hence the dry-summer, subtropical climate not only experiences cool, dry winds blowing equatorwards in summer, but has a cool-water current flowing equatorwards offshore. This "cool water coast" is the second major ingredient in the creation of a Mediterranean climate.

It is typical for the "cool-water coasts" to be enveloped in prolonged fog in summer. Relatively warm, moisture-laden oceanic air flowing shoreward is cooled as it passes over the upwelling, colder "California Current" near the land. The moisture in the air is condensed into fog, and then, as the marine air moves inland, it is warmed and reabsorbs its moisture. This phenomenon may be observed nearly any normal summer day in Northern California on Interstate Highway 80 between Vacaville and Vallejo.

Our basic Mediterranean climate has both "coastal" and "interior" aspects. Along the coast, the cold offshore current acts as a climate-tempering device. Almost daily fog affects the daily temperatures — ask any tourist who drives across the sweltering Great Valley in July and then finds himself and family shivering an hour later on the Bay Bridge! The fog also delays the seasonal cycle by slowing the earth's warming by the sun. The characteristics of this coastal-type Mediterranean climate are cool summer weather that reaches maximum warmth in September; mild, almost frost-free winters; and minimal temperature fluctuations.

Inland, where marine air does not easily penetrate, the temperature range is more extreme. Clear, dry summer air permits maximum sunlight penetration, and days become hot. After sunset, this same clear, dry air permits maximum heat radiation and the nights are cool by comparison with the days; a drop of thirty degrees after sunset is not uncommon. Frost is frequent in winter, the growing season is shorter, and rainfall is less than along the coast.

Two of the four remaining American-flag vessels in international passenger trade meet beneath the Golden Gate Bridge — en route to and from South America.

— *Courtesy Delta S/S Lines, S.F.*

The usual differences between coastal and interior Mediterranean climate types are greater and more evident in the central portions of the Great Valley. This intensification is due to the existence of the Coast Range, which virtually bars the movement of marine air into the interior except through the "wind gap" of Carquinez Strait, where the waters of the Sacramento and San Joaquin rivers enter San Francisco Bay. Engineers have estimated that shaving some hundreds of feet off the tops of the Coast Range ridges east of Richmond, Berkeley, and Oakland would change quite drastically the climate of the central Great Valley, and require a momentous shift in its agricultural economy. Thus we introduce the third major ingredient affecting California's climate — the mountains that bound the Great Valley.

Mountains make excellent moisture catchers, because their ascending slopes and summits are cooler than the valley or seacoast below. As masses of warm, moist air are pushed up the slopes of these mountains by storms, the air is cooled and its moisture content is precipitated in the form of rain or snow — a squeezing process like wringing out a sponge. After the storm has been relieved of its moisture and pushed over the mountains, its air then warms rapidly as it drops down the other side. Precipitation falls sharply, and the warmed air, as it expands, may even absorb existing moisture from the ground over which it passes. The resultant dry areas in the lee of the mountains are called "rain shadow" areas, and California has them on the east side of all its mountain ranges. The pattern of rain shadow and squeezing is graphically demonstrated by the fact that Coalinga until very recently had to haul its drinking water from elsewhere, while Fresno just across the valley receives 12 inches annually; Blue Canyon on the ascending Sierran slope gets 60 inches annually, while Owens Valley is lucky to have 8 inches, and the Mojave Desert rejoices over but 2 inches.

Because of the normal storm track pattern out of the North Pacific, the rain shadow area in the western part of the Sacramento Valley is less arid than the rain shadow area of the western San Joaquin Valley. The rain shadow east of the Sierra is most pronounced in the Mono Basin-Owens Valley country, simply because the Sierra Nevada has higher elevations as you come down its crest from north to south.

It should be noted here that both the Los Angeles Lowlands — to use geographers' terminology — and the San Diego area have distinct variants of the basic Mediterranean climate. San Diego's is classified as "fog desert," wherein the scanty annual precipitation is compensated for in part by persistent fogs. The Los Angeles Lowlands, owing to their mountain-girt location, suffer an air-inversion pattern which makes itself felt in recurrent "smog alerts." Both regions endure sporadic invasions of air masses from the deserts to the east, which are most hazardous in the Los Angeles Lowlands.

Meteorologists do not fully understand why at times a tremendous mass of dry air becomes stalled above the Great Basin between the Rocky Mountains and the Sierra Nevada. It forms a stationary dome of high barometric pressure that may last for several days before collapsing with a tremendous surge in an inexorable search for a lower-pressure area. The towering barrier of the Sierra Nevada forces this collapsing mass southwestward towards the lower mountains that separate it from a low-pressure trough off the coast of Southern California.

This desert air is pushed through the mountain passes and across the Los Angeles Lowlands, where it is known as the "Santa Ana" because it rushes down Santa Ana Canyon at speeds up to one hundred miles per hour. As the air mass moves downward, it is heated and compressed, gaining five degrees for every thousand feet of descent. Humidity readings in the Lowlands have reached as low as 1 percent, this factor, plus the velocity of the Santa Ana, explains the horrendous fire damage that often results. This is a high price to pay for the fact that the Santa Ana does sweep away the smog shroud from the Lowlands.

Similar winds from similar causes are known as the *foehn* in Austria and Germany, as the *chinook* in Montana and Wyoming, and as the *khamsin*

Sculptured by rain, wind, ice and snow for more than 4,000 years, the Bristlecone pines in Inyo National Forest are threatened by smog from the Los Angeles Lowlands.

Leland J. Prater / Courtesy U.S. Forest Service

in Israel. Wherever they occur, by whatever name they are known, such winds have been charged with accentuating asthma, increasing high blood pressure, magnifying irrational behavior, and stimulating suicides, general lassitude, and crimes of passion. The behavior of freeway traffic while a Santa Ana is buffeting the Southland seems to support these charges. A similar equalization of tremendous barometric pressure differentials afflicts the Sacramento Valley, but less dramatically than does the Santa Ana. This results in a parching north wind that seems to turn plums into prunes on the tree in just one day. And on occasion, this can cause the "cool, gray city" of San Francisco to swelter in unaccustomed summertime heat by preventing its fog-borne air conditioning from operating.

The climate of central and northern California holds the key to both the state's present level of development and its future prospects, simply because past, present, and future have been, are, and will be concerned most urgently with water. San Francisco is dependent upon the Sierra Nevada for its water or life, which comes from Hetch Hetchy Valley, north of Yosemite, via aqueduct to San Francisco's peninsular appendage. The burgeoning East Bay conurbation draws its water requirements from Pardee Dam on the Mokelumne River. The City and County of Los Angeles would not, because it could not, have grown above 500,000 persons without Sierra Nevada water from Owens Valley; and subsequent growth required Hoover Dam on the Colorado River. California agriculture, with its "Peach Bowl," and "Rice Bowl," and "Salad Bowl" aspects, has grown by grace of stored water from the Sierra Nevada. Southern California, *where the votes are*, soon will be unable to enjoy the use of substantial amounts of Colorado River water when the Central Arizona Project diverts that state's allocated share of the river's flow to its own use. With a very few exceptions, which are discussed in the later chapter on "The Water of Life and Growth," the Sierra already has made its major contributions to California's ever-growing water needs. What now?

One more internally controlled major source of surplus water remains to California; and even as the Sierra Nevada, it stems from the evolution of the California landscape. The North Coast Region, stretching from San Francisco to the Oregon border, between the main Coast Range massif and the sea, annually receives about 40% of the state's annual supply of developable water of about 70,000,000 acre feet. For ready reference, one acre-foot of water contains 326,700 gallons, or enough to flush about 60,000 suburban toilets simultaneously. The North Coast Region uses a minuscule amount of this water and the rest flows largely unchecked and unused into the sea. Under the ultimate optimal development foreseen for this region, it will require not more than 4% of all the water consumed in the state.

The first step in saving this presently wasted water already has been taken on the headwaters of the Trinity River by the Lewistown-Whiskeytown dam-and-tunnel complex, which diverts water through the Coast

A summer fog creeps in through the Golden Gate   *Courtesy the Bancroft Library*

Range into the Sacramento River for ultimate use along the west side of the San Joaquin Valley and in Southern California. The next steps in utilizing the surplus waters of the North Coast Region would require damming and diverting the waters of the Eel and other rivers in the same manner. These steps have been considered and dropped because of opposition from groups as diverse as die-hard environmentalists and subdividing developers. The water potential, however, has not been forgotten.

Wrinkled by time and weather, the ridge-ribs of the Coast Range plunge down to meet the sea from whence they came. — *Courtesy Standard Oil Co. of California*

A summary of the effect of California's physical geography upon its developable supply of water makes a simple equation: about 80% occurs north of a line from San Francisco Bay to Lake Tahoe, which includes about 40% of the state's land mass and 30% of its population; south of this line, 70% of the population and 60% of the land mass get 20% of the natural developable supply. This natural maldistribution explains more clearly than any amount of political oratory the interdependence of the state's sections; inasmuch as the area south of our imaginary line, primarily because of the urban complex in Southern California, furnishes the major portion of the state's taxes. Herein is found the taproot of the conflict between urban needs and agricultural needs, between megalopolis and "cow county"; between preservationists and pragmatists in developing water supplies and allocations within the state.

Ten years ago, the desalination of ocean water was regarded as the millenial answer to meeting Southern California's water needs without depriving the northern counties of origin of their own life-giving fluid. At that time, a major plant was being planned for construction at Huntington Beach by a consortium of private utility companies and the federal government. This did not materialize and today the best information available indicates that while some experimental and research work continues, the future of desalination remains open to serious questions because of the costs and the ecological factors involved.

California's future, to say nothing of any future growth, depends upon the zealous protection of its watersheds; further and expensive development of its remaining internally controlled water potentials, including the underground aquifers of the upper Sacramento Valley, and the procurement of additional water outside the state. The latter is a national matter and is discussed more fully following the chapter on the growth of Southern California — a growth that makes the most significant historical, political, economic and cultural development in the history of California in the Twentieth Century.

CHAPTER TWO

THE FIRST IMMIGRANTS

California's treasure trove of resources demanded a technology to unlock them that was not possessed by her first human inhabitants and her first in-migrants, the California Indians. Passive in all of its potential plenty, the environment compelled no change, the environment prevented no change. Here humans resisted change and the first Californians lived in a culture lag, changing remarkable slowly over a vast period of time.

They lacked the dash and derring-do of the Cheyenne and Comanche and Sioux; they were without the fierce cruelty and political organization of the Iroquoian peoples of the eastern woodlands; the Hopi and Zuni of the Southwest were far above them in social organization and cultural accomplishments. Between the Indians of California and the Mayan and Aztec civilizations, the cultural, social, and political gulf yawns gaspingly. Yet these people had a harmony with, and a stability within, their environment that would stand modern man in good stead.

To the Indians of California, the plants and animals around them were members of the same one world; each and all were a part of nature. When they came to the inexplicable in this natural world, they did precisely what humans have always done; they invented myths and legends to explain the inexplicable, so that they and all the unknowns all about them could live harmoniously together. Perhaps this mystico-religious structure, which kept intact the psychic envelope of being, explains the lag in material cultural accomplishments.

Given the ethnic writhings in the nation's bowels today, it may be impolitic to present the California Indians as they actually were. Compounding the problem of presenting them in their true light, without malice or rancor but in the pursuit of ethno-historical truth, is the hard matter of myth. Every American Indian — come hell, high water, or the Immaculate Conception — is too often pictured riding an ear-notched war pony, wearing a double-tailed, eagle feather war bonnet, and living in a skin tipi surrounded by herds of buffalo. We simply have to face the facts that there were no horses, as we know them, in California until the Spanish arrived in 1769. There were no buffalo in California in historic time; and the prehistoric mammals were gone, as far as we know, before the first human wanderers came across from Asia.

Depending upon what anthropologist you hear and what book you read,

Portrait of a Pomo. Photo by E.S. Curtis, *Courtesy of Southwest Museum, Los Angeles*

the erratic migrations out of Asia to North America range from 10,000 to 40,000 years past. Sometime during the last glacial retreat, probably between 15,000 and 10,000 years ago, small bands of nomadic hunters came by way of the Bering Strait, either on a land bridge caused by a glacial withdrawal of water, or on an ice bridge, or by paddling crude rafts between closely situated islands. The date at which the first of these immigrants entered California is moot, to say the least. Shell mounds around San Francisco Bay indicate, through carbon dating, that inhabitants were there at least 3,000 to 4,000 years ago. One of these has been estimated at being 30' high by 460' long and 250' wide, which is a lot of clams!

The most reliable estimates of their number — and they are estimates — places the total number of Indians in California at between 180/250,000 when the Spanish first encountered them. Whatever figure is used, California was one of the most densely populated Indian areas in the entire North American continent north of Mexico, with perhaps four to eight times the human density per square mile of any other aboriginal population in what is now the United States.

Diversity is the key word to remember about the 500 Indian groups of California. Their maximum estimated population, about enough to fill two

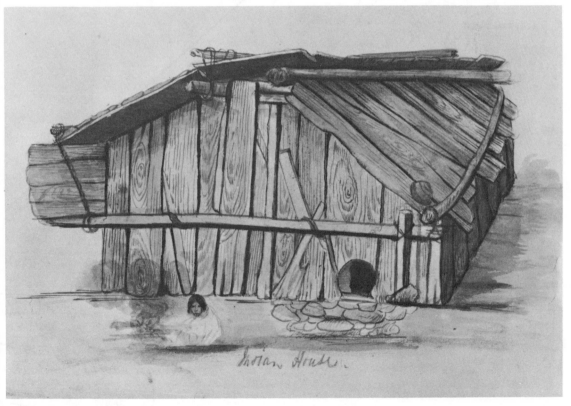

A house of the coastal people near Trinidad, Humboldt County   — *Courtesy The Bancroft Library*

Indian

Territories

ATHABASCAN
LUTUAMI
KAROK
YUROK
SHASTAN
● EUREKA
WIYOT
● REDDING
WINTUN
YANA
ATHABASCAN
YUKI
MAIDU
POMO
WASHO
YUKI
☆ SACRAMENTO
MIWOK
MIWOK
SAN FRANCISCO ●
● SAN
JOSE
COSTANOAN
● FRESNO
☆ MONTEREY
ESSELEN
YOKUTS
SALINAN
SHOSHONEAN
CHUMASH
SANTA
BARBARA
● LOS
ANGELES
YUMAN
SAN
DIEGO

Super Bowl stadiums today, spoke 130 dialects of the basic Indian linguistic families — language grouping being the commonly accepted means of classifying the "Amerinds." Thus, we have from one to two thousand human beings, on an average, sharing a basic dialect, which contained variations within its basic structure from village to village within the language group. Communication between these linguistic fragments was about as difficult as it might have been between a Greek of Periclean Athens and a courtier of Kublai Khan.

The usual Indian village, or *rancheria* in Spanish idiom, contained perhaps 200 persons. The method of constructing dwellings varied as widely as did their dialectical differences. The Karok along the Klamath River made houses of crudely split planks, using stone axes and elk-horn chisels to cleave the redwood, which runs true to its grain for many lineal feet at a stretch. The Maidu in the Sacramento Valley made houses sunk half into the earth with a thatched framework above-ground. The Cahuilleno people of the southeastern deserts made a crude wickiup, little more than a windbreak. This diversity in shelters was repeated in differences of dress, customs, and artifacts.

Long before the days of saunas and hot tubs, the sweat house was common to the cultures of many California tribelets. This is Peewan Sweathouse of the Hupa.
— *W. Erickson / Courtesy The Oakland Museum*

The words "tribe" and "chief" are to be used sparingly, if at all, in relation to these peoples. Perhaps the Mojave and Yuma along the Colorado River were the only ones to whom the political connotation of "tribe" could be applied. The numerous bands of the Yokuts in the San Joaquin Valley also had a proper tribal structure based upon a common clan, or totemic name, but the word "tribelets" seems more appropriate for the various dialectic groups.

Each tribelet shared a common dialect and a common geographical use territory, or range, thus being politically and territorially independent. This use territory usually was so circumscribed that an individual could be born, live and die without ever leaving the boundaries of the tribelet's use range, perhaps as much as one hundred square miles. One Indian woman moved at least eight times during her life-span of more than sixty years and yet stayed within an area six miles in diameter. Socially and economically, the tribelets were self-sufficient, and whatever warfare occurred between them generally stemmed from trespass upon one another's use range to hunt, or fish, or gather seeds and acorns. Such trespass, or food stealing, was serious inasmuch as the exigencies of life within the ancestral territory did not permit the luxury of sharing its productive capacity with outsiders. The use of witchcraft by a neighboring tribelet was another cause of strife.

With all their diversities, the naturally fragmented California Indians had certain common characteristics. They were a Stone Age people, who did not have the wheel, or beasts of burden, or written records. They all were hunters and gatherers, except on the borders of California along the lower Colorado River, where the Yuma and the Mojave were flood-plain agriculturists. Most of them practiced a crude form of public sanitation by the simple expedient of leaving their fouled dwellings when they became too noisome, often burning them, and then constructing new dwellings within their territory. The use of the *temescal*, or sweathouse, was widespread, and many of the first Californians bathed each day, which was far more frequently than European or white-American custom dictated for many and many a year.

The California Indians by and large made superior baskets, the Pomo of Lake County excelling in this craft; and this skill in basketry is advanced as one reason for the lack of any skill at all in pottery-making. Another reason offered is the absence of suitable kaolin which their level of technology could employ. The Chumash of the Santa Barbara Channel made sea-going canoes out of split planks caulked with asphaltum, and the Yurok and Karok of the Trinity-Klamath river complex made dugout canoes by fire-hollowing windfall tree trunks. The Choinimni made 50-foot long tule rafts, with clay fireplaces, upon which they lived for weeks at a time in the marshes of the San Joaquin river.

A complex system of mystico-religious cults was widespread, and the "toloache" cult, based upon the psychedelic qualities of Jimsonweed,

A woman of the Yokuts, among whom age was to be respected.

— Courtesy Southwest Museum

originated with the tribelets south of the Tehachapi Mountains and spread northwards, just as fads from that region today sweep the state and often the nation as well. Their religious leaders were shamans, individuals with a personal pipeline to their supernaturals, who cured disease by dancing and incantations, and by feats of sleight of hand. The greatest cultural accomplishment, perhaps, was the widespread use of acorns as a dietary staple, those from the foothill species of oaks being favored over those from the Great Valley's grasslands. This involved the leaching-out of the tannic acid in the acorns, which boasted a fat content that gave acorn mush or cakes a high caloric value. It may be said that the lowly acorn was indeed the corn-bean-squash of the California Indians.

Within a tribelet's use territory, the land generally provided its hunting-and-gathering culture with abundance: salmon and trout in the streams, sky-darkening flocks of waterfowl, acorns, grass seeds, grasshoppers, the larva of flies and insects, stately elk if they were lucky, fleet antelope if they were luckier, and grizzly bears so numerous as to be a daily hazard. Only rarely did the Indians tackle "old Ephraim," and then generally when he was found asleep. They then would ring the sleeping monster with fire and arrow him to death.

With such natural largesse in all save abnormal years, the land made no demands upon them and imposed no obstacles. Why seek "progress" such as agriculture when for millenia your ancestral people have been able to survive, generally at a comfortable subsistence level, simply by harvesting what Nature provided in her seasons? It has been suggested that California's physical environment, rather than cultural forces, inhibited the adoption of agriculture by the Indians. This suggestion holds that the winter rain-summer drought pattern would not permit the introduction of crops from the lower Colorado River agricultural complex. My own feeling is that the beneficent environment of California did not present a challenge requiring such an innovative response.

Another factor in the culture lag was the isolation imposed by the desert and mountain barriers. It should be remembered, however, that the California Indians did not know that they were isolated. It is known that the Paiute of Owens Valley raided the Chumash of the Santa Barbara Channel, and that the Washo of Lake Tahoe traded pine nuts with the tribelets of the Great Valley. Iridescent abalone shells found their way into a trade route that took them to the *pueblos* of the tribes along the upper Rio Grande River in New Mexico. These contacts produced no measurable cultural explosion, simply because all of those involved in direct contact were at the same general level of accomplishment.

By and large, the Indians of California were short, flat-nosed, broad-faced, and roundheaded. They did not practice scalping as an indigenous custom, or torture of captives, or human sacrifice. Only the peoples along the lower Colorado River had a specific war weapon in the form of a club, and pressure from the aggressive southwestern tribes caused them to develop warlike values in their culture. They and the Modoc varied the most from the introspective, mystic peoples of the rest of the state and sometimes are not included among the state's original Indian population. Slavery based upon debt was practiced along California's northwest coast; and the Modoc of northeastern California were slave raiders for profit; trading their captives into the trade route that ran northward east of the Cascade Range to Celilo Falls on the Columbia River. With these exceptions, the Indians of California did not wage aggressive warfare; and none of them rode horses or lived in skin tipis, or wore flowing-tailed feather bonnets, or hunted the buffalo. And it should be pointed out here and remembered well that there is no such person as a "Digger" Indian. The word is a derisive epithet to be shunned.

Spain's contacts with these people were confined, as were her settlements, to the coastal strip between Sonoma and San Diego. The missions were built along this strip because that is where the Indians were, perhaps 150,000 of the total Indian population. The Indians lived there because that's where the living was the easiest for them, and today almost 95% of the state's population live along this same coastal strip. The missions baptized perhaps 55,000 of these people, but only 31,000 more-or-less Christianized neophytes were said to be in the care of the missions when they were secularized (reduced to parish church status) in 1834. There is no record of how many Indian lives were lost in the smallpox epidemics of 1827-28 and 1837-39. Another disease, believed to have been malaria and to have been introduced into the Great Valley by trappers of the Hudson Bay Company from Canada, killed between 20-30,000 in 1832-33. This did not affect the coastal peoples, because the coastal mosquito then in California was not a malaria carrier as was the anopheline mosquito of the Great Valley, where the mosquito pool was infected by the malaria-carrying trappers aforementioned. Assuming that there were 250,000 Indians in California in 1769, there probably were no more than 100,000 remaining at the time of the Gold Rush. The full force of this influx fell upon those tribelets who had been beyond the reach or influence of Spain and Mexico. The impact was made more brutal because the California Indians did not have the cultural resiliency to provide a cushion against the arrival of thousands of gold-seekers bearing the Industrial Age and bearing, too, a deeply ingrained animosity towards Indians that was the result of the more than two centuries of warfare between the two peoples that followed establishment of the first European settlements in North America.

The human warmth of the history of the California Indian is learned best perhaps through the story of Ishi, the last of the Yahi, who were a sub-group of the Yana tribelet that ranged the foothills east of Red Bluff. Ishi, about fifty years of age and still living in the Stone Age, was captured in the corral of a slaughter-house near Oroville in 1911.

During the next five years, until his death from tuberculosis in 1916, he was a ward of the University of California, working as a janitor at the University of California Hospital in San Francisco. The great story in his life, its urgent message to modern man, is the manner in which he made the transition from his Stone Age milieu into the twentieth century, for he made it with great dignity and unafraid. This was the aspect stressed in my brief telling of his story for the American Museum of Natural History in 1948. A full-scale treatment of his life, *Ishi in Two Worlds*, by Mrs. Theodora Kroeber, widow of the distinguished anthropologist A.L. Kroeber, is well worth your reading.

Ishi with a deer he killed while on a camping trip with Berkeley scientists in 1914.
— *Courtesy The Bancroft Library*

Today, the most tangible legacy from the California Indians to mark their long existence here is found in place names, including those of nine California counties: Colusa, Modoc, Mono, Napa, Shasta, Tehama, Tuolumne, Yolo, and Yuba. An intangible legacy surrounds Mount Rubidoux in Southern California, which is said to have been sacred to the peoples of the San Gabriel Valley as their altar to the Sun, which gave their whole world life. The first Easter sunrise service in Southern California made its joyous way to the summit of Mount Rubidoux on Easter Sunday, 1909.

The social, political, and linguistic fragmentation of the California Indians prevented their making any unified or sustained opposition to Spain's penetration and settlement. Their lack of cultural skills, including that of applied homicide, also worked in Spain's favor. Evidence of this is to be found in the fact that the total strength of Spain's military forces, to

A man of the Mohave people

protect the province from Napa-Sonoma to San Diego, often fell below 100 soldiers. On the other side of the coin, the Indians' ability to absorb simple instructions, to learn and to execute the basic tasks associated with the society that Spain transplanted to California, made them indispensable to this colonization. In summarizing the Indian role in the Europeanization of California, it may be said that they were vital to spain, useful to Mexico, and an annoyance to the United States.

Bateau du port de S.ⁿ Francisco.

It is worth noting here, however, that the United States has made two awards to the California Indians for the value of the lands they lost, either by the eighteen unratified treaties of 1851-52, or by simple dispossession. These awards were based upon the value of the lands lost at the time they were lost, which is the standard government practice in condemning lands from any citizen today. These awards, plus interest accumulated and less attorneys' fees and offsetting amounts for government services rendered, totalled $43,000,000. There were 69,911 people of California Indian blood eligible to share in this amount, which makes an arithmetical average of $614.60 each. However, the amount each individual did receive was determined by the various Indian governing groups. Additional awards were made to the lower Colorado River peoples and to the Modoc, because these were not regarded as being among the California tribelets covered by the awards mentioned. So far as is known, no other country in recorded history has undertaken to indemnify the people it conquered for any part of what they lost. Certainly, neither Spain nor Mexico has considered making any reimbursement or even verbal acknowledgement of what their conquests cost the California Indians. This becomes more noticeable when it is considered that without *los Indios* Spain would have been unable to make Alta California the isolated outpost of empire on the very "Rim of Christendom" that it became.

The bells of Mission San Gabriel, the mother of Los Angeles, 1897.   — *Courtesy Los Angeles County Museum*

CHAPTER THREE

SPAIN'S FARTHEST NORTH

Alta California made a final sunburst of accomplishment in the deepening twilight of Spain's imperial glory. Two and one-half centuries elapsed between the beginning of Cortes' conquest of Mexico and the raising of Spain's brilliant banners above the site of San Diego in 1769. Interestingly enough, these same banners had been raised over New Mexico in 1598. When one considers that California was admitted to the Union in 1850, sixty-two years before this same privilege was accorded the Territory of New Mexico, the impact of the Gold Rush upon California's destiny becomes apparent.

By 1540, less than twenty years after Cortes had conquered Mexico, Spanish mariners had sailed to the head of the Gulf of California, and one of them had ventured some distance up the turbulent Colorado River. In 1542, Joao Rodriguez Cabrilho (a Portuguese, which fact irks Hispanophiles, who have changed his name to *Juan Cabrillo*), set forth on a voyage of discovery from Navidad, a vanished port which in its glory days lay about twenty miles up the coast from present-day Manzanillo, Mexico.

He discovered and landed at San Diego Bay and battled the adverse winds and currents as far north as Monterey Bay before turning back to Cuyler's Harbor on San Miguel Island, off Santa Barbara. There he died from a fall and was buried about January 3, 1543. His successor, a Levantine named Bartolome Ferrelo, resumed the voyage northwards to about Cape Mendocino before turning back for Navidad. Spain's later northward voyages to Monterey from Acapulco, and then from San Blas, took between thirty-five and fifty days against the winds and currents. Rolling home before the prevailing winds and with the currents, the voyage consumed only about one-third of this time.

It should be remembered that these ships were not the *Queen Mary*, or the "Love Boat" seen on television. They were built on the west coast of Mexico from native timber, designed in accordance with marine architecture then prevalent, which called for three feet of length to one of beam. Thus, a vessel sixty feet long would be about twenty feet wide at the waist. Ships were undecked for the most part, sat low in the water, combined square and lateen sails, and generally were unhandy, and uncomfortable, and all too often, unsound. The galleon type of vessel was larger and relatively more comfortable and more seaworthy. The sea in those days quickly separated the *hombres* from the *ninos*!

In 1565 a monk-turned-mariner, Urdaneta, pioneered the round trip from Acapulco to Manila. Thereafter, Spain's artery of communication with Manila pulsed via the Atlantic and Caribbean to Vera Cruz, thence by a royal road across Mexico to Acapulco, and then across the lone leagues of sea to Manila. On the return voyage — the *tornariaje* — Spain's galleons utilized the wind and current pattern of the North Pacific to raise the California mainland at about Cape Mendocino and then roll down the offshore swells to Mexico.

Long at display at the University of California, Berkeley, the authenticity of Francis Drake's plate of brass now is quite questionable.   *— Courtesy The Bancroft Library*

The "master thief of the unknown world," so the Spanish called him with good reason, appeared on the California coast in June, 1579. He had plundered several Spanish vessels on his slow voyage up the ladder of the latitudes from Cape Horn, and among his acquisitions were three Negroes, one named "Maria," who became the first of their people to set foot on the "back side of America." He stayed ashore for five weeks, repairing his vessel for the voyage home to England, the first circumnavigation of the world made under a single command. Francis Drake's voyage gave England its first approximate knowledge of the width of North America and when the Virginia Company of London was given its charter, it was granted land all the way to the Pacific. The controversy as to just where Drake landed and careened his ship in California still rages among certain scholars. The most likely candidates are Drake's Bay, Bolinas Lagoon, and San Quentin Cove, but only foolhardiness will permit making a positive selection and, indeed, the actual site of his landing may never be known. The "plate of brasse" that Drake affixed to a "greate poste" above the beach to claim the land for England as New Albion long was believed to be an authentic relic of his visit. This, too, is under severe questioning today and the preponderance of evidence indicates that it is a very clever forgery.

The need for a safe harbor on the California coast, where "the lonely horror that was the Manila galleon" could obtain fresh water and anything that would combat the ravages of scurvy, brought about the next Spanish contact. This occurred in 1587 when Unamuno anchored in today's Morro Bay, near San Luis Obispo, and explored a short distance inland. This resulted in the first known skirmish between Europeans and California Indians, the first opening of the time capsule that contained the conflict between Stone and Iron.

In 1595 a Manila galleon under the command of Sebastian Cermenho (Cermeno), a Portuguese merchant-adventurer in Spain's service, was exploring the California coastline on its homeward voyage when it was wrecked in Drake's Bay. In a superb feat of seamanship, Cermeno and his survivors sailed a small open boat to Acapulco, continuing coastal explorations as they went. The loss of the galleon and its cargo put an end to using these vessels for coastwise probings, probably to the great relief of Spain's mariners.

In 1602 Sebastian Vizcaino, a Basque who had made a previous voyage to Manila, rediscovered San Diego Bay and gave it the name it bears today. He then voyaged northward, giving the names we now use to many of the points and headlands that he passed. He rediscovered Monterey Bay and described it as a fine harbor with such exaggeration that when Portola viewed it more than a century later he was unable to recognize it from Vizcaino's description. For all practical purposes. Viczaino's voyage ended Spain's efforts to establish a harbor of refuge for the Manila galleon on the California coast. There are no known voyages thereafter until the settlement of San Diego in 1769. One explanation for this hiatus is the morass of problems, both at home and in the New World, in which Spain found herself, coupled with a slow but steady rundown of her imperial energy under the Hapsburgs. Another stems from Spain's relations with her New World colonies. *GOOD* colonies produced precious metals, and after the failure of Cabrillo, Cermeno and Vizcaino to find wealth in the "Northern Mystery," why bother?

The hazards of sea voyages northward from the west coast of Mexico have been demonstrated. The exploring vessels, as well as the Manila galleons, often returned home with half their crews dead and the other half so weak from scurvy as to be unable to stand on deck. These difficulties — and the word seems inadequate at best — operated throughout the age of sail, although the toll from scurvy was later reduced by the use of citrus fruits and juices.

The other isolating barrier, the Colorado and Sonoran deserts, began to be breached in 1691 when Fray Eusebio Kino commenced his years of missionary labors in *Pimeria Alta*, which included present-day southern Arizona, that ended with his death in 1711. Kino was a Jesuit, and that order was expelled from the New World by order of the Crown in 1767. Kino's pioneer work in unlocking the geography of the deserts, however, was carried on in 1768 by Fray Francisco Garces, a Franciscan, and it was on their findings that Juan Bautista de Anza built when he established an overland route from Sonora to California in 1774-76. This was done after Spain became suddenly galvanized into action regarding California, an action stemming from dramatic international developments.

In 1740-42, Vitus Bering, a Dane in the service of the Russian government, began his voyages from Siberia toward Alaska and the Arctic. These resulted in Russia's colonizing Alaska and sending sea otter hunters south-

Outpost of Empire on the "Rim of Christendom" — the Presidio at Monterey.
— Courtesy The Bancroft Library

ward from Sitka. In 1763 as a result of the Seven Years War in Europe, for which the Great French and Indian War in America was the trigger, England replaced France as master of the eastern Mississippi River Valley. Thus, despite her possession of Texas and French Louisiana — a buffer against England in physical mass only — Spain was in danger of having her New World empire outflanked on both the northeast and the northwest. This threat loomed at a time when Carlos III was seeking valiantly to revivify Spain's fading glory. Pursuant to his instructions, the Viceroy in Mexico organized an expedition to colonize California.

The entire colonial party — both the two groups by land and the vessels by sea — was under the general command of Gaspar de Portola. Fray Junipero Serra, a Franciscan who was chaplain of the land expedition, was charged with overseeing the establishment of religious activities in the new colony. However, so strong has been the religious motif in the writing and teaching of California history that poor old Portola, a brave man, competent and loyal, frequently has been overshadowed by Fray Serra. Certainly, the mission role in establishing Spain's farthest north settlement in the New World can hardly be overstated, but it was Portola who was the overall commander of the first expedition.

Spain's plan of settlement for California essentially was a plan tested and proven effective on Spain's frontier in Mexico. It rested upon three legs, each with its own special function — the "presidio," the "mission," and the "pueblo."

The presidio was the military leg and comprised the fort and its garrison. Its function was to defend California against external aggression, to quell Indian uprisings, and to supress civil insurrections should such occur. Spain's presidios were established at Monterey, San Francisco, Santa Barbara, and San Diego, and military towns grew up around them in time. Each of these presidios fought a losing battle against apathy and the elements under both Spain and Mexico, and that at San Francisco boasts the distinction of never having had a shot fired in anger from its batteries to this day. It was erected on the general site selected by De Anza, who did not, however, participate in its construction.

The mission was the religious leg of the tripod of settlement. Its functions were to convert the heathen *Indios* and train them in useful skills; about 55,000 converts is the estimated gross harvest from Franciscan labors during the heyday of the missions. The missions also became the granary of the province, thus freeing the presidial forces for their primary defense functions, which included protecting the missions and enforcing discipline in cases which the religious could not handle. Civilian towns grew up around the mission nucleus at San Luis Obispo, Sonoma, San Juan Bautista and San Juan Capistrano. Sonoma was the only mission established under Mexico, being founded in 1835 by Mariano Guadalupe Vallejo under instruction from the governor as a bastion against the Russian settlement at Fort Ross.

Mission Santa Barbara has been in the hands of the Franciscans since its founding, and is the *only* one continuously in use for religious services despite earthquakes, uprisings, and revolutions. Santa Barbara is also distinctive in that it reflects the earliest phase of Spanish Renaissance architecture and thus differs from the exuberant and lavishly ornamented *churriquesque* of Old Mexico, which is said to have influenced the general mission style. The latter style influenced the design of the buildings for the San Diego Exposition of 1915 and spread from there into general California use between the world wars.

The *campo santo* at Mission Santa Barbara contains some 4,000 graves of Indians, and has led to charges that the Franciscans were guilty of coercion, brutality, and genocide. The record of history disproves these charges. There never were enough Franciscans, even reinforced by soldiers, to coerce the Indian population of California in such a manner as charged, let alone to practice genocide, which, in all truth, was contrary to the teachings of the Church of both Franciscan and soldier. Smallpox took a heavy toll, as did the dread strangling of diptheria (*el garrotillo*). Perhaps even more deaths were caused by the lack of even such primitive sanitation methods as the Indians had practiced by moving and burning their houses at sporadic intervals, which were not possible in the fixed abodes of the missions.

The pueblo was the civil leg of the tripod, designed to attract civilian colonists. Each pueblo was granted four square leagues of land — about 17,600 acres — with which to provide its residents with homes, garden plots, and common grazing grounds. Only two true pueblos became operational in California: San Jose and Los Angeles. A third, Branciforte, was begun across the river from Santa Cruz by a party of destitute colonists from Guadalajara, but it did not survive into the American period. Other pueblos grew up around both presidios and missions, and were granted lands as noted above; but these pueblos were outgrowths of the initial nuclei of settlement provided by presidio and mission, and were not originally established as parts of the civil leg of Spain's plan.

Founded as a pueblo on November 29, 1777, the city of San Jose is the oldest continuously inhabited civilian community in the state. Its initial settlers were nine *soldados*, five *pobladores* (settlers) with their families, and one *vaquero*. Every settler was given two each of cows, oxen, mules, sheep, and goats, plus some seeds and crude farming implements, and was promised the equivalent of ten dollars per month for the first two years of residence. It was a notably independent community, exemplified by the fact that its citizens did not recognize Mexico's independence from Spain until May 10, 1825, three years after the formal act of allegiance to Mexico had been taken by the Spanish government of California. Prickly with independence though it was, San Jose's European population grew slowly, numbering but 524 persons by 1831. When Los Angeles was founded in 1781, more than half of its 46 settlers had some African ancestry. The famous Pico family of

Southern California was descended from a mulatto mother, and one of her sons, Miguel, sired 15 children who gave him 116 grandchildren and 97 great-grandchildren. By 1791, however, Los Angeles could boast of all of 139 inhabitants.

This growth rate supports the statement that the mission was the most effective and certainly the most important segment of civilization in California during the Spanish regime, 1769-1821. The mission complex not only became the granary of the province but served as the educational center, the religious center, and the cultural center. The mission chain also became the main arm of Spanish expansion in California. It has been said too often in California history that the missions were established a day's horseback ride apart. They came to be about this distance apart, given a good horse and a durable seat, but the dates and locations of their foundings show clearly that they were not a day's ride apart in the beginning. The missions were established where there were Indians, and the Indians were found where natural conditions were most favorable for their way of life.

Out of the twenty-three missions in California, only one, as noted, was founded during the Mexican regime, 1822-46; all the rest were born under Spain. All of the missions were established by the Franciscan order, and from its beginnings until final secularization in 1834, the mission record is one of friction between the Franciscans and the military. The friars felt that the soldiers corrupted their converts, and the military felt that the religious encouraged their charges to be insubordinate to military authority. Mission San Diego was moved five miles from its original site to escape the pernicious influence of the garrison troops, and Mission San Carlos Borromeo was moved from Monterey to the Carmel Valley for the same reason.

Added to the basic friction was a matter of practical economics. While Spain was willing to make the down payment of men and materials to establish the first settlement of California, she did not make the subsequent installments that might have made California what she intended it to become: a sturdy defense bastion on the northwest flank of her New World empire. When 1773 came to an end, there were but two presidios and five missions established, and 61 Spaniards had the task of controlling all of Alta California. Until the missions attained adequate food production, about 1780, the struggling colony was dependent upon supply ships from Mexico. These often were long delayed by the hazards of vavigation; many were lost at sea, and there were times when the infant colony was on the brink of starvation. Dependence upon maritime communication forced the search for an overland route between California and Spain's outposts in northern Sonora, and this is where De Anza built upon the desert explorations of Fray Kino and Fray Garces.

In 1774-75, De Anza blazed an overland trail from Sonora to Mission San Gabriel, near Los Angeles, and used it in 1775-76 to lead 240 colonists' (of whom 166 were women and children) and livestock to California. This

It was a fair and gentle land to which Spain's *pobladores* came.   *— Courtesy Library of Congress*

movement resulted in the founding of San Francisco around Mission Dolores and of the Presidio of San Francisco. De Anza's journey must rank as one of the epic feats of travel on this continent, if for no other reason than that he arrived in California with more people than had left Sonora: births along the way more than offset the few deaths. The first white child born in California, Salvador Ignacio Linares, arrived on Christmas Eve, 1775, while the expedition was encamped at Coyote Canyon in today's Riverside County.

The key to the overland route was the Yuma Crossing of the Colorado River, and as long as the Yuma Indians remained friendly, the crossing was usable. However, relations between Spaniard and Yuman worsened. In 1787 the Yuma warriors, jealous of their gardens and their women, wiped out the Spanish garrison and missionaries at the crossing and closed the overland link with California for many years. This step apparently had a most deleterious effect upon Spain's ability to reinforce the California colony with civilian settlers. For the rest of California's period of control by both Spain and Mexico, its stoutest lifeline with, and window upon, the outside world was the sea.

The safest snug harbor on the California Coast in the hide-and-tallow days — San Francisco Bay.
— *Courtesy The Bancroft Library*

Dependence upon the sea, coupled with the availability of substantial Indian populations along the coast and accentuated by the lack of population pressures owing to the lack of colonists, explain why neither Spain nor Mexico expanded its perimeter of settlement inland. There simply was no compelling pressure to do so.

The Franciscans, zealous in the quest for souls to be saved, did make many journeys into the San Joaquin Valley seeking possible mission sites. Several such seem to have been selected where the Indian populations promised a harvest of souls and a source of labor, but no missions ever were established within the Great Valley. The present-day community of Los Banos acquired its name from Fray Arroyo de la Cuesta's habit of bathing himself there on his journeys from San Juan Bautista over Pacheco Pass to the Valley. Water storage behind the great San Luis Dam, a vital link in the state's master water plan to slake Southern California's thirst, now hides the sturdy friar's bathing pool.

After the closing of the overland route from Mexico, the main source of civilian colonists was provided by several hundred ex-convicts from Mexico and discharged soldiers from the military garrisons, many of whom found wives among the Indian converts of the missions. Richard Henry Dana would note in later years that one drop of Spanish blood carried with it all the rights and privileges of Spanish subjects — and these were few enough by modern standards of civil rights. The rate of growth in Spanish California is eloquently portrayed by the fact that in 1820 the colony's total European population approximated 3,720 persons, including thirteen "foreigners," meaning non-Spanish.

Another reason for slow growth was the lack of any real economic incentive for individual enterprise in Spanish California. The government in Mexico controlled all trade and it forbade commercial intercourse with vessels of other countries. California's internal market for agricultural produce was the presidios and pueblos, and here the individual had to compete with mission production as well as with fixed prices established by the government. All imported goods were subject to this same price-fixing and regulation. Under Spain, the residents of California were bound by rigid controls that provided no reward for individual economic initiative.

It must be remembered, too, that down all its days under both Spain and Mexico, California had no manufacturing, save simple handcrafts. The *Californio* was dependent upon importation for all the survival artifacts of western civilization: knives and axes, forks and spoons; soft cloth that did not scratch as did the home-loomed product; coffee and tobacco, salt and pepper, and the cones of hard sugar called *panocha*; mission bells, altar cloths, and priestly vestments, fireworks for *fiestas*, wine, and rum — everything that was needed came from outside, except for the basic, and limited, foodstuffs and rather rudimentary handcraft manufacturers. It is not surprising, then, that smuggling by foreign vessels became common during

Spain's tenure, and that under Mexico it changed to conniving with officia-dom. It is in this context that the United States' maritime trade with California, immortalized in Richard Henry Dana's *Two Years Before the Mast*, must be considered.

Here it is well to dispose of another rampant figment of California mythology: the "Spanish" land grant. During Spain's entire tenure, perhaps twenty-five grants of land were made by the Crown to individuals, the bulk of them being in Southern California around Los Angeles and San Diego. Of the some eight hundred land grants that were adjudicated by the United States after its acquisition of California, the overwhelming majority were made by Mexico between 1822 and 1846; and the preponderance of Mexican grants was made after the secularization of the missions in 1834. It should be noted here that grants of land by the Crown to the missions were not made to the Church per se. Rather, they were grants to be held in trust until such time as the Indians had been converted and trained in the simple survival tasks and skills of a feudal society. Then these lands were to be given to the Indians for their own subsistence. In this context the oft-made statement that the missions were despoiled of their rightful property by secularization falls apart.

The San Fernando Valley when the Mission was its major habitation.

— Courtesy The Bancroft Library

In essence, Spain transplanted a feudal society to the beneficient wilderness that was California. It was a society lacking completely in the technology necessary to unlock California's resources, although if the placer (surface) gold that caused the Gold Rush had been found in the Spanish period, the mission dwellers could have handled it quite well. It was a society with agricultural techniques of the most primitive kind, a society without internal banking or commerce, and one lacking in the arts, in communications, and in libraries, to say nothing of schools as we know them.

In a very real sense, the following twenty-four years as a province of Mexico did little to change the basic nature of California's society, although at least one aspect of it was expanded greatly.

This map was attached to the petition for Rancho San Vicente, near Santa Cruz, granted to Blas Escamilla in 1846.
—Courtesy *The Bancroft Library*

CHAPTER FOUR

RANCHEROS y EXTRANJEROS

The isolated province of Alta California played no part in the long years of struggle that dissolved Spain's New World empire into sovereign nations. California did experience one almost comic-opera incident in this period, when Hippolyte Bouchard, the Argentine privateer or pirate or revolutionist, as you prefer, seized Monterey in 1818 and looted it of everything that was usable, portable, and potable. One of his sailors, a young American named Joseph Chapman, was captured later by the *Californios* when Bouchard sent a landing party ashore at the Ortega *rancho* near Santa Barbara. He was the first known American to take up permanent residence in California and became a shipbuilder and vineyardist in Southern California.

During the Mexican period, 1822-46, California experienced a "population explosion," in that its population grew from some 3,700 persons to about 9,000, including perhaps 900 non-Hispanic foreigners. This "foreign" element at first was comprised of British, American, and Russian deserters from trading, naval, and whaling vessels. The earliest of these in 1814 was a Scot named John Cameron, who took the name of Juan Bautista Gilroy and left that name on a community in the Santa Clara Valley. He is believed to be the first permanent non-Hispanic resident of California. Wandering trappers from Canada and "the states" added to this "foreign" element in the 1830's, and beginning in 1841, a thin trickle of emigrants from the United States seeped across the natural barriers.

Secularization of the missions — that is, stripping them of all functions save that of parish church — was the most significant internal development during the Mexican period. The idea appeared first in 1813, when the Spanish *Cortes* (parliament) passed a law calling for secularization. This became ignored in the turbulence of the colonial struggles for independence, but surfaced again after Mexico won her freedom. Personal freedom for *los Indios* was the goal of the liberal faction in Mexican politics, while there were others in Mexico and Alta California, who saw the property of the missions as a golden opportunity for personal profit. Between these forces, pressure built up and the decree ordering secularization was passed by the Mexican Congress in 1833.

Jose Figueroa then was governor of Alta California, perhaps the ablest of all the Mexican governors and from the evidence the most humanitarian. He saw clearly the problems confronting *los Indios* under secularization, and when he ordered the first ten missions secularized, he decreed that one-half the property of each be divided among its resident Indians, who were forbidden to sell their land or chattel property, while the other one-half was entrusted to an administrator to be conserved and used for their benefit. Six more missions were secularized in 1835, the year that Figueroa died, and the remaining five in 1836. With Figueroa's death, the situation deteriorated to say the least. Greedy and incompetent administrators, plus the political upheavals that racked the province, resulted in the despoilation of the Indians' inheritance from the missions.

Secularization removed the one cohesive force in Alta California, the church, which had combined spiritual authority with its functions as the fountain of education and the cultural transmission belt. It also deprived the mission Indians of the only cultural and psychic stability many of them had ever known, and the population of "Christianized" Indians declined from about 30,000 to perhaps 10,000 in a scant ten years. Those that were left made the labor force for the *rancho*, which became the basic social, cultural, and economic unit of Mexican California.

Using the mission livestock as a foundation — the missions owning more than 400,000 head of cattle in 1833 — the *rancho* system flourished. Mariano Vallejo, one of the largest of the *rancheros*, pastured upwards of 14,000 head of cattle, 7,000 horses, and 2,500 sheep on his acreage, while his work force consisted primarily of 300 Indians and their families. This was the period of "pastoral Arcadia," which gave California the hazed and nostalgic heritage of dashing *caballeros*, beautiful *senoritas*, and the "cattle on a thousand hills." In all truth, Mexican California made one of the largest, non-nomadic pastoral societies the world ever has known.

Independence from Spain removed the interdiction against trade with foreign countries, although rather high import and export taxes were levied at Monterey, the only legal port of entry, to finance the provincial government. Mexico virtually insisted that California's costs of government be met internally, and taxes upon foreign commerce were the principal means to this end. A minuscule tax on each head of livestock slaughtered was the only internal revenue measure, and the lack of real property taxes was most appealing to the earliest emigrants from the States. The emphasis upon import taxes in all their nuances brought about the switch from smuggling under Spain to conniving with officialdom to gain more favorable treatment in the matter of levying duties and tonage taxes upon cargoes and vessels.

The relaxing of trade restrictions enabled the *rancheros* to dispose of their principal commercial product — hides and tallow — and this period coincided with the growth of industry in New England. The infant United States needed hides for leather and tallow for soaps and candles, particularly the latter. It also needed a market in which to dispose of its manufactured products. Although the English had been the first to trade legally with California after it gained independence from Spain, which brought William *"Don*

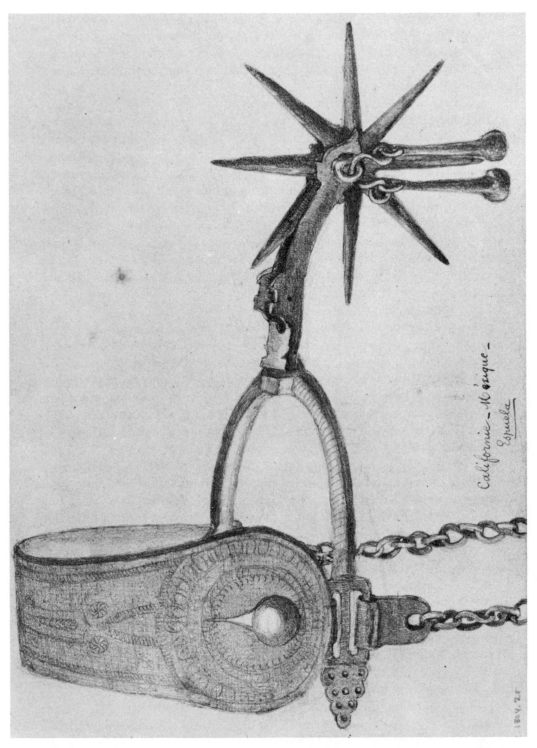

Sketch of a *ranchero*'s spur by Fritz Wikersheim, 1851. The pendants from the rowel made tinkling music as he rode.
                                                        — *Courtesy The Bancroft Library*

Guillermo" Hartnell to California, it was not long before American vessels out of New England ports, especially Boston, dominated the California trade. San Diego became the principal place for collecting and curing the hides obtained all up and down the coast, and the "hide houses" there contained a polyglot assortment of the world's seafarers.

The hide-and-tallow trade was the mainstay of the California economy during the Mexican period. Estimates of the total number of hides exported from California during the twenty-five years of Mexican tenure veer wildly from 600,000 to 1,250,000. The peak year appears to have been 1838, when it is believed that 200,000 hides were shipped to Boston alone. There were other aspects of commerce that became prominent in this period as well. American whalers plied the coast and reaped a rich harvest from the migrations of the California gray whale. Livestock from California were driven to Oregon and shipped to Tahiti, while cattle and horses from California, with *vaqueros* to instruct the Hawaiians, laid the foundation of the cattle industry on the Big Island of Hawaii; the Hawaiian word for cowboy still today is *paniolo*. An early trade in lumber developed during this period and is dealt with in a subsequent section.

In the beginning of the hide-and-tallow trade, each ship traded for itself along the coast, sending a supercargo riding inland to persuade the *rancheros* to bring their produce to the nearest beach. Under these conditions, a vessel might be all of two years on the coast getting a full cargo of 40,000 hides. This evolved into a resident-merchant system, the most prominent members being Americans such as Henry Delano "Enrique" Fitch in San Diego, Abel Stearns in Los Angeles, and Thomas Oliver Larkin in Monterey. These men purchased whole cargoes of imported goods and acted as purchasers of produce the year round centralizing the business and providing California with a steady market, as well as a constant supply of goods. A concomitant of this arrangement was the beginning of California's first banking system, in that the merchants provided credit and advanced funds against future production by the *rancheros*, whose word was indeed their honor, not alone their bond.

One result of the rise of the *rancho* system was the eruption of violent sectionalism between Northern and Southern California, a matter that has modern connotations. Monterey always had been the capital of California under Spain, and it remained so under Mexico. With secularization of the missions, the most rapid growth in both population and livestock occurred between Santa Barbara and San Diego, and inland toward today's San Bernardino. It was the modern cry of "the most people need the most attention," and for the last decade of California's existence as a Mexican province, it was racked by sectional political strife.

Compounding this internal turmoil, California felt herself to be the unloved, idiot stepchild, so to speak, of the Mexican Republic. She resented having the governor appointed from Mexico, and she resented even more the quality of the soldiers (all too often ex-convicts whom the *Californios* dubbed *rateros* and *cholos*) that Mexico sent north to protect the province. What California wanted was home rule, and in 1836 Juan Bautista Alvarado actually declared California to be an independent republic. This status did not become permanent, but California remained unimpressed with Mexico's appointed officials right up to the Mexican War and her acquisition by the United States. This governmental instability within California, coupled with an even greater political chaos in Mexico proper, was a factor in the calculations that the United States, Great Britain, and France — especially the former two — made about California in the decade preceding the Mexican War.

The *gente de razon*: Southern California's Lugo family.   — *Los Angeles County Museum*

The basic social unit in Mexican California was the *rancho* family, widely separated from its neighbors. It was a patriarchial unit, and respect for parents was so deeply ingrained that grown men of forty, with their own grandchildren, thought it proper to submit without protest to their parents' disciplinary measures. In a land and time unafraid of excess humanity, Secundino Robles and Maria Antonia Garcia became the parents of twenty-nine children on their *rancho* where Stanford University stands today. William Hartnell married the beauteous Teresa de la Guerra and sired nineteen progeny, while Tomas Sanchez, who married Maria Sepulveda in her thirteenth year, became the father of twenty-one offspring.

It was an isolated life on the *ranchos* but a life of boundless hospitality. It has been said that you could ride from one end of Hispanic California to the other, from San Diego to Sonoma, without a purse or a horse of your own and exist comfortably, and travel astride, simply from the bounty of the families along the way. It was a life of pastoral simplicity, incredibly simple by today's standards, but it was socially and culturally self-sufficient. Economically it was profitable, thanks to the hide-and-tallow trade.

In a very real sense, the land made no demands upon the *Californios* and imposed no obstacles in their lifeway. Man again was the determinant in California. As Sir George Simpson of the Hudson's Bay Company acidulously observed, "Idleness can find both subsistence and recreation" in California. The *Californio* rode superlatively, feared God, honored his parents, worried not about the morrow, and cherished his *dignidad*. What else was there?

The seemingly idyllic lifestyle of the *Californios* survived the Mexican War intact, and the processes of history under normal conditions would seem to have favored its gradual, generational assimilation into the technologically superior culture of the conquering Americans. The best parts of both styles of living might have been combined thereby through progressive acculturation. But such a development was not to be. The lifeway of the *Californio* first was inundated, then swept away forever by the flood tide of gold seekers.

It is proper to note here that the Hispanic influence in contemporary California, where Los Angeles contains one of the largest Mexican centers in the world, is not due to California's slumberous days under Spain and Mexico, except in regard to place names and a bastard architectural style. Neither is it due to the influx of people from Mexico and Latin America during the first two years of the Gold Rush; most of these went home, willingly or for survival. Today's Hispanic influence stems primarily from the migration of people from Mexico during and between the two world wars, to meet the state's demand for labor. The *bracero* program, terminated in 1966, was a manifestation of this historic influx, and this influx continues with both legal and illegal immigrants.

As a grace note to the above, it well may be that we speak glibly today of "bulls" and "bears" because of California's Hispanic heritage. One of the legendary *vaqueros* of Southern California, Ramon Ortega, is said to have roped and subdued more than seventy grizzly bears while riding rangeland now within the Los Padres National Forest. Contests between wild bulls and grizzly bears, both captured by skillful use of *la riata*, were a staple entertainment for the *Californios*. Horace Greeley, the thunderous editor of the New York *Tribune*, is said to have witnessed one of these encounters while visiting California and thereafter to have applied the names of the antagonists to the embattled denizens of Wall Street's wilds after his return.

LOS EXTRANJEROS

There is no doubt of early visitations by Asiatics to the New World. A Chinese legend holds that a Buddhist monk visited Mexico before Cortes and remained among the Aztec several years before returning to Cathay. Juan Bautista de Anza saw the wreckage of a "foreign" (non-European) vessel on the rocks near Carmel in 1776. At least two Japanese trading voyages reached the west coast of Mexico during the early years of the seventeenth century. A Japanese vessel has been reported as drifting ashore near Santa Barbara in 1815, after a derelict year at sea, with three men still clinging to life aboard her battered hulk. Here again, the winds and currents of the North Pacific enter the picture, even as they do today when the glass floats of Japanese fishing nets wash ashore on Pacific Coast beaches.

Despite the evidence of such voyages, the fact remains that nothing effective came of them. They belong in the same category as Thor Heyerdahl's drift voyage to Tahiti, which proved that it was possible. Nothing more. The outside world's first meaningful contacts with California, both by sea and by land, came about because of the quest for the pelts of fur-bearing animals.

The first of these animals to spur the avarice of the world was the mammalian sea otter, one of the most appealing of all the sea's creatures, which ranged the Pacific Coast from the fog-shrouded Aleutian Islands to the slag-barren headlands of Baja California. Its rich, lustrous pelt, a sensuous, chocolatey blackish-brown, could yield a fur sixty inches long by half that wide. As early as 1774, Spanish sailors learned that the Pacific Northwest Coast Indians would trade sea otter pelts for abalone shells, but it was left to Captain James Cook of the Royal Navy, on one of his great voyages of discovery into the Pacific, to bring the world's attention to the profits to be derived from marketing sea-otter pelts in China. In 1789 American vessels were trading with the seafaring Indians around Vancouver Island; and in 1792 an American shipmaster out of Boston, William Gray, gave the name of his vessel to the Columbia River. This was the United States' first claim to what became the "Oregon Country" and marks our first national interest in the western lands washed by the Pacific Ocean.

A round-the-world trade quickly developed for New Englanders, who brought out their crude manufactures, particularly iron products, and traded them on the Northwest Coast for sea otter pelts. Thence they sailed down the latitudes to the Hawaiian Islands to get fresh foodstuffs and fill their water casks, and to take on sandalwood, highly prized in China, in exchange for ironware. In Canton, the principal Chinese port, they traded sea otter and sandalwood for spices and silks and ceramics. Then they sailed down between the emerald islands set in the equatorial girdle, out into the Indian Ocean down around the Cape of Good Hope, and home to New England, sometimes three years on the voyage.

As the northern sea otter was hunted out, the California coast came into the picture, because one of the otter's favorite haunts was the kelp beds and rocky ledges of the Santa Barbara Channel. William Shaler, in the ship *Lelia Byrd*, traded so flagrantly for sea otter pelts in San Diego, in violation of Spanish law, that he had to fight a bloodless battle to win his way down the San Diego River to open sea. Captain Ebenezer Dorr in 1796 became the first American known to have landed officially in California when his ship *Otter* entered Monterey Bay, and he took advantage of international law to remain two days while getting wood for cooking and water. Dorr had come up from Australia, and when he departed surreptitiously, he left ashore some convicts from the Botany Bay penal colony "down under." These were sent off to Mexico and disappeared from recorded history.

The sea-otter trade created one of the first peaceful collaborations between Americans and Russians on record. The Russian-American Fur Company in Alaska would supply a crew of fierce Aleut hunters, the "Cossacks of the North Pacific," to American shipmasters in return for a proportion of the catch. The men of this combined operation hunted down the California coast, fighting pitched battles whenever necessary along the Santa Barbara Channel with Indians hunting otter for the missions, and then returned to Sitka to divide the spoils.

A variant of this collaboration saw the American ship *Juno* bring the dashing Baron Rezanov to San Francisco for the purchase of foodstuffs to protect the Russian-American Fur Company's posts in Alaska from starvation. Spanish law, of course, prohibited all such purchases, but the beautiful Concepcion Arguello, the teenaged daughter of the *commandante* of the Presidio of San Francisco, fell in love with the Russian Baron. So the legend goes. Her father then shut one eye or winked it just long enough for the foodstuffs to be acquired. Rezanov and Concepcion were bethrothed when he sailed from San Francisco, but he was killed on his way across Siberia to seek the Czar's permission for his marriage. In due time, "Concha" Arguello became Sister Mary Dominica and ended her days on December 23, 1857, in a convent at Benicia, where she is buried.

Another outgrowth of this trade was the establishment by Russia of Fort Ross, an illegal settlement under international law, for the unlawful purpose of poaching sea otter. The fort also was expected to grow food for the Russian outposts in Alaska. Spain was powerless to prevent its establishment; Mexico was powerless to expel it. Fort Ross endured until its contents were purchased by John Sutter, the founder of New Helvetia, the compound that became today's Sacramento.

The Russian River, a favorite summer haunt of San Franciscans, commemorates the onetime Russian presence in the land. So does Mount St. Helena, brooding above the vineyards of the Napa Valley, which was named either for Princess Helena de Gargarin, the wife of the Russian governor of

Alaska, or for the Empress of Russia. The Monroe Doctrine took warning notice of the Russian presence in California, and the California Poppy was given its botanical name (*Eschscholtzia californica*) to honor a German zoologist, Johann Friedrich Eschscholtz, who visited California in 1816 while in the service of Russia.

The sea otter trade passed its peak by 1822, although a flurry of renewed activity seems to have occurred in San Francisco Bay during the early 1830s. The sea otter today is a protected creature, under supervision by the Federal Fish and Wildlife Service, both in Alaskan waters where the herd now numbers more than 100,000, and in California where the herd is estimated at about 2,000 head. Killing a sea otter is a federal offense, punishable by a fine up to $20,000 and up to one year as a guest of the federal government. Despite this, sea otters have been shot by wrathy abalone fishermen in Morro Bay, where the abalone population has been decimated by the sea otter's taste for this delicacy, so the fishermen claim. A contributing factor has been the human pressure on the abalone beds, brought about by the use of wet suits and aqua-lungs.

Like the shark in "Jaws," the sea otter is an eating machine, and an adult otter, weighing up to eighty pounds, will consume up to 35% of its body weight daily. As the sea otter spread down the coast, they threaten the clamming beds at Pismo Beach, upon which the economy of the town depends, because Pismo Beach to the sport clammer is Yankee Stadium, the Pro Bowl, and Indianapolis all rolled into one. The California Department of Fish and Game (DFG), which is responsible for protecting and maintaining the clam beds from overuse by humans, is powerless to combat the sea otter because of its federal protection. Biologists for DFG estimate that nine adult sea otters at Pismo Beach will eat the same numbers of clams as are taken ALL year by sport clammers, and the sea otter does not observe the size limits which the DFG enforces for human clammers. So a confrontation is shaping up between the state's 100,000 or more sport clammers and the city of Pismo Beach on one side and the 4,000-member Friends of the Sea Otter on the other. The confrontation is inevitable simply because you can have an unlimited number of sea otter or you can have a shellfish fishery, but you cannot have both today.

The quest for beaver skins brought the first Americans overland to California — "men with the bark on," who were able to surmount the formidable natural barriers, including the resident aborigines, that long had protected California's eastern marshes. They came as a result of the brass-knuckled competition for beaver skins in the trapping grounds along the Continental Divide. Their conquest of the mountain fastness gave a nasty shock to the then governor of California, a "thin and juiceless man" named Echeandia. What they represented was the cutting edge of the American frontier; and what they learned about the overland routes to California, what they learned about California's vast and untapped potential, contributed to the yeasty ferment bubbling in the collective consciousness of the American people. It was a ferment that would come to a head in the year of the War with Mexico, the year of "Manifest Destiny," the year 1846.

James Ohio Pattie, whose reminiscences are not to be believed as Holy Writ, trapped west-southwest from Taos, New Mexico, in 1826 and apparently reached as far west as the east bank of the Colorado River on this journey. He did not, so far as is known, then set foot on any part of what today is California. The first American we know to have done so was unique among the mountain men.

Jedediah Strong Smith was a praying and fighting Methodist, who did not use profanity, who eschewed tobacco, who took wine only upon ceremonial occasions, and who did not follow the custom of the mountains in making temporary alliances with assorted Indian wives-by-courtesy-only. He first went to the Rocky Mountains in 1822 from St. Louis, headquarters of the emerging American segment of the fur trade of the Far West, and by the year 1826 he was a full partner with David Jackson and William Sublette in what became the Rocky Mountain Fur Company. Competition from the great Hudson's Bay Company for the fur riches west of the Continental Divide caused Smith to seek new beaver streams. With a small party of trappers, he left the vicinity of Bear Lake (Utah) in midsummer of 1826 and made his way southward across Utah to the mouth of the Virgin River, where he crossed the Colorado. Recrossing this silt-laden stream near what is today Needles, California, he traversed the waterless waste of the Mojave Desert and entered California by way of Cajon Pass, arriving at Mission San Gabriel. Here he and his men were received hospitably by the resident Franciscans, but his reception at San Diego was a different matter.

Jose Maria Echeandia, a man of astringent personality, was the Mexican governor of California; and he had established his personal headquarters at San Diego because the climate at Monterey was, he believed, injurious to his health. His ego had suffered in San Diego from the loss of his suit for Josefa Carillo to the dashing American seafarer-merchant Henry Delano Fitch. In the governor's jaundiced view, Smith was a spy, and he had him plunked into the local *juzgado* until he could decide his fate. American shipmasters then in San Diego interceded for Smith, and the governor released him on Smith's solemn promise to leave California by the way he had entered it. Rejoining his men at San Gabriel, which they were sorry to leave, so equable was the climate and so refreshing the wine made there, Smith led his little band back over Cajon Pass, thus seeming to follow his promise to the governor.

He then turned northwest across the Mojave Desert to Tehachapi Pass, crossed it, and entered the San Joaquin Valley early in 1827. Here he found rich beaver streams and trapped up the east side of the valley to the mouth of the Stanislaus River. Leaving the bulk of his party encamped there to trap, Smith and two companions made the first known crossing of the main range of the Sierra Nevada by Europeans. Then they traversed the unknown wastes of the Great Basin, almost dying of thirst, and were reunited with Smith's partners at Bear Lake, in the first week of July, 1827. Smith had proven that California could be reached overland, and even though his route did not become a major one in the later migrations to California, the information he had gained became most valuable to his country in its restless, westering urge.

Before July, 1827 had run its course, Smith set out again for California with another party of trappers. Following his previous route, he came to the Mojave Indian villages on the Colorado without incident. These Indians, most peaceably inclined on his first trip, apparently had had a bitter encounter with American trappers from New Mexico shortly before Smith's second arrival in their lands. They avenged this encounter by surprising Smith's party and killing ten of its members. With the eight other survivors, Smith made his way to the men he had left encamped at the mouth of the Stanislaus River. Because the combined party needed supplies, Smith journeyed to Monterey to obtain them and again was incarcerated as a spy.

Again he was released through the intercessions of American merchants and shipmasters on his promise to the governor to leave California. This time he kept his promise. Obtaining the supplies he needed, he led his party from the Stanislaus up the east side of the Great Valley to above Sacramento. Here he turned westward, at about today's Chico Landing, and crossed the Coast Range folds to the ocean. Turning northward along the coast, which he found to be poor fur country, he and his men were nearly wiped out in a surprise attack by the Umpqua Indians in Oregon. Only Smith and two of his men survived. Making their way to the Columbia River, they were hospitably received by Dr. John McLoughlin, the Hudson's Bay Company's resident eminence at Fort Vancouver. (This lay across the Columbia River from what is now Portland, Oregon.)

After this experience, Smith sold out his interest in the firm of Smith, Jackson & Sublette and entered the Santa Fe trade out of Independence, Missouri. He was killed in his thirty-second year by Comanche in the Cimarron Desert on his first trip to Santa Fe.

Smith was the first American to reach California overland from the east, and the first of any nationality to traverse the approximate full length of the state. These accomplishments, added to his earlier participation in the discovery of South Pass (Wyoming) — the most feasible way for wagons to cross the Rocky Mountains — give him an honored place in the roster of American explorers of the Far West. He also gave his country its first accurate information about much of the Far West and Pacific region, which is an added laurel wreath.

After Smith came other Americans. James Ohio Pattie, mentioned earlier, entered California on a trapping junket from New Mexico with his father, Sylvester Pattie, and was jailed in San Diego, where his father perished. A smallpox epidemic ravaged California at this time, and Pattie later claimed to have earned his freedom and the undying gratitude of the *Californios* by vaccinating them by the thousands against the dread disease. Thereafter he departed California for good and all, and found a publisher for his reminiscences in Cincinnati. Hyperbolic though they were, and despite a hopelessly snarled chronology and geography, they played their part in quickening American interest in the sleepy land called California.

Ewing Young trapped out of New Mexico into California in the late 1820's and early 1830's, giving his first lessons in wilderness skills to a runaway saddler's apprentice named Christopher Carson and nicknamed "Kit." The route used by these trappers out of New Mexico to the Gila River in Arizona became one of the principal overland trails to California during the Gold Rush.

In 1834 Joseph Reddeford Walker led a party of trappers west from the Rockies by way of the Humboldt River, which was destined to become the major overland sluceway to California before, during, and after the Gold Rush. In his efforts to cross the Sierra, Walker became the first white man known to have looked down into Yosemite Valley, although he did not enter it. He also discovered Walker Pass in the Tehachapi Mountains. He and his party wintered at Monterey, where they were well received, or at least not molested. This may have been because their rifles represented more effective firepower than the entire Mexican military establishment in California could muster. Walker returned again to California during its golden heyday and was buried at Martinez, where his long trail finally reached its end.

In the late 1830's, a group of American ex-trappers headed by "Peg Leg" Smith and a mulatto master of wilderness craft, James P. Beckwourth or Beckwith, combined with the Ute Indians under their great war leader Walkara to make some of the largest horse thefts known in the annals of California. Leaving the Ute homeland around present Spanish Fork, Utah, the raiders would traverse southern Nevada and the Mojave Desert to enter California by Cajon Pass. The *ranchos* along the San Gabriel and Santa Ana rivers were their targets, and they are said to have stolen hundreds of horses at a time in these forays, driving their booty as far east as Pueblo, Colorado, for sale.

Americans were not the only overland adventurers to enter California in this period. The Hudson's Bay Company began sending trapping expeditions down from the Columbia River into the Great Valley as early as 1829. Traveling southward, east of the Cascade Range peaks in Oregon, they entered California near Goose Lake, angling thence across the juniper barrens and lava flows to Pit River, and into the Great Valley by a pass east of present-day Redding, California. Trapping well down the valley, they left a record of their presence in French Camp, near Stockton, which commemorates the French-Canadians in their expeditions. That beaver were plentiful in the Great Valley is supported by the fact that one of the Hudson's Bay Company parties trapped one hundred beaver in one day at the Sutter Buttes.

That they were formidable competitors for the fur riches of the Far West and California is supported by the wry American comment that H.B.C. stood for "Here Before Christ!"

It was the need for some kind of resident authority in the Great Valley, unsettled by either Spain or Mexico, to check these poaching intrusions by foreign trappers that caused another adventurer to earn the honor of erecting the first effective inhabitation there. This was the Swiss dreamer, Johann August Suter, whom we know today as John Sutter.

Sutter arrived in California from the Hawaiian Islands after a disastrous financial involvement in the Santa Fe trade. Rumor still emanates from his past that he was not a model of probity in handling funds entrusted to him by Swiss friends for investment in the United States. That he had a tremendous personality seems certain, and this may have been his major asset in obtaining an enormous land grant at the confluence of the American and Sacramento rivers. Here in 1839 he began the erection of Sutter's Fort, which was to be the economic and military center of his dreamed-of personal empire and to which he gave the name of New Helvetia in honor of his homeland. Sutter's reach was always longer than his grasp was strong; his dreams were always too large for his capabilities; and he had an appalling appetite for credit at ruinous rates of interest. Nonetheless, no man was turned from his door hungry, and instead of checking the flow of immigration when it began, he encouraged it. Ironically, Sutter, whose sawmill spawned the Gold Rush, was ruined by it.

Immigrants may be distinguished from adventurers, such as the fur trappers, and from drifters, such as the deserters from foreign vessels, by the fact that they set forth from their homes with a compulsion to find new land and there settle down. Also, their orientation primarily was agricultural.

It should be remembered that the bulk of the American movement into the Far West in the period 1840-47 was bound for, and went to, Oregon, not California. Oregon in this period was a disputed region under "joint occupancy" by Great Britain and the United States. California, on the contrary, was the possession of a foreign power, Mexico. Another factor in the Oregon emphasis was that for many years it had benefited from Protestant missionary publicity in the eastern part of the United States — publicity which had combined the virtues of bringing light to the heathen and adding territory to the United States. Underlying these reasons was a definite feeling among Americans, regardless of sectional or other phobias, that "perfidious Albion" (England) should be prevented from in any way gaining a solid foothold on land that belonged to the United States by divine right.

The first party of avowed overland emigrants from the States to reach California got its principal impetus from glowing accounts of the climate and fertile soil, sent east by John Marsh — called "Doctor" on insufficient grounds. Marsh had a certificate of completion of a classical education from Harvard when he reached California after unfortunate personal experiences

Californie . Rancho près du bois Rouge .

Wilkersheim's sketch of a *rancho* building and corrals, 1851.   — *The Bancroft Library*

elsewhere. Finding a shortage, actually a vacuum, of medical men in California, he used his Harvard certificate to establish his claim to be a licensed physician and acquired a grant of land from the Mexican governor near Mount Diablo. His letters back to friends in Missouri, coupled with accounts of conditions in California by Antoine Robidoux, who had visited California as a trapper, triggered the so-called Bidwell-Bartleson Party's emigration from Missouri in the spring of 1841.

John Bidwell, a young man in his early twenties, became a mainstay of the group, even though he was not its elected trail captain. As far west as

Fort Hall (Pocatello), Idaho, they followed the trappers' route, using South Pass to breach the Rocky Mountains. From Fort Hall to California they used some of the information derived from Joseph Walker's journey in 1834 but had God's own time of it, having to abandon their wagons en route. They crossed the Sierra in the vicinity of Sonora Pass, with Bidwell getting credit for being the first American to see the Big Trees *(Sequoia gigantea)* in the process, probably what is known today as the Calaveras Grove. In this party was the first American woman, teenaged Nancy (Mrs. Benjamin) Kelsey, to enter California overland, and her infant child has a comparable distinction. Bidwell made a truly distinguished career for himself in California, and his residence in Chico, which he founded, is now a historical monument administered by the state. Charles M. Weber came with this party and became the founder and benefactor of Stockton, while another member, Josiah Belden, became the first American mayor of San Jose.

The first wagons to reach California came with the Stephens-Townsend-Murphy Party of 1844. Under the guidance of Caleb "Old" Greenwood, some wagons were forced up and over the sheer granite face of what was later called Donner Pass before the party bowed before the threat of too much winter too soon. They left the rest of the wagons, about thirteen, at the east end of what came to be called Donner Lake, under the care of a seventeen-year-old named Moses Schallenberger. This teenager guarded the wagons and their contents all winter, and all alone, which is no mean feat. The crude cabin that he occupied was used in 1846 by the tragic fragments of the emigrant party that left the name of Donner for all time on the central pass through the Sierra Nevada.

"We crossed the prairies as of old/The Pilgrims crossed the sea . . ." and it was no easier for these wayfarers than it had been for the Pilgrims. — *The Bancroft Library*

Donner Pass — last great hurdle on the overland trail — scene of tragedy, depravity, and calm courage—
synonym for fun in the snow today — arterial east-west funnel north of Tehachapi; Espee tracks and
snowsheds, right foreground; snake-breaking curves of old highway, left foreground; scars of multi-
lane 1-80 far left.   — *Courtesy California Dept. of Transportation*

Cannibalism clings to the Donner Party's legacy and gains irony from the story that one Keseberg, said to have been the chief practitioner of this very ancient human survival act, later opened a restaurant in Sacramento. What is little known is that this party was so delayed before reaching the Sierra that an early severe snowfall caught them before they could cross the pass that bears their name. Their major delay occurred in the rugged Wastach Mountains east of Salt Lake City, simply because they believed a guidebook written by a young man *who had not even traveled* the shortcut he recommended at the time his book was published in Cincinnati, Ohio in 1845. This young man was Lansford W. Hastings, and his handbook to disaster for the Donner Party was *The Emigrants' Guide to California and Oregon.* By far the most appealing aspect of this tragedy of human disintegration is the heroism of Tamsen Donner, who stayed with her injured and much older husband knowing full well what her fate would be, and the heroic, literally superhuman efforts of the successful relief parties sent out from Sutter's Fort to rescue the survivors.

Donner Pass, which was a terrible obstacle at best to wagons and livestock, and their owners, gained an unsavory reputation as a result of the Donner tragedy. Despite its reputation, Donner Pass was used in the Gold Rush by those in a greater hurry than was wise. The main Gold Rush pass appears to have been Carson, after its route was laid out by eastbound Mormons in 1848, and Henness Pass, north of Donner was used by others. It should be borne in mind that the Sierra Nevada passes get progressively higher as one goes south down the range. Thus, Ebbets, Sonora, and Tioga passes were not favored by wagon travelers. From Tioga to Tehachapi and Walker passes, the High Sierra was not breached by wheels, and is not today. Current demands to open this segment of the Sierra Nevada to motorized recreationists are being opposed right stoutly by conservationists and to date successfully.

It may be well to remember that wagons by and large can go only straight up or straight down. Their center of gravity is too high for contour following, and the physical labor involved in making a "dugway," which is a trench on the uphill side of slopes for wheels to use (thus lowering the center of gravity) was too exhausting and too time-consuming for people in a hurry to reach the Promised Lnad. Going up, they would double, treble-, or quadruple-team each wagon. Coming down, they tied a tree behind the wagon for a drag brake, rough-locked the wheels by chaining them into immovability, and sometimes let the wagons down by snubbing a rope around a tree trunk and paying it out as needed, against too precipitous a descent.

In order to gain title to land in California after their arrival, the immigrants had to become Mexican citizens, and this seems to have been a matter of leaving their consciences somewhere east of the Sierra. Many of them did not go through this formality — remaining "enemy aliens," so to speak — but simply squatted on land that looked good to them and began subsistence farming. The beginning trickle of immigrants in the early 1840's and the independent attitude of many of them caused the Mexican government to fear that California would be the scene of another Texas-type usurpation of Mexican territory.

Another group of those who sought their Canaan in California deserves inclusion here. For one distinction, they came by sea, the only pre-Gold Rush party of settlers to do so; for another they were all Latter-day Saints (Mormons) seeking religious freedom under the leadership of Samuel Brannan. They arrived in San Francisco by the ship *Brooklyn* from New York *after* California had been conquered by the United States, and their landing date is recorded variously between August 30 and September 5, 1846. Twenty members of this contingent founded New Hope, the first agricultural settlement in the San Joaquin Valley, on the Stanislaus River.

Extranjeros and entrepreneurs extraordinary (left to right); Jacob P. Leese, Talbot Green, Thomas O. Larkin, Sam Brannan, W.D.M. Howard. — *The Bancroft Library*

It is this arrival of Mormons, fleeing persecution and pillage in Illinois and elsewhere in the East, that has given rise to the claim that they conducted the first Protestant church service in California. Omitting any remembrance of Francis Drake's chaplain, the question here well may be whether the Church of Jesus Christ of Latter-day Saints accepts membership in the Protestant community.

This group, plus the "Mormon Battalion," which arrived in 1847 as part of the United States' military forces under Colonel Philip St. George Cooke, put a substantial number of Mormons in California before the Gold Rush. Mormons were among the work force building Sutter's sawmill in 1848; Mormon Island on the American River, until it was submerged beneath the waters of Folsom Dam, commemorated their presence in the earliest days of the rush; Sam Brannan, leader of the sea-traveling Mormons, is credited with making the sleepy, fog-washed, sand-drenched, flea-bitten hamlet of San Francisco accept the fact of the discovery of *gold*! The question arises as to just how important a part the Mormons played in the Americanization of California that truly began with the Rush.

Sam Brannan was an ambitious man. So was Brigham Young, the leader of the Church. The two men split violently over their respective dreams and ambitions, and there is strong rumor that Brannan did not remit the tithes he collected in California in the name of his Church to Brigham and that Church in Deseret (Utah). Brannan left the Church as a result of these differences and suspicions, and wrote a fantastic personal chapter of life in California before he died — a broken, semi-alcoholic dreamer.

The majority of Mormons who came to California before the Gold Rush obeyed the dictates of Brigham Young and moved back to Utah while the Rush was at flood tide. This is a remarkable tribute to their religious fidelity. It also prevented the Mormons from exercising any substantial influence upon the early Americanization of California.

The major interrelationship between the Mormons and the Gold Rush seems to have been in the economic advantage the brethren in Utah derived from trading with travelers to California. It was substantial and contributed to the initial expansion of the Mormon establishment in the Great Basin, which included Mormon Station (Genoa, Nevada) and a settlement at today's San Bernardino, which was linked to Salt Lake City by the Mormon Trail.

Captain John Charles Fremont, Topographical Engineers, pathmarker and "conqueror" of California — a portrait taken probably about 1850.

— *Courtesy The Oakland Museum*

CHAPTER FIVE

HALLS OF MONTEZUMA: CALIFORNIA CHAPTER

Thirty years ago, it would not have been thought unusual to describe American acquisition of the Far West below 42 degrees north latitude as a necessary and an inevitable expansion to fill the "divinely ordained" boundaries of the republic. Today the conquest of California — indeed, the whole Mexican War — is apt to be denounced as an exercise in aggressive imperalism. This is especially true of politicians seeking votes in what once were Spain's Borderland Provinces — California, Arizona, New Mexico, Texas.

The conquest of California is further clouded by the state's Bear Flag mythology. What popular belief holds to be the "Bear Flag Republic" was never a government *de jure*, despite William B. Ide's proclaiming its independence, and most certainly it never was a government *de facto*. It existed between June 14 and July 7, 1846, primarily on paper and primarily in the minds of the handful of men involved. We are confronted in this matter with conflicting views as to the motives of those who *were* the Bear Flaggers, called *"los Osos"* by the *Californios*. One view holds that they were dedicated patriots, determined to raise the banner of individual freedom and political democracy above an alien and outlandish batch of Papists; the opposite view maintains that they were a bunch of brandy-happy ex-trappers and recent in-migrants who sought absolution from the crime of horse theft by declaring themselves revolutionaries against political despotism. A third view holds that they were essentially land-hungry immigrants who were disturbed by the fact that during the early months of 1846, land grants in the Sacramento and San Joaquin valleys by Pio Pico had totalled 373,000 acres and unless they acted swiftly, there would be little good land left for them to acquire however they could. One thing is certain: California would have been acquired without *"los Osos."*

An added emotional snare is set by the figure of John Charles Fremont, misnamed "the Pathfinder," who was in actuality a "path follower and marker." One view holds that Fremont was the hero who single-handedly conquered California by cutting his way through a wall of human flesh, while trailing the robes of Caesar in the gushing gore. The other view holds him to be an insubordinate young army officer, who belongs among the gaudiest popinjays in American history. No matter which view one cares to espouse, the fact remains that Fremont's experiences in California made him one of the state's first two U.S. Senators and made him the infant Republican

Party's first presidential candidate in 1856, as well as a major-general in the Civil War. Even as Sitting Bull, Billy the Kid and Little Annie Oakley, Fremont got a good press early and kept it far too long.

The fact remains that Texas and California are linked indissolubly in the tangled skein of events leading up to the Mexican War. The protection of Texas against reconquest by Mexico is the ostensible trigger of these hostilities, while the necessity of obtaining the harbor of San Francisco, which to the commercial and political powers in the East meant California, seems to have been the finger on that trigger. President Andrew Jackson had sought to acquire California by purchase as early as 1835, and the matter never was absent thereafter from the calculations of American statesmen and politicians and traders.

In addition, Mexico itself was an unstable, weak, and impoverished political entity. Such governments always are a menace to their near neighbors, and Mexico's chaotic internal political and economic structure gave the young United States good cause to fear that Mexico would fall easy prey to the designs of European powers such as England and France. This was compounded in the case of California by the fear, fed by rumors along the diplomatic grapevine, that Mexico would cede California to England in order to liquidate her indebtedness to the British. Such a happening would forever limit the United States to the land east of the Rocky Mountains; it would drastically affect the possibility of obtaining Oregon; it would place an exponent of monarchial absolutism in a position to threaten, perhaps even more than by its presence in Canada, the liberties and political principles of the United States. This was compounded by the plan of a young Irish priest, Eugene McNamara, to colonize California with Irish Catholics before it could be seized by the United States, "an irreligious and anti-Catholic nation." He won the approval of the Archbishop of Mexico to bring 10,000 colonists to California, and Pio Pico gave him a grant of 3,000 square leagues which latter was held to be illegal. Added to these was the widespread feeling among individual Americans that the Almighty had ordained it to be the mission of the United States to spread the glories of an enlightened political system wherever possible. These political and emotional forces coalesced into what became known most conveniently as "Manifest Destiny," a concept that provides a context for certain events in California history.

In 1842 Commodore Thomas ap Catesby Jones, a fiery American officer of Welsh extraction and long in the naval service of his country, commanded the U.S. Pacific Squadron, which was stationed at Callao (Lima), Peru. In September of that year, Jones received faulty intelligence that war had broken out between Mexico and the United States. This posed the threat that England's Pacific fleet would seize California forthwith. Jones sailed immediately for Monterey, sent his marines ashore without meeting resistance, and claimed California for his country. Afterward he discovered that there was no war. Somewhat embarrassed, he hauled down the American flag, restored the Mexican ensign to its place, and made profuse apologies all around. The tolerant residents of Monterey did not seem to take the affair too seriously, and Jones was given a farewell ball before he sailed out of the harbor. Official Mexico, however, took Jones' action to be an insult to the *dignidad nacional*, and Mexico City's newspapers made much over this insult by "ape" Catesby Jones. In a larger sense, Jones' action precluded any success for President Tyler's efforts to acquire California by paying off Mexico's creditors in England and the United States. It also brought a halt to negotiations between the countries over the boundary of Texas, and generally increased Mexico's fears over the future of California.

Daniel Coit made this drawing of San Francisco and its Bay as it looked before the Gold Rush.
— *The Bancroft Library*

In 1843 Thomas Oliver Larkin, the principal American merchant in Monterey, was appointed his country's consul at that only official port of entry in the province. In 1845 he was appointed the confidential agent of President James K. Polk, who had been elected in 1844 on a platform dedicated to expanding America's territorial boundaries. In the latter capacity Larkin was instructed to promote a revolution with California that would create an independent republic favorable to the United States. In time this entity would be expected to petition for annexation to the United States, as had Texas under conditions which seem to have provided the pattern for the proposed gambit in California. Larkin found allies among prominent *Californios*, primarily in the north, and especially General Mariano Guadalupe Vallejo at Sonoma. Larkin's position as the leading merchant and dispenser of credit in northern California did not hamper his machinations. Fremont did.

As a lieutenant in the Corps of Topographical Engineers, then the Army's *corps d'elite*, Fremont had made two exploring expeditions beyond the Rocky Mountains, which brought him the title of "Pathfinder." The fact is that ex-mountain men such as Kit Carson and "Broken Hand" Fitzpatrick had been the guides for Fremont's expeditions, and they *knew* at all times where they were and how to get from there to the next place. Fremont, however, does deserve laurels for his reports of these two expeditions, because these gave his country solid scientific data, by that day's standards, of the lands he had traversed. Fremont had been in California on the second of his wayfarings, in 1844, and had been hospitably received. Also, he had refrained from making an unmitigated nuisance of himself on this visit.

In the early weeks of 1846, Fremont returned to California, crossing the Sierra at Carson Pass in the dead of winter, and coming down to sanctuary at Sutter's Fort. His official orders did not instruct him to visit California at this time, but Fremont was the son-in-law of one of the most powerful senators in Washington, Thomas Hart Benton of Missouri, and a large body of questionable evidence has been presented to support the claim that Fremont was acting on secret instructions, suggestions, or thinly veiled hints from his father-in-law.

Fremont squattered about California for several months, having a bloodless run-in with Jose Castro, the military commander at Monterey, which knocked Larkin's secret negotiations in the head. This involved Fremont's construction of an alleged "fort" on Gabilan (Hawk) Peak, southeast of San Jose, and its abandonment. Fremont then moved slowly up the Great Valley toward Oregon, where he was supposed to have been pursuant to his general orders. In the vicinity of Klamath Falls, he was overtaken by a lieutenant of U.S. Marines, Archibald Gillespie, who was bearing dispatches to both Larkin and Fremont from Washington, dated in October, 1845 — many, many months before the War with Mexico erupted. Gillespie also brought letters from Fremont's family, and these allegedly contained secret instructions in a family code upon which Fremont subsequently acted. Whether they did or not, Fremont turned back to California, making his camp at the Sutter Buttes; and the Bear Flag Revolt began to swirl about his presence.

American settlers in the Sacramento Valley, between Sutter's Fort and today's Hamilton City, in Glenn County, were fearful at this time that Mexican officials were going to expel them from California. Some of these were Mexican citizens only for purposes of land acquisition; others were recent arrivals who had not deigned to become more than squatters, after the American frontier tradition. When a herd of horses was dispatched from Sonoma to Monterey, under the escort of a Mexican officer and several *vaqueros*, it was imagined that this presaged an army with fire and sword to drive the Americans out. Therefore, a group of settlers led by a stuttering ex-trapper named Ezekiel Merritt determined to prevent this by capturing the horses. Among his party was Robert "Long Bob" Semple, whose height allegedly caused him to fasten his spurs to his calves, not his heels, that he might tickle his horse without undue contortions. They asked Fremont to join them and to take command in his capacity as an army officer. Fremont refused. The settlers went right ahead and captured the horses at Murphy's

Ranch on the Consummes Rver in the Sierra foothills. Flushed with this success, they then determined to capture Sonoma and again asked Fremont to lead them. They got another refusal.

Securing recruits from recently arrived immigrants, including William Todd, a nephew of Abraham Lincoln's wife, and William Brown Ide, a mill-wright who was suspected of Mormonism, they rode for Sonoma to rinse away the blot of horse theft in the waters of patriotism. In the early morning of June 14, 1846, they demanded the surrender of Mariano Guadalupe Val-lego, whose title of "General" made him the ranking and only Mexican military force in that region. This was Vallejo's first intimation that war was loose in his land; after accepting this fact, he surrendered with great hos-pitality. The result of this hospitality was that Ide, a teetotaller, drew up a Proclamation of Independence, the only state document resulting from the capture of Sonoma, and a crudely fashioned flag — bearing the Lone Star from Texas and a grizzly bear, with the legend CALIFORNIA REPUBLIC — was hoisted above the captured citadel of despotism. The bear was so badly drawn that it looked like a pig to the *Californios*, but this has been rectified in the state flag that floats over California today.

In consequence of the Bear Flaggers' success, Fremont brought his party of ex-trappers, Delaware Indians, and plain military men over from Sutter Buttes and assumed command of the forces of the new republic — *after* the fact, be it remembered. Fremont's true contribution to this im-broglio was psychological. He was an army officer; he had been junketing about California for months; he had left and then returned, and he had powerful connections in Washington. It was natural for the settlers to feel that there was more to Fremont's presence in California than scientific curiosity, and their course of action undoubtedly was influenced by some expectation that he would support them with his armed might if events caught the revolutionaries between a rock and a hard place.

While Fremont was riding up and down and around in California, major events were taking place outside California. War with Mexico actually came to pass along the lower Rio Grande, when a Mexican cavalry patrol defeated a similar American force allegedly trespassing on Mexican ter-ritory. Word of war filtered across Mexico to Mazatlan, where Commodore John D. Sloat had the U.S. Pacific Squadron at anchor. Sloat was a sluggish man, and cautious, but he finally set sail for Monterey. Arriving there, he took a few days more to make up his mind to act. Then, on July 7, 1846, the Stars and Stripes were raised above the ex-capital of Mexican California for all time. Fremont and his enlarged command rode down to Monterey to be mustered into Sloat's forces; as the "California Battalion," they took part in the bloodless American conquest of California.

The small amount of real fighting that occurred in California came about after this initial seizure because of heavy-handed actions by American forces and officers, and it erupted and had its main center in Southern

Mariano Guadalupe Vallejo — "The Lion of the North" — with daughters.
— *Courtesy The Bancroft Library*

California. American occupation troops were expelled from Los Angeles in the skirmishing, and the one real battle of the entire Mexican War in California was fought at San Pasqual, some miles northeast of San Diego, on the foggy morning of December 6, 1846. Here the American "Army of the West," about two hundred men coming overland from New Mexico under Stephen Watts Kearny, was defeated by a force of *Californios* under Andres Pico, whose superlative horsemanship made their lances and *riatas* most deadly weapons. Rallying from these setbacks, the American sea and land forces reconquered southern California with a minimum of bloodshed. Thereafter, the governance of the conquered land degenerated into an unseemly bickering between Kearny, Fremont, and Commodore Stockton (who had relieved Sloat), which resulted in Fremont being court-martialed on charges of insubordination. While the charges were not proven, Fremont resigned the service in a huff and Kearny's reputation has been diminished ever since by pro-Fremont partisans. This bickering would have made it possible for the *Californios* to expel the *Americanos*, at least temporarily, had they not been equally divided among themselves.

California remained under a military government after the conquest, and in 1847 more emigrants from the States went to Oregon, and to Utah, than to California. Of the less than 2,000 Americans who did enter California in that year, the majority were soldiers of the Third New York Regiment of Volunteers, which gained a reputation for rowdiness, and of the "Mormon Battalion," most unrowdy, both of which arrived too late for any fighting but served as occupation and garrison troops until their enlistments expired.

By the Treaty of Guadalupe Hidalgo, Mexico was paid $15,000,000 for the lands she ceded and the United States also assumed claims of American citizens against Mexico in the amount of $3,250,000. It seems worth noting here that payment by a conqueror for what it has acquired by force of arms is not common practice in international relations.

California eventually would have been given offical status as an American territory, and would have followed the procedures pertaining to the transition from territory to state. How long it would have taken for these steps to have brought statehood must remain forever unknown. The Gold Rush settled the question with speed and finality.

Even more important than bringing California statehood, virtually by Caesarian section, the Gold Rush set in motion the acceleration of growth based upon the interaction between technology, population and bounteous natural resources that changed the isolated province of Mexico into the equivalent of a nation-within-a-state in an incredibly short time.

"I would not for ten thousand dollars have stayed [at home] and lost what I have seen . . ."
It was, indeed, a time when "the hearts of the young men were touched with fire."

— *Courtesy The Bancroft Library*

CHAPTER SIX

THE GOLDEN STONE
IN THE POOL OF HISTORY

Gold made the golden trout the state fish and the golden poppy the state flower. Gold brought to California men to match the mountains where the gold was found, and brought them in such numbers as to transform San Francisco from a desultory haven for 500 persons to frantic human hive of 25,000 in two years; to lift California from less than 14,000 total population to 264,435 by the state census of 1852.

Economically, gold gave California a self-contained source of capital that not only prevented it from sharing the common far western fate of exploitation by the financial east but enabled California to become an investor in, and exploiter of, the Far West in her own right. This does not mean that great hordes of prospectors struck it rich in Shirt Tail Gulch or wherever, and thereafter invested their gains in ranches or other mines or real estate in Nevada or Oregon or Idaho or Arizona. Rather, it was the merchants, the men who mined the miners, who accumulated the initial investment capital and reinvested it elsewhere.

Socially, gold transformed California from a sleepy, isolated, pastoral land into a bustling, basically urban, very cosmopolitan, and socially fluid member of the world community.

Politically, gold enabled California to bypass the territorial period, simply by implying that if California were not admitted to the Union on her own terms, she was quite able, and more or less willing, to establish herself as an independent entity until such time as the Union wanted her.

It is interesting to note here that the first Constitutional Convention at Monterey in September, 1849 drew up a state constitution, not a territorial document; that a full slate of state officers was elected; and that a state government was functioning some months *before* California was granted membership in the Union.

It should be noted also that this first constitution carried an anti-slavery section and that California was admitted as a "free" state, thus upsetting the balance of power between free and slave states in Congress. This action had a considerable effect upon fixing more rigidly than before the lines of sectional cleavage that culminated in the Civil War.

It is necessary to point out that the antislavery proviso in the first constitution did not represent a moral indictment of slavery on the part of Californians, many of whom were from the Deep South. Negroes in

California, there being about one thousand of them in the census of 1850, or about 1 percent of the total population, did not get any true semblance of civil rights, such as the franchise and the right to testify in court cases involving white Americans, until 1863, after the Republican Party had risen to political prominence in both the nation and the state. The antislavery section seems to have been inserted simply to prevent the use of slave labor, be it chattel Negro, or trinket-happy Indian, or *peon Latino* in the mines.

The first years of the Gold Rush were years of individuals seeking on an individual basis a fair share of "anybody's gold." It was, indeed, *anybody's gold*, for the land was not yet surveyed, nor had any arm of any government any means to enforce no-trespass laws on the public domain. In these first years, say 1848-50, any individual was entitled to as much gold as he could find anywhere by his own exertions, but it was not right, or fitting, or American to use slaves, or servants, or employees to gain an unfair advantage over one's fellow-seekers who did not have such extra arms and hands.

California remained the world's leading gold-producer for the balance of the century, giving the United States its first great source of precious metal for both coinage and currency support. Of world importance, gold from California was the first major infusion of new precious metal since the Spaniards had tapped the accumulated hoards of Aztec and Inca.

Perhaps $500,000,000, more than twenty times that amount at today's gold prices, flowed from California's mines in the years before the Civil War, and this almost exactly equals the amount invested in new industrial capacity in the eastern states over the same span. It is presumptuous to make a one-for-one relationship here, but California gold can be said to have

ARRIVÉE D'UNE FAMILLE EN CALIFORNIE.
Ah! mon Dieu...... voilà déjà nos domestiques qui nous abandonnent pour courir aux mines !.... faudrait peut-être leur promettre une petite augmentation de gages !......

Ship captains lost their crews, merchants lost their clerks, French *bourgeois* lost their servants — all to the lure of the golden Lorelei.
— *The Bancroft Library*

The *arrastre* technique for crushing quartz ore was borrowed from Mexico. Note the miner with his "cradle" at right and the "panner" in foreground.
— *Courtesy The Bancroft Library*

played a substantial part in creating the industrial supremacy that was so vital to the Union's ultimate victory over the Confedracy. The lure of California and the nation's expanding economy also caused emigration from Europe to the United States to double between 1848 and 1850 and to maintain this new level for several years. The bulk of these newcomers settled in states that came to the Union's support; thus California may be said to have contributed another substantial element to the preservation of the Union.

All down the millennia before the Gold Rush, the forces of nature had been extracting gold from the quartz ledges in which it had been formed in the Sierra Nevada. Erosion had exposed the ledges; frost had split off chunks of gold-bearing rock; rains and snow-melt had carried these into stream beds; and the force of falling water had carried them downstream for varying distances, pounding and crushing out the gold between the rolling native-rock boulders in the process. Gold is one of the heaviest of metals, nineteen times heavier than water; a fact obvious to the forty-niner but unknown to most of today's urban residents. This fact is basic to the extractive processes, from miner's pan to modern concentrator, and played its part in the distribution of gold in the watercourses — the "free" gold that made the placers of the forty-niners.

The finest, or "flour," gold was found farthest down the streams, sometimes into the eastern edges of the Great Valley. Then, working upstream, the golden placer flakes got bigger — grain gold, pea gold, nut gold, nuggets, gobbets, and chunks. This progression gave rise to the belief that somewhere, high in the shimmering heights of the Sierra, there must be the *Veta Madre*, the one great "Mother Lode" whence all this golden treasure sprang.

In the spring of 1850, the rumor that someone had found "Gold Lake" high in the Sierra fastness — a lake whose sands were pure gold — unhinged some 2,000 miners sufficiently that they spent fruitless weeks in seeking it. Today, the Lakes Basin Recreational Area in the Plumas National Forest boasts a Gold Lake, among its numerous glacial tarns, in the same region that was traversed by those who sought the mythical lake so many years ago.

California's main gold belt extended from Mariposa in the south up the western slope of the Sierra to Oroville, where the North Fork of Feather River became regarded as its northern terminus. From this demarcation north into the southern Cascade Range, the volcanic activity discussed earlier had overlaid the late Tertiary (15,000,000 year-old) formations so deeply with lava that natural forces had not been able to perform the work of extraction and distribution as in the main California auriferous belt.

From the North Fork of Feather River, the gold belt jumped northwestwardly across the Great Valley into western Tehama and Shasta counties, into Trinity County around Weaverville, and thence ranged northward toward and into southern Oregon's Klamath Mountains. This put western Siskiyou County also into the secondary gold belt. Isolated pockets of

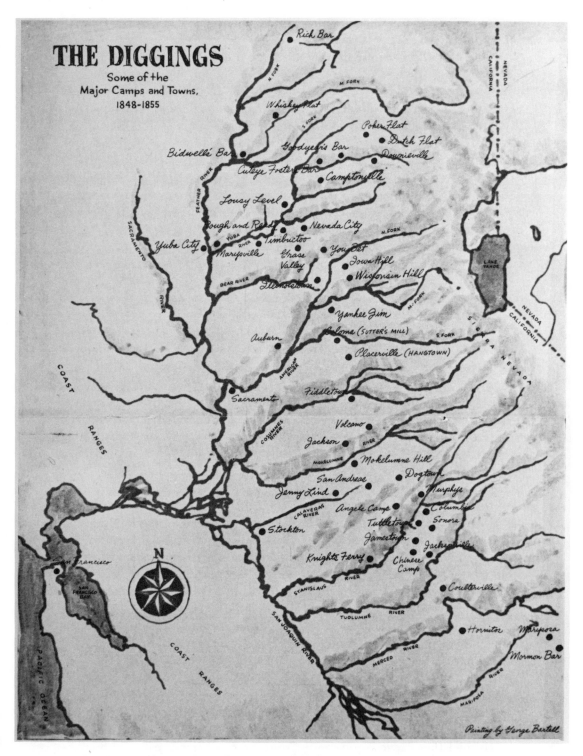

The Mother Lode where Dame Fortune was a fickle lass.
— *Courtesy of WESTWAYS — The Auto Club of So. Calif.*

placer gold were found in southern California, but these were of small import to the state, or its growth.

Few important deposits of gold were found on the eastern slope of the Sierra within California's present boundaries, although the town of Bodie — now preserved in a state of arrested decay by the Division of Parks and Recreation — had a hectic life as a gold camp both promotional and productive. Indeed, the major mineral east of the Sierra summit was silver, a fact emphasized by the later chapter on the Comstock Lode beneath Virginia City, Nevada.

The existence of gold in California was known at least in the Mexican period, for small shipments of placer gold were made to New England during the heyday of the hide-and-tallow trade. They seem to have been brought to the missions by Indian converts, or by wild Indians from the Sierra for trading purposes. Such minor amounts, however, did not stimulate any gold-seeking expeditions of consequence — some say because the Franciscans had seen the evils wrought by mining upon the native population of Mexico and did not wish to see such havoc repeated in California.

The first, repeat *first*, veritable discovery of gold in California was made near present-day Newhall, where a roadside marker commemorates the event and slightly misplaces it. The date was March 9, 1842, and the discoverer was a *vaquero* named Francisco Lopez who, according to legend, pulled up a bunch of wild onions to flavor his dried meat (jerky) and found gold flakes clinging to the shallow roots. Legend or not, the fact remains that shallow placers were worked in that area for several years, and relatively substantial amounts of gold extracted, some of which was shipped to the Philadelphia Mint by Abel Stearns. For reasons still unclear, none of the great *ranchero* families of the Southland — Pico, Lugo, Yorba, Sepulveda, Dominguez, del Valle — got excited about it. The majority of the working miners in these placers were from Mexico, and when the shallow deposits were worked out, about 1845, they went home to Mexico. They returned by the thousands in 1848-49. Even though this first discovery was vastly overshadowed by the discovery of January 1848, it must be mentioned, simply to keep the more rabid Southern Californiacs from unseemly protest.

The discovery that triggered *the* Gold Rush was set in motion by John Sutter's need for lumber at his seat of power called New Helvetia. His quest for a sawmill site convenient to this establishment had been carried on for several years before one was found in a bend of the South Fork of the American River at a spot the Indians called *Culloma* (beautiful vale), which is today's Coloma, in El Dorado County. A cadaverous, introverted Yankee millwright and carpenter, James W. Marshall, was Sutter's partner and superintendent in building this mill — a vertical saw powered by a waterwheel that operated a Pittman rod off an eccentric on the wheel. In the mill's "tailrace" (the channel that carries water away from the revolving wheel as its buckets discharge their contents), Sutter's workmen, Marshall being the first, discovered a "mettle" that looked to them like "goald." Debate still continues over whether the exact date of this discovery was January 19 or Jaunary 24, 1848. The commonly accepted date is the latter one, although the argument seems academic. The operative fact is the timing of the news affecting the rest of the world, which would not have been affected by the earlier date in any measurable way.

Even though the knolwedge of gold's existence became widespread, several months elapsed before it had discernible impact upon California. Sam Brannan, not yet an apostate Mormon, is said to have started all the excitement by riding through the sandy somnolence that was San Francisco, holding aloft a bottle filled with flakes and shouting, "Gold! Gold! Gold from the American River!" The fact that Brannan had just opened a store at Sutter's Fort may have stirred him into stimulating transient trade.

In the wake of Brannan's ride, the adult male population of California decamped in a body, it seems, for "the diggin's." The memoirs of a young army lieutenant then stationed in California, the immortal William Tecumseh Sherman of later Civil War fame, bear witness to the reduction virtually to nothing of U.S. Army forces in California by desertions of those who sought sudden fortune in the gold-rich streams of the Sierra Nevada.

New York's lithographers had a field day lampooning the greedy hysteria that gripped the East Coast in 1849.
— *The Bancroft Library*

Rumors of the gold find trickled eastward in the ensuing months but did not find wholehearted acceptance there. The same rumors rippled northward into Oregon, and westward across the Pacific to Hawaii and to Australia, and made their way southward to Mexico and on into Chile and Peru. Men from all these regions, unlike the skeptical Yankees, forthwith made haste to California, and the "forty-eighters," perhaps 14,000 of them, came from these places, a very large proportion of them from Mexico. Many of the firstcomers, especially the Oregonians, went home when the panning season ended with the advent of the winter rains, and who can blame them, with flour at $800 a barrel and whiskey at $100 a gallon, and merchants giving but $6-8 per ounce for their gold.

Gold production in this first year has been estimated at ten million dollars, but the existence of gold in quantities beyond belief did not impress the residents back in "the States" until President Polk's message to the Congress on the State of the Union in December 1848. His message contained official information from Colonel R.B. Mason, commanding what army he had left in California, that gold had been discovered, and that in quantity. Then the roof fell in, and the astonishing pattern of human movement to California was established, a pulsating migration that has continued throughout her history, as human beings have sought to better their condition in life beside the Golden Shore.

Perhaps 100,000 Americans or more comprised the starting "argonauts of '49"; and barring such esoteric promotional schemes as a hot-air ballon line, they ventured by land and sea, and by a combination of these hazards. Leaky, worm-eaten old tubs were hastily refurbished, and tickets to disaster were sold to the frenzied throngs seeking sea passage to the Golden Shore. New York alone cleared 775 vessels for California in 1849. In the outfitting points along the Missouri River — Independence, Westport, St. Joseph, St. Louis — the prices of horses, mules, wagons, salt pork, flour, powder, and lead went out of sight. And wagons were rigged with sails to attempt a lumbering navigation of the Great American Desert.

The first of the Americans to reach California did so via Cape Horn, a passage of 18,000 miles that consumed six months — with luck. In later years, both *Flying Cloud* and *Andrew Jackson* made eighty-nine-day passages from New York to San Francisco; but these were clipper ships, the finest flowering of American genius under sail, which were far, far different from the "butter tubs" that carried the forty-niners on the Cape Horn passage.

Crowded quarters, poor food, and the resultant scurvy and other disease took their toll on this artery, by which perhaps 16,000 reached California in '49. By July 1, 1850 more than 600 blue-water vessels, abandoned by their crews, lay rotting and forgotten in San Francisco Bay and its tributaries.

The quickest route, and the one that remained the fastest communications link until the transcontinental railroad was completed in 1869, was by

The hazards of an uncharted coast are all too plainly seen in the wreck of the *Glenesslin* which drove ashore under full sail.

— *Courtesy National Maritime Museum at San Francisco*

sea and land via Panama. This required sea passage from eastern and Gulf ports to Aspinwall (Colon), then a tortuous overland trek across the Isthmus, then passage in an overloaded sidewheel steamer to San Francisco. It ate up at least six-to-eight weeks and cost $500 at first. A variant of this route ran by way of Nicaragua. Chagres (yellow) fever, dysentery, malaria, and bandits killed many of those who used this route, but perhaps 20,000 of those who essayed it won through to California in '49.

These routes were used chiefly by those who resided near salt water. Argonauts from the Mississippi River Valley generally took the overland trails. There were several of these to California, some 9,000 taking the Gila Trail and other thousands crossing Mexico to its Pacific and Gulf of California ports. The bulk of the traffic in '49 used the old Emigrant Trail, the so-called Central Overland Route, which later was followed generally by the Union Pacific-Central Pacific rail linkage. The Central Overland required from sixty to ninety grinding days on horseback, or from three to five months of even more abrasive travel by wagon. Cholera swept the trail in '49, some 5,000 graves bespeaking its ravages; and the young men of the Plains tribes acquired status and improved their skills by picking off stragglers and ill-guarded livestock. Perhaps 30,000 won through on the Central Overland, but even these did not do so unscathed. Across the forty death-dry Nevada miles between the Sink of Humboldt River and the snow-fed, life-giving waters of the Truckee, one observer who survived its crossing counted 362 abandoned wagons, 350 dead horses, 280 dead oxen, and 120 dead mules along this *via dolorosa*. In addition, these miles were littered with abandoned household treasures; one mound by the wayside was composed of 600 pounds of jetisoned bacon.

We do not know the total human losses on the routes to California in '49. Between 90/100,000 in all won through to the Golden Shore, and it is believed that 20% of these died within six months of their arrival from accident, disease, and malnutrition. That this influx was predominantly masculine is attested by the Army register kept at Fort Laramie in 1850, which showed 39,506 men, 1,421 women, and 1,609 children through August 14 of that year. This same period tallied 9,927 wagons, 23,172 horses, 36,116 oxen, and 7,323 cows. Another 35,000 reached California by the sea routes in 1850, while 26,593 men and 8 women LEFT the state in the same year. Dame Fortune had not smiled upon them.

Whether in '49 or '50, the men were young, virile, lusty and aggressive, for this was a time when "the hearts of the young men were touched with fire," and they represented in many respects the cream of young American manhood of the time. There was a high proportion of literate men, of educated and professional men among them, and this gave a distinctive flavor to California's first tidal wave of humanity from the older states.

They brought their homegrown political allegiances with them, Whig and Democrat, and it was never settled beyond a reasonable doubt which

"Abundance of gold does not always beget . . . a grasping and avaricious spirit. The cosmopolitan cast of society in California, resulting from the commingling of so many races and the primitive mode of life, gave a character of good-fellowship to all its members."
— *Courtesy California State Library*

persuasion held the hardest drinkers, men who were to be shunned as "hopeless casks." Whig or Democrat, they held firmly to the fixed belief that every man had an equal right to an equal chance to his fair share of fortune; and it should be remembered well that this was the very first time in America's history that Dame Fortune had extended to the individual the prospect of sudden riches, of gold for the grasping, without let or hindrance or seemingly much effort. Whig or Democrat, they were fundamentally and irrevocably Protestant, cherishing an active mistrust of Popery in every form; and they brought with them an animosity towards Spain and her descendants that went back in time to the Spanish Armada.

They held that God's bounty belonged to native-born Americans, and white at that, and this was reflected in the laws they passed levying a special tax upon "foreign" miners in California. The gold-seekers brought with them the frontier's tradition of free land for the squatting and an ignorance of the property rights of the *Californios* and such as John Sutter — rights which had been acquired pursuant to the laws of Spain and Mexico, and rights that the United States had pledged its honor to uphold in the Treaty of Guadalupe Hidalgo. As a result, they overran lands granted under the preceding governments. Poor, portly John Sutter, the open-handed dreamer, once the self-styled Baron of New Helvetia, was destroyed financially by their locust-like invasion of his broad acres near Sacramento.

When the Argonauts reached California, they quickly expanded the known extent of the "diggin's" from its first center at Coloma. In this expansion, some of them satisfied their avarice with rich discoveries. To meet their needs, and the needs of the teeming thousands of less fortunate seekers, became the destiny of San Francisco, and it soon possessed 46 gambling joints, 48 brothels, and 537 saloons.

The heart of the city first beat frantically along the curving little beach of Yerba Buena Cove, which was the city's principal landing spot. Its northern extremity was today's "foot of Broadway," currently the center of an exposure of female flesh for the tourist trade; its southern extremity was Rincon Point, where the western buttresses of the Bay Bridge stand today. The waters of the cove lapped against the line of the present Montgomery Street at the foot of the California Street hill. Thus, the financial heart of today's San Francisco, from Montgomery Street to the Embarcadero, is built on "fill" from the then near-by sand hills and other, less prosaic materials.

Deserted sailing ships were burned to the water's edge and then scuttled to make more fill. Commodities that arrived to find a glutted market also were consigned to the bottom of the Bay; stoves, bales of cloth, hogsheads of tobacco, barrels of flour, and assorted jars, boxes, bundles, and parcels of almost anything you care to name became part of modern San Francisco's underpinning.

One of the deserted ships became California's first state prison, before more formal quarters were constructed at San Quentin. Other vessels were driven up onto the beach of the cove to serve as warehouses, hotels, and restaurants. In these usages, the hard fact is reillumined that gold-crazed California's umbilical link with the outwide world was the sea, even as it had been in Hispanic days.

Among the more exotic shipments said to have reached San Francisco in '49 was a bevy of *senoritas* from Mazatlan to bring solace and excitement to the Argonauts. Another was a shipment of several hundred cats to combat the hordes of rats — brown, black, gray, all large, all hungry, and all incredibly agile — that infested San Francisco. They were a more obvious pest, although no more voracious, than the sand fleas for which the city was notorious.

San Franciscans who had more than one shirt sent their laundry to Honolulu in the beginning. Some, it is said, sent it clear to Canton, China. Perhaps the first "service" industry in San Francisco was the laundry business; and its first practitioners were brawny Irishwomen, who resented, often forcibly, the later intrusion of the Chinese "washhouses."

The lure of gold for the peoples of all the world is shown clearly in the first accurate federal census for California, that of 1860. In this year, the state's total population was 379,800 persons, of whom 162,855 were men between the ages of twenty and fifty, while there were but 50,000 women in this same age bracket. It has been said that "the dynamite of California in these years was composed of one part vigor and one part unsatisfied passion." *Quien sabe?* This census showed 4,086 American Negroes in the state, while almost 40% of the total population were foreign born: China, 34,935; Ireland, 33,147; Germany, 21,646; England, 12,227; Mexico, 9,150; France, 8,462; Canada, 5,438; Scotland, 3,670; Italy, 2,805; and 2,250 from South American countries. The cultural diversity these seekers brought to California has given the state a distinctive flavor ever since.

The Chinese, mainly from the southern provinces where there had been rebellions against the Peking government, largely had come on a credit system, whereby their passage was paid by wealthy Chinese, who in turn sold their labor through Chinese sub-contractors to various Chinese mining and manufacturing companies. These victims of debt peonage were known as *Gum Shan Hok*, "guests of the Golden Mountain." When the Foreign Miners Tax was re-installed in 1852, it was aimed directly and primarily at the Chinese in the mines. First levied at $3.00 per head per month, later raised to $4.00 until its repeal in 1870, it brought the state 40% of all monies collected, while 40% went to the county where collected, and 20% to the sheriff who did the collecting. It financed almost one-quarter of the total state budget in some years, and *all* of the budget for such mining counties as Plumas, while making the sheriffs of such counties the highest paid officials in the state.

The Oriental Americans by Brett S. Melendy is a standard work on this subject.

The native-born *Californios*, perhaps 11,000 in 1849, were relatively unaffected by the first flush years of the Gold Rush, although many of them profited from the demand for livestock that the Rush engendered. For one thing, their land holdings were not in the gold regions of the state; for another, very few of the *Californios* actively participated in the Rush after the earliest months of 1849. By and large, the area of major *Californio* influence remained un-Americanized until after the Civil War. This was Southern California, especially Los Angeles, which became a place of refuge for those who felt that continued residence in San Francisco or the mines would subject them to a fatal attack of "hemp fever." For twenty years after the Rush began, Los Angeles was as tough a little town as California history affords, and it tallied forty legal hangings and thirty-seven impromptu ones in this period — to say nothing of the ones who got away.

The resident Indians suffered most from the Gold Rush, simply because their ancestral honelands either were on the roads to or contained the "diggin's." There never was what properly could be called an Indian War in California, despite rampant local legends to the contrary, until the reduction of the Modoc in the Lava Beds of northeastern California in the 1870's. Neither was there an organized campaign of genocide against the Indians, despite the rhetoric of today's Native American orators and activists. Wherever the Indians were in the way, they were removed to reservations; even so there *was* violence incident to the clashes between Stone Age and Industrial Revolution. The disruption of the Indians' environment, coupled with the introduction of diseases such as measles, against which there were no hereditary immunity, and the introduction of alcohol, for which the Indians had no tolerance to equal their affinity, did far more to reduce their numbers than any other factors. Only in the deserts of Southern California, along the eastern slopes of the Sierra, and in the far northern mountains, did the Indians escape the initial culture-shock of the Gold Rush. To a lesser degree, they escaped it in the Coast Range intervales in Lake, Mendocino, and Humboldt counties, which were not within the gold belt described earlier.

Blacks, as noted earlier, made up about 1% of the Gold Rush population. Many were freedmen from New England; some were slaves accompanying their owners and permitted to work on their own to purchase their freedom and that of the families they had left behind, and some, although slaves, had been permitted to come alone to California to earn enough to buy their freedom. A negro known only as "Dick" made a phenomenal success in the diggin's and blew it all in a riotous stay in San Francisco. Others reacted differently to good fortune, as did the seven men who made a good find in Brown's Valley on the Yuba River drainage east of Marysville. They named it the "Sweet Vengenace Mine," and used its proceeds to become successful businessmen, barbers, hotel keepers, and leaders of the Black community outisde of San Francisco. One of these fortunate miners, Edward Duplex, became the first Negro to be elected mayor of a California community, when

Wheatland so honored him in 1888. Throughout the nineteenth century, the numbers of Negroes in California were so small in relation to total population that there was no economic competition to engender racial animosity, and it also seems evident that anti-Chinese sentiment acted as a lightning rod to divert racial antagonisms from the other minority segments of the populace. The story of the early Blacks in California has been well told by Rudolph M. Lapp in *Blacks in Gold Rush California*.

The major foreign element in the first two years of the Rush were Latin Americans, many of them from Chile but most of them came from the north Mexican state of Sonora, which fact is preserved in the foothill city of that name today. The majority of these proficient *placeros* were concentrated in the so-called "Southern Mines," from Sonora to Mariposa. So numerous were they that the first anti-foreign legislation in California, the Foreign Miners License Law of 1850, was passed with them in mind. It imposed a special monthly tax of $20 per head on non-native Americans and was designed to reduce competition for the gold from this source and to raise revenue for the state by taxing those who employed foreign-born miners for their own benefit. While the law applied to *all* foreign-born, it appears that English, Germans, and British colonials escaped its enforcement. By the end of 1851, most of the *Latinos* in the Southern Mines had returned to their homelands. As noted earlier, the tax on foreign miners was reinstituted to apply to the Chinese.

It is a commonplace of California folklore and in all too many history texts that the corporate ancestor of the Southern Pacific Railroad imported the first Chinese for construction purposes. This is clotted nonsense! The Central Pacific Railroad *did* employ thousands of Chinese after 1865 to do construction work that no one else wanted to do, what with job opportunities abounding elsewhere. These Chinese were drawn from the existing thousands already in the state, where they had been hospitably received at first, as is indicated by the fact that a Chinese contingent was invited to participate, and did so, in the Fourth of July parade in San Francisco in 1852.

It was not until the Chinese began to compete in the mines, and to do so as the chances for quick fortune faded, that their persecution began. This was aggravated by the economic willwaws of the 1850's and 1870's, when the Chinese became branded as horrible, alien, and outlandish creatures who were taking the bread from the mouths of honest American workingmen and their families. This made the basis for the state's long friction with the federal government over restrictive immigration legislation directed against all Asiatics, and it laid the psychological foundation for the emotional hysteria that sanctioned the internment of the Japanese during World War II. Ironically enough, the earliest agitation against the Chinese was sparked in part by other immigrant groups, the Irish being prominent among them.

The Gold Rush came at an opportune time to solve some of Europe's human problems. Ireland had been in the grip of a potato famine for some

Merchants' Express Line of Clipper Ships
FOR
SAN FRANCISCO!

NONE BUT A 1 FAST SAILING CLIPPERS LOADED IN THIS LINE.

THE EXTREME CLIPPER SHIP
OCEAN EXPRESS

WATSON, COMMANDER,

AT PIER 9, EAST RIVER.

This splendid vessel is one of the fastest Clippers afloat, and a great favorite with all shippers. Her commander, Capt. WATSON, was formerly master of the celebrated Clipper "FLYING DRAGON," which made the passage in **97 days,** and of the ship POLYNESIA, which made the passage in **103 days.**

She comes to the berth one third loaded, and has very large engagements.

RANDOLPH M. COOLEY,
118 WATER ST., cor. Wall, Tontine Building.

Agents in San Francisco, DE WITT, KITTLE & Co.

NESBITT & CO., PRINTERS.

No flying fish were available for the Cape Horn passage but the message was plain to those in a hurry to reach the golden shore.   — *Courtesy The Bancroft Library* years in the late 1840's, and it was better to emigrate than to starve beyond the pale of an English landlord's mercy. The Irish element in San Francisco did the brute labor of the port, and their wives did the city's washing and domestic chores, thus competing with the Chinese at the bottom of the urban economic ladder. The Irish quickly became important in the city's politics and long remained major players on the city's political stage.

France had internal problems in this period, and the French government went so far as to establish a state lottery in which the chief prizes were free passages to California. The Gallic presence in California was expressed quickly in a French-language newspaper, and the great tradition of fine cuisine in San Francisco had its roots in this element. The French encountered anti-foreign sentiment in the mines, and a pitched battle between American and French gold seekers was fought near Mokelumne Hill, on the Mother Lode.

Germany, too, experienced an abortive revolt in 1848. Many of its leaders and partisans fled to the United States, including California, where a German-language newspaper sprang up in San Francisco. The bulk of the German segment seems to have eschewed the mines in favor of urban trades, small businesses and professions. One of the first savings banks in San Francisco was organized by a group of Germanic immigrants, and Anaheim was founded as a cooperative colony by a band of German farmers in 1857.

Trace elements of many another ethnic group can be found in the Rush. Hawaiians, being magnificent seamen, had been in California ever since the hide-and-tallow trade. The cadre of Sutter's initial working force at Sutter's Fort had come from the Islands. Place names, such as Kanaka Bar, reflect the Hawaiians' presence in the mines, and the name of Owyhee County in southwestern Idaho derives from their homeland islands.

The Australians, other than the "Sydney Ducks," who came to California in the Rush were a national rather than an ethnic minority, and constituted an important influence in their own country's later development after their return. What they had seen and learned in California prompted the Aussie "diggers" to look for gold in their own backyard, and their strikes at Ballarat and Bendigo triggered a smaller Gold Rush to Australia, which helped to lift it out of its penal colony heritage.

The strong Italian flavor that still exists in parts of San Francisco appears to have been a post-Gold Rush development. So, too, the Portuguese element at Half Moon Bay; the Finish enclave at Fort Bragg; the Armenian group at Fresno; and the Italian-Swiss grape growers in Sonoma County.

The Japanese influx began in the middle 1890's, encouraged by the need for "stoop labor" in the developing sugar beet industry; the majority of this initial Japanese segment coming from Hiroshima. In this century, the Fillipino element in the Salinas Valley was another response to the demand for agricultural labor, this time in strawberries and lettuce. There is a Sikh (Indian) enclave at Yuba City-Marysville that stems from the same need. The influx from Mexico during and after the two world wars already has been noted.

All of these groups, as well as the steady torrent of in-migrants from within the United States, simply highlight California's constant need for labor and her capacity to absorb it because of a continually expanding economy. How true this will be in the future — or is even today — for un-skilled labor is thrown into serious question by the Watts riots and by the fact that California's growth in every sense has brought her to the impasse of labor versus technology a great deal sooner than a somewhat less violent and certainly a less sustained acceleration would have done. This is clearly seen in the increasing mechanization of agriculture.

Popular fancy, as well as many a media presentation, commonly depicts the Gold Rush as a saturnalia of unbridled licentious lust — for gold, for women, or whatever. It warn't necessarily so! At least, not during the first flush times — say, from 1848 to 1850. Personal opinion extends the halcyon days into early 1851; equally competent opinion limits it to 1850.

Whatever its length, this period was the Golden Age of good fellowship in the mines, foreigners excluded. There were isolated murders, plus brawls, fights, horse-whippings, and the like, but in the main, the diaries and letters from the mines at this time reflect a camaraderie that seems unbelievable today. Men could leave their pans of nuggets and dust unattended in their crude brush-and-canvas shelters without fear of loss. The same applied to their tools, which were vital to the task of gold-getting, and to their supply of foodstuffs. Men helped one another, shared with another, in the golden haze of plenty-of-gold-for-all. As Charles H. Shinn once noted of this period, "It was certainly easier to earn your money than to steal it, and infinitely safer."

Even after the division of the state into counties, each with its duly established and elected officiadom, the men in the mines handled their own problems in a crude but effective working democracy. And it was not a democracy based upon brute force or physical prowess, foreigners again excluded. All the miners (and they were a transient lot) that were assembled at any camp or river bar or gulch comprised the Miners Association of that place at any given time. They drew up their own code of laws applicable to the particular locale; regulated the size of claims, thus equalizing oppor-tunity for all; passed laws regarding the use of water; and, in general, made a constantly shifting congeries of self-governing entities. Heinous crimes were punished either by banishment from camp or by flogging, in the tradition of Captain Bligh. Occasionally, there was a hanging, after the local Miners As-sociation had heard the evidence and the accused's testimony, and less frequently there was a lynching. The record made a remarkable demonstra-tion of self-discipline by men who were under the cruellest of compulsions, that of material gain for the seizing. It was an extra-legal democracy in the Jacksonian sense and it was infinitely better than the anarchy which otherwise would have ensued and much to be preferred to the corruption that marked the early stages of organized government in San Francisco.

This almost idyllic time drew to a close as the easy-to-get placer gold petered out. Its demise was hastened by the civic housecleaning in San Francisco effected by the First Committee of Vigilance in 1851, which inspired an unsavory exodus to the interior mines. Thereafter, the inland incidence of what we now call crimes of violence increased. The actions of the Committees of Vigilance of 1851 and 1856 in San Francisco, incidentally, may be considered as essential surgery to restore the health of the body politic, a view long held; or, they may be considered examples of Fascist totalitarianism, a contemporary view among more gentle souls, and among those who seek to judge the past by the standards of a complex legal system influenced by psychological explorations of human behavior under stress.

In the realm of outlaws, a matter dear to the media mythologists, California can present three — Joaquin Murrieta, Black Bart, and Tiburcio Vasquez — who have been fixed right firmly in the public consciousness. Joaquin Murrieta, sometimes spelled Murieta, today is as much figment as fact. His story, and it has been repeated *ad nauseam*, was born in the 1852 writings of a half-Cherokee newspaper editor at Marysville, John Rollin "Yellow Bird" Ridge. That there was an actual fleshly body with the name of Joaquin Murrieta is indisputable; that he did all the things Ridge attributed to him is highly questionable. In fact, he seems to have gotten the credit for a number of hair-raising stunts perpetrated by other Hispanic gentry such as Joaquin Carillo, Joaquin Valenzuela, Joaquin Ocomorena, and Joaquin Gonzalez — all of whom had a deficient sense of property rights. This may explain why the legislature offered a reward for the capture of "Joaquin," patronym unspecified.

A company of California Rangers was organized under Harry Love, the so-called "Black Knight of Zayante," and in due time a severed head preserved in alcohol was exhibited as the veritable visage of the "Robin Hood of El Dorado." The hard core of the Joaquin legend seems to be in the creation of a folk hero, and his virtual enshrinement in the Hispanic lore of California may indicate his role in assuaging their sense of dispossession and persecution by the Anglo-Americans. He has become something of a folk hero in contemporary Chicano literature and the Chilean poet Pablo Neruda wrote a play which cast Murietta as a fellow *Chileno* resisting *gringo* racism.

Black Bart — who signed himself "The P O 8," in a truly awful pun — was one Charles E. Bolton, or Boles, who holds the distinction of staging the first successful stagecoach robbery in the state, and this not until the early 1870's. He was a mild-mannered little man of incredible endurance, who lived most of the time in San Francisco, enjoying its amenities, and only took to the road when his purse was becoming bare. He told his friends in the city, including members of its police force, that his absences were occasioned by having to look after his "mining properties" in the mountains.

Over a span of years, he robbed about twenty-six stages, never killing any-one, never wounding anyone, never retaining ladies' purses, and always using an unloaded shotgun as his means of moral suasion. Legend holds that in each looted treasure box, he left a derisive bit of doggerel, or "P O 8-try" (poetry). Wells Fargo, which bore the brunt of his extractions, has but two of these verses, and his reputation as a practicing poet seems to have been exaggerated. The following sample may support this premise:

> "I've labored long and hard for bread
> For honor and for riches
> But on my corns too long you've trod
> You fine-haired sons of bitches."

Black Bart finally was apprehended because he dropped a handkerchief bear-ing a San Francisco laundry's mark. He had just stopped his last stage with the time-honored shout of "Throw down the box!" when he was shot in the rump by the rifle of a youngish rabbit hunter who was nearby. A hoary legend holds that Bart was released from prison on his promise not to com-mit any more crimes, including the writing of verse!

Tiburcio Vasquez ranged California in the 1870's, from San Benito to Fresno to Los Angeles and the Mojave Desert. That he was able to do this in a day of intrastate telegraph and railroad communications is a tribute to his horsemanship, to his daring, and to the Hispanic Californians who befriended him, partly out of fear, partly as a despoiler of *los gringos*. Vasquez was an outlaw, nothing more or less, and a cutthroat as well. His enshrinement is of a piece with the maudlin process that has made a social activist out of the buck-toothed, murderous little thug we call "Billy the Kid." Vasquez was "jerked to Jesus," as the saying then had it, in 1875 at San Jose, after a lengthy trial attended by many female admirers.

Many of the men who won through to California in the Rush were veterans of the Mexican War; many more of them would fight in the Civil War that grew out of the one great failure to date in the essential democratic process of compromise. No matter what material goods they had to abandon along the trail to the Golden Shore, their cultural baggage held intact a sense of personal honor that could be satisfied in but one way: "Pistols for two and coffee for one!"

The men who framed the state's first constitution recognized this habit in their fellows by inserting an anti-dueling provision in that document. It was honored more in the breach than the observance, and between 1850 and 1860 California counted more fatal duels than any other state in the Union. Among these was the notable encounter on September 13, 1859, between the Chief Justice of the California Supreme Court, David S. Terry, and U.S. Senator David C. Broderick, in which the latter was mortally wounded. This has been said to constitute the "Fourth most noted duel in the United

States." More importantly, Broderick's death gutted the Democratic Party in California, inasmuch as the quarrel had its origins in a brass-knuckled battle for that party's control; its outcome was of no little assistance in bringing the Republicans to a position of dominance within the state. The anti-dueling provision was kept in the New Constitution of 1879, and remains there to this day. There also are specific penalties provided for killing an enemy in a duel in both the civil and penal statutes of the state. These should be consulted *before* indulging in any "affair of honor."

Each successive American frontier in our westering surge was marked by a slow evolution from raw wilderness to stable society, a process that was accelerated tremendously in California. On our other frontiers, the transition required a generation or more; in California it took perhaps five years.

The heyday of the happy individual gold-seeker — when the surface gold could be harvested with pan, pick, and shovel — dawned in 1848 and flourished at least through 1850. Then, after loose gold had been depleted from the stream beds and gulches, it became necessary for the miners to band together in associative groups, or partnerships, to accomplish the physical tasks necessary to obtain the less accessible gold. By 1853 the search for gold had entered the corporate stage because of the amounts of capital required to engage in relatively sophisticated types of mining. Thus, the three stages in the transition, in terms of the individual, were: (a) self-employed placer miner; (b) member of an associative group; and (c) wage-earning employee of a corporation. In 1852, gold production approximated eighty million dollars, which marks the peak of the placer period in stages (a) and (b) above. Thereafter, production declined steadily to about $17,000,000 annually and stabilized at this figure for the remainder of the century, as mining itself became stabilized in stage (c). The values of gold production are given in terms of its then maximum price of $16 per ounce. To determine its value in today's metal mania, the values given can be multiplied by twenty for a reasonable approximation. Gold is measured by the Troy ounce, of which 14½ make an avoirdupois pound.

The advent of the third stage began the stabilization of the Mother Lode communities. The mining camps that had vast gravel beds to be sluiced away by the hydraulic technique, those that had quartz ledges to be exploited by shafts and hoists and mills — these were the ones that endured, the ones that brought schools and churches and other appurtenances of social community to themselves and the area around them. The purely placer camps became trodden dust, of each one of which it can be said, "'Twas lively while she lasted." Most of these today are not even ghost towns.

Between stages (b) and (c) above, the slow erosion of population in the Mother Lode counties began. This was not swift enough to prevent the location of the state capital at Sacramento in 1854, after some political peregrinations between San Jose, Vallejo, and Benicia over the preceding four years. The gold counties wanted the seat of government where they could reach it

"You can scarcely form any conception of what a dirty business this gold digging is," one miner wrote to the folks at home. The slow daguerotype lens could not "stop" the rushing water.
— Courtesy of Robert A. Weinstein

more easily than by traveling to tidewater; perhaps, too, they wanted it away from the cosmopolitan corruptions of San Francisco. Whatever the reason, they had the political muscle to gain their point; in 1854, for example, El Dorado County boasted four state senators, out of sixteen total; and eight assemblymen, out of thirty-six total. The city and county of San Francisco in the same year had but one more legislative member, an assemblyman, than did El Dorado County. It should be remembered here that between 1850 and 1928 California elected both houses of the legislature on a population basis, not by the so-called "federal" system.

The continued flow of people out of the gold counties gave an impetus to agricultural settlement and community development in the Great Valley. The major internal market for the valley's crops was the urban nucleus of the San Francisco Bay area, and the port of San Francisco was the valley's major means of access to world markets. The financial and commercial dominance of the state by San Francisco would remain unchallenged until the emergence of Los Angeles in this century. Similarly, the political dominance of the state would be exercised practically continuously by its northern urban areas, principally San Francisco Bay, until the balance of population shifted to Southern California, which is shown clearly in the tables at the back of the book.

It is the speed of the transition from self-employed placer miner to wage-earning corporate employee, coupled with the growth of the urban areas in the north, that enables us to say that California was the first truly urbanized state in the whole Far West. A great measure of social stratification and class consciousness would have come to California with this rapid transition and the population shift it promoted had it not been for the Comstock Lode. Erupting out of the almost lunar landscape of western Nevada, the Comstock gave California an infusion of new capital and an impetus to all forms of production that kept the fluidity of its social structure alive.

Technological changes wrought by gold came more slowly than social changes, simply because the basic techniques of initial mining endeavors in California were as old, at least, as the Phoenicians. By and large, the refinements of these techniques in California were only adaptive and expansive. Further refined on the Comstock Lode, they spread throughout the whole mining frontier of the Far West, which is to say, roughly, the vast expanse between the summits of the Rocky Mountains and the Sierra Nevada-Cascade Range. Needless to say, California capital was instrumental in developing these other mining operations.

Very few Americans with any experience in gold-mining came to California in the Rush. Cherokees and whites from Georgia, where a minor gold rush had developed in the 1830's, were the very few native Americans with any proficiency in the skills of placer mining. Other Argonauts from the Michigan Peninsula brought with them the skills they had acquired in the copper mining excitement that began there in 1846. The most experienced body of gold-miners were the Sonorians from Mexico, who were adept at "dry washing" auriferous sands in a shallow, circular wooden bowl (*la batea*) very similar to the pan used in wet washing. The *batea*, too, was rotated in a circular motion, but instead of washing away the lighter material with water, the Sonorian blew it out very carefully. Much fine gold was lost by this process. Another dry-washing technique of the Sonorians was to toss gold-bearing gravel on a blanket, just as in winnowing wheat in olden days, letting the wind blow the lighter dirts away and then carefully hand-sorting what was left to get the gold. Again, this was a wasteful and time-consuming process.

Water was the *sine qua non* for those who groveled in the golden gravels of the Mother Lode, and the pattern of California's climate, with its marked dry and wet seasons, greatly limited the continuity of placer mining at first. It was confined of necessity to those periods when there was enough, *but not too much*, water in the streams — say April to July, and again between mid-September and the heavy rains of winter in late November. These time spans, of course, varied with each year and with the specific locale in the Mother Lode, because of the "micro-climates" of the region. These climatic limitations on placer mining brought corresponding influxes of miners into the urban areas of the Great Valley and San Francisco, which accentuated the transient nature of the state's population in these first hectic years.

James Marshall and his helpers at Sutter's ill-starred sawmill extracted their first gold by the simple expedient of prying it, with a knife blade, out of the crevices in the native rock where it had been deposited and held fast by its weight. The belief that this was a common practice in California became so widespread that people arrived with specially made tongs, very like ice-bucket tongs today, to extract their share; some even brought padded stools upon which to sit in comfort while they did so.

The basic placering instrument at first was the "miner's pan," which can be purchased today in many a foothill town's hardware store. A common frying pan would serve, and do double duty when the day's work of getting gold was done. The favorite spots were gravel bars and terraces beside running water. The pan was filled with gravel, sand, and water, and rotated between the hands to spill out these elements gradually and gently until nothing was left but the heaviest particles, including the gold, if there was any.

As the readily accessible treasure troves were depleted, it became necessary to build dams to divert the stream flow through canals (dug by hand) in order to get down to the bedrock where the gold concentration was always heaviest, or believed to be. (As early as 1918, marine diving suits were used to reach bedrock beneath deep pools on the Middle Fork of Feather River, and today's enthusiasts use scuba-gear and suction equipment for the same purpose.) These efforts took more capital than one could muster; they required more muscle and sweat than any one man possessed. Hence, these ventures became associative ones.

Concomitantly, the miner's pan was replaced by a more efficient instrument, the cradle. This was shaped just as its name implies, with an inclined floor, crossed with cleats to act as riffles to catch the gold. Dirt was shoveled in at the upper end, and water was poured in, too, while the miner rocked the cradle and speeded the extraction process. A very strong or a most determined man could work a cradle alone; two men were better and processed more dirt per day. The cradle was so short that much of the finer gold was lost in the process.

The cradle evolved into the "Long Tom," or sluice box. It consisted of three-sided sections, dovetailed into one another to get whatever length was necessary to prevent undue loss of fine gold. The length of the sluice box was crossed with cleats, as in the cradle, and a refinement was to coat the bottom of the sections with mercury, which has an affinity for gold. (The riffle-quicksilver technique was an improvement over the Golden Fleece which Jason sought, which was simply a sheepskin laid with the grain of the fleece against the water flow. The lanolin in the fleece acted to trap the gold and the fleece was taken out when saturated, dried, and then shaken carefully to free the golden particles it had ensnared.) The recovery rate was much improved by this method, and the mercury amalgam was distilled in iron retorts to get the gold. The mercury was recovered for re-use by means of a vapor condenser. Here again, the sluice-box technique was too much for one man to build and operate properly. The existence of quicksilver deposits at New Almaden, near San Jose, and at New Idria, in San Benito County, were of great value to gold mining in the state.

There was never any single, great "Mother Lode" in the Sierra, but many, many lodes, or veins. One man could sink a shaft on one of these veins by himself, but once he dug deeper than the length of a long-handled shovel plus his own height, the task of getting the rock out of the hole became tedious. Even two or three or four men could go down only so far with windlass and bucket before the necessity of mechanical hoisting energy and equipment became mandatory. Also, crushing quartz rock by hand was a laborious way of making the ore fine enough to be washed by pan, cradle, or sluice box. Lode or shaft mining, as it is often called, thus became a partnership venture from its beginnings, and evolved into a corporate one.

The Empire Mine in Grass Valley began as a group effort about 1850 and produced more than $80,000,000 in its century of operations. Its shaft eventually probed 7,000 feet beneath its mountain surface and bottomed 1,500 feet *below* sea level. In Amador County, where about one-half of all the lode gold mined in California has been produced, the Argonaut Mine yielded more than $25,500,000 between its beginnings in the latter 1850's and 1942; its shaft had a vertical depth of 5,570 feet. Forty-seven men perished underground when fire swept the Argonaut's workings in 1922. In this same county, the Kennedy Mine produced some $45,000,000 in its life-time out of a shaft that went down 6,000 feet. Wooden bucket-wheels, forty-eight feet in diameter, lifted the tailings (waste) from its mill into flumes that carried them away to ever-increasing spreading grounds.

Lode or shaft mining gave tremendous impetus to the state's young ex-plosives industry, which thus meshed with its and the state's needs. The Cali-fornia Powder Works began operations near Santa Cruz as early as 1865 and produced the state's first smokeless powder. Two years later, the Atlas Powder Company produced the state's first dynamite, because of its rights to use the patents of the Swedish inventor of nitroglycerine. Dynamite's early versions killed many of the miners that used it.

Drilling machinery using steam and compressed air was infinitely quicker than hand sledge and drill steel for putting in the holes to hold the powder. Better rock-crushing machinery, such as the steel-shod stamp, the agitating table, and other extractive equipment were just as necessary to quartz mining as hoisting and blasting equipment. These demands both nourished California's heavy industry and were supplied by it.

Gold-bearing gravels were sometimes found in great bodies well away from any living water with which to wash them by any of the usual pro-cesses. The finder of such "dry diggin's" originally had the back-breaking task of shovelling his dirt into a leather bucket or a canvas sack and carrying it on his back or in a barrow, if he could afford one, to the nearest stream. This was hard work and slow. It was more practicable to bring the water to the gravel. This solution, however, conflicted with the basic English com-mon-law doctrine of "riparian rights" to water, which prohibited the diver-sion of water from a stream unless it was returned undiminished, save for domestic consumption. To meet their needs, the miners evolved their own law of waters, which became known as the doctrine of "appropriation and beneficial use." While Spanish law had permitted the appropriation and diversion of waters to non-riparian lands, this does not appear to have been the ancestor of mining camp laws on the same subject.

The new doctrine permitted water to be diverted from its normal course to be used benefically elsewhere, without necessarily having to be re-turned to the stream of origin. This solved the problem of profitably work-ing many dry diggings and laid the basis for California's present water laws, basically the Wright Act of 1887, without which diversion for irrigation would be impossible. For this reason, it has been called "the single most im-portant contribution to the growth of California agriculture." A growing sentiment exists to revise most drastically *all* of California's water laws.

The new doctrine also laid the foundation for hydraulic mining, which California made a standard part of mining technology. All up and down the Sierra's western slope, particularly along its northern reaches, lay tremen-dous bodies of gold-bearing gravels that were too low grade to be worked profitably except in great volume. The miners therefore utilized the force of

The hydraulic "monitors" or "giants" sluiced down mountainsides, silted up rivers, and left the land laid waste.
— *Courtesy The Bancroft Library*

falling water to cut down whole hillsides, hundreds of feet high, and send the liquid muck (called "slickens") through sluice boxes that reached thousands of feet in length. The water was played against the bluff or hillside through gigantic nozzles (called "monitors"), often more than six feet long, that threw as much as a nine-inch stream up to four hundred feet under tremendous pressure. These gigantic undertakings left dramatic remains — tall spires and minarets and fluted columns — of which the most startling examples are to be seen at Cherokee, Butte County, and near North Bloomfield, Nevada County. Hydraulicing in California is credited generally to Edward E. Mattison, who pioneered it in 1853 at American Hill, Nevada County.

Water from the higher reaches of the Sierra Nevada was what made possible these monster operations; some 425 of them were operating at the peak of the hydraulic industry in the latter 1870's, and they consumed 72,000,000 gallons of water per day. Storage dams were developed in the high country to provide water for year-round operations, and this water was delivered to the monitors by an extensive network of canals, flumes, ditches, and pipes. The Middle Yuba and Eureka Lake Company alone had more than 700 miles of delivery system. Water sales to others were often more profitable to this company than its own gold recovery. Two years after Alexander Graham Bell received his first patent, another gigantic water supply firm, the South Yuba Canal Company, strung 184 miles of telephone line to maintain contact with its water sources and delivery systems; this is said to have been the world's first long-distance network. Today many foothill towns owe their present water supply to the original hydraulic developments.

In just one year's operations, the hydraulic mines of the northern Sierra dumped 46,000,000 cubic yards of slickens into the streams that fed the Sacramento River. This was the equivalent of a solid mass one mile long by one mile wide by forty-five feet high. In 1850 Marysville had perched nineteen feet above the level of Feather and Yuba rivers. By 1878 hydraulic debris had raised the bed of the Yuba River more than thirty feet, and the city of Marysville found itself *beneath* the level of the river and dependent upon levees for protection. The problem was aggravated downstream as the bed of the Sacramento River was continually built up by the influx of slickens, with resultant flooding of agricultural acreage. The farmers built their levees higher; the hydraulic monitors relentlessly washed down more of the Sierra foothills; more flooding ensued.

This brought about a bitter conflict that pitted farmer against miner, and violence flared before it finally was settled by legislation and court action in 1883-84. A requirement of the settlement, that hydraulic operations construct their own catchment areas to prevent ensilting of the Sacramento and other watercourses, proved so costly that hydraulic mining came to an end. It is said that some four-hundred million dollars could be recovered from the North San Juan Ridge (Nevada County) if hydraulic mining could be resumed.

Gold dredging often is said to be a California invention in the millenia-old evolution of gold extraction, but such is not the case. Gold dredges first operated in New Zealand, and operated in Colorado before being introduced into California, where they were refined, improved, and greatly enlarged. The dredges were used mainly in the lower foothills and along the rim of the Great Valley, as they required reasonably level terrain in which to pursue the task of garnering the "flour" gold in the gravelly soil. Once more, volume was the key to profits and, as dredge capacity increased, it became feasible to work ground that returned as little as 33¢ per cubic yard.

"Turning" a river was a major undertaking and there was no guarantee that the bedrock exposed by the turning would make it worth the time and sweat and funds expended.— *The Bancroft Library*

The monster dredge was a boat hull floating in its own man-made lake. It held machinery that caused a boom-supported, revolving bucket-chain to lift up the gravel and dump it onto a revolving cylindrical screen where water washed the finer materials down onto mechanically agitated riffle tables coated with mercury. The vast quantity of waste was ejected in windrows behind the dredge, filling in the lake behind as the dredge gnawed its way forward with its revolving buckets. Rock rindrows are a common sight throughout the Sierra foothills, and it is noteworthy that debris from dredging operations was the major source of material for the gigantic Oroville Dam, which impounds water for delivery to Southern California and the west side of the upper San Joaquin Valley.

Today's Natomas Corporation began as a gold-dredging operation, and

Gnawing into dirt containing as little as 33c per cubic yard of gold, the monster dredges left behind mountains of rock to mark their passage.

— *State Library, Sacramento*

dredges designed or made in California found use all over the world, for tin as well as for gold. Three specially designed dredges were air-lifted into the New Guinea highlands in the 1930's for Bulolo Goldfields, Ltd. The last of these monsters to work in California came to the end of its operations near Marysville in 1969. The increase in world gold prices since then may bring the dredges back to re-work ground they have mined before.

The flush years of the Rush saw California without any adequate medium of exchange. The first state constitution prohibited banks from issuing currency, and a branch of the United States Mint was not established in San Francisco until 1854. Even though coins from all over the world circulated freely, coinage was so scarce that a man with minted Mexican dollars could swap them for dust or nuggets at eight dollars an ounce. Scales for weighing gold were not as common in the Rush as is often imagined today, save at express company offices, banks, and the larger mercantile firms. A "pinch" of dust, the amount that could be lifted between thumb and forefinger, was commonly accepted as an ounce, worth sixteen dollars at par. Thus, the saying "How much can you raise in a pinch?" acquired its meaning. Gold from different sections brought different prices per ounce; that from the "southern mines" around Sonora and Columbia being more valuable than that from the "northern mines" around the Yuba and Feather rivers' drainage. Unscrupulous fellows were given to mixing copper or brass filings with their dust to increase its weight and offset low values received in exchanging it for coinage or goods. An unfortunate inability to distinguish between the gold from the different regions of California is said to have played a part in the collapse of the banking firm of Page, Bacon & Company, triggering the financial panic of 1855 in San Francisco.

To meet the state's need for coinage, private firms built around assay offices that had smelting or refining facilities minted their own coins — illegal under the federal Constitution but allowed by necessity. Coins struck off by these private mints, especially the $50 octagonal gold slugs, are collector's items today; the author has fondled two of these, each valued at more than $1,500 in today's fiat currency. Even after a branch of the federal Mint was established in San Francisco in 1854, private assay offices continued to transform raw gold into bars for their customers at charges lower than those levied by the Mint for the same service.

Very few of those who participated in the buoyant, boyish Jasonic quest for the Golden Fleece that was the Gold Rush made fortunes from it. One miner's wife made $18,000, far more than her husband ever did, by baking pies made from dried fruits and anything else she could scrounge on top of open-hearth wood fires, without even a tree for shade. A thrifty German on one of the roads to the diggin's set out a melon patch which soon made him enough to open a brewery which made him more than even the pie-maker had earned.

A day's work, waist-deep in the rushing icy waters of a Sierra stream *might* average out at sixteen dollars. With eggs at one dollar each, flour at three to five dollars per pound; boots and blankets at fifty dollars per pair; shirts at sixteen dollars; and whiskey in proportion — this did not leave much room for saving, even by doing one's own cooking. The *big* finds — the nameless Chinese who scratched out a nugget worth $5,000 near Bed Bug; the single lump worth $43,534 that was found near Carson Hill — were just like today's jackpot winners at Reno or Las Vegas. We refuse to remember, or even to think about, the small winners and the inevitable losers. Yet, for the men who made the Rush, it was the great adventure of their lives, and the memories of it warmed their hearts until they died.

The Gold Rush laid the foundations for California's industrial manufacturing, for its banking and transportation systems, for its commercial activities. It gave a tremendous impetus to agriculture, and it shed a golden haze across California that affected the minds and hearts of people all around the world, and still does. It was the catalytic agent between land, man, and growth in California, and it affected the nation's political future.

Even before the Gold Rush, there was agitation in California to end the military rule that had followed the state's actual conquest. The military governor, Colonel R.B. Mason, did not want the task of governing a bunch of militant civilians, and both he and the civilian population were prone to damn Congress for its failure to provide suitable territorial status and officials as provided by law. Federal failure to act promptly was due to the growing schism between the slave states and the non-slave states. A congressional bill in 1848 would have granted Territorial status to the lands acquired in 1846 — basically Oregon, New Mexico, Arizona, California — but would have left the matter of slavery in these territories up to the Supreme Court, which Northerners felt was dominated by Southerners. A new bill covering Oregon only and barring slavery therein did pass on a quibble that it was above 36° 30" north latitude, fixed by the Missouri Compromise of 1820 as the northernmost limit of slavery in the Louisiana Purchase lands. That Oregon was not a part of the Louisiana Purchase was conveniently overlooked in passing the bill and securing President Polk's signature. All that California got from Congress in 1848 was to make San Francisco a Port of Entry for customs purposes and revenues and to make Monterey and San Diego Ports of Delivery. A small subsidy bill was responsible for bringing steam-powered, side-wheel steamers around the Horn just in time to be swamped by the Gold Rush horde at the western end of the Panama route.

Early in 1849, before the Gold Rush torrent inundated the state, local mass meetings at San Francisco, San Jose, Santa Cruz, and Sutter's Fort expressed the inhabitants' desire for a constitutional convention. In April, Colonel Mason's successor was replaced by General Bennett Riley, who did not like the idea of governing civilians any more than had Mason. He willingly agreed to the notion of a constitutional convention and issued a proclamation calling for the election of delegates to such a meeting. The convention of forty-eight delegates, in which the *Californios* were over-represented in terms of population, met at Colton Hall in Monterey on September 1, 1849. They had copies of the New York and Iowa constitutions to guide them and some definite ideas of their own. They did a large job in a short time with better results than are usual in such cases.

Distrusting paper money after the financial fiasco of 1836-37, they provided that no banks could issue paper money and that the state could not operate a state bank. They retained the Mexican law of community property, which descended from the "dower right" law of Spain, and provided that all future legislation be written in both English and Spanish, which was done until the second language was dropped by the New Constitution of 1879. Their biggest problem arose over the eastern boundary of the state. The "big state" faction wanted it placed at the Rocky Mountains; the "small state" faction wanted it at the crest of the Sierra, Nevada, which was thought to be along the 120th Meridian West of Greenwich, England. The small state faction won out and it was agreed to leave the determination of the eastern boundary to the federal government.

Before the line was run and agreed upon, it produced the so-called "Sagebrush War" between Plumas and Lassen counties, over whether Lassen was in California or in Nevada, where it wanted to be. After the line was run, it left Lake Tahoe, then known as Lake Bigler, divided between the two states, which has led in recent years to the growth of gambling casinos on the Nevada side and urban sprawl and pollution throughout the Tahoe Basin. This has led to considerable disagreement between the states over future growth, and raises the strong possibility that only federal intervention will prevent the Tahoe Basin from becoming a slum in the sky, rather than "The Jewel in the Sky."

There was another major disagreement between the two states over the exact location of the boundary as officially surveyed. The Houghton-Ives Line of 1863 has been recognized by both the states in their statutes and it is about one mile west of the Von Schmidt Line of 1872, which is the generally accepted but *unofficial* boundary. The Houghton-Ives Line, official but unaccepted, would give about 207 square miles of California to Nevada, which initially agreed with California to have the Supreme Court tidy up the matter, based upon more than a century of acceptance, by making the Von Schmidt Line official. Then larceny raised its lovely head in Nevada, as its legislators and developers looked at those 207 square miles of California real estate and found them good. Also they became aware, and only *le bon Dieu* knows why it took them so damnably long, of yet another survey made in 1868 which would give Nevada even more California real estate, by slicing off the eastern ends of eleven California counties for a gain of more than 1,000 square miles. California then countered with a proposal for a new survey which would shove the line eastward into Nevada as much as 1,700 feet. The matter went before the Supreme Court and United States Judge

Robert Van Pelt, Nebraska was appointed Special Master to ajudicate the matter. Then common sense apparently prevailed and the long *accepted* Von Schmidt line continues to be used.

More important than the eastern boundary was the anti-slavery section of the first state constitution, certain aspects of which have been discussed earlier in this chapter. On the national scene, this became of major importance because it upset the balance in Congress between slave and free states that had been maintained since 1820. As the debate over admitting California into the Union waxed hot and heavy, California calmly went ahead with ratification of its constitution, which was approved by 12,604 to 811, a total which represented about 14% of those eligible to vote. It rained most of the day, November 13, and most eligible voters were too busy mining to take time off at their own expense, so to speak. Thereafter, California went again to the polls, elected a slate of state officers, Peter Burnett from Oregon being the first governor, a legislature, which in turn elected two U.S. Senators, William M. Gwin and John C. Fremont; and was in business as a state, without being a member of the federal union.

What finally came out of Congress has become known as the "Compromise of 1850." Under its provisos, California was admitted as a free state, the territories of New Mexico, which included Arizona, and Utah, which included Nevada, were created without restrictions on slavery until they were eligible for statehood, at which time a popular vote would determine whether they would become free or slave states. The Texas boundary with New Mexico was fixed as it stands today, and Texas was paid $10,000,000 compensation for her alleged loss of territory. This was a Godsend to the bankrupt state of Texas. Slave trading was prohibited in the District of Columbia, and a more severe federal fugitive slave law replaced the old one of 1793. In the long view of American history, the Compromise of 1850 provided a space of ten years in which the North could take advantage of the industrial stimulus and population expansion caused by the Gold Rush to lay the foundations for the successful preservation of the Union during the Civil War.

Sacramento as it looked during the great flood of January, 1850.   *— The Bancroft Library*

CHAPTER SEVEN

GREEN GOLD: ETERNAL ASSET?

Truly can it be said that Colonial America was trees; a dense hardwood forest that covered the eastern one-third of the nation, except on the rolling grassland prairies of western Indiana and Illinois. It was a forest so dense that a squirrel could travel from Mussel Shoals in Tennessee to Niagara Falls without ever having to touch the ground! The English colonists learned, from the Swedes and Finns along the Delaware River, how to build log cabins. Lumber became the first export commodity of England's colonies, and the axe and the saw were as indispensable as the long rifle in the westward movement between the Atlantic seaboard and the Mississippi River.

Beyond that rolling river, west of eastern Kansas, the environment changed to semiarid, then arid, as the land lifted slowly towards the snow-covered crests of the Rocky Mountains. Only in the higher elevations abutting the Continental Divide, only along the beds of streams whose waters were "too thin to plow and too thick to drink" were there "timber islands" to provide the settler with the building materials that he knew and needed. Between the Rockies and the Sierra-Cascade summits, the timber situation was even worse, thanks to the climatic changes wrought by the upheavals of geologic time. Thus, the formation of the California landscape provides another example of Nature's generosity in its magnificent timber stands.

These include the cathedral-column redwood, the world's tallest living plant, the *palo alto* of the Spaniards, one specimen of which has been measured as soaring skywards for 367 feet; and the "Big Tree" of the Sierra, the world's largest living plant. In the White Mountains across Owens Valley from the forbidding granite scarp of the Sierra, the world's oldest living thing, the bristlecone pine, clings tenaciously to life as it has for almost five thousand years. Together with these superlatives, California's timber largesse includes oaks and pines and firs and cedars — all useful to man's past and present needs, and vital to California's future. This natural resource demanded a superior technology to permit its development in the service of the state, the nation, and the world.

With the exception of the canoe-building peoples of the Santa Barbara Channel and along the Klamath River system, if one Indian used up one tree in one lifetime, he was guilty of conspicuous waste. The California Indians made little use of timber, except for the windfalls or branches they gathered for firewood and shelter framework. The Spanish and the *Californios* of

An ox-team drags a "turn" of logs down a skid road, not skid row, on its way to the mill. Note the men straddling the log for a dusty ride.

— *The Bancroft Library*

Mexico's regime took but little more advantage of this tremendous natural resource.

Beams for the missions, for the presidios, and for dwellings were hacked painfully from the coastal timber stands, but the basic building material of Hispanic California (1769-1846) was the sun-dried *adobe* brick. The crude, two-wheeled cart (*la carreta*) that was the bulk transportation vehicle of Hispanic California had a framework of poles, covered with hides, and its wheels were sections of tree trunk. Doors, window frames, tables, benches, and chairs were virtually unknown in California until the advent of "foreigners" — Russian, English, and American — introduced the first crude tools and techniques of lumber processing.

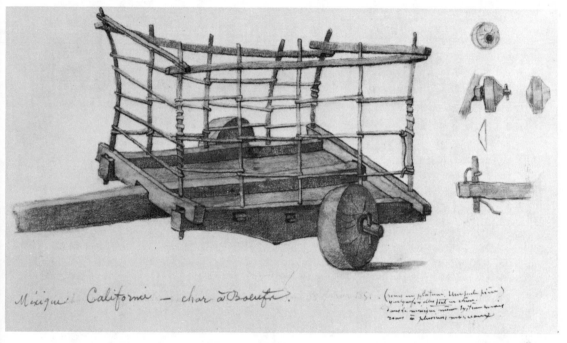

La carreta, the basic vehicle of Mexican California, was sketched by Wilkersheim in 1851. No iron was used in its construction, just rawhide and wooden pegs.　　　　*— Courtesy The Bancroft Library*

The Russians at Fort Ross appear to have been the first to make commercial use of the towering redwood (*Sequoia sempervirens*), one adult specimen of which today can yield enough lumber to construct twelve two-bedroom houses. At the time of their first utilization, the redwood groves spread along the coast from Crescent City to the Santa Lucia Mountains below Carmel, and reached inland with the coastal climate belt along the San Francisco Peninsula, the Marin and Sonoma hills, and in the Coast Range folds behind Oakland and Berkeley. By 1827, it is believed, the Russians at Fort Ross were whipsawing and splitting redwood planks and timbers that were sold in the Hawaiian Islands. They also are reported to have manufactured prefabricated houses by erecting them, marking and numbering the pieces, and then knocking them apart for export. One of John Sutter's reasons for buying Fort Ross was to get the lumber that it represented.

A branching oak clings to a hillside along the Mother Lode.   *— Courtesy Library of Congress*

In the 1830's, Thomas Larkin, the U.S. Consul at Monterey, began developing an export trade in redwood, using whipsaws and splitting tools, and it is well to remember here that mature redwood follows its grain for seemingly incredible lengths. His source of supply was the redwood groves of Santa Cruz County, and his markets were in Southern California, Mazatlan, and Hawaii. In this same period, an Englishman known as "Bill the Sawyer" began whipsawing and splitting redwood near today's community of Woodside.

To meet California's insatiable demands for lumber, great cigar-shaped log rafts were towed down from the Pacific Northwest. — *Page Collection / Nat'l. Maritime Museum, S.F.*

Who established the first powered sawmill remains open to question. A water-powered mill was erected by Juan Bautista Roger Cooper, Larkin's half-brother, along the Russian River before 1837. An ex-trapper turned *ranchero*, George Yount, erected another water-powered mill northeast of present-day Yountville and in this same period, a water-powered mill was built near Zayante in Santa Cruz County, either by Isaac Graham or Peter Lassen, the perdurable Dane who left his name on a volcanic peak, a county, a national park and a national forest in northeastern California. Edward T. Bale gave 3,000 acres of land to Ralph Kilburn in payment for the sawmill Kilburn built near Calistoga in 1846. This is not be confused with the flour mill built by Bale which stands beside the road between Calistoga and Napa and has been restored and maintained by the state. The first steam-powered sawmill was brought from Baltimore by sea captain Stephen Smith, who erected it in 1844 on Salmon Creek, near Bodega Bay.

The state's timber stands became the first natural resource to be exploited commercially after gold, although it also can be said that it was exploited concurrently with gold. It can be said further that, without the magnificent stands of timber in close proximity to the gold belt, the production of gold would have been far smaller.

At the time the Rush began, the virgin stands of coniferous timber grew much lower down the western slope of the Sierra than today. The best of these stands (best because they were the most easily worked into planks and beams and timbers) were the two great pines: the three-needled yellow pine (*Pinus ponderosa*) and the five-needled sugar pine (*Pinus lambertiana*). The availability of these species in quantity throughout the Mother Lode provided the raw materials for cradles and sluice boxes, for water flumes and diversion dams, and for the timbers and planks so vital to both shaft and hydraulic mining. For building and for fuel as well, the Mother Lode's timber resources were indispensable.

Sawpits were the first means of converting timber to lumber for the mines. A hole was dug and heavy timbers, or small tree trunks, were laid across it, onto which a log was rolled. Then one man got on top of the log and another underneath, in the pit, and they used a crosscut saw, a "whipsaw" to those who used it, to inch their way slowly through the log, making planks. The bottom man, of course, got the sawdust down his neck, but he also might find gold in the pit while waiting for a new log to be rolled into place. The sawpits were soon followed by water-powered, then by steam-powered, mills. The first were the same as Sutter's mill: a crosscut saw set in vertical guides, and pushed up and down by a Pittman rod working off an eccentric on the water-wheel, or later off the action of the steam cylinder piston rod. Ironically enough, had Sutter retained title to his saw mill, he might have salvaged a financial gain from the disaster that the Gold Rush brought him. Lumber from these early Sierra mills brought one dollar per linear foot, regardless of width, and a common price in 1851 was around

$650 per thousand board feet, which would be perhaps ten times as much in today's currency. A board foot is a foot-square piece, one inch thick; thus a plank 1"x12"x12' equals 12 board feet, and today about 10,000 board feet go into the building of a new home with 1,500 square feet of floor space.

Although lumber from the Sierra Nevada stands was vital to the mines and camps of the Mother Lode, the terrain of the foothills and the Great Valley precluded its utilization elsewhere until the subsidiaries of the present Southern Pacific (Espee) system began to traverse the valley floor in the 1870's. The roads down into the Great Valley and on the valley floor itself were classed as "impassable, not even jackassable" most of the winter months, and were hub-deep in dust come summer. Thus, hauling costs were prohibitive. And the courses of the rivers plunging down from the Sierra imposed additional transportation obstacles to transporting lumber across the valley floor.

Wet work on the Klamath River, ca. 1895. — *The Bancroft Library*

Men from New England, where log-driving on the rivers was basic to lumbering operations, tried to float or raft logs and timbers down the California rivers with a notable lack of success. As might well have been said by these hopeful "river pigs": "Of all the variable things in Creation, the most uncertain are the actions of a jury, the workings of a woman's mind, and the conditions of California's rivers. The crookedness you see ain't but half the crookedness there is." Too, the basic weather pattern in California left the streams with insufficient water in the summer months to make the rivers suitable for consistent log or lumber transportation. And winter logging was not practiced in California as it was in New England and the Great Lakes region, again because of the weather pattern.

The "donkey" and the mule in the woods. The first Dolbeer donkey had a single, horizontal cylinder which turned a gypsy head on a vertical shaft. The mule carried water to the buckets along the skidroad. Wire rope later replaced the Manila haul line.   —A.W. Ericson — Calif. Redwood Association

Today's version of John Dolbeer's "donkey."   — *Courtesy Louisiana-Pacific Corp.*

California's first urban needs for lumber were met in part by importations around Cape Horn from New England, and even by camphorwood planks from China. Prefabricated houses, both of lumber and of iron, were shipped to San Francisco in the 1849-51 period. The main source of supply was the redwood stands of the coastal mountains, where the sea provided a ready and usable route to market. Six so-called sawmills were operating in the Santa Cruz Mountains by the closing months of 1849; two years later there were fifteen in the Woodside area, and Redwood City acquired its name because it was the shipping point for their production. Across the Bay, along the *contra costa*, the lumbering settlement of Clinton became the nucleus of today's Oakland. San Francisco was swept by fire six times during the first two years of the Rush, and each time it was rebuilt largely with redwood lumber, which is more fire retardant than pine or fir or cedar, among other advantages. The importance of accessible redwood stands, and of the sea access route to market, is demonstrated by the fact that 90% of the lumber consumed in Sacramento in 1858 came from the Redwood Coast and from the Puget Sound and Columbia River timber stands.

The interaction of the Puget Sound and Columbia River regions with California should not be overlooked. It was particularly important to the growth of Los Angeles and the resultant sustained demand for lumber. The basic timber of these two regions was, and is, Douglas fir, which possesses far more structural strength than redwood or pine — a characteristic vital to construction. Too, these regions had the great advantage of sea transportation the length of the Pacific Coast, which required no other investment than a vessel and the crew's wages. Later on, when the seaports of San Francisco and Los Angeles were joined by rail with the Great Basin and southwestern states, Douglas fir from the Pacific Northwest became important in the development of towns, mines, and industries in these inland regions. California was more than a market for the Pacific Northwest's lumber. From its gold, it furnished much of the initial investment capital to develop the lumbering industry in that region, and it played a major role for many years in distributing the production of this industry to other parts of the Far West.

The need for ships to transport lumber stimulated shipbuilding in both California and the Pacific Northwest; this in turn led to a unique contribution to naval architecture, the so-called "steam schooner." With engines and boilers located aft, like a miniature oil tanker, these vessels were admirably suited to carrying cargoes of long timbers and were very "handy," in maritime parlance, when it came to navigating into and out of the dangerous "dog-hole" ports of the Mendocino and Humboldt coasts.

This lumber trade evolved techniques of loading lumber that provide a classic demonstration of the uses of industrial technology. Inasmuch as a through rail connection between San Francisco and Eureka on Humboldt Bay did not materialize until 1915, the importance of sea transportation to both the redwood lumber industry and the urban growth of California was tremendous.

The "Big River" plows through San Francisco Bay with a load of lumber, which made her and her kind hard to sink if the binding chains held fast.   — *Courtesy The Bancroft Library*

Steam carried men to the woods and logs to the mills.   — *Special Collection, CSU, Chico Library*

Before the Sierra timber stands became a major factor in California's internal development, they were vital to the successful development of the Comstock Lode. The eastern slope of the Sierra and the contiguous territory in Nevada is timber-deficient, because of the "rain shadow" effect discussed earlier. The Comstock Lode — literally the bowels of Mount Davidson — could not have been worked safely or profitably without ample supplies of timber to shore up its miles of tunnels and stopes and winzes and shafts, the last of which became among the deepest in the world. The steam-powered hoisting machinery, the ore reduction plants along the Carson River, the construction and domestic needs of Virginia City and Gold Hill and Carson City — all were dependent upon forest products. After the eastern slope of the Sierra had been denuded, these needs were met by timber from the Lake

Pine logging in the northern Sierra, with the "jerk line skinner" riding the near wheel horse. The solid-wheel logging "truck" was still in use after the turn of the century in isolated "pineries."
— Author's Collection

Tahoe basin. The eastern rim of the basin around Glenbrook was cut out first; then log rafts were towed across the lake from the western shore to meet the insatiable demand of the Comstock for lumber in all its forms and uses. The logs were sawed at Glenbrook; then the lumber was hauled up to the crest of the mountains by rail and sent *whooshing* down the slope to the Carson Valley in V-shaped flumes made of lumber.

Peeling tan bark on the Mendocino Coast for use in the leather factories of San Francisco, ca. 1900.
— *Courtesy Forest History Society*

Transplanting the V-flume technique to the western slope of the Sierra solved one of the major problems that heretofore had prevented true commerical utilization of that region's magnificent timber stands, the problem of prohibitive hauling costs from mountain sawmill to valley floor. Another problem, that of getting Sierra lumber to the state's and the world's markets, was solved concurrently by the coming of the railroad to the Great Valley. The V-flume and the railroad made Sierra lumber a dependable commodity at a competitive price and greatly stimulated the development of inland California. This impact was felt first in the Sacramento Valley communities of Chico, Red Bluff, and Redding, and then worked southward along the central and southern Sierra slopes.

The southern Sierra holds another phenomenon of California's forest bounty, the Big Trees (*Sequoia gigantea*). While never commercially important in the growth of California, the Big Trees certainly are amongst the most awesome experiences Nature provides to keep egocentric man properly humble. The preservation of stands of Big Trees will be appreciated by generations to come.

It cannot be denied that during the Gold Rush and for many years thereafter, the lumbering industry was incredibly wasteful. The soaring trunks went one hundred feet to the first limb, but the initial rule of thumb was "take three logs and leave her." More lumber than was used was left to rot on the forest floor in these early years of primitive harvesting. Forest fires were left to burn unchecked, except when they threatened the sawmills and other appurtenances of the industry. The record of dedicated conservationists and public-minded forest products firms in curbing this waste is an inspiriting chapter in the state's history. It is a chapter which requires constant writing and rewriting.

It was concern for the natural beauties of the Tahoe basin that sparked the first efforts at legislation to protect its timber resources in 1883. These efforts gained momentum in 1885, when Governor Stoneman of California established the first State Board of Forestry in the United States. The agency seems to have succumbed to economic and political pressures in 1893, when the legislation that established it was repealed, leaving a gap in official conservation concern that was partially filled by private groups.

Among these early groups, the Sacramento Valley Development Association and the Water and Forest Association of San Francisco both pointed out the relationship between sustained forest cover and the water-retaining capacity of the Sierra Nevada, upon which California's life depended then and depends today. These local efforts benefited tremendously from the presidency of Theodore Roosevelt, which gave national impetus and immense prestige to the whole conservation movement. Conservation, as Roosevelt understood it, meant conserving vital natural resources in order to permit their use over the longest period of time to bring the greatest good to the greatest number of people. This concept of sustained use was at the heart of the thinking behind the formation of the National Forests, administered by the U.S. Forest Service, which encompass 20,234,327 acres in California alone. This concept of conservation for use is not to be confused with the "preservationist" attitude that has ardent supporters today, because the latter seeks to preserve what exists for the benefit of those who can afford to enjoy it, without the regard for the benefits of intelligent utilization to humanity as a whole.

The Roosevelt era was accompanied in California by the election of a new governor, Dr. George C. Pardee of Oakland, whose inaugural address of January 7, 1903 contained a long passage devoted to forest conservation.

During his administration, a State Board of Forestry was again created, with E.T. Allen as State Forester, and the first redwood grove to be preserved, Big Basin near Santa Cruz, was set aside as the first state park. Pardee has been called with reason "the father of conservation in California."

During the Civil War, an interesting facet of California's forest bounty was developed when supplies of turpentine, resins, and other so-called "naval stores," which had come from South Carolina, were cut off. Turpentine was the basic ingredient for a lamp fuel called "camphene," made by distilling turpentine over fresh lime. Camphene at this time was the leading urban illuminant, surpassing tallow candles and whale-oil lamps, so the need for turpentine was quickly felt.

Rebuilding San Francisco in 1906 at the corner of Van Ness Avenue and Post Street.
— B.D. Johnson — Nat'l. Maritime Museum, S.F.

To meet it, the stands of yellow pine (*P. ponderosa*) in the Sierra were tapped, and turpentine distilleries and collection depots became concentrated along the higher foothills of Butte County, where the community of Dogtown (Magalia) became the industry's center. Production bounties offered by the state legislature stimulated the infant industry's growth. But with the ending of the Civil War, supplies from South Carolina reentered the market, and by 1866-67 the local turpentine industry came to an economic end.

It left an interesting legacy to the Gasoline Age, because during the turpentine "rush" some distressing accidents had resulted from turpentine stills exploding. These finally were traced to their having been charged with pitch from Jeffrey pines (*Pinus jeffreyi*). The trouble with this pitch was simply that it contained a high amount of hydrocarbons, a chemical matter foreign to other species of pine.

In 1926, largely owing to the improvement of the gasoline engine and its application to air transport, the need for better fuels arose and with it the need for a standard of measure to determine their octane rating. The peculiarly consistent and measurable hydrocarbons from the Jeffrey pine, obtained by tapping a stand of this species in Lassen National Forest, proved most valuable as the required measuring agent.

The effects of the lumbering industry continuously widened throughout California's development after the Gold Rush. Early manufacturing was given a great impetus by the lumbering industry's needs for machinery and equipment. Transportation both affected the industry and benefited from it, in construction and in traffic. Agriculture found a market in the provender needs of lumbering and provided a market for that industry's products in such things as citrus fruit containers, dried-fruit boxes, grape stakes for vineyards, and fencing. The components of urban growth — domestic, industrial, and service industry construction — long affected, and were affected by, the lumbering industry.

The plenitude of lumber, coupled with the salubrious climate, made it feasible to adapt the "bungalow" style of dwelling from Asia for use in Southern California. A variant of this style, dubbed "Bay Area Redwood Shingle," became fashionable in the San Francisco region. As with the "San Diego Moorish" style, the sustained influx of other cultural mores and technological advances dissipated these rudimentary gropings toward a distinctive regional, or typical "California," architecture, especially in residences. Lumber's plenitude, too, permitted the lavishly ornamented residences, all fretsaw and scrollwork, of the nabobs atop Nob Hill in San Francisco. The best surviving example of what can be termed "carpenter Gothic" architecture is the Carson House in Eureka.

California's "green gold" includes a major attempt to augment it by raising eucalyptus, of which 300 species exist in its native home of Australia. The one brought first to California was the blue gun, which was raised

Too many forest fires are man-made through carelessness. Others are set deliberately for reasons known only to the arsonists. — *California Department of Forestry*

for sale by nurserymen in San Francisco as early as 1856, and by other nurserymen near Santa Barbara and Los Angeles shortly thereafter. The boom began about 1900 in a manner remarkably like other "booms" that have been a part of the California scene. The idea was that by planting 10 acres to eucalyptus, a family could live comfortably for the next several generations, so quickly did it grow, so durable was its wood, so easy was its cultivation, and so valuable its oil. The Santa Fe Railroad succumbed to the lure of getting cheap cross-ties that would last and planted a large acreage near San Diego that became the community of Rancho Santa Fe when the boom became a "bust." The blue gun, unfortunately, was the wrong species for hardwood production and it raised all kinds of manufacturing problems, even for railroad ties, while the right species for commercial use took 200 years to reach marketable growth. But the trees remain to brighten the

landscape and to fill the summer air with their unmistakable and unforget-
table pungency. In the coastal regions, they trap the summer fog and the
drip from their glossy leaves replenishes the water table in the ground beneath them. Energy conscious Californians have revived the fast-growing
Eucalyptus as a source of residential heating material.

Lightning is an immemorial hazard to California's timberlands.   — *Author's Collection*

With all the climate has done and continues to do for California's
"green gold" resource, it brings the certainty that each year the forests will
burn and more than once and in more than one place. In keeping with the
state's reputation, its forest fires are bigger, more numerous, and hotter
than in any other state. In the world of wildland fire fighters, California is
the ultimate proving ground for both the men and the machines that fight
them. Good forest land in California generally is computed at $50,000 per
acre in terms of timber production, watershed protection, and recreational
value, and its protection is of major concern to all those involved in forest
management.

The more that is learned about wildland ecology, the more it becomes
apparent that fire can be a beneficial tool, as well as a destructive menace.
Thousands of acres of forest/grazing lands are covered, "clogged" is a better
word, with brush — ceanothus, manzanita, and the like. By controlled burning of manageable plots, deer and quail population is increased, and so are
water resources. For about seven years after a controlled burn, the deer

Helicopters open up previously inaccessible terrain with minimal damage to the environment.
— *Courtesy Louisiana-Pacific Corp.*

browse on what to them are "ice cream," the shoots of new growth, while water that was tied up in nourishing the old scrub enters the watershed instead and is percolated downstream to reservoirs in the amount of about 100,000 acre feet per burn, depending upon its size. This water increase also holds for about seven years, although on a declining basis. The use of helicopter "torch" ships to start and control these burns was pioneered on the Mendocino National Forest, of which about 60% is brush land susceptible to this treatment. Alumigel — gasoline mixed with aluminum powder and soap to attain a gel consistency — is squirted out of a tank beneath the helicopter in golf ball-size globules which are ignited as they leave the tank. The fire they start does the rest. Other beneficial effects of controlled burns include fertilizing the soil with ashes, consuming accumulations of needles, leaves and other combustibles that increase the danger of uncontrolled fires, and destroying insect pests, which in itself is of major importance.

Dangling below the "chopper" is the alumigel container and the igniter. Smoke cloud shows what happens when the blazing blobs of 'gel hit tinder-dry brush.   —*Kevin Turcotte/Chico Enterprise-Record*

As a result of the two years, 1975-77, of reduced rainfall, which was given the designation of "drought" by excitable Californians, there was a marked upsurge of damage from the ravages of the Bark Beetle family in the coniferous timber stands, made much more vulnerable by water starvation. Some 12,000,000,000 board feet were lost in the state's national forests alone, which is more than double the board feet of lumber produced annually in California. The magnitude of this insect loss can be approached by again remembering that it takes 10,000 board feet of lumber to construct a home of 1,500 square feet of floor space. Also, that eight or more jobs in the lumber industry exist for every 1,000,000 board feet produced, to say nothing of the cash flow effect upon communities that depend for their economic life upon lumbering. It also should be remembered that while national forest lands pay no property taxes, the county that contains federal forests receives 25% of the proceeds of all sales of national forest timber in that county. These funds are earmarked for public schools and roads, and California counties receive approximately $50,000,000 annually from this source.

National parks do not remit any direct revenues to the counties in which their lands are located, although an indirect economic effect stems from local seasonal employment and the sales tax collected by concessionaires operating within the parks. With this in mind, the impact upon the counties in which it is located of adding 48,000 acres in 1978 to Redwood National Park can be appreciated. This acreage was removed from the tax rolls of the counties and its removal abolished 1,500 jobs of loggers, truckers, and mill workers, which was a severe blow to the local economies and to the lives of those affected. It also removed approximately 1,500,000,000 board feet from commercial use, which is equivalent to about eighteen month's output of the entire redwood industry. The price of redwood lumber went up even more than it has in the past five years and this was high enough, as any homeowner with a redwood deck or grape stake fence in mind has learned. The total cost of this national park is estimated to exceed *one billion dollars*, which is more than the cost of *all* the other national parks combined. This latest addition brings the total redwood parkland in California to 229,000 acres, making the redwood the most protected tree species in the United States. In the aftermath of Proposition 13, the state tried to turn over its three state parks in the redwood region to the National Park Service, but the offer was declined, as the Park Service saw no reason to interfere with what already was a functioning operation.

The redwood hot tubs of today are just a more recent usage of this rot-resistant lumber for water containment and transportation. The first public water system in the United States was installed at Boston in 1652, of the bored-log type using local hardwoods. Redwood stave piping became available about 1880 and for many years made most of the state's conveyance systems for low-pressure water lines. One of these, more than one mile long and 18" in diameter, was dug up near Dominguez, between Compton and Long Beach, where it had been in service for more than fifty years, and was found to be as sound as the day it was laid in the ground.

California today ranks third after Oregon and Washington as a lumber producing state. Its "green gold" industry is rooted firmly in millions of acres of commercial timberlands, of which federally owned lands comprise about two-thirds of the total. These lands are managed on a "sustained yield" basis, which means that under ideal conditions no more is cut per year than is grown, either by natural afforestation or by reforestation plantings. One acre of young, vigorously growing conifers takes in five-to-seven tons of carbon dioxide a year and returns four tons of oxygen. This is important in reducing the so-called "greenhouse effect" caused by too much carbon dioxide in the atmosphere, which admits incoming solar radiation but partially blocks the longer heat waves emitted by the earth. Thus, intelligent forest management practices by all owners of timberlands is of more than economic benefit. As the foothills of the Sierra sweep along its length, they contain thousands upon thousands of acres of various oaks, which have thwarted almost every attempt to turn them into commercial lumber. Now, however, these oaks possess the potential of meeting some of the growing need for heating energy, and this "green gold" benefit also can be replenished *ad infinitum* by sound forest management practices.

Intelligent forest conservation provides the only surety that the "green gold" of California's economic base will endure. And intelligent conservation means something more than an emotional reaction that every stump is an unpardonable crime against nature. The tree that is harvested under sound forest management practices is embarked upon a new and useful life in the service of humanity. Then it must be and can be replaced by another over a sixty-to-eighty year cycle. Too few citizens are aware that trees are a vital natural resource that can be replenished, even increased, by human intelligence and ingenuity. Even fewer citizens are aware that without the products, influences, and services of the forests, Californians could not maintain their present standard of living, let alone meet the challenges of the future in this regard. It is well to note, and to note well, that without the forest cover on the Sierra Nevada, its capacity to receive, to store, and to release water would be so diminished as to cast an ominous shadow across the future of generations yet unborn.

Equally important — perhaps even more important as the urbanization of the state continues apace — are other values that result from sound forest management. Love of land demands that every Californian accept *responsibility* for conservation. This is given greater emphasis by the realization that the world's forests shrink by an area the size of Hungary each year. Thus one of the world's most important tasks may be to plant trees and California is no exception to this need.

Tree Farms are a sure way to ensure adequate timber supplies for future generations, but a tree farmer must have the patience to harvest his crop every 40-to-80 years, depending upon the species. — *Courtesy Louisiana-Pacific Corp.*

CHAPTER EIGHT

AGRICULTURE: AN IMMIGRANT SAGA

Two centuries ago, the bulk of California's land mass properly could be classified as semi-desert. It has been transofrmed into North America's most varied and productive agricultural region, which produces more than 200 agricultural commodities; leads the nation in 44 of them; produces 40% of the nation's fresh fruits and vegetables; 25% of *ALL* table foods consumed in the nation; and for 30 consecutive years has led the states in the farm-gate value of agricultural production. No other economic sector in the state so directly affects every Californian; agricultural expenditures for goods and services create and maintain one of every three jobs in the state. No other economic sector occupies so much land; uses so many natural resources; involves so many people in the food chain from farm field to consumer's table, and yet seems *so much to be taken for granted*.

From cultivation's beginnings two centuries ago to today's "factories in the fields," California's soils and climates have welcomed seeds and seedlings, cuttings and rootstock from all the world. Against this backdrop, the story of California agriculture is a saga of transition: first, the transformation from subsistence farming during the Hispanic period to one of the world's great grain producing regions within 15 years after the Gold Rush; and second, the change from basic cereal grains to the intensive and diversified cultivation of high-value row and orchard crops.

Certain factors are common to both stages: (a) relatively large-scale operations, such as today warrant the term "agri-business"; (b) the need for quantities of supplemental labor at harvesttime — first human, now increasingly mechanical, and (c) an export market, both inside and outside the United States.

Stage One above may be illustrated clearly in several ways. The first of these is the shift in the number of Californians engaged in mining and agriculture between 1850 and 1870.

YEAR	MINING	AGRICULTURE
1850	57,800	2,000$^{\pm}$
1860	82,600	35,800
1870	36,340	47,900

Vineyard irrigation with overhead sprinklers.   — *Pacific Gas and Electric Co.*

This human shift was accompanied by an economic shift, in that the value of agricultural production by 1870 exceeded the value of gold production in the state's economic mix. The political implications of this shift caused the original vast extent of Mariposa County, as defined in 1850 when Gold was King, to be carved into the additional counties of Fresno, Kings, Madera, Merced, and Tulare, when agriculture replaced gold as the dominant economic force.

Stage Two in California agriculture stems directly from the expansion and improvement of irrigation, which, by and large, was and remains possible only because of the huge water-storage capacity of the Sierra Nevada. The expansion of irrigation, as we have noted earlier, had its roots in the water doctrine of "appropriation and beneficial use" developed by the miners during the Gold Rush, because the ancient English common-law doctrine of

Self-propelled and computer-controlled, these sprinklers march across fields that could not be flood irrigated. — *Automated Farm Systems, Stockton*

riparian water rights precluded its use for irrigation. As early as 1862, the legislature granted ditch and canal companies the right to condemn private land for right-of-way purposes. For the next quarter century, the conflict between riparian and appropriative rights was fought out in the courts on a case-by-case basis. In 1887, the basis of today's irrigation was laid down by

The *Sierra Estrella*, a Cape Horner in the grain trade from California to Europe.
— *Courtesy San Diego Historical Society / T.I.T. Collection*

the Wright Act, which gave legal status to mutual, cooperative irrigation districts in taking advantage of the "appropriative" doctrine.

Among their many solid accomplishments, the Franciscans must be credited with practicing the first irrigation in California. Some twenty miles of ditches made Mission San Gabriel one of the most productive of them all, although extensive irrigation works were also constructed at other missions. The *Zanja Madre* that gave Los Angeles its first water supply was three feet wide by four feet deep, and the *zanjero* (water-master) was more important than the *alcalde* (mayor) in the town's affairs. Despite their pioneering role, it does not seem historically sound to date irrigation, as we know it today, from the Franciscans. Though there is some evidence that the *rancheros* of Southern California in part restored and used some of the missions' irrigation works, it appears that any extensive practice of irrigation was non-existent after the breakup of the mission system by secularization. Irrigation was equally foreign to the experience and practices of the Americans who made the Rush, with one notable exception.

In 1851, an outpost of Brigham Young's "Great Basin Kingdom" was established at what is now San Bernardino by the purchase of 35,509 acres from the Lugo family for slightly more than two dollars per acre. By 1855 this outpost boasted a Mormon population of 1,400 and had 4,000 acres under irrigation, thus deserving the accolade of being the first widespread practice of irrigation in California's American period. When the settlement was abandoned in 1857 because of the so-called "Mormon War" in Utah, these irrigation works passed to the purchasers of the Mormon buildings. By 1879, more than 110,000 acres were under irrigation in Southern California, and the importance of this technique to the growth of grape and citrus fruit production in that region cannot be overestimated. Approximately 68% of the state's irrigated acreage today is south of the imaginary line mentioned earlier that divides the state into water-*Haves* and water-*Have Nots*, and the bulk of this acreage is in the San Joaquin Valley, a matter of great importance in the continuing controversy over water distribution in the state.

As noted earlier, the Indians of California harvested Nature's bounty by hunting and gathering; but they were not agriculturists, save for the Yuma and Mojave peoples along the Colorado River. These practiced flood-plain planting to produce crops of melons, corn, and squash, which had been foundations of the much earlier Maya and Aztec agricultural civilizations in Mexico and Central America.

The Spanish introduced agriculture to California, and the Franciscans again deserve the credit for providing the transmission belt. At the missions that were strung like beads along the coastal strip of California, the *padres* introduced the basic cereal grains, the basic vegetables, and the basic deciduous fruits of their civilization. They also introduced the first grapes, the first citrus fruits, and the soft-shell English walnut which had its origins in Persia. They also cultivated hemp for shipment to the rope walks of Mexico.

Don Ignacio del Valle of Rancho Camulos, Ventura County, was famous for hospitality in a society noted for it. — *Los Angeles County Museum*

Corn was ground on primitive grinding stones, adopted by the Spanish from the Indians, to make the raw material for *tortillas*, and other grains were ground into flour in the same fashion. In the case of wheat or barley or oats, the grain was separated from the straw by piling the cut grain on a corral floor (usually of hard-packed earth) and then turning a band of horses into the corral. Driven around and around atop the mass, the horses trod out the grain from the straw; winnowing was done by Indians, and the precious kernels were collected and stored for use.

After the breakup of the missions during the Mexican period, agriculture declined to the status of subsistence farming at each *rancho*. The life and economy of the *rancheros* revolved around their herds of beef cattle, while sheep were limited to flocks large enough to provide wool for homespun cloth and to afford a change from the almost constant beef diet. Many *ranchos* had orchards of deciduous fruits and the "Mission" orange, and most had vineyards of Mission grapes for making wine and brandy. Ignacio del Valle of *Rancho Camulos* (Ventura County), where Helen Hunt Jackson gained much of her data for *Ramona*, was noted far and wide for the products of his trees and vines — fresh, dried, and liquid.

The Gold Rush spawned a demand for meat that between 1850 and 1853 drew perhaps 60,000 head of cattle from Texas to the mines, where they sold at prices from fifty to one hundred and fifty dollars each. In this same period, upwards of 100,000 "American bullocks" made their plodding way from the Mississippi River Valley to the slaughter pens of the Mother Lode camps. The Gold Rush also brought what truly can be called their "golden years" to the *rancheros*. Whereas in the 1830's an animal had been worth $1.25, the price of its hide and tallow, it brought forty times that amount, and more, in the mining camps. Stockton was the great cattle trading center in this period.

Great herds were trailed up from Southern California to the diggings, either over Tehachapi Pass or via the coast route and then over Pacheco Pass. The *rancheros* then rode sedately homeward with bulging saddlebags of raw gold. This welcome prosperity was reflected in the horse hardware of one of the Lugo *gente*, which was said to be worth more than $5,000; and by the great coach, ornamented in silver, in which the De la Guerras were wont to journey from their town house in Santa Barbara to visit their far-flung holdings, more than 300,000 acres, accompanied by outriders dressed in velvet livery. When beef production in Northern California began to catch up with the demand, about 1856, the hard times of the Southern California *rancheros* began.

During the first flamboyant years of the Rush, California's flour was imported from Oregon and Chile and became the great speculative commodity in the frenzied mercantile life of San Francisco and the inland supply towns. Wheat did not do well along the coastal plains because the moist air promoted "rust." Barley was the basic coastal grain crop, but even its tolerance for moisture often required that *vaqueros* be sent riding through the fields at sunup, with a *riata* stretched between them to sweep fog droplets from the ripening heads. It was not until grain farming worked its way into the hotter, drier reaches of the Great Valley that California attained ample cereal and feed grain production, although barley today is grown on more than 1,000,000 acres of largely unirrigated land.

The state neared self-sufficiency in wheat, the basic source of foodstuffs, about 1856; by 1860, it was producing some 6,000,000 bushels, more than the combined wheat production of all the other Far Western states. When the disruption of world commerce by the Civil War had ended, the great grain days in California got underway. By 1870, almost one-third of the state's 16,000,000 bushels of wheat was exported to Australia and England. In 1873, California was the largest wheat producing state in the nation and held this rank again in 1877; while in 1882, more than 550 tall-masted, blue-water vessels sailed from San Francisco Bay carrying wheat and flour to the world's markets.

In 1890, the state produced about 40,000,000 bushels of wheat; thereafter the financial "Panic" that swept the nation in this decade, coupled with the fact that Australia, Argentina, and Canada began to pour their wheat onto the world's markets, caused a sharp drop in wheat prices. This stimulated conversion of wheat acreage to less competitive crops, more intensively cultivated and irrigated. It should be borne in mind that California wheat

Believe it or not, there are thirty-eight mules hitched onto this harvester in the Sacramento Valley, ca. 1885. — *Courtesy of John Nopel, Chico*

Before the combined harvester made its appearance, grain was cut and then hauled to the threshing machine. This idealized scene was painted by Andrew P. Hill on Dr. Hugh J. Glenn's gigantic wheat ranch in Colusa County, 1876.
— *Author's Collection*

always found its export market in the world at large, because it could not compete in the eastern urban markets with wheat from the Great Plains. Today, the state produces more wheat than it did in 1890; basically winter planted and thus avoiding the necessity of irrigation.

The climate of the Great Valley was admirably suited for wheat cultivation. Hot, dry summers permitted the grain to ripen evenly, and to be stored in the open for weeks before shipment without fear of spoilage. It was a wheat well-suited for withstanding the rigors of ocean transportation and for milling, and became known as "California White Velvet" on the world's principal wheat market at Liverpool, England.

Wheat and flour both were exported from California, through Port Costa, Vallejo, Crockett, Benicia, Oakland, and San Francisco itself, to the world beyond the Golden Gate. At the peak of the wheat trade, Port Costa, where the inland waterways met the Bay, shipped approximately 1,000,000 tons of wheat and flour annually. Some said it was the largest grain port in world; certainly it was the largest on the Pacific Coast between Bering Strait and Cape Horn. Its glory days declined as the price of California wheat at tidewater sagged from $1.48 per hundredweight in 1888 to but $0.90 in 1894. It should be noted that many a California community had its own flouring mill, of which the Starr Mills at Vallejo was one of the largest for both export and local use.

These were the days of the "bonanza grain farms" in the Great Valley — days when Hugh Glenn of Colusa County could envision producing 1,000,000 bushels of wheat in one year from his own land. The great reapers were drawn by thirty mules, moving like an army through the square miles of waving wheat. Threshing crews worked from sunup to dark, their cooks even longer; and the mountains of chaff rose high enough, it seemed, to tower above the Sutter Buttes. On both the Sacramento and San Joaquin rivers, barges or shallow-draft, "dew-skimming" steamers took the golden grain down the rivers to the Bay, which led to the world beyond.

Pheasants explode out of the cover provided by rice land vegetation.
— *California Dept. of Fish and Game*

Because most of California's wheat was winter planted, the millions of migratory waterfowl in the Great Valley liked nothing better than to feed on the succulent green shoots when they popped above the ground. Men were hired as goose-herders, using eight-gauge shotguns to protect the crop from the gabbling, honking, quacking foragers. Even today, men use airplanes and flares and smoke bombs to keep the now-protected waterfowl from damaging the valley's crops.

Vineyards that descended from those introduced to California by the Franciscans gave Los Angeles County a production of 500,000 gallons of wine in 1858. It was from grapes of the Mission variety that Luis Vignes, pioneer Southern California vintner, produced his celebrated "Sparkling

California" to challenge the supremacy of champagne among the state's elite. The foundations of California's now world-famous wine industry were laid down by a Hungarian who backed the wrong side in a revolution at home and found it advisable to emigrate. He was Agoston Haraszthy — flamboyant, visionary, talented beyond most men when it came to grapes and wines. He settled near Crystal Springs in San Mateo County but found the climate more to his liking in Sonoma County and removed his operations there. The Buena Vista Winery he founded is said to be the oldest continuous wine operation in the state. In 1862 Haraszthy was authorized by the legislature to represent the state on a collecting tour of Europe's most famous wine regions. The legislature, however, did not see fit to appropriate any funds for his traveling expenses, and Haraszthy made his great contribution to the state at his own expense. He returned with 100,000 cuttings and rooted vines of literally hundreds of varieties of Europe's best grapes, and saw many of these become adapted to California before his disappearance in Nicaragua in 1869.

The interior coastal valleys of California — Napa, Sonoma, Livermore, Santa Clara — were admirably suited to wine-grape cultivation. In fact, these are among the most favored wine-grape regions in the world; their soils and climate making for less variation in vintages from year-to-year than their European counterparts, and the varietal wines which they produce have carried California's name afar. Under the pressure of today's urban sprawl, several famous vineyards have brought thousands of new acres into wine-grape cultivation in San Benito and Monterey counties. Had anyone thought to use the 30,000,000 gallons of wine stored in San Francisco's cellars in 1906, the disastrous fire that followed the quake might have been much less damaging than it became due to the lack of water to fight it.

While the varietal wines are the most famous of California's grape products, the larger dollar value over the years has come from lesser-known wine grapes and from raisin grapes in the Great Valley and Southern California. Leland Stanford once had the largest brandy distillery in the world on one of his ranches at Vina, Tehama County, which became part of his bequests to found the university that bears his son's name. Raisins from California have become world famous under the Sun Maid brand name, and it was the raisin industry, by and large, that carried California's viticulturists and viniculturists through the traumatic experience of Prohibition.

Since 1971, the acreage planted to wine grapes has doubled, with Zinfandel and Cabernet Sauvignon leading the red wines and French colombard and Chenin blanc the whites. Despite the gains in varietal acreage, the Thompson seedless accounts for the largest acreage planted to grapes, with some 270,500 acres which yield both raisins and a wine used in blending with other types.

Citrus fruits, even more than grapes, have spread California's name and fame afar. One of these wrought a drastic change in the dietary habits of the

When Orange County was the citrus groves that gave its name.　— *Courtesy Sunkist Growers*

nation, under the lash of finding an outlet for the productive capacity of Southern California's peculiarly suitable climate and soils. "California for health, Oranges for wealth" became the promotional cry at the turn of the century, and orange juice for breakfast became a part of the American way of life because of popular response to this siren song.

The so-called "mission" orange introduced by the Franciscans was thick-skinned, pithy, stuffed with seeds, and often sour. Despite these drawbacks (by modern standards), William Wolfskill, an ex-trapper who had settled in Southern California, planted about 2,500 mission orange trees in what is downtown Los Angeles today, and became the state's first commercial citrus orchardist. Wolfskill also is credited with making the first shipment of California oranges to the East, in 1876, a coup made possible by the advent of rail transportation into Southern California that year.

Given the mission variety's liabilities, it seems most likely that oranges would have remained a *curiosa California*, had it not been for the U.S. Department of Agriculture. In 1873, this agency received a few budded trees of a sweet and seedless orange from Bahia, Brazil, whence it apparently had been transplanted from China by parties unknown. Some of these precious seedlings were sent to Florida, where they expired. Fortunately for California, those that were consigned to it became entrusted to Luther C. and Eliza Tibbetts, residing at Riverside. Their efforts in propagating the new variety made "Washington navel" oranges the true Golden Apples of the Hesperides for California.

The expansion of orange groves was rapid and steady thereafter, as attested by the fact that California boasted more than 1,000,000 navel orange trees in 1890, and more than 5,600,000 in 1900. Most of the individual groves were small, about ten acres; and the problems of production, marketing, pest control, and frost protection led to the formation of growers' cooperatives, for which Sunkist may stand as exemplar. This method of association-handling of individual problems proved so successful — the first enduringly successful agricultural cooperative of any magnitude in the nation — that its pattern has been followed by growers of other farm commodities, such as walnuts, almonds, raisins, rice, and eggs.

Even though the word "navel" was for many years too indecent for advertising exposure, the promotional campaigns conducted by the citrus cooperatives played an important part in publicizing California throughout the rest of the nation. This contributed both directly and indirectly to the popular, albeit mythical, image of the state in other less favored climes. Certainly, their role in inculcating the belief that Southern California was the "Italy of America" and the "Riviera of the Pacific" is undebatable.

While the Washington navel made the foundation of today's citrus industry, this base was broadened immensely by the introduction of the Valencia orange from England in 1876. A summer-ripening variety, it was adaptable to the foggy coastal climate, which the winter-ripening navel was not.

The citrus base established by oranges was expanded by the rise of lemon acreage, stimulated both by a disastrous freeze in the Florida groves in the winter of 1894-95, which set lemon orcharding there back for many decades, and by development of the "Eureka" lemon, which is free of thorns. The Limoneira Ranch near Santa Paula, Ventura County, became the largest lemon grove in the world, and its production contributes to California's second-place rank in world lemon production, just behind Italy. Grapefruit entered the citrus picture when the Imperial and Coachella valleys were opened to cultivation by Colorado River water after the turn of the century, while mandarin oranges and tangerines are comparative latecomers to California's arsenal of citrus fruits.

Today, urban sprawl in Southern California and the prevalence of smog have forced most of its citrus acreage into the upper San Joaquin Valley, where climatic and other growing conditions are less favorable. The oft-heard dirge that citrus is dead in California is belied by the fact that a million acres of new citrus plantings have been made, and production per acre is higher. In dollar value, citrus fruits still rank high among California's crops, and their margin of profit, enhanced by frozen concentrate products, still depends upon an export market, primarily within the United States.

Factories in the fields — lettuce harvesting in the Salinas Valley.   — *Pacific Gas & Electric Co.*

California's agricultural productivity is the result of its transportation facilities and its agricultural diversity; this diversity in turn stems from the variety of favorable soils and climates — plus always *irrigation* — that the state affords. Asparagus in the peat islands of the Sacramento Delta; avocados along the favored slopes of Southern California, early melons and lettuce in the Imperial and Coachella valleys, dates at Indio; Christmas strawberries from Thermal; artichokes in the fog-belts of Santa Cruz County and up the Pajaro Valley and along the Skyline Drive south of San Francisco; 85 *tons* of garlic; a veritable ocean of lettuce from the Imperial Valley and the steady procession of maturing crops up the climate zones of the Salinas Valley, plus strawberries and carrots as well; the nation's "Peach Bowl" in the Sutter Basin; pears and apricots and nectarines and peaches elsewhere in the Great Valley; apples at Sebastopol; the nation's largest production of short-grain rice in Sutter, Butte, Glenn, and Colusa counties; almonds and walnuts galore, tomatoes, a multi-million ton crop that gives Stockton and other interior processing centers the rich smell of catsup for weeks at a time during their harvesting; and cotton in the San Joaquin Valley providing the raw material for Japanese textile mills. Cotton — fiber and cottonseed together — is the largest cash money crop raised in California. The advantage of longer staple and better spinning quality that California cotton enjoys over cotton produced elsewhere in the United States is threatened by artificial fibers, polyester chief among them. Added to these must be the celebrated "Spice Islands" herbs and condiments, many of which are grown near Dixon, California. The Kiwi (Chinese gooseberry) from New Zealand and the Pistachio from Iran have joined the roster of California's commercial crops since the first appearance of this book. Possibly the most exotic crop of all is the cut-flower and flower seed crop, as well as agricultural crop seed production.

To these exotic crops (exotic in the sense that their market demand seems based upon an affluent society in the main), one must add such staples as hay and grain, potatoes and sugar beets. Each one of these takes full advantage of California's diversity of soils and micro-climates. To these advantages must be added the basic research conducted by the federal government and the University of California in improving irrigation and growing techniques and in developing new and better varieties of major crops. Nothing illustrates this more dramatically than the delectable strawberry. The average production per acre in California is 20 tons, versus the national average of but 3 tons per acre, and another new variety developed by University scientists yields up to 50 tons per acre. California produces 77% of the total United States strawberries on but 33% of the total acreage devoted to this crop. At the peak of the season *twenty tons* of plant-ripened strawberries leave California each day for other markets.

Suburbanites who purchase homes adjacent to orchards are apt to get wrathy when they or their children learn the painful lesson that blossom

A steam harvester in the great grain fields of the San Joaquin Valley, ca. 1890.
— *Courtesy L.A. County Museum*

time is bee time. Bees are indispensable for pollination of fruit and nut crops; for all of the crops that depend on pollination for edible and profitable results. Almonds, for example, are susceptible to pollination only for a 3-5 day period after blossoming. If cold, windy, or rainy weather discourage the bees from their appointed tasks, the almond grower faces a lean year. Bees also are raised for export, particularly to western Canada, where the winters are such as to decimate the bee colonies.

Population growth and affluence, not climate or soil, has spawned the state's production of mushrooms, which must be cultivated in buildings where humidity, temperature, and air movement can be controlled most carefully. Estimates of the state's mushroom production exceed 10,000,000 pounds annually. About one-half this total is consumed fresh, while the remainder goes into cans, and there have been times when fresh mushrooms were air-freighted from Pennsylvania to meet the California demand.

The net result of this diversified productivity is to make California the *leading agricultural state* in the nation, in terms of raw farm production value. The *annual value* of this production *exceeds* the total value of *all the gold* mined in the state since 1848, and exceeds $9,000,000,000. This raw worth, or farm-gate value, plus the millions more added by the manufacturing and distributing processes in the food chain, make agriculture a major support of the state's economy. It also gives California a direct and vital interest in worldwide markets and international tariff agreements.

The state's larger-than-average-size farms and relatively higher labor costs have had direct and important effects upon agricultural machinery. In 1867, a Martinez mechanic, Philander Standish, invented a steam monster with rotating blades instead of plow shares. It *"tickled the bosom of Mother Earth in vigorous fashion,"* according to one account, but it was not a practical success. It did, however, herald the dawn of steam mechanization of California agriculture. By 1890, steam powered, combined harvesters that reaped and threshed in one operation were lumbering across the grain fields of the Great Valley. These steam rigs supplanted the thirty-mule teams for harvesting, and were supplanted in turn by another California-born development, the track-laying "caterpillar" tractor, which took full advantage of California's then plentiful supplies of petroleum energy. The "Stockton gang plow," three or more plow shares on a single frame, was evolved to meet the need for quicker and more efficient turnover of more acreage for planting.

Today the need to replace hand labor at harvest time has produced the mechanical cotton picker and machines that pick row crops and dig potatoes and sugar beets. Other machines cut and bale hay in a single operation, while pulling a mechanical stacker that loads the bales onto trucks for haulage to market or storage barn. Looking like a friendly Brontosaurus, a machine moves through alfalfa fields, scooping up the alfalfa, chopping it fine, and compressing it into bite-size cubes for livestock feeding. The cubes are easier to handle than baled alfalfa, and livestock eat more, get fatter faster, and

An olive picking crew takes a "picture break."   — *The Bancroft Library*

Waiting for work — migrant workers in camp, ca. 1918.   — *Los Angeles County Museum*

return more profit. Mechanical nut-tree shakers are in common use, together with mechanical sweepers to collect the nuts from beneath the trees. Machines that shake peach and other soft-skinned fruits from their trees have proven reasonably successful, thus obriating much of the laborious, ladder-climbing hand work, and machines successfully harvest the bulk of the wine grape crop.

The work of the University of California in primary research on mechanization equipment and processes has been invaluable, and has brought it severe criticism from labor and social activists who see mechanization as threat to the livelihood of farm workers. While reminiscent of the Luddites, who destroyed textile machinery in England, 1811-1816, because it reduced employment of hand weavers, this criticism overlooks the fact that there can be social benefits of mechanization. Dr. Charles Hess, University of California — Davis cites the case of the mechanical harvester used in the canning tomato crop. Development and adoption of this harvester prevented the canning tomato growers from moving to Mexico, where there was ample hand labor. The harvester, as well, has made possible five times as many jobs in the canning tomato fields as there were in 1963, while harvest wages have more than doubled and the consumer has benefited in lower prices. The entire field of argument over agricultural mechanization highlights a salient aspect of California agriculture, past, present and future.

With the rise of the "bonanza wheat farms" after the Civil War, agriculture became dependent upon large quantities of farm labor at both planting and harvesting seasons. This demand continued after the transition to intensively cultivated specialty crops, and was accentuated as the size of the average California farm increased steadily to today's plus-or-minus 600 acres. California's sustained population growth always gave it a plentiful supply of largely unskilled labor and agricultural employment was the beginning or the last resort of many such. Beginning with the Chinese after 1869, ethnic minorities have made an element in this seasonal labor force, with workers from Mexico becoming prominent during the labor shortage of World War I and the "boom" years that followed. During the Great Depression, fugitives from the Dust Bowl regions of the Great Plains swelled the migrant work force, the so-called "fruit tramps," who followed the crops as they ripened throughout the state and often went on into Oregon and Washington. Throughout these years, efforts to improve the economic and social conditions affecting these essential human components of the state's agricultural productivity produced flaring violence; the most notorious incident being the "Wheatland Hop Riot" of 1913, in which two hop pickers and the sheriff and district attorney of Yuba County were killed, and many more injured. The National Guard was called out to maintain an uneasy peace and Governor Hiram Johnson appointed a commission to investigate the plight of the migrant workers.

Another labor shortage during World War II saw the U.S. Department of Agriculture negotiate with the Mexican government to recruit, transport, house and feed Mexican agricultural laborers, who became known as *los braceros*, "the strong-armed ones." Under the agreement with Mexico, *los braceros* were guaranteed the same wages as were paid domestic laborers in agriculture in the area where they worked. The contractual agreement between the United States and Mexico regarding wages, housing, and feeding laid a firm basis for the later efforts of Cesar Chavez to organize California's farm laborers to gain what the *braceros* had enjoyed, because it showed that such standards were economically possible for California's employers of

From the grain days to the present, supplemental labor at harvesttime is a necessity. A migrant worker of the 1930s.
— *The Bancroft Library*

seasonal farm labor. There were two great advantages for the employer in the *bracero* program: the men were dependable and there was no threat of strikes at the critical times in the agricultural cycle; when their contracts were up, they went back to Mexico and thus eliminated the social and economic problems that always plagued transient farm laborers and their families and communities during the slack employment months.

The *bracero* program lasted from 1942 to 1963, with an average of 100,000 employed in California during those years. The ending of this program saw the beginning of Cesar Chavez's dedicated efforts to do what had been tried and had failed so many, many times before: construct an effective union to represent the farm workers of the state. By his patient energy and compelling personality, he did what he set out to do; attracting widespread support from clerical and political activists both statewide and nationally, surviving jurisdictional fights with rival labor organizations, and winning several crucial strikes, one of which dragged on for three years and brought his farm workers for the first time in American labor history a health insurance program. California's Agricultural Labor Relations Act of 1975 was a tribute to Chavez's efforts and a recognition of his political muscle. Its long-term effect upon California agriculture is yet to be determined. Both the farm employer and the farm laborer, however, remain at the mercy of the Teamsters Union, which holds bargaining rights for the cannery and distributive workers. A strike at the processing level during the peak harvest season can spell ruin for both the crop grower *and* the farm laborer who is dependent on harvest time for peak employment and income.

It commonly is assumed that the millions of illegal aliens in this country, mostly from Mexico, are the backbone of farm labor in California today. The available data show that most of these go from rural to urban employment just as soon as they can, but it should be remembered that in no phase of California agriculture is hard, factual data more scarce than in the area of farm labor. Another little known fact is that mechanization has affected farmers and their families more than it has their hired hands. This is due to the expansion of average farm size, which in turn is due to the pressures of higher costs and taxes, and this expansion means that there are fewer family members to handle the expanded operation, thus, requiring a larger proportion of hired labor.

California's main agricultural advantage remains today what it always has been: its climate. This is not enough if less expensive labor areas, such as Mexico and certain South American countries, can compete with California on a cost basis and they already do, threatening the state's floriculture industry, which is labor-intensive and the tenth most valuable crop in the state. Future projections indicate a decline of 1-1½% per annum in farm labor requirements, mostly in cotton, sugar beets, tomatoes and grapes, where mechanization has been most effective. Mechanization in tomatoes has brought about a drastic shift in the labor force composition, from

(Above) The pilot, in crash helmet, signals his ground crew that he has another load in the hopper. (Below) Dark swathe on water is rice seed. Paddies are flooded before planting and the rice grows up through the water to greet the sun.

— Courtesy of C.W. High, Richvale, CA

predominantly male to two-thirds or more female. The trend towards more ready-to-eat foods and towards more eating out, rather than at home, also has speeded the processing of tomatoes in the field, due to the expansion of pizza parlors and other "fast food" outlets across the nation. The rise of diversified agricultural cooperatives, such as Tri-Valley Growers, represent an option for economic survival for the farmer by giving him a home for what he grows, and by "home" is meant the processing, distributing and marketing of his products, with the grower sharing in the profits from the integrated operation.

It should be noted that rice growing is one of the most mechanized of all agricultural operations. Seeding, fertilizing, and fresh water shrimp control are done by air, harvesting and threshing in one operation by self-propelled machines on very broad treads. The paddy (field) layout also is done

Track-laying rice harvesters at work in the Butte Basin. These machines cost more than $100,000 each and can operate in ground so soft that it "would bog down a blanket."
— *Butte County Rice Growers Assn.*

by machinery, as is the drying of the harvested rice. The only handwork in rice cultivation is in irrigation control. The chaff from harvesting and the standing stubble must be burned, as rice straw will not readily decompose when plowed under. This has led in recent years to the imposition of fees for burning the fields, as well as outraged cries from urbanites who feel that the resultant air pollution is inimical to their health.

The development and expansion of rice growing in California played a major part in the successful introduction and propagation of the ring-neck pheasant. The irrigation checks and canal banks provided the essential cover for what has become the state's most popular upland game bird. The sale of hunting rights on rice lands provides supplemental income for many rice growers. Fallow paddies often are used to raise catfish for the urban market, yielding about 1,600 pounds per acre. Fish fanciers point out that one pound of fish protein can be raised on only 10% of the water required to raise one pound of beef protein, and say that this should be encouraged because of the environmental gains through the lessened use of water.

The place of rice in the agricultural mosaic of California brings up the fact that development of deep-water ports at Stockton and Sacramento is linked directly to the industry and diversity of the Great Valley, which these cities serve, today as in the past, as distributing centers. The natural waterways reaching inland from San Francisco Bay make it possible to ship rice in specially designed vessels to Pacific Basin and Caribbean nations. They also make it possible for the best California malting barley to be shipped directly to Scotland, whence it returns to those ports in the form immortalized in the late Guy Gilpatric's fiction as "Duggan's Dew of Kirkintilloch." The world's largest corn processing plant has been constructed at Stockton.

No outline of California's agricultural growth would be complete without a mention of what can be termed without apology "agri-silliness." The mythical properties of the state's climate have led to ill-starred schemes for the raising of such crops as bananas, coffee, and lichee nuts. One of the wildest of such schemes was that of planting and cultivating mulberry trees to make the base for a silkworm, hence silk, industry. This almost bankrupted the state from the overly generous bounties offered by the legislature for production both of silk and marketable cocoons. More than 1,000,000 inferior cocoons were raised in 1868 with a bounty of $300 for each 1,000 of them. Governor Haight got the legislation repealed in 1869 when the state had 1,750,000 mulberry trees and cocoons threatened to drain the state's coffers. Tobacco cultivation was stimulated by the Civil War, which cut off supplies from the seceded southern states, but encountered severe problems in curing the leaves because of California's drier climate. James D. Culp claimed to have solved this problem by 1872, and had about 1,000 acres planted to tobacco in the Gilroy area. His venture was ruined by the financial crash of 1875, and there has been little commercial interest in tobacco growing since that time. This lack of interest does not presently apply to at

The airplane virtually is indispensable to California's specialized agricultural products. Here an almond orchard gets sprayed against disease. — *Ty Barbour — Chico Enterprise-Record*

least one other smokable weed, which makes the largest cash crop in several coastal and mountain counties.

Of more national concern was the effort to produce rubber from the Mexican *guayule* shrub, which began during the rubber shortages caused by World War I. After lengthy searching and experimentation, suitable soil and climate for *guayule* cultivation was found in the Salinas Valley. Some 15,000 acres were planted there between 1926-1931, and a processing plant was constructed. The development of cheap synthetic rubber from petroleum derivatives doomed this venture to failure. New experiments are underway today to reduce the growing time to maturity of the *guayule* shrub from four to one year. With natural tree rubber decreasing in supply and the cost of synthetic rubber soaring from increased petroleum costs, the *guayule* could become a new and valuable commercial crop, as well as a decided asset to the nation's need for rubber-tired vehicles.

Protection of the oceans' whales by every nation except Russia and Japan brought about a shortage of sperm whale oil for delicate lubrication and pharmaceutical purposes. A once lowly shrub from the arid southwestern deserts now promises to yield oil equal to that of whale oil. This is the *jojoba* which has been planted commercially in Kern and Tulare counties and in the Southern California desert region. The San Carlos Apache in Arizona have been selling *jojoba* oil to Japan for many years, and it has made a widespread appearance on the cosmetic shelves and counters here at home.

Agriculture's transition is epitomized by the change in dairying since 1850, when butter was packed in snow and ice for wagon shipment across the Sierra from the Mormon dairies in the Carson Valley to Sacramento. In our time, gigantic milk tank trucks roll out of Modesto early each morning to meet the needs of Los Angeles and its satellite communities. In our time, too, the barefoot boy who used to bring the family cow home at milking time each night earns a degree in dairy science or business management, or both. "Bossy, the Moo Cow" now spends her life on concrete or asphalt; she is fed a scientifically balanced and mechanically weighted allotment of feed; her milk output is tabulated daily by a computer, and when it falls below the profit point, Bossy winds up as hamburger in a fast food drive-thru.

The same change is reflected in the old-time family flock of hens that the farmer's wife used to raise for egg money. Today they are antiseptic and cage-bound batteries of laying pullets, 35,000,000 of them producing *nine billion* eggs annually in flocks ranging from 30/100,000 each. Their brothers became broilers under similar conditions, without ever touching the ground or chasing a hen. Similar conditions govern the production of thousands upon thousands of turkeys around the year in California, and those gobbling bundles of nerves have raised particular problems for the state's sheep industry. Turkey meat can be produced and processed for the consumer at about one-half the cost of lamb. The once familiar farmyard sight of a brood sow with her piglets happily snuffling their way to the nearest mud wallow is no more. The hog farmer has taken a leaf from the poultry raiser's book and as many as 10,000 porkers are handled by two men on a minimum of land in air-tight and air-conditioned buildings, quiet, well-lighted, even solar heated. This requires a hefty investment and demands careful attention to disease control. In both the dairy and poultry installations, a waste-heat recovery unit that recoups heat lost from compressors reduces energy consumption by as much as 83%, which is no small saving.

As was noted earlier, the Gold Rush created a demand for meat in California that the herds of the *rancheros* could not fill, and the state has been an importer of meat-on-the-hoof ever since. Millions of cattle, sheep, and hogs are imported each year from states as far away as Texas, Louisiana, Nebraska, and Missouri. Thus today, as in the past, much of California's hay and grain production is used to put weight on imported livestock. Bakersfield early became the "feeder cattle" capital for the livestock producers of the Southwest and remained so for many years.

Cattle and sheep provide a direct link with the nostalgically romantic days of the *rancheros*. The transition from those days of hide-and-tallow slaughtering, of open range and of daring *vaqueros*, to today's automated and computerized feedlots — such as the one at Coalinga that has a capacity of more than 100,000 cattle and wafts its fragrance over the traffic on Interstate 5 — is as dramatic as the changes in crop production and dairying. The old days are preserved — or prostituted, as you prefer — in the professional sport known variously as "rodeo" or "stampede" or "Frontier Days."

Such words as "buckaroo" from *vaquero*, "hackamore" from *jaquima*, "hoosegow" from *juzgado*, "chaps" from *chapareras* reveal the Hispanic influence upon the modern language of the fence-mending, feed-weighing, jeep-riding cowboy. And Hispanic horse hardware, such as the center-fire saddle, the spade bit, the rawhide *riata*, spread from California into Nevada and western Arizona, into eastern Oregon and Idaho, as California ranchers and cattle buyers extended their interests into those regions.

Economic problems that beset the *rancheros* following the decline of cattle prices in 1856, which was a year of deficient rainfall as well, were compounded by others that could be attributed only to the Will of God. These natural catastrophes affected all of rural California, and all of those who lived by the land and its bounty.

Beginning in the Christmas season of 1861, California was swept by a procession of moisture-laden Pacific storms that continued virtually without cessation for thirty days. Los Angeles saw the sun but once, and that briefly, during this period. The Great Valley became in effect a great inland sea and so remained for seemingly interminable weeks. When the sun returned, the grass and weeds grew luxuriantly; the surviving herds grew sleek and fat, and the glutted cattle market sagged even lower.

More importantly, no beneficial rains blessed California's farms and pastures *for more than thirty months* after the deluge ended. More than 75,000 head of cattle perished in Monterey County, 50,000 in Los Angeles County, and almost 200,000 head in Santa Barbara County. The buzzards became too gorged to fly, the coyotes too insolent to flee, and the dessicated carcasses of dead cattle, bony racks under flint-hard hides, were spread across the pastoral landscape from Monterey to San Diego. For *rancheros* and plain farmers alike, this destroying drought burned away land and hope and the psychological bulwark these two had provided. This dry spell, the longest in California's recorded history, had a shattering impact on the independent farmer and contributed to the growth of tremendous agricultural-pastoral enterprises, several of which have endured, albeit on a reduced scale, to this day.

Among these is that founded by Henry Miller, an immigrant German butcher boy, who had reached San Francisco in 1853 and subsequently laid the foundations of the state's meatpacking industry at "Butchertown" (South San Francisco). To meet San Francisco's expanding needs for meat, Miller plowed his profits into buying ranches and raw land around Hollister and in the San Joaquin Valley and turning them into livestock-producing units. He bought other acreages for the production of hay and grain for feeding purposes, was an extensive user and developer of irrigation systems, and is credited with being the first large-scale grower and user of alfalfa in the state. He also is credited with amassing three fortunes: one for himself, one for his associates, and one for his lawyers. The legend holds that at the peak of his holdings, Henry Miller could ride from Mexico to Oregon and sleep every night on his own land. Not quite true, but pretty close to it, as his holdings in Nevada and eastern Oregon were vast.

Lloyd Tevis and James Ben Ali Haggin, two lawyers from Kentucky, obtained their initial risk capital as moneylenders and private bankers in San Francisco during the Gold Rush. They ventured risk capital in the Comstock Lode and saw it returned manyfold. They then began to acquire vast landholdings in the upper San Joaquin Valley, centering around Bakersfield, and created a grasslands empire of more than 1,400,000 acres in Arizona and New Mexico. The latter was operated for "feeder" cattle production. They combined their agricultural production in California with their livestock production in the Southwest, via railroad linkage on both the Southern Pacific and Santa Fe lines, to make Bakersfield important in meeting the ever-growing market for meat in ever-growing Los Angeles.

Edward Fitzgerald Beale was a certified hero of the California phase of the Mexican War, and a man who treated the California Indians humanely. The other side of his coin is depicted by the legend that President Abraham Lincoln refused to reappoint him as U.S. Surveyor-General for California because "Beale became Monarch of all he surveyed." What he began is known today as the Tejon Ranch Company, which controls a tremendous acreage in the Tehachapi Range, extending south and east from the present swooping route of Interstate Highway 5 through those mountains.

The native Hispanic cattle, introduced to California with the De Anza expedition, were inbred descendants of the original importations from Spain, the first of which reached Mexico about 1520. Long of horn and colored even as was Joseph's cloak, they were cat-hammed, wasp-gutted, and deer-legged, with shoulders that could split a hailstone. They also managed, even as their Texas counterparts, to walk incredible distances to market; and they were fierce enough to contend against varmints on the unfenced range, be they coyote or mountain lion or grizzly bear. Improvement of this native stock by the use of imported bulls from Europe and the East (Durhams at first, then Herefords) was due to a demand for better beef and for greater efficiency in converting grass to meat. This pattern of upgrading, of meeting increased operating costs with better meat-producing animals per pound of feed, is reflected today in such strains as the Santa Gertrudis from Texas, and the Charolais and Simentel from Europe.

The Hispanic sheep was the Spanish merino, and in California before the Gold Rush it was an inbred, long-legged, scanty-fleeced animal called *churro*. The improvement of sheep seems to have started before that of beef cattle. In 1851, the partnership of Flint, Hollister & Bixby left St. Louis with some 6,000 head of American sheep, a basically French merino strain; they reached Southern California some twenty months later at a cost of more than half their flock. The movement of sheep from the Mississippi River Valley to California in the 1850's appears to have been of some magnitude, perhaps reaching 500,000 head by 1860, but it is a largely un-recorded and certainly an untold story in the livestock annals of California. It did work a substantial improvement in the quality of California's flocks. Given impetus by the cattle losses aforementioned and by the cotton short-age during the Civil War, the number of sheep in California increased to some 3,000,000 head by 1870.

There was a major movement of sheep from Arizona and New Mexico into Southern California in the 1850's of several hundred thousand head. After the California sheep had been upgraded, as noted above, rams and breeding-ewes were sent back into the Southwest to improve the flocks in that region. Sheep from northern California stocked the ranges of eastern Oregon and Idaho beginning in the middle 1860's, and there are numerous instances of bands of sheep from California trailing as far east as Wyoming and Colorado, sometimes requiring two years for the journey. The sheep industry in Montana gained its start about 1869 with sheep trailed from California.

Until well into our present century, an almost biblical scene was en-acted yearly in California by herds of wandering woolies. Flocks in South-ern California, each about 2,500 sheep, with a herder and his dogs, moved north across the Mojave Desert in the spring, as soon as the first vegetation was up and while the scattered waterholes still held moisture from the winter rains. Moving up the Owens Valley, they grazed along the eastern slope of the Sierra until the snow melted in the passes. Then they worked up and over the Sierra's spine and down the western slope into the upper San Joaquin Valley, whence those that were not sold for meat or breeding replacements turned southward across the Tehachapi into Southern California. The seasonal migration came to an end with limitations upon the number of animals that could be grazed upon the national forests and other public lands.

These so-called "tramp" bands of sheep provoked animosity among settled, tax-paying residents of the lands they traversed. Even so, it is hard to find anything in California's past comparable to the bloody range wars between sheepmen and cattlemen that pocked the history of Arizona, Colorado, and Wyoming.

The sheep industry is primarily responsible for the Basque element in California's ethnic mix, for these were and are sheepmen par excellence. They are a most important factor in the state's contemporary sheep industry, and Sheepherder Bread quickly becomes a favorite of recreation seekers in the Bishop-Lone Pine area. It may even surpass San Francisco's famous sourdough variety in flavorful durability.

Horses were introduced to California by the Spanish, and were of the mixed Arab-Barb strains that were predominant in northern Mexico. These were riding types, light horses; and there is no evidence that California had any kind of draft horse during the Hispanic period. For one thing, they had no need for them; oxen were the main tractive power. For another, they had no harness; and the only wheel they employed was a slice of tree trunk used for their two-wheeled *carretas*. Juan Bautista Alvarado, while *el gobernador* of California in 1838, is said to have been given a proper carriage, brought all the way from Boston, by a shipmaster desirous of cementing friendly relations. Alvarado had two mounted *vaqueros* affix their *riatas* to the carriage shafts and pull the vehicle, while he sat serenly inside. This vehicle later was owned by Jose Arnaz, who planted the apple orchard that long purveyed cider and fruit in season to motorists between Ventura and the Ojai Valley.

The burro, too, was a Spanish introduction, as was the hybrid we call the mule. It is believed that the ancestors of the famous Missouri mule reached the "Show Me" state from California or New Mexico in the course of the Santa Fe trade. The feral stripes on the burro's back often form a crude cross at the shoulders, and Hispanic folklore holds that this dates from the time when a burro carried Our Savior's mother on her way to Bethlehem.

The native California horses were quite suitable for the first stagecoach lines, once they had been educated to look through a collar, but they lacked the heft and stamina for tractive power. The improvement of horseflesh by imported draft-type stallions became a necessity. Horses and mules were *the* motive power in California's development during its first seventy-odd years as a state. They drew the city's delivery wagons and its first municipal transit cars; they powered the great grain harvesters and did the heavy work of plowing and cultivating. They were essential to the high-sided freight wagons that dominated much of California's inland transport even after the railroad spanned the length of the state. Horses, and mules, and burros (the prospector's *confidante* and the sheepherder's friend) gave man in California a controllable source of energy until they were replaced by the internal combustion engine in all its manifold mutations. The twenty-mule teams of Death Valley, actually 18 mules and 2 horses, probably symbolize this fact in the public consciousness.

It is hard to find a draft horse anywhere in California today. But horses do play an important part in the leisure time of our affluent society. No parade is complete without its mounted units, and the state's numerous trail-ride groups — of which *Los Rancheros de los Visitadores* at Santa Barbara is the most famous — could not function without horses. Neither could the producers of Westerns for cinema and television audiences. These are play-world horses, but they should not be overlooked, especially in view of the tax revenues derived from horse racing.

Newspaper headlines and television commentators often give the impression that California's farmland is being swallowed up by foreign investors, who offer abnormally high prices to acquire it. There is no solid evidence that foreign buyers are sending the state's farmland prices out of sight, nor is there any solid evidence that foreign buyers are acquiring substantial amounts of the state's cropland. Seventy percent of all California farmland sales are made to neighboring farmers who bid up the price per acre through competing with other neighboring farmers.

Another myth is that California agriculture is dominated by absentee landlords and multinational corporations. As the old song says so well, "It ain't necessarily so"! What is happening in California, as well as in the nation as a whole, is that the *number* of farms is increasing, while the percentage of *large* farms, those annually producing more than $40,000 at the farm gate, is increasing. This increase is larger for the nation as a whole than in California. It also is a reality that $90\%^{\pm}$ of the state's farm gate value comes from 20,000 *large* farms, which probably sired the notion that great agri-business corporations dominate the state's agricultural industry. More than 70% of *all commercial farms* in California are family owned; 14% are owned by partnerships, and 15% by corporations. Of these corporations, less than 5% had more than 10 stockholders, which means that most of the corporate farms in California are owned by family corporations, which have adopted this business structure for tax and accounting purposes. In addition, a substantial percentage of the partnership farms are family partnerships. A family operation, too, may have separate corporations for each segment of its activities — cotton, grain, row crops, fruits and livestock.

It should be remembered and remembered well that the agricultural

If it grows anywhere on earth, it presumably can be grown in California.—*Bureau of Reclamation*

food chain from farm field to consumer table is a mainstay of California's economy and thus puts a firm foundation under what often is termed the "California lifestyle." As Daniel G. Aldrich has expressed it so well, "The whole process of economic advancement begins with reducing the amount of human effort it takes to provide the basic necessities of life and then using the work power thus released to produce other kinds of goods, more comfortable living, more leisure, the arts." In 1850, it took 20 man-hours to produce one acre of wheat, while today less than 2 man-hours will do the job and do it better; in the hand-and-hoe days of 1880, it took 344 man-hours to raise 100 bushels of corn — the most valuable crop of all in terms of efficient conversion of the sun's energy into food and feed value — while today the most efficient farmer can raise 100 bushels with less than 4 man-hours.

This remarkable achievement has been accomplished by the use of energy and it is estimated that the energy equivalent of 200 gallons of oil are necessary to provide one American's yearly food consumption. If a 50% cut in fossil fuel use by California farm tractors and harvesters was mandated, a recent study has shown that it would reduce the value of irrigated farm production by $462,000,000 per year, while saving only $63,000,000 in fuel costs. Only 5%+ of the total energy consumption in the state is required in producing, transporting, and processing farm products, and three-fourths of this energy is consumed *after* the commodities leave the farm.

You pitchforked the hay onto the wagon and you pitchforked it off to build the stack, while the horses got a rest and a few mouthfuls. The youngsters in the stack are not the farmer's kids, or they'd be working.   — *The Bancroft Library*

There is increasing debate today about the highest and best uses of rural land. Urbanites, paradoxically, are concerned about rising food prices, while not realizing that onerous regulations governing such things as size, weight, and packaging cause about a 30% loss between farm and table. There are eighty-three federal "maturity color standards" for California peaches, for example. They also prefer homes in rural settings, thus removing productive land from the food chain. The urban/agricultural conflict was dramatized in 1980-81 by the "Medfly crisis," as it came to be called. Among the most voraciously destructive pests that afflict agriculture, California had been free of the Mediterranean fruit fly for some years, until they were found in Santa Clara County in 1980. The state's then Governor, Edmund G. "Jerry" Brown, delayed authorization of malathion spraying because of vocal and prolonged opposition from urban dwellers. As a result, the infestation did reach a "crisis" point and spraying had to be done over a wider area and for far longer than otherwise would have been the case. Urbanites view the role of agriculture in California as providing them with abundant, high quality food at the lowest possible prices. They view food costs and farm efficiency from the consumer's perspective. Farmers and ranchers, however, see their role as an attempt to combine a profitable livelihood with a preferred way of life. They see costs and efficiency from an entirely different point of view. The marketing orders that regulate the quality of most of the state's fruit, nut, and vegetable shipments are viewed by urban consumers as un-American, monopoly tactics. The rural producer, on the other hand, views them as essential to survival, because they promote an *orderly* flow of produce to market, rather than a succession of seasonal gluts. Also, these marketing orders are initiated by the growers themselves; they are *not* subsidized, as are crops such as wheat and tobacco, and they ensure *quality* in the market-place, not half-spoiled, worm-ridden junk. And it should be remembered that Americans spend on the average only 14c out of every dollar for *food consumed at home*, although eating out is much more widespread today than it was when eating meals together at home was a ritual for most families.

The urban devouring of farm land between 1965-1982 approximated 1,000,000 acres, of which about 800,000 acres came from productive agricultural acreage. Until 1972, however, California had an annual net gain of 56,000 acres of agricultural land, despite urban enroachments, through the development of water supplies for previously non-irrigated acreage. Despite continued urban growth, California will have *more* productive farm land available over the next decade than there is water to irrigate it. Here, then is another major conflict between urban and rural California, because agriculture presently requires about 85% of all the water used in the state. Should dry years come again, as they have often done in California's past. the urban dwellers have the votes to bring about a drastic change in water allocations throughout the state.

The utilization of sprinkler, rather than flood irrigation, is one means of more effective water utilization in agriculture. Another is the "drip irrigation" method pioneered in the Negev Desert of Israel, which consists of equipment that delivers a measured amount of water at regular intervals directly to plant or vine or tree roots. Application of fertilizers and pesticides are made through this system, which, while costly, is said to increase crop yields up to 40% in tomatoes, with lesser gains in others. Still a third method of water conservation is the "deficit high frequency," or "stress," system, which irrigates at rates less than the daily estimated evaporation and crop need, with soil-stored water offsetting the deficit. This method is usable only on certain crops and certain soil types, but where it can be used, it reduces water usage by as much as 50%.

Extensive use of the hydroponic technique, in which plants are grown in liquid nutrients, not soil, may be a partial answer to the urban/rural conflict over land and water use, although commercial utilization of this technique has not been as successful as its promoters might have wished. Another palliative is the technique called "high density seeding," which amounts to putting crop rows closer together and putting more seed per acre in the ground; from 12,000 seeds per acre for tomatoes to 20,000 and more per acre. And still another is the continued development of improved crop strains that are more drought and disease resistant, and higher yielding.

Within the context of the conflicting urban and rural demands for land and water usage, together with the burden of urban-dictated environmental controls, it is sobering to remember one of the principal thoughts in the late Chairman Mao's "little red book." This stressed the necessity of capturing the countryside as a prelude to the final and victorious assault against the cities. If California's cities reverse this premise by capturing the countryside, what then for California? Another point to be remembered is the fact that California agriculture plays an important part in the export of agricultural products overseas which in turn affects the American balance of international trade. California's strategic position for trade with the expanding economies of the Pacific Basin nations bodes well for this balance of trade in future years.

Coal — an essential ingredient for heavy industry — is unloaded on the San Francisco docks, 1887.
— *Courtesy The Bancroft Library*

CHAPTER NINE

WEBS OF INDUSTRY
AND TURNING WHEELS

Rich as she was in other natural resources, California lacked practicable amounts of the two essential ingredients of the Industrial Revolution — coal and iron. She still does. The state did not have an integrated steel operation (from raw materials to fabricated products) until the Kaiser interests constructed the Fontana complex during World War II. Although this plant uses iron ore from within the state at Eagle Mountain, coal comes from New Mexico. In this reference, the manner in which the Santa Fe Railway runs its specially designed and operated coal trains from York Canyon, above Santa Fe, New Mexico, to Fontana is a triumph of modern railroading.

Despite these lacks, California quickly established a basic heavy industry because she had to. The impetus of the Gold Rush, and of the continuing population explosion it set in motion, triggered an exploitation of natural resources that could move in only one direction.

Iron pigs (ingots) from the East and from England and Europe made ballast for the tall-masted Cape Horners, sometimes whole cargoes. A bigger problem in respect to bulk was obtaining the coal to convert these ingots into usable products.

Coal was imported from Nanaimo, British Columbia; from Australia; from the eastern seaboard; and from Scotland, Cornwall, and Wales. The best coking and forge coal, essential to iron foundry and blacksmith alike, long sold for $40 per ton in cargo lots, alongside San Francisco's wharves. Inland transportation costs increased this price to $53 at San Jose, and to a whopping $110 in Marysville. Increase in cost at inland points gave San Francisco an industrial supremacy it held for many years. Heavy industry in Los Angeles was hampered by its distance from the seaport of San Pedro, and this effect was compounded farther inland in Southern California until the advent of petroleum.

Some coal was mined within the state, principally at the predominantly Welsh hamlets of Nortonville and Somerville on the slopes of Mount Diablo, Contra Costa County. The shipping port for this coal was the town that began as New York-of-the-Pacific and became in turn Black Diamond and today's Pittsburg. More coal was mined at Corral Hollow, near Tracy, where the Tesla Mine sent coal to San Francisco by river barge in the 1890's. Local production never seems to have exceeded about 2 percent of the state's requirements, which totalled 1,650,000 tons imported by sea in 1888, plus the undetermined tonnage brought in overland by the Southern Pacific and Santa Fe lines both for commercial consignees and to fuel their motive power.

The state's ability to import the required tonnages of both iron and coal to meet the steadily growing needs of its economy was aided immeasurably by the export trade in grain. Coal, iron, and wheat are all bulk commodities, which generally speaking require the lowest possible freight rate. With a two-way cargo virtually assured by the exportable surplus of wheat in California, ships brought coal and iron from the world's sources and lifted outward cargoes of the golden grain from California's fields. This ocean trade continued after the so-called transcontinental railroad was completed in 1869 simply because of the lower rates ships provided to and from the world's markets.

The first effective component of heavy industry in California was the Union Iron Works, in San Francisco, established by the three Donahue brothers from Scotland. Peter Donahue was twenty-seven when he left Glasgow for the Gold Rush; his brother James soon followed. They opened a blacksmith shop in an *adobe* on Montgomery Street, at the foot of Telegraph Hill, where they were joined by a third brother, Michael. The three men's skills were wonderfully complementary: Peter was a machinist; James, a boilermaker; Michael, a moulder, or pattern maker. San Francisco's numerous fires provided scrap metal, which they melted down to get the iron they needed to make cooking and heating stoves, their first major product. By 1851, they had prospered sufficiently to move to larger quarters at First and Mission Streets in San Francisco, doing business there as the Union Iron & Brass Foundry. There they made the first quartz mill and the first railroad locomotive produced in California.

Other forge and foundry firms arose in San Francisco — Pacific, Vulcan, Sutter, Fulton, to name a few — and Sander's Copper Works soon became the largest manufacturer of brandy distilling equipment in the nation to cope with the productivity of the vineyards and the thirsts of the citizens. Forge and foundry firms arose, to a lesser degree, in the principal valley supply towns of Stockton, Sacramento, and Marysville, which were the *entrepots* respectively to the southern, central, and northern mines. The Mechanic's Monument on Market Street in San Francisco, erected by the Donahues' descendants to honor their forebears, is in effect a memorial to the whole industry and the men who made it.

This was the Age of Steam, and the devices that both generated and controlled its power were made of iron. Boilers for river steamers and offshore vessels; boilers to generate steam for mine hoists and mills; boilers to power sawmills and flouring mills; boilers to power the main shafts that drove the belts that turned the tools in factories making shoes, and woolens, and furniture, and horseshoes, and wagons — all these were made in San Francisco. Steam engines were needed to use the steam these boilers generated,

Mechanics Monument and Fountain, Market Street, San Francisco — Douglas Tilden's tribute to Peter Donahue and the men who forged the beginnings of heavy industry in California. Picture circa 1910.
— *National Maritime Museum, S.F.*

and these engines, too, were made in San Francisco. Miles and miles of heavy-gauge iron pipe, carefully hand-riveted with a double seam in short sections, were needed to deliver water to the hydraulic monitors that blasted whole hillsides of gold-bearing gravel into liquid muck.

In 1881, John Dolbeer, founder of the great redwood lumbering firm of Dolbeer & Carson in Eureka, invented the "Dolbeer donkey," which brought steam to the brute force task of handling the insensate mass of a "soggy" redwood log. This "donkey" had a vertical boiler, burned wood, and spewed sparks like a roman candle; it generated steam to turn a vertical capstan, or "gypsy," around which several turns of thick, hawser-laid Manila rope afforded the friction necessary to haul in logs from the woods along greased chutes. Rope soon gave way to wire cable, and steam greatly accelerated the productive capacity of the lumber business.

Brought to California from his native England at age sixteen, Andrew S. Hallidie became a pioneer in bridge building and transporting freight and ore across yawning chasms by the means of an endless moving cable, similar to those that take skiers up the slopes today. Appalled by the injuries to horses pulling street cars up San Francisco's hills, one of which has a slope of 22°, Hallidie put his experience to good work. He adapted his system of endless cable powered from a central plant to operate what have been known ever since as "cable cars." By 1880, San Francisco was criss-crossed with 112 *miles* of cable car lines. The three lines that remain in operation in San Francisco today are one of that city's great tourist attractions, and give headaches to the city's insurance carriers.

Rails and rolling stock for all sorts of transportation facilities came out of San Francisco's industrial capacity and know-how. In time, the Southern Pacific established its largest shops at Sacramento, using coal from its own fields in Washington, and gave that city a firm industrial base to complement its ever-growing governmental payroll.

San Francisco's needs for skilled labor in the forge and foundry business, as well as in other trades and crafts, were met at first by disappointed gold-seekers, for there were men of every skill and profession among the Argonauts of '49. This background of industrial labor established San Francisco's position as a strong union town, a position that has endured largely unabated ever since. Los Angeles remained an "open shop," anti-union community for many years, which made another difference and source of conflict between the two urban centers.

The demands of inland waterway navigation and coastwise and trans-Pacific trade gave the state a shipbuilding industry from the time of the Gold Rush. The availability of lumber for hulls, decking, and superstructures was another natural advantage. San Francisco's strategic position and the deep-water reaches of the Bay, coupled with the necessities of national defense, led to the establishment of the Mare Island Naval Shipyard in 1854 and the Hunter's Point drydock in later years. In 1859, Mare Island built the first

(Above) United States Navy Yard at Vallejo, ca. 1870. (Below) Refining plant of the Arctic Oil Works, San Francisco, where whale oil was processed for shipment to the world's markets.
— *Courtesy The Bancroft Library*

warship constructed on the Pacific Coast, the *Saginaw*, and today it is the only Pacific Coast yard capable of constructing nuclear submarines.

California's shipbuilding saga reached its peak in the tremendous production records set during World War II. The Permanente yard at Richmond and Calship at Wilmington accounted for 45 percent of all the Liberty-type vessels built in the United States. The nation's record for Liberty ship construction was set by the Permanente yard in building the *Robert E. Peary* from keelson to completion in just eight days.

Wartime needs for manpower in heavy industry, especially in shipbuilding, brought California a tremendous number of young immigrants; Vallejo, for example, jumped from a population of 20,000 in 1941 to 100,000 in 1943. This influx completed the political transition already in progress from a preponderantly Republican electorate to one preponderantly Democratic by registration. It was the wartime influx, too, that brought the state its first substantial Negro population.

Another early and important California industry was its fisheries. This industry had its true beginnings offshore when the American whale fleet, primarily out of New England ports, had to flee the whaling grounds of the Atlantic during the War of 1812. The enormous "pods" (herds) of California gray whale attracted whalers to the California coast. La Perouse, the French navigator who visited Monterey in 1786, probably witnessed the annual migration from their breeding grounds in Scammon's Lagoon, Baja California, when he wrote, "It is impossible to conceive the number of whales that surround the ship." For many years before the Civil War, a whaling fleet left San Francisco every summer for the Arctic whaling grounds, thus heralding the later salmon fleet of the Alaska Packers and directly stimulating American interest in the acquisition of Alaska. The annual migration route along the California coast also made it profitable for land-based whaling stations to arise during the American period.

Stations were located at Ballast Point, near San Diego; at Portuguese Bend, near today's Marineland-of-the-Pacific; at San Simeon, beneath the ostentatious display of Hearst's Castle; at Moss Landing and Davenport at Monterey Bay; at Point Reyes-Bolinas and at today's exotic enclave known as Sausalito. At one time during the 1840's, sidewalks and patios at Monterey were paved with whale vertebrae. The extensive onslaught against the gray whale — the female of which yields twenty gallons of milk at a time to give her calf a rate of growth approximating two hundred pounds per day — led to American conservation measures, beginning about 1900, and today thousands of gray whale have been tallied on their immemorial migration. Protecting the whales also requires international cooperation, which has not been whole hearted as these lines are written.

The *Californios* do not appear to have been notable fish-eaters, perhaps because they could not fish from horseback, but the later population of San Francisco, owing to the Irish and Italian influxes, has provided a market

Bringing a touch of the Mediterranean to Sausalito in the 1880's, these lateen-rigged Italian fishing boats were the work horses of the industry. — *W.A.Scott/Nat'l. Maritime Museum*

for table fish since the Gold Rush. One of California's greatest delicacies moved the tragic poet George Sterling to a famous outburst:

Some folks boast of quail on toast
Because they think it's tony;
But my tomcat gets nice and fat
On hunks of abalone!

Another of California's great seafood delicacies, crab, often is taken in the amount of 20,000,000 pounds per year. This is about twice the average annual take, a reflection of what crabbers have come to accept: that there are fat years and lean in crabbing.

The lean years have descended upon Monterey's "Cannery Row," the scene of some of John Steinbeck's most famous and appealing tales. That port's sardine industry once took upwards of one billion pounds of sardines annually for processing into food, fertilizers, and feed supplements. A shift in the ocean's sardine population in 1952-53 virtually eliminated this industry, and Cannery Row now processes tourists, not sardines.

There was a time when the coastal streams of California were clogged with hordes of salmon seeking their ancestral spawning grounds and salmon contributed heavily to San Francisco's economy. This once mighty asset succumbed to a chain of diminutions that began with the hydraulic "slickens" and was compounded by industrial water pollution and exploitative commercial fishing. After the local supply was diminished, ships of the Alaska Packers Corporation for many years sailed out of the Bay for the northern fisheries. The state's Department of Fish and Game is making strenuous and reasonably successful efforts to bring the salmon back, and the towns of the Redwood Coast, Eureka chief among them, are major fishery centers, processing rock fish and crab as well as salmon. Restoration and conservation efforts are hampered by the presence of fishing fleets from other nations, chiefly Japan and Russia.

Frenzied fish-seekers throng to Southern California's beaches in frantic throngs during certain high tides each spring when the tiny grunion comes ashore to spawn. By law, the grunion must be taken by hand, an act that gains a certain hectic quality because the female grunion comes in on a wave, flirts a hole in the sand with her tail, deposits her eggs, and is gone — *in thirty seconds*! The grunioneers are either quick or fishless.

The sea offshore occasionally affects Southern California in a less appealing way. So-called "red tides" cover the beaches with a layer of the microscopic sea life known as "plankton"; it decays, the prevailing winds blow the aroma inland, and Los Angeles has "smish," which is smog with a fish flavor. More importantly, the wide-ranging tuna clippers, which can stay at sea for months and cruise clear to the Peruvian coast, land about 300,000,000 pounds of tuna at Terminal Island each year. Here again, international complications have beset the tuna fleet, as several South American countries find a source of revenue in levying fines on tuna boats allegedly trespassing inside their national water boundaries. Los Angeles is the nation's leading fishing port, landing more tonnage annually than do Boston and Gloucester, Massachusetts, combined.

Commercial and sport fishing only scratch the surface of the sea, which is still more mysterious than outer space. Whether one is "hanging ten" at Malibu or wet-suiting after abalone, the sea has an intimate relationship with all those who seek it for profit or pleasure. In the past, the kelp beds off California's coast have been harvested for iodine and stomach emollients. This was a primitive forerunner of what today's scientists foresee as "aquaculture" — the farming of the sea, which is self-renewing by natural forces, and the mining of this same sea for its vital minerals. There is a determined school of thought that holds that the true frontier of the future is the vast circulatory system of the sea, whence came all life. California's 1,264 miles of coastline lend added meaning to the future importance of "aquaculture" and facilitate marine research by such institutions as Stanford University, the University of California at San Diego, and University of the Pacific. Such a combination of natural assets with the reservoir of scientific and technological knowledge in California's institutions has explosive potentialities for the future, and this field of endeavor currently is attracting hopeful entrepreneurs to explore its possibilities.

Solar energy was used in the beginnings of California's dried fruit industry, with wooden trays by the thousands covered with raisins, apple slices, and split halves of peaches, apricots, and pears drying in the constant sun of the state's long harvest season. Patient Chinese were the mainstay of this work, and enough of the sulphur used in the curing process clung to the finished product to give the consumer a taste of one aspect of the Hereafter. Steam drying plants sprang up during the 1870's, but the sun remained important until after World War I. Today, such processes as vacuum-drying, dehydration, and quick-freezing make an industry all their own in California's complex of agricultural processing.

As we have said, the industrial growth of Los Angeles was hampered by the higher costs of imported coal in that city. Another deterrent was the South's lack of the hydroelectric power, which Northern California enjoyed in abundance, thanks again to geology, geography, and climate. The Sierra rivers had cut their gorges fast and deep, falling up to 130 feet to the mile, whereas rivers such as the Hudson in geologically older lands fall but 14 feet, and the great muddy torrent of the Missouri falls only 17 feet.

The energy of falling water was first used to turn waterwheels, such as that in John Sutter's sawmill. Most of the early flouring mills and other industrial developments in the towns of the Great Valley and the Mother Lode also used falling water for power. The alternative source of domestic and industrial energy in these communities was firewood, which was plentiful and cheaply obtained, albeit its BTU efficiency was not outstanding. The first locomotives in California, the "muzzle loaders," burned cordwood; and even with spark arresters on their balloon- or diamond-shaped stacks, they were rolling fire hazards to forest and grainfield alike.

The Helms Project, the state's largest pumped-storage plant is completely encased within Sierra granite, and operates as follows:

- A. Water from upper lake flows into horizontal tunnel
- B. It then falls more than 1,500 feet vertically to turbines
- C. Flowing through vanes of fan-like turbines it spins them at some 360 rpm
- D. Turbines spin the generators that make electric power
- E. Water then flows into lower lake. At low-demand periods, the generators become motors to pump water back to upper lake for re-use when needed
- F. Vertical columns are surge chambers which reduce "water hammer."

Even when it came to firewood, Los Angeles suffered from a supply inadequate for the phenomenal growth that began in the middle 1880's. The natural supply never compared with that of the Sierra or the oak parks of the Great Valley, or the timber stands along the central and northern coasts. Charcoal burners and woodchoppers for the domestic market had made such

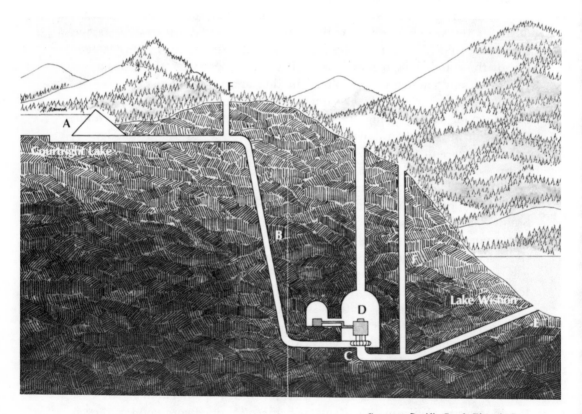

Courtesy Pacific Gas & Electric Co.

inroads upon this scanty natural resource that in 1880 stove wood was commanding $15 a cord in Los Angeles, a price that was exorbitant to the average householder.

The state's first use of waterpower to generate electricity appears to have occurred in northern California on April 10, 1879, when Excelsior Water Company used a cumbersome waterwheel to generate enough "juice" to light three 3,000-candlepower lights, which enabled them to work their hydraulic operations by night and by day, thus doubling their "cleanup" from the riffle boxes.

This crude beginning was given a tremendous assist by an invention of Lester Allen Pelton, a millwright and carpenter at Camptonville on the Mother Lode. His compact turbine-type wheel with a double row of buckets and a "splitter" to get two jets of water from the same orifice, was first perfected to power the sewing machine of Mrs. Margaret Graves, Pelton's landlady. When he patented his invention on October 26, 1880, it marked a major breakthrough in the efficient utilization of falling water as an energy source. A statue commemorating Pelton's discovery stands today at Camptonville in Nevada County.

The invention was first used to develop energy for the mining operations along the North San Juan Ridge. When the South Yuba Water Company lost its hydraulic mining customers, owing to restrictive legislation, it used Pelton's wheel to generate electricity. By August 4, 1887, the firm was illuminating streetlights in Nevada City, and just 23 days later, it had streetlamps in Grass Valley with a total of 14 miles of transmission lines. A major achievement was made in 1895, when Folsom Powerhouse on the American River sent current a then record distance of 22 miles to Sacramento. The use of hydropower in California has increased immeasurably since these beginnings, and improvements in Pelton's wheel continue to convert falling water's force into one of the state's essential servants.

The title of the state's "hardest working river" is claimed by Southern California Edison Company for the South Fork of the San Joaquin River, where its eight generating plants use and re-use the river's flow to generate about 700,000 kilowatts for transmission to Southern California. A counterclaim to this title is asserted by Pacific Gas and Electric Company on behalf of the North Fork of Feather River where its multiple plants make a "staircase of power" that develops 780,000 kilowatts for central and northern California. To put these capacities in perspective, it is noted that the power generated by the falling water of the Feather River's North Fork will meet the needs of 78,000 two-bedroom homes with all electric appliances, including air conditioning. In another perspective, it would require the energy of 867,000 barrels of oil per year to replace this capacity.

The bitter sectional squabble over California's water has received a new dimension from its generating capacity. Existing utility company-owned power plants on northern California's Feather and Mokelumne rivers are objects of takeover attempts by municipalities in both the northern and southern sections of the state. These attempts are based upon an interpretation by the Federal Energy Regulatory Commission of congressional legislation concerning power plant licensing. Should these attempts prove successful, they will have the effect of serving far less households than the plants do today and will increase substantially the costs of electricity to those households who currently depend upon the plants for their energy needs.

Even as Lester Pelton used a "low head" fall of water to turn his first turbine-type wheel, so today the utilization of "low head" hydroelectric plants is seen as another means of reducing the state's dependency upon imported oil, be such from Alaska or elsewhere. The term "low head" means simply that the vertical fall of water necessary to generate electricity, admittedly in small increments, can be as little as ten feet. Such low-head hydro plants can be easily and *preferably* installed at existing dams and canals owned by irrigation districts and other water agencies. The economic incentive for building these plants is the same as the incentive for building the "windmill farms" discussed in a subsequent chapter: federal legislation *requires* existing utility companies to purchase whatever "juice" they produce at the companies' cost for producing electricity. Evangelical enthusiasts for this alternative source of electricity, meaning energy, claim that if all the potential sites in the state for such plants were developed, they would generate electricity requiring 4,000,000 barrels of oil to duplicate. Such a saving would enable California not to import oil for just eight days. Despite the enthusiasm and despite the number of applications for such plants, most of them filed by out-of-state entrepreneurs, it is unlikely that the maximum number of plants or the petroleum savings envisioned will come to pass. Whatever is gained, however, is another reminder of the old Scottish proverb, "Mony a mickle makes a muckle."

Another weapon in California's arsenal of hydroelectric generation is the "pumped storage" generating plant. The hydro plants mentioned earlier as "staircases of power" use falling water which then goes on downstream, meaning *downhill*, to another power plant and so on *ad infinitum* until the downhill slope becomes too slight for "high head" generation. Pumped storage, however, puts a different twist on the downhill flow of water for power generation. A reservoir below the powerhouse collects the water that is run through the plant during the peak load, or peak demand periods. Then during the slack demand period, late at night into the small hours of the morning, the plant's turbines are reversed to become motors and pump the day's water back uphill to the reservoir or lake whence it came. Then it is used again when demand begins to pick up as the day's activities begin. This reverse pumping uses electricity generated by plants that otherwise would be idle or partly idle, which reduces the cost of pumping and makes for more efficient plant utilization all around. The largest such pumped storage plant in California became operable in 1982 on the North Fork of Kings River, some 80 miles east of Fresno. Unusual in that the entire generating plant is constructed underground, the plant will generate 1,125 Mew at designed capacity, which is enough to serve a city the size of San Francisco, and save additional multi-millions of barrels of oil. (see p. 186)

Long-distance transmission lines march across the California landscape on stilt-like legs. In addition to carrying electricity from the Sierra powerhouses to the urban consumers, these lines also tie California into the Northwest Power Grid along the Columbia River to provide supplemental supplies of this non-polluting energy source at "peak load" periods.

While northern California was blessed with initially adequate supplies of falling water, the first hydropowered dynamo apparently was installed in Southern California. It is said to have been installed by George Chaffey, a Canadian-born pioneer irrigation engineer, in San Antonio Canyon near Etiwanda, whence he ran a transmission line to Pomona. This plant and the few others that followed it in the water-short region below the Tehachapi Range were not adequate to meet its need for power.

At the very heart of Los Angeles' ability to enter the state's industrial complex was the discovery of petroleum in Southern California, and to develop it in such quantity as to make it a much cheaper and more readily available and infinitely more flexible source of energy than any other. In fact, petroleum provided the whole state with its first self-contained source of fossil fuel (its coal deposits being negligible and of inferior quality at that) and gave tremendous impetus to the industrial growth of California in the twentieth century. The importance of the petroleum story merits a separate chapter later.

The state lacks a self-contained source of uranium or other fissionable material. However, the energy potential per ounce of such substances makes them far less costly to import than the coal, with which the state's true industrial complex began.

California's size and shape would have precluded the development of its diversified assets without adequate transportation. Indeed, it can be said that each of the great surges in the state's growth has been both stimulated and accompanied by the expansion and improvement of transportation facilities. These facilities have been both internal and external, and both got their start from the impact and influence of gold.

California's Hispanic years did not produce a road worth the name between San Diego and Sonoma. A few cart tracks around the missions, presidios, and pueblos, served for such hauling as their needs required; similar cart tracks from coastal *ranchos* to the nearest beach served to convey hides and tallow to the waiting ships. For all its years Hispanic California was a land where transportation meant an animal's back or human feet, and it was thus that travel largely used *El Camino Real*, later dubbed the "Mission Trail" and now followed generally by U.S. Highway 101.

The Gold Rush generated a need for transportation; not more and better transportation, just *transportation*! Consider how different the gold-accelerated years would have been if San Francisco Bay had not existed, and if the only other safe, natural harbors on the coast, Eureka and San Diego, had been the main portals of ingress to the gold-bearing interior.

San Francisco Bay gave safe harbor to blue-water ships from all the world and in any number imaginable. The inland reaches of that bay, via Carquinez Strait, gave access to the waters of the Sacramento and San Joaquin rivers. A look at the map of California will demonstrate most vividly the immense value of this inland waterway system. If humans continue to fill-in the Bay for industrial and subdivision purposes, its esthetic and climatic values will be destroyed, and it will become little more than a commercial sluiceway between the interior and open sea.

Swift sailing launches were the fastest means of Gold Rush communication along these inland waterways until the steamers came. The *Sitka* from Alaska was the first of these and she and her arthritic little steam engine succumbed after just one voyage to Sacramento. Shortly thereafter, a side-wheel steamer, *Senator*, made her way around Cape Horn to put steam on the inland waterways to stay. She is said to have netted her owners the tidy sum of

Double-ended ferries like the *Amador* tied the San Francisco Bay communities together.
— *Nat'l. Maritime Museum, S.F.*

$600,000 during her first year of operation. This is well within reason, because her first steam competition, *Pioneer*, charged two ounces of gold for deck passage from San Francisco to Sacramento. By the end of 1850, some fifty steamers were plying the inland waterways. In short order, these vessels evolved into luxurious craft, built in San Francisco, that would have done credit to the more celebrated paddle-wheel packets of the Mississippi River.

Stockton, Sacramento, and Marysville were the main interior towns, and they were sired by easy water access to San Francisco Bay out of their proximity to the Mother Lode mines. Of these three, Sacramento was the most important from the start, and long remained the hub of interior transportation in the Great Valley.

When horsepower required horses, scow schooners brought hay from the Delta and Marin County and anywhere else it was grown around the Bay to fuel the motive power. — *The Bancroft Library*

Crossing the Santa Ynez River was not always a pleasant pasttime.
— *Courtesy Calif. Historical Society — T.I.T. Collection*

Mike Bustillos was the driver of this winter express team when he and it were photographed in March, 1911. Iron snowshoes with rubber soles also were used on both horses and mules.
— *Courtesy Calif. Historical Society — T.I.T. Collection*

Red Bluff was the head of navigation on the Sacramento River, which dictated its growth as the transshipment point between steamer and wagon train and muleback for the mines and settlements of Trinity and Shasta and Siskiyou counties. When the railroad reached Redding in 1872, that city became the transshipping point for many more years. Red Bluff, however, remained the head of navigation, since the gorge of Iron Canyon, just above the town, precluded successful upriver commercial navigation.

On the Feather River, Oroville was the ostensible limit of navigation, but this position was jeopardized by the commercial rivalry and machinations of Marysville downstream. It can be said that river traffic never was significant in the development of Oroville or the region that it supplied.

Sustained commercial navigation of the San Joaquin River above Stockton never was as important as that on the Sacramento. Of some significance to the upper, or southern, San Joaquin Valley was the fact that the Tulare Lake, now reclaimed, was navigable in wet years by shallow-draft sternwheelers, called with some reason "dew skimmers."

From the valley centers, independent little stage lines and freight services fanned out into the gullies, gulches, river bars, and ridge-spine camps of the Mother Lode. James Birch started the first stage line from Sacramento to Mormon Island in 1849. The celebrated Concord coaches, among the finest examples of American craftsmanship, reached their peak of utility in response to the demand from California. The first Concord, which took its name from its place of construction in Concord, New Hampshire, arrived by sea on June 24, 1850, costing about $1,500, plus freight, for its 2,500 cunningly contrived pounds. By 1851, Sacramento was the hub of stage lines that reached almost to the Oregon boundary, and by 1854, the frenzied competitors had been consolidated into the California Stage Company which came to control almost 80% of the 3,000 miles of stage routes in 1856. In 1854, too, a similar consolidation on the inland waterway system saw the California Steam Navigation Company gain control of 75% of the operating steamers.

Three-dog teams, hitched fan-fashion to a sleigh, were used in winter on the mountain run between Oroville and Quincy; and horse snowshoes were developed for the stage teams and pack strings that braved winter travel at the higher elevations. As late as 1937, John Ahlgreen and "Hooligan" Johnson were using snowshoes on animals carrying mail and supplies over Salmon Summit (between Etna in Siskiyou County and Forks of Salmon in Trinity County). These snowshoes were also used on horses harvesting asparagus on the peat lands of the Delta until the "caterpillar" tractor was perfected.

There does not appear to have been any consolidation — monopoly, if you prefer — of freighting operations such as developed in staging and steamboating. The high-sided, high-wheeled freight wagons, owned individually in in the main, were the bulk carriers for foodstuffs and machinery needed in the major foothill communities. The point at which they could go no farther became the head of "Whoa-Haw" navigation, and long lines of pack animals took up the transportation burden into truly isolated sections.

During the first years of the Rush, the miners' desperate yearning to hear from home and to write to the homefolks led to the custom by which individuals, armed with lists of miners' names, would make the journey to San Francisco, there to collect mail for all from the one and only area post office. (Only 34 post offices blessed the state by June 1851.) These they took back to the mines and delivered, charging as high as two dollars per letter and five dollars per newspaper for their services. This evolved into the performance of shopping chores for men too busy to leave the "diggin's," and to the carrying of gold dust down for deposit with some reputable merchant who had a good, stout safe. Probably the first of these carriers, Alexander Todd is said to have transported more than $250,000 in dust for his customers, using a small butter keg for his brief case. Out of these beginnings evolved the express business, which came to be dominated by Wells Fargo & Company after the financial panic of 1855 had ruined its principal competitor, Adams & Company.

By 1851 the gold country, which was then the economic heart of California — the heart with the most human heartbeats — had been tied together by a combination of inland waterways and wheeled-vehicle and animal transportation. Through San Francisco Bay, it had access to the world.

Transportation was somewhat different along the coast and in Southern California, because there were not the golden gravels to pay for it and to attract the population that required it. The importance of coastwise shipping to the redwood lumber industry and to the early growth of San Francisco has been noted. This shipping remained Southern California's chief communication link with San Francisco and the state capital at Sacramento until 1876, when the Southern Pacific Railroad linked the two sections by rail.

The sea continued even longer to provide an economic lifetime for Santa Barbara and San Diego. The Coast Stage Line was established by Flint, Bixby & Company in the middle 1850's, but this was uncertain and far too expensive for anything heavier than mail and express, and those passengers not in an uncommon hurry and blessed with a durable physique. The sea was Santa Barbara's artery of communication for the first thirty-five years after the Rush; San Diego relied on it even longer. It continued to be of importance to the coastal settlements and ranches well past World War I, as the steam schooners that carried lumber down the coast to meet urban building needs returned northward with cargoes of grain, sheep, hogs, and sometimes cattle, as well as honey, butter, and cheese. It should be remembered that Southern California was economically dependent upon San Francisco virtually until the turn of the twentieth century. Its markets and its sources of capital were in Northern California.

Construction on California's first railroad began from Sacramento in

February, 1855 and reached its eastern terminus at Folsom, 22 miles distant, on February 22, 1856. The road's basic equipment came around Cape Horn at a cost exceeding $700,000, all of which was raised within the state, thanks to the surplus capital accumulation made possible by the Gold Rush. The San Francisco & San Jose Rail Road began construction in October 1860, but was not opened for service to San Jose until January 16, 1864. This provided infinitely faster service between the two points than the original stage line in 1849, which had taken nine hours to make the journey.

A real live brass band greeted the first Southern Pacific train to reach Los Angeles in 1876.
— *Historical Society of So. California*

This enabled San Francisco's wealthy to begin the urbanization of the Peninsula and provided the first segment of the Southern Pacific's coast line, which was finally completed to Santa Barbara in 1902. A rail link between San Pedro and Los Angeles was opened in the early 1860's, but San Diego had to wait for its rail connection with the outside world until 1885, when the California Southern extended its lines to meet those of its parent corporation, the Santa Fe, at San Bernardino.

The development of the Great Valley, the unlocking of its full agricultural potential, and the utilization of the timber treasures in the adjacent mountains began in the decade of the 1870's with railroad construction its entire length by companies that became subsidiaries of the Southern Pacific.

A rail link between Sacramento and Oakland was opened for traffic in

1869. The California & Oregon Railroad north from Roseville, up the east side of the Sacramento Valley, reached Chico via Marysville on July 2, 1870, crossed the Sacramento River at Los Molinos to reach Red Bluff in 1871, and inch on to Redding in 1872. Redding was its "end of track" for many years before construction was resumed up the Sacramento River canyon, climbing out of that meandering chasm in the shadow of Mount Shast on its way to surmount the Siskiyou Mountains and enter Oregon.

Construction of the Southern Pacific Railroad — the name later applied to the whole rail network that developed from the original Central Pacific — began from Tracy in 1869. Its tracks forged slowly up the east side of the San Joaquin Valley, a choice probably stemming from the unproductive nature of that valley's west side, which is in the rain shadow of the Coast Range. A later rail line up the west side of the valley is said to have been a result of Henry Miller's development of irrigation in that section. The greatest engineering feat of the original line was the "loop" by which it surmounted the Tehachapi Mountains; its worst problem was tunneling through the San Fernando Mountains to gain access to the Los Angeles Lowlands.

The "Saugus tunnel" was "holed through" in 1876, giving Los Angeles its first rail link with Northern California and the nation at large. Its initial impact has been noted previously in Wolfskill's celebrated first shipment of citrus fruit to the East via rail. The Southern Pacific's line was continued eastward via San Gorgonio Pass, and reached the Colorado River at Yuma in 1877, thus blocking the Espee's ill-starred rival, the Texas & Pacific Railway, from gaining access to Southern California. In 1883 another extension of this line was built from Mojave to Needles, thereby blocking the Santa Fe from access to California until negotiations between the two roads smoothed the Santa Fe's entry into Southern California.

In 1887, a Southern Pacific branch line from Saugus via Ventura reached Santa Barbara, giving it a rail link with the outside world and starting its long career as a winter haven for monied easterners. The coast line of the Espee, which had been completed from San Francisco to Santa Barbara in 1902, was not extended into Los Angeles, via the Chatsworth Tunnel under the Santa Susana Mountains, until 1904.

It cannot be denied that the Espee's interstate rail construction was vital to the state's growth and development. It also cannot be denied that in some respects the Espee was economically oppressive and politically undemocratic. Frank Norris' great, naturalistic and turgidly Gothic novel, *The Octupus*, etched in excruciating detail these aspects of the company's operations.

Interior northern California had to wait until 1909 for effective competition with the Espee to materialize with completion of the Western Pacific Railroad from Salt Lake City down the North Fork of Feather River to Sacramento and Oakland. This opened up the lumbering industry in the mountain counties it traversed. Extreme northeastern California had to wait

(Above) Seven schooners waiting to load lumber under the chutes at Westport, when it was a two-sawmill town with a "dog hole" port on the Redwood Coast. (Below) The steam schooner evolved to meet the lumber carrying needs of California. One of the largest of these is the s.s. Wapama shown here. Representative vessels of California's early days are preserved by the Department of Parks and Recreation at the foot of Hyde Street, San Francisco.

— Courtesy Nat'l. Maritime Museum, S.F.

even longer, until the development of its timber stands by lumbermen from the Great Lakes states brought a branch of the Espee into Lassen and Modoc counties in 1912. Lumber traffic, too, brought the last major railroad construction in California to these counties, as well as eastern Shasta County, when the Western Pacific and the Great Northern completed a link between the Columbia River and Keddie (Plumas County) in 1932.

The story of internal transportation would not be complete without mentioning the famous San Francisco Bay ferries, of still sweet memories to this writer's generation. Of equal nostalgia, although more noisome in memory's circuitry, are the "Big Red Cars" of the Pacific Electric, which made one of the most efficient interurban transportation systems ever known. It was the Pacific Electric, operating 3,700 trains a day over 1,200 miles of track, that enabled the urban sprawl of Los Angeles to begin its sprawling, giving rise to the saying that "Los Angeles is about thirty-seven suburbs in search of a city hall." Both the Bay ferries and the Pacific Electric were essential to the growth and development of the urban centers that they served.

A similar, although less dramatic role was played in the urban complex of San Francisco by the Key Route electric interurban system, which competed for many years with the Southern Pacific's ferry-interurban complex in expanding the Oakland-Berkeley portion of the Bay Area. In all truth, this intercity network gave the "mysterious East Bay," as Herb Caen used to call it, a functional entity of its own that aided its transition from a purely "bedroom" function for San Francisco into a metropolis with a major league baseball team.

Ferry days on the Bay came to an end with completion of the two great bridges that spanned it in 1936 and 1937. A minor league revival of ferry boating between San Francisco and Marin County may be helped along by the costs of gasoline and bridge tolls.

Construction of electric railways from Oakland to Sacramento by the Oakland, Antioch & Eastern, and thence to Chico by the Sacramento Northern, gave residents of the upper Sacramento Valley better public transportation to the capital city and the Bay Area than they enjoy today. (So it is remembered from personal experiences both in the 1920's and the present.)

Like the Pacific Electric in Southern California, the electric transit systems in the north were killed by the internal combustion engine. Currently we seem to have strangled ourselves in the coils of concrete freeways; and those concomitants of the Internal Combustion Age, air pollution and parking space, are forcing us back into systems of mass transit remarkably similar to those that our passion for personal indulgence in transportation convenience destroyed. The Bay Area Rapid Transit System (BART), long plagued by technical problems, today transports some 160,000 commuters to-and-from San Francisco and the East Bay communities. One who has

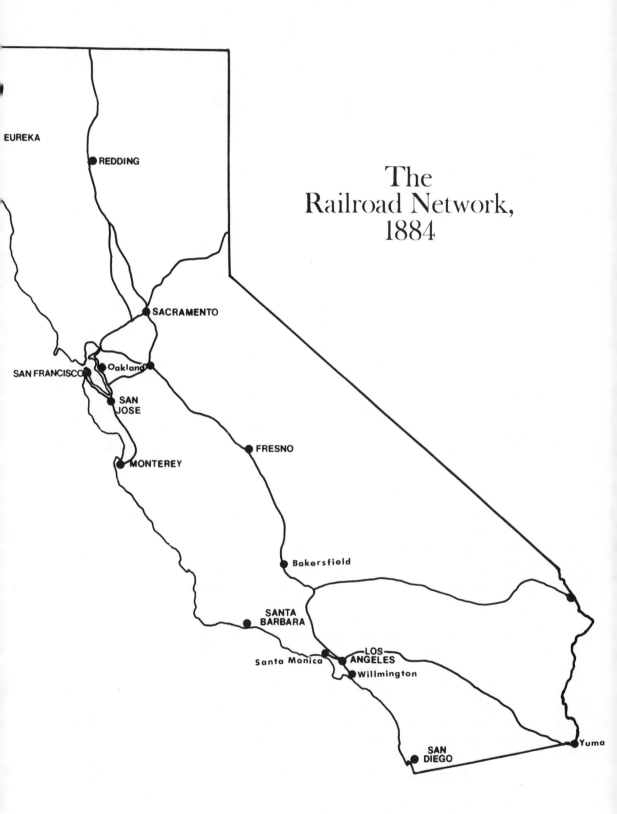

EUREKA

REDDING

The
Railroad Network,
1884

SACRAMENTO

Oakland
SAN FRANCISCO
SAN
JOSE

FRESNO

MONTEREY

Bakersfield

SANTA
BARBARA

Santa Monica
LOS
ANGELES
Willmington

SAN
DIEGO

Yuma

ridden both the Big Red Cars and the rocketing, third-rail coaches of the Sacramento Northern will bear witness that they had more to offer in comfort, almost in elapsed transit time, than do the "Blue Pooch" buses or the "feeder" airlines of today.

Today, Roseville in Northern California contains the largest railroad assembly yard west of the Mississippi River, where trains are made up and disassembled by electronic aids. It serves the operational needs of the Espee at the strategic spot where its main east-west and north-south lines intersect.

Northern California's internal transportation complex was enhanced in 1915 by completion of the Northwestern Pacific Railroad from Marin County to the Redwood Coast at Eureka. The line gave that region its first overland link with San Francisco and opened the interior of Mendocino and Humboldt counties to profitable settlement by agriculturists, lumbermen, and livestock raisers.

The roster of so-called "short-line" railroads within California is extensive. Perhaps the best known were the lines that linked Nevada City and Grass Valley with the Espee's main line over the Sierra; the Sierra Railway to Oakdale and Sonora, which has been used in many motion pictures; and the "Slim Princess" line in Owens Valley.

Logging railroads were essential to the lumbering industry, and their story is a conglomerate of multitudinous details that are of interest only to specialists in railroad lore. One of these logging lines, the California Western, survives today as a lumber-hauler, operating the diesel powered "Skunk" train over its forty-mile length between Fort Bragg and Willits in Mendocino County, which has become a major tourist attraction as well, especially in the summer-time.

The greatest individual saga of California's internal transportation is that of "Snowshoe" Thompson, an immigrant from Norway, who wrote an incredible chapter in the annals of winter travel. He was not yet thirty in 1856 when he fashioned his famous "snow skates" (skis) from valley oak. Each one was ten feet long, with an eight-inch upward curve at the toe, and tapered from a six-inch width at the toe to four inches at the heel; their maximum thickness was two inches at the toe strap (the only binding), and the pair weighed twenty-five pounds. Using these ponderous planks and a balance pole, which he rode astride as a brake on downhill reaches, Snowshoe Thompson carried the mail over the snow-locked Sierra between Placerville and Genoa, Nevada, for almost fifteen winters.

On his first trip, carrying an eighty-pound mail sack, he made the eastward crossing in four days. He then reduced his average time for the 110-mile journey to three days eastbound and only two days westbound, where the long downhill slope of the Sierra was in his favor. Traveling alone, subsisting on dried beef and hard biscuits, he was the communications link when winter settled its grip upon the upper heights of the Range of Light. He saved James Sisson's life by making the round trip from Genoa to Placerville in less than five days to get medicine that was needed for Sisson's gangrenous leg. In 1858, the type for the *Territorial Enterprise*, Nevada's first newspaper, went over the Sierra on his sturdy back and equally sturdy skis.

Thompson charged nothing for his services, including carrying the mails; and when he sought compensation from the government in his declining years, his requests became so ensnarled in bureaucratic knots that nothing tangible transpired. On his death, May 15, 1876, he was buried in the little cemetery at Genoa, and crossed skis were carved into his gravestone. In the mountain light as evening falls, they speak eloquently of at least one man who met California's cry for men to match her mountains.

"We may now look forward with confidence to the day when the Pacific will be bound to the Atlantic by iron bonds . . ."
— *Southern Pacific Company*

CHAPTER TEN

BINDING CALIFORNIA TO THE NATION

Within a few years after the Gold Rush, northern California, which was all the California that mattered then, had an internal transportation network surpassing anything in any of the other states and territories beyond the Mississippi. What California wanted was safe, dependable, efficient, fast and relatively inexpensive overland linkage with the rest of the nation. It took some years for this demand to be satisfied.

Even as the offshore winds and currents had dominated Hispanic California's lifeline with the outside, world, so was the sea basic to California's life until the misnamed "transcontinental" railroad was completed. The route via Panama, always superior to that via Nicaragua which was not used after 1856, was improved markedly by completion of the Panama Railroad from Colon to Balboa in 1855. This shortened transit time across the Isthmus, lessened exposure to disease along the way, and made it possible to journey from San Francisco to New York in about four weeks with luck.

This railroad was built by American capital, and it was built simply because the volume of traffic to and from growing California would make it profitable. It was the first demonstration of California's ability to demand and to get faster connections with the rest of the nation; it had its logical culmination in 1903 with the beneficial little revolution, which had the tacit assistance of President Theodore Roosevelt, that created the Republic of Panama and gave the United States the Canal Zone within which to construct a trans-isthmian canal, an enterprise that previously had defeated French efforts.

Severance of the overland link between Alta California and Sonora at the Yuma Crossing had drastically affected Spain's ability to expand her initial beachhead of missions and presidios. Lack of an overland link with Mexico had affected Alta California's position in and relations with the Republic of Mexico. Had the state's demands for adequate communication ties to the rest of the nation not been met, the history of the nation might have been quite different.

It is hard for those who have grown up in an age of jet propulsion to understand that distance was a greater problem to the people and technology of the mid-nineteenth century than it was and is to the space probes of the present day. A jet aircraft covers the same distance in one hour that a plodding oxteam covered in six-to-seven *weeks*. Sixty miles per hour on a freeway today equals five days travel by that same oxteam. The point is that the *jet plane of the nineteenth century was the railroad train!*

In 1849, not a single rail had crossed the Mississippi River. The golden lure of California and the demands of its swelling population gave a violent impetus to the westward thrust of the nation's rail network. But for thirteen years after '49, railroad construction beyond the Mississippi River was delayed by disputes in Congress between pro-slavery and anti-slavery forces over the route of the Pacific Railroad, as it then was called.

It must be remembered that from the Atlantic Ocean to the "Father of Waters," the railroads had *followed* settlement. Beyond the Mississippi, west of eastern Kansas, railroad construction faced a barren waste, still shown on some maps of the time as "The Great American Desert," a vast expanse without revenue-producing settlements or crops to be hauled until Utah was reached, and Utah was not, shall we say, over-populated. From the Mormon sanctuary to the golden shore of California, there was another, even less inhabited and more inhospitable waste, which culminated in the formidable granitic barrier of the Sierra Nevada. Because construction of a railroad across these wastes to the Pacific promised to be and to remain an unprofitable venture for many years, it did not attract private capital. In hard fact, there was not enough private capital in the United States to construct such

This welcoming sign graced the Espee depot at Yuma, Arizona as a prelude to California
— *Calif. Historical Society — T.I.T. Collection*

— 204 —

a line without foreign investment help, and foreign investors were not enthusiastic about financing a railroad to serve mainly jackrabbits, prairie dogs and buffalo.

Federal assistance was essential to make initial construction possible; just as federal land grants had made possible wagon roads and canals in the states east of the Mississippi, and as federal subsidy had made possible the mail route via Panama. Whenever legislation was introduced in Congress to aid a railroad along the "central" route of the old Emigrant Trail by the Platte River and South Pass, it was blocked by southerners who feared that such a route would increase the power of the anti-slavery North. Conversely, legislation that proposed to assist a road from Memphis or Fort Smith or New Orleans to California, was killed by northerners who feared that such a

A cab-ahead "Mighty Mallet" snakes a string of refrigerator (reefer) cars eastward across the Sierra.
— *Southern Pacific Co.*

road would multiply the power of the South's "slaveocracy." Regardless of the squabbles in Congress, the demands of California continued to be voiced in strident tones. They were met, in part, by several enterprises, which were financed directly or indirectly by the federal government.

In 1853, Congress passed a bill authorizing a survey of all possible rail routes to California by the Army's Corps of Topographical Engineers, and demanded that it be done within ten months. Thus, the central route of the Platte and the southern route along the Gila River were not surveyed, as they had been well laid out by emigrants. A northern route from Minnesota to Puget Sound was investigated and discarded because of bitter winter weather

Donner Pass is never easy! Here a powerful rotary snowplow, pushed by a cab-ahead Mallet, struggles to clear the track to reach the stalled streamliner "City of San Francisco" in the record snowfall of 1952.   — Southern Pacific Co.

No. 1] **[Sep. 16th, 1858.**

OVERLAND MAIL COMPANY.

THROUGH TIME SCHEDULE BETWEEN

ST. LOUIS, MO., MEMPHIS, TENN. } & SAN FRANCISCO, CAL.

GOING WEST.

LEAVE.	DAYS.	Hour.	Distance, Place to Place.	Time allowed.	Av'ge Miles per Hour.
St. Louis, Mo., & Memphis, Tenn. }	Every Monday & Thursday,	8.00 A.M	Miles.	No. Hours	
P. R. R. Terminus, "	" Monday & Thursday,	6.00 P.M	160	10	16
Springfield, "	" Wednesday & Saturday	7.45 A.M	143	37¾	3 7/9
Fayetteville, "	" Thursday & Sunday,	10.15 A.M	100	26½	3 7/9
Fort Smith, Ark.	" Friday & Monday,	3.30 A.M	65	17¼	3 7/9
Sherman, Texas	" Sunday & Wednesday,	12.30 A.M	205	45	4½
Fort Belknap. "	" Monday & Thursday,	9.00 A.M	146½	32½	4½
Fort Chadbourn, "	" Tuesday & Friday,	3.15 P.M	136	30¼	4½
Pecos River, (Em. Crossing.)	" Thursday & Sunday,	3.45 A.M	165	36½	4½
El Paso,	" Saturday & Tuesday,	11.00 A.M	248½	55¼	4½
Soldier's Farewell	" Sunday & Wednesday,	8.30 P.M	150	33½	4½
Tucson, Arizona	" Tuesday & Friday,	1.30 P.M	184½	41	4½
Gila River,* "	" Wednesday & Saturday	9.00 P.M	141	31½	4½
Fort Yuma, Cal.	" Friday & Monday,	3.00 A.M	135	30	4½
San Bernardino "	" Saturday & Tuesday,	11.00 P.M	200	44	4½
Ft. Tejon, (Via Los Angeles.)	" Monday & Thursday,	7.30 A.M	150	32½	4½
Visalia, "	" Tuesday & Friday,	11.30 A.M	127	28	4½
Firebaugh's Ferry, "	" Wednesday & Saturday	5.30 A.M	82	18	4½
(Arrive) San Francisco,	" Thursday & Sunday,	8.30 A.M	163	27	6

GOING EAST.

LEAVE.	DAYS.	Hour.	Distance, Place to Place.	Time allowed.	Av'ge Miles per Hour.
San Francisco, Cal.	Every Monday & Thursday,	8.00 A.M	Miles.	No. Hours	
Firebaugh's Ferry, "	" Tuesday & Friday,	11.00 A.M	163	27	6
Visalia, "	" Wednesday & Saturday,	5.00 A.M	82	18	4½
Ft. Tejon, (Via Los Angeles)	" Thursday & Sunday,	9.00 A.M	127	28	4½
San Bernardino, "	" Friday & Monday,	5.30 P.M	150	32½	4½
Fort Yuma, "	" Sunday & Wednesday,	1.30 P.M	200	44	4½
Gila River,* Arizona	" Monday & Thursday,	7.30 P.M	135	30	4½
Tucson, "	" Wednesday & Saturday	3.00 A.M	141	31½	4½
Soldier's Farewell,	" Thursday & Sunday,	8.00 P.M	184½	41	4½
El Paso, Tex.	" Saturday & Tuesday,	5.30 A.M	150	33½	4½
Pecos River, (Em. Crossing.)	" Monday & Thursday	12.45 P.M	248½	55¼	4½
Fort Chadbourn, "	" Wednesday & Saturday	1.15 A.M	165	36½	4½
Fort Belknap, "	" Thursday & Sunday,	7.30 A.M	136	30¼	4½
Sherman, "	" Friday & Monday,	4.00 P.M	146½	32½	4½
Fort Smith, Ark.	" Sunday & Wednesday,	1.00 P.M	205	45	4½
Fayetteville, Mo.	" Monday, & Thursday,	6.15 A.M	65	17¼	3 7/9
Springfield, "	" Tuesday & Friday,	8.45 A.M	100	26½	3 7/9
P. R. R. Terminus, "	" Wednesday & Saturday	10.30 P.M	143	37¾	3 7/9
(Arrive) St. Louis, Mo., & Memphis, Tenn. }	" Thursday & Sunday,		160	10	16

This Schedule may not be exact—Superintendents, Agents, Station-men, Conductors, Drivers and all employees are particularly directed to use every possible exertion to get the Stages through in quick time, even though they may be ahead of this time.

If they are behind this time, it will be necessary to urge the animals on to the highest speed that they can be driven without injury.

Remember that no allowance is made in the time for ferries, changing teams, &c. It is therefore necessary that each driver increase his speed over the average per hour enough to gain the necessary time for meals, changing teams, crossing ferries, &c.

Every person in the Company's employ will always bear in mind that each minute of time is of importance. If each driver on the route loses fifteen (15) minutes, it would make a total loss of time, on the entire route, of twenty-five (25) hours, or, more than one day. If each one loses ten (10) minutes it would make a total loss of sixteen and one half (16½) hours, or, the best part of a day.

On the contrary, if each driver gains that amount of time, it leaves a margin of time against accidents and extra delays.

All hands will see the great necessity of promptness and dispatch: every minute of time is valuable as the Company are under heavy forfeit if the mail is behind time.

Conductors must note the hour and date of departure from Stations, the causes of delay, if any, and all particulars. They must also report the same fully to their respective Superintendents.

* The Station referred to on Gila River, is 40 miles west of Maricopa Wells.

JOHN BUTTERFIELD.
Pres't.

What this timetable does NOT tell patrons is the suggestion that each passenger be equipped with a "good rifle" and 100 rounds of ammunition as a form of traveller's insurance.

— Courtesy History Room, Wells Fargo Bank

conditions. Another route through central Colorado via Cochetopa Pass and one from Arkansas to Albuquerque were surveyed in a hurry; the Colorado route getting little support, save from John Charles Fremont and his father-in-law. The route via Albuquerque and the one using the Gila Trail were those favored by the South, while the Platte River route remained the favorite of the North. Stalemate again!

George Chorpenning may have been foolhardy but he was no quitter! In May, 1851, encouraged by a federal subsidy, he set out from Sacramento with a string of pack mules to carry the mail to Salt Lake City. He reached it more than five weeks later, two of which were spent battling the snow-locked Sierra. He tried again in May 1852. This time he spent *two months* on the trail and had to walk the last 200 miles into Salt Lake City. He licked his wounds and bided his time. The Sierra's winter hazards caused the federal subsidy to be diverted to the "Mormon Trail" during the winters of 1854-58. Mails from Northern California went by steamer to San Pedro and then by way of San Bernardino, Cajon Pass and the deserts of southern Nevada to Salt Lake City.

John B. Weller, who had succeeded Fremont as Senator from California and would become the fifth governor of the state, presented Congress with two enormous, leather-bound and gold-stamped volumes in 1856. These contained the signatures of 75,000 Californians petitioning Congress for a federal assistance to construct a real wagon road along the route of the central Emigrant Trail. By asking for only a humble wagon road, the way would be prepared for a later railroad along the same route; furthermore, with government help the wagon road could be kept open all year long, thus removing any practical southern objections to the central route. The wagon road was to end at the Nevada/California boundary, because it was held then that federal aid was constitutional in the Territories but not in the states. Weller added other wagon road routes to the bill he introduced in Congress, in order to attract sectional support, and a road was scraped out from El Paso to Yuma, and another that ended in Honey Lake Valley, now in Lassen County, within the next few years.

While this was going on, certain Californians got tired of waiting and built their own wagon road from Murphys in Calaveras County, now known as the capital of the Ancient Order of E Clampus Vitus, to the Carson Valley in Nevada. This was opened in August 1856, and got most of the traffic over the Sierra for the next two summers. Spurred on by this profitable example, the citizens of Sacramento and Placerville raised their own funds and built another road to the Carson Valley in 1858. In the Fall of this year, Frederick Bee completed stringing telegraph wires, using trees for poles much of the way, between Sacramento and Genoa, thus extending the telegraph line that had linked Sacramento to San Francisco in 1851. None of these ventures, of course, did what Californians demanded — link them with the nation.

In an effort to by-pass the mountain hazards of the central route, a federal contract was given in 1857 to the "Jackass Mail," which used mules ✷ to cross the sandy wastes west of the Colorado River crossing at Yuma. This line ran from San Antonio, Texas via El Paso and Tucson, through the very heart of *Apacheria*, to San Diego — a route aptly described as extending "from nowhere through nothing to no place." While it lasted, twenty-seven days was its scheduled running time.

In 1857, the government sponsored the importation of camels (drome-✷ daries, in reality) from Asia Minor, to see whether they could overcome the transportation hazards of the Great American Desert. These beasties were located at Indianola, Texas, where what today would be called a Basic Camel Training School was established to teach American soldiers and civilian packers the mysteries of the odorous creatures. Under Edward Fitzgerald Beale, they made a successful journy from Indianola to El Paso, thence to Albuquerque, and across Arizona to Los Angeles.

They could travel twice as far, and four times as fast, on a given amount of water as mules, and they gained weight on natural forage that gave a burro acute indigestion. They also scared hell out of the Indians along the way. Despite these virtues, camels simply were not accepted because of their smell, their malevolent dispositions, and their ability to frighten all other types of livestock they encountered. They were used intermittently in Southern California to carry mail and supplies to isolated army posts along the Colorado River, and Beale is said to have broken a pair of them to pull his buckboard from Rancho El Tejon into Los Angeles. In the end, the government auctioned them off at a public sale at Benicia Arsenal in Northern California, and they wound up in Nevada, where their purchaser used them fitfully to haul salt and cordwood to the smelters of Carson Valley below the Comstock Lode atop Mount Davidson.

In these same years, a San Francisco importer, Otto Esche, brought in some genuine, double-humped Bactrian camels from Mongolia. He planned to use these in an all-year, all-weather mail and express service to Utah. Again, the nature of the beasts defeated their utilization as planned, and these Bactrian camels also were retired to Nevada.

The chief result of the camel experiments, it seems, was to give a gushing fount of folklore to the Far West. Among them is the legend of the great red-roan bull camel that roamed the southern Nevada deserts with a skeleton lashed to its back — a version, perhaps, of the "Flying Dutchman." As late as 1946, a story emanated from Tonopah, Nevada, about a wild-horse hunter who claimed to have caught an animal that was half-horse and half-camel. Near Quartzite, Arizona, is a monument to "Hyjolly," born Hadji Ali, one of the imported Syrian camellers, who became a prospector after the experiment failed.

The most successful of the early overland links was the justly famous and well subsidized Butterfield Overland Mail, which used 100 Concord ✷

coaches, 1,000 horses, 500 mules, and 800 men to traverse the 2,795 miles (some say 2,812 miles) between its terminals at Tipton, Missouri, and San Francisco. The scheduled contract time for this journey was twenty-five days. Butterfield coaches ran without overnight stops, changing teams at way points, which meant that every passenger had to possess a durable *derriere* to make the journey. They also had to have $200 gold for the one-way fare, for which 40 pounds of luggage were carried free, and they were advised to equip themselves with a good Sharps rifle and 100 rounds of ammunition.

The Butterfield line used the railroad between St. Louis and Tipton, Missouri, whence the stages swung southwestward via Fort Smith, Arkansas; Sherman and El Paso, Texas; to Las Cruces, New Mexico; Tucson, Arizona; the Yuma Crossing, and Los Angeles. From Los Angeles, they followed the route of *El Camino Viejo* across the Mojave Desert and Tehachapi Pass to Visalia and Firebaugh's Ferry in the San Joaquin Valley, whence they crossed the Coast Range via Pacheco Pass to Gilroy and rolled up the valley to San Francisco.

The Espee's wooden sleeping cars were lighted by candles and kerosene lamps, and heated by coal stoves. Travel books of the day said that you slept "amid the easy roll of the car as sweetly and refreshingly as ever upon the home bed." The Railroad Museum adjacent to Old Sacramento, which is under the supervision of the Department of Parks and Recreation, displays beautifully restored railroad rolling stock and locomotives. — *Southern Pacific Company*

The first westbound Butterfield mail left St. Louis on September 16, 1858 and arrived in San Francisco on October 10, 1858, for an elapsed time of twenty-three days and twenty-three hours. So far as has been ascertained, the Butterfield always ran within its specified contract time, and by 1860 it was carrying more overland mail to and from California than went by way of Panama. With the outbreak of the Civil War, the Butterfield contract was transferred to the central route, with a subsidy of $1,000,000 per year, to avoid benefiting the Confedracy.

It was over this route that Ben Holladay, now the stagecoach magnate of the Far West, made the fastest long-distance stage run known: from Folsom, California to Atchison, Kansas in twelve days and two hours, at a considerable cost in horseflesh over the 2,030-mile journey. Passenger fares over Holladay's line, which began at Atchison, Kansas, were $75 to Denver; $150 to Salt Lake City, and $225 to Placerville. By 1865 these rates had doubled, and Holladay sold his far-flung operations to Wells Fargo in time to avoid competition from the westward thrusting rails.

California's demands for even speedier overland transportation gained new urgency from the exigencies of the Civil War, among them a fear that the state might be swayed toward espousing the cause of the Confederacy, or at best remaining neutral. A vicious fight for the government contracts developed between various overland freighting firms. The result of the combined pressures was the creation of the glamorous Pony Express.

Several points should be borne in mind about "the Pony." Among these is that the *first* pony express on the Pacific Coast had pitted the two express company titans, Wells Fargo and Adams & Company, in a head-and-head contest to deliver President Fillmore's "State of the Union" message from Sacramento to Portland, Oregon. Adams & Company triumphed; the year was 1854. Another point is that another pony express involved several transportation firms in a contest to deliver President Buchanan's State of the Union message from St. Louis to San Francisco in 1858. George Chorpenning was involved in this contest, using the central route to prove that he could beat the time of the Butterfield line. This he did in actual road time but not in being first to deliver the message to San Francisco.

The 1860 pony express was the brainchild of the great western freghting firm of Russell, Majors & Waddell, which long had prospered from government hauling contracts to army posts west of the Missouri River. The purpose behind their pony express was to prove that the central route could be used all year 'round and this, hopefully, would enable them to wrest the mail contract away from the Butterfield line. During much of the "Pony's" hoof-drumming career, the express and banking firm of Wells Fargo & Company had a large financial interest in its notably unremunerative operations.

Truly can it be said that the symbolism of the "Pony" is fundamental to our image of the pioneer West. It embodies such figures as the wiry

Interior of sleeping car, 1900. Bottom seats slid forward at night to make mattress for bed; concave segments above dropped down to make another bed, and curtains divided each "section" into semi-privacy, but did not prevent loud snoring in another berth from keeping you awake. Porter provided a ladder to reach the upper berth, which required some agility.

— Courtesy Southern Pacific Co.

teenagers who later became "Buffalo Bill" Cody and "Pony Bob" Haslam, riding almost 400 miles in less than two days, changing horses every half-hour, vaulting from saddle to saddle with the mail-stuffed *mochilla* as they did so; not to mention outriding, outfighting, and outwitting road agents and Indians in the process. Some facts should be set beside the legends.

At $5 per half-ounce letter, the Pony averaged perhaps 35 letters each way each trip. Its scheduled running time between St. Joseph, Missouri and Sacramento was ten days for the 1,936 miles. The first westbound rider left St. Joe on April 3, 1860; the first east bound rider spurred out of Sacramento on April 4, and covered the fity-five miles to Placerville in one minute less than three hours. By July 1, 1860, the Pony's western terminus was at Folsom, and its eighteen-month life came to a close with completion of the Overland Telegraph Line, constructed with governmental assistance, which reached Sacramento on October 4, 1861.

The telegraph was another step in the moves to bind California to the federal Union, and another step in the long struggle to give California the fastest possible communication with the East. Its building is a saga in itself, and it antedates in time the building of the overland railroad.

Some historians have stated that both freight and passenger traffic along the Central Overland Route was of paramount importance to California during the Civil War, bringing the state supplies and transporting the mineral wealth of California east to bolster the exchequer of the Union government. This writer simply disagrees and believes that the sea lanes, via both Cape Horn and Panama, were the primary arteries between California and the Union, despite Confederate sea raiders.

Interestingly enough, the Alabama Hills, just west of Lone Pine in Owens Valley, commemorate the *Alabama*, most famous of these Confederate raiding ships. Just so does Kearsage Pass across the Sierra in this region commemorate the name of the Union vessel that ended the *Alabama*'s career. Many a television "western" has been filmed in the Alabama Hills.

California's prolonged demands for a railroad link with the other states received an added fillip from the riches of the Comstock Lode. Its silver was of importance to the federal treasury, and this stimulus to governmental interest in a western rail line came at an opportune time for legislation to be passed. Secession had removed the South's representatives from both houses of Congress and they could no longer obstruct railroad assistance that might favor the North. In 1862, Congress passed a measure providing financial assistance to railroad construction along the central route. The Union Pacific was formed to build westward from Omaha, Nebraska and the Central Pacific was born to build from Sacramento east. Congress later had to specify where they would meet in order to prevent unnecessary duplication of construction.

Although long called a "transcontinental" railroad, the title is erroneous, because the nation never has had and probably never will have a *single* railroad that runs from coast-to-coast. One of the tantalizing dreams connected with this initial railroad to the Pacific was that, by providing rapid transit — seven days — across the country, it would give the United States a stranglehold on the trade between the Orient and Europe, which at this time had to make the long sea voyage around the Cape of Good Hope or Cape Horn. This dream evaporated in the same year that the rails were joined in Utah, because opening of the Suez Canal enabled maritime commerce between Europe and the Orient to by-pass the Cape routes, thus so reducing the transit time by sea that the route across America lost its great advantage. A portion of this dream seems to have come true for California in the years since World War II, in that up to 40% of her exports go to Pacific Basin countries and up to 30% of her imports come from those same countries.

Differing views are held as to the merits of federal assistance to these railroads. One view holds that their builders were capitalistic looters of the public purse. Another view holds that their builders were sincerely interested in the national welfare at a reasonable profit to themselves. The controversy seems bootless for valid reasons.

The Republican Party was engaged in the grim business of preserving the Union by winning the Civil War, an effort immensely aided by California's contributions mentioned in the Gold Rush chapter. It did not intend that the Democratic Party, the party of secession in Republican eyes, would dominate the nation after the war was over. One good way to prevent this was to settle the unoccupied public domain lands of the West — lands unoccupied because they lacked transportation — by providing what these lands lacked in the form of railroads. Also, railroads would make these lands saleable, where they had been unsaleable before because of no transportation, and thus bring revenues to liquidate the debts incurred by the Civil War. Thus, the nation as a whole would benefit from railroad construction by increasing its taxable wealth, increasing national production, adding value to the public domain lands retained by the government, and unifying the nation by stitching it together with rails.

The Pacific Railway Act of 1862, as later amended, provided that the federal government would extend assistance to the railroad companies in the amounts of $16,000 per mile of level construction, $32,000 per mile for foothill construction, and $48,000 per mile for mountain construction, with a maximum of 150 miles in the last category. No payment was to be made until 40 miles of track had been completed, and payment thereafter would be made on the basis of each 20 miles completed. These payments were not in cash but in government bonds, bearing interest at 6%, and they were *a loan, not a gift*, which was to be repaid with accumulated interest.

In addition, the roads received an outright grant of land from the unoccupied public domain at the rate of 12,800 acres for each mile of track built, as well as a right-of-way 400-feet wide, and the right to use timber and stone free of charge from the public domain for construction purposes. As noted earlier, land grants had been made to wagon road builders and canal companies long before 1862, and the purpose of all these grants was the same — to encourage the builders of transportation facilities to take the risks that such projects entailed. At this point in our national history, the federal government was selling the public domain in the western Territories for $1.25 an acre or less, and as noted before, it was not selling, because no sane person would buy land that did not have means of transportation to and from it.

The Central Pacific and other companies that became the Southern Pacific received a total of $64,623,512 in government bonds (loans) and repaid a total of $167,746,490. In common with all roads that received federal land grants, they carried the U.S. Mail at a reduced rate and transported government freight and passengers at one-half the tariff price. The California & Oregon Line, from Roseville to Portland, carried government traffic *for nothing*. These reductions continued until abolished by Congress in 1946, after World War II had ended. The Interstate Commerce Commission reported a total payment by these roads of $1,250,000,000 through these reductions, which the railroad says is ten times the value of the public lands it received as an inducement to undertake the awesome and hazardous task of construction.

As a matter of interest, the government bonds the roads received had to be sold in order to raise more money for more construction. If the Union was preserved, the bonds would be good as gold; if it was not, they would be worthless paper. So, buyers of the bonds simply offered 75% or less of their face value to shorten the odds against possible loss. These bonds were sold in the East for paper currency, while the Central Pacific's bills in California had to be paid in gold, and the nation's paper currency during the Civil War was discounted up to 60% in California for the gold coins that were the state's medium of exchange. When it came to selling the bonds of the Central Pacific Railroad, they were discounted for cash up to 50% of their face value. One other item affecting the men who financed the Central Pacific may not be amiss: under California law, stockholders in a corporation were liable for the corporation's debts, should it fail, in the proportion that the number of shares they held bore to the total number of shares issued. With all these matters well in mind, it perhaps can be appreciated that financing the Central Pacific was no game for the faint-hearted or the nickel-nurser.

The story of the Sacramento merchants — Collis P. Huntington, Leland Stanford, "Uncle" Mark Hopkins, Charles Crocker — who became "The Big Four" of the Southern Pacific companies is one of the standard subjects of California history. So is the epic of construction across the Sierra Nevada by *"Cholly Clockeh's pets*," the thousands of industrious Chinese he began to employ in 1865, two years after the first dirt had been turned at Sacramento for the long climb "over the hill," as railroaders still refer to Donner Pass. What is not so well known is the initial impact joining of the rails in Utah in

1869 had upon California.

There is an estimate, no more than that, which indicates that within two years after the rails were joined in 1869, the railroad brought more than 250,000 persons into Northern California. A large proportion of these were single men and unskilled laborers, which aggravated an already declining job market due to the closure of local manufacturing plants brought about by the influx of cheaper goods from the east that the railroad had made possible. This was further aggravated by a drought in the winter of 1869-70, which proved runious to many interior farms. Joining of the rails released some 12,000, -15,000 Chinese laborers and about 80,000 more entered California between 1870-75. When the "Panic of 1873" staggered the eastern cities, the rails permitted thousands of unemployed and their families to reach California in seven days, because the special "immigrant fares" offered by the railroads made it possible for them to scrape the funds together. This would have been impossible in the old days of overland wagon travel, because such would have been beyond their means or their abilities. In this deluge of humans seeking to better their condition in life at a time of economic depression is to be found one deep root of the animosity towards the Southern Pacific.

Another root of this animosity was put down by the Big Four's moves to maintain a monopoly of rail transportation within the state. Having taken extraordinary risks, they sought to reap the rewards of hazard, and to ask them to have refrained from doing this is to ask of them more than most mortal beings can ask successfully of themselves. The California & Oregon line was thrust up and out of the Sacramento River canyon above Dunsmuir to block a threatened approach by other railroads. The Espee, building east from Los Angeles via Yuma, met the Santa Fe, building down the Rio Grande Valley from Albuquerque, at Deming, New Mexico in 1881. This gave Los Angeles its first direct rail link with the east, and blocked the Santa Fe from entering Southern California via the Yuma Crossing.

The Santa Fe then built westward from Albuquerque to the east bank of the Colorado River at The Needles in Arizona, reaching that spot in 1883. The Espee already had built a line from Mojave to the west bank of the river, thus blocking the Santa Fe unless it could obtain trackage right from the Espee, which would give that road the whip hand regarding rail access to Southern California. The Santa Fe then began to build a line from New Mexico to Guaymas on the Gulf of California, which would give it its own direct access to the sea routes to the Pacific Basin countries.

By relinquishing this line to the Espee, the Santa Fe obtained the Espee's track from Needles, California to Barstow, and it appears that the Espee, which already had located a line down Cajon Pass, believed that the Santa Fe could not find another roadbed through the narrow defile. To the Espee's chagrin, the Santa Fe did find a way down the canyon below the Pass, and then had its linkage to tidewater at San Diego through its

Where the "transcontinental" rails met the sea—Oakland's Long Wharf.— *Nat'l. Maritime Museum, S.F.*

subsidiary, the California Southern Railway. Thereafter, the Santa Fe gained access to Los Angeles over its own tracks and gave that city competitive rail transportation to the East, a matter of great importance in creating the "Boom of the Eighties" in Southern California. Los Angeles gained another competitive rail link with the East in 1906-06 with completion of the Los Angeles, San Pedro & Salt Lake road, now part of the Union Pacific system.

Opposition to the Espee caused the so-called "People's Road" to be organized in the 1890's to build from Stockton through the San Joaquin Valley, giving that region access to tidewater free of Espee domination. This line encountered financial problems, and eventually was acquired by the Santa Fe, which extended it to Richmond on the deep water of San Francisco Bay. The Santa Fe then secured trackage rights over the Espee line across the Tehachapi Mountains and gave the Bay Area a competitive rail link with the East, albeit this route required a longer transit time than did the Espee mainline over the Sierra. Completion of the Western Pacific in

The mighty Mallet, sixteen driving wheels, was King of the Road when steam ruled the rails. Cab was located ahead to avoid danger to crew from fumes and smoke when traversing the miles of tunnels and snowshed over Donner Pass. It also provided greater visibility. A beautifully restored specimen of this type locomotive is on display in the State Railroad Museum at Old Sacramento.
— *Courtesy Southern Pacific Company*

A westbound Emigrant Train in 1883 pauses at Mill City, Nevada. From left to right — Head Brakeman (shack), Conductor, Engineer (hog head), Fireman (tallowpot) and Second Brakeman. The dog kept the crew company in the caboose (crummy).
— *Courtesy the Bancroft Library*

1909 already has been noted.

The rail network's long-lasting and vital importance to California's internal development and external markets has been eroded by airlines and trucks and buses, and by the ubiquitous private automobile. Short-haul and express freight, to say nothing of passengers, have been siphoned away from the rails by these more flexible and convenient forms of transportation. As late as 1960, 90% of California's fresh fruits and vegetables that went East did so by refrigerated rail cars; today that figure is down to 10%. With oil shortages and truckers' strikes, it may return to the rails. Since 1960, air transport of fresh fruits and vegetables to eastern markets has increased more than twenty-fold; shipment of high-value, perishable commodities has reached one million pounds in one day from California airports, while fifteen tons of cut flowers have moved by air from San Francisco in one year alone.

The railroads' success in fighting back is typified by the "piggy-back" operations using laden truck trailers on specially designed flat cars to get them between terminals. Less visible to the general public are specially designed freight cars for specific commodities; automated and electronic improvements in train operations; the tremendously increased efficiency of the diesel locomotive, and the expansion of the railroads into other forms of common carrier activity. The railroads today are the most efficient, least polluting means of moving great quantities of freight over long distances that the nation possesses. It well may be in the future that they will again occupy the place of importance that they once held in binding the nation together.

A step in this direction has been taken by Californians in their increasing use of the governmentally subsidized passenger system known as Amtrak. It provides passenger service the length and breadth of the state, as well as interstate service to the Pacific Northwest, the East and the Southwest. Among the most heavily patronized of any Amtrak service in the nation is that provided between Los Angeles and San Diego with eight trains each way per day. At San Diego, this service connects with the "light rail" system known affectionately as the "Tijuana Trolley" which links the two cities. Amtrak's passenger equipment is operated over trackage of the existing railroads and uses those roads' train crews, except for the personnel directly involved with Amtrak's passenger services.

While opening of the Suez Canal ruined the American dreams of dominating the Orient's trade with Europe, rail connections with the Pacific Coast did promote a substantial growth in transpacific merchant shipping. It had gained an initial impetus from the opening of Japan to western commerce, an event almost simultaneous with the Gold Rush. Lumber was a staple item in this trade and still is. A California lumberman, Robert Dollar, expanded his export of lumber into the famous Dollar Line of transpacific and round-the-world steamers, which operates today as American President Lines. Similarly, the Matson Navigation Company grew out of the importance of the Hawaiian Islands' commerce to California. When the Suez

With a capacity of 1,212 containers on deck and below, including 300 refrigerated containers, the *Maui* reflects the changes in cargo handling and vessel design that containerization has brought.
— *Courtesy Matson Navigation Co.*

Canal was blocked to the world's trade by Arab-Israeli conflict, American railroads captured much of the Europe-Orient traffic by offering special rates and services across the continent between Atlantic and Pacific ports.

The adaptation of petroleum to maritime uses was a tremendous asset in the growth of transpacific shipping, and this, coupled with construction of the artificial, deep-water harbor complex at San Pedro-Wilmington, enabled Los Angeles to surpass San Francisco as the leading tonnage-handling port in California.

The opening of the Panama Canal in 1914 gave California a relatively fast maritime connection with the eastern seaboard. This was especially vital to the transportation of bulk commodities such as lumber, which needed all the price advantage they could get. Here again, the internal combustion engine has eroded the intercoastal trade almost to the vanishing point, except for petroleum from Alaska to east coast refineries, and for specialized commodities.

Among vessels specially designed for such commodities are wine tankers and bulk cement and wheat and rice carriers. Other such vessels bring liquid sugar from Hawaii to Crockett on Carquinez Strait, while others bring paper pulp from the Pacific Northwest to manufacturing plants on San Francisco Bay. Vessels specially designed for automobile-carrying are used in shipping vehicles to Hawaii and the Pacific Islands, as well as to bring other vehicles from Japan, while containerization of non-bulk cargoes has revolutionized maritime cargo handling and maritime labor.

Long-distance sea transportation for these and other commodities that need no time advantage in transportation seems destined to remain a function of the blue-water vessels that have played such a major role in California's past. Long-voyage passenger traffic has succumbed to jet-powered air transport. Today's ocean-borne passengers are those who can afford the time and the cost to savor the leisurely life aboard ship. The *only four* American-flag vessels that qualify as true passenger carriers in international trade today voyage from California around South America under the house flag of Delta Steamship Lines of New Orleans and their days seem numbered.

The city that waited for the rails to come — San Francisco's Market Street. — *Courtesy Nat'l. Maritime Museum, S.F.*

A large-scale "associative" operation brought everybody into this picture of its river workings near Marysville. — *San Diego Historical Society — T.I.T. Collection*

CHAPTER ELEVEN

THE SILVER THREAD
IN PLENTY'S TAPESTRY

In the full flush of the Gold Rush years, many immigrants to California used the Carson River Valley to approach the forbidding wall of the Sierra that loomed beyond the Nevada wastes. Some found small amounts of gold in the sands of streams tumbling down from the snows that clung late to the slopes of a mountain above the valley. This they named Sun Peak (now Mount Davidson) because its crest caught the first glints of the rising sun before they touched the peaks of the Sierra Nevada to the west.

More traces of gold were found by the first true settlers in the Carson, Washoe and Eagle valleys between the Sierra and Sun Peak. They were Mormons, establishing an outpost of what Brigham Young envisioned as the inland empire of his Latter-day Saints. The Mormon War of 1857 called these settlers back to Utah to defend their church on its home grounds, and drifters from California established themselves in this region. Among them were many who had found it wise to leave California for their health; among the others and earlier were two young brothers — honest, hard-working and God-fearing Vermonters — named Hosea and Ethan Allen Grosch.

The brothers had come to California in the Rush but had not found fortune. Seeking that will-o'-the-wisp, they arrived at the Sun Peak diggings in the latter part of 1853. They found that the gold they sought was not too plentiful, and worse than its scarcity was the abundance of a heavy blue, clayish stuff that clogged the sluice-

"Myriads of swarthy, bearded, dust-covered men are piercing into the grim old mountain . . ." Miner and ore car, Savage Mine, 1867.   — *The Bancroft Library*

The Diedesheimer "square-set" method of timbering the cavernous "glory holes" of the Comstock Lode was an engineering marvel of its day.
— *Courtesy The Bancroft Library*

box riffles. The Grosch brothers are credited with discovering that this stuff was silver — something quite foreign to the Gold Rush in California and, indeed, new to the American experience anywhere.

It apparently took them several years to come to this conclusion, and they did not live to capitalize on their findings. One of them died of gangrene resulting from driving a miner's pick into his foot by accident. The other, after burying his brother, tried to cross the Sierra in mid-winter. He succeeded, but was so exhausted by his exertions, compounded by frostbite, that he died shortly thereafter. So far as is known, they had confided their secret to none of the other inhabitants of the Sun Peak country.

In 1859, about two years after the brothers' deaths, James Finney (called "Old Virginney" for his native state) and Manny Penrod were working a claim at the head of one of the canyons that seamed Sun Peak's slopes. Here they had found a ledge of decomposed gold-bearing quartz handy to a spring of water and were making a fair haul by Sun Peak standards. This led another drifter, Henry Comstock (known as "Old Pancake" because he was too shiftless to make proper biscuits), to assert ownership of the spring and thus to a share in the claim. The two discoverers for undetermined reasons acceded to Comstock's demand. So far as the scanty records show, Comstock had nothing to do with the initial discovery of this gold claim and certainly does not appear to have done any work on it.

The ledge of quartz petered out into a stratum of the "damned blue mud," causing a cessation of profits. Samples of this bothersome stuff got across to California, where competent assayers in Nevada City and Grass Valley found that the disdained "blue mud" contained as much as $867 in gold and $3,000 or more in silver per ton. The "Rush to Washoe" was on, and the Comstock Lode took its name from "Old Pancake's" voluble assertions that he and he alone was responsible for the whole shebang.

George Hearst, who had walked to California in 1850 and not had much luck thereafter, was one of the first to "rush" to the new diggings. Before winter locked the passes, he mulebacked some thirty tons of the "mud" back to California for a return of $91,000! In the spring of 1860, perhaps 10,000 men took the road from Placerville, trudging over Johnson Pass, down the Kingsbury Grade, across the Carson Valley and up the slopes of Sun Peak. By the end of 1863, the Comstock had produced more than $22,000,000, the bulk of which filtered back across the Sierra to San Francisco. By 1880, it had pumped another $280,000,000 into the economic lifestream of the nation.

The Comstock gave the nation its first great supply of silver. This supply introduced bimetallism into our currency and made silver coinage a major factor in our politics for the remainder of the century. Comstock silver was filtered through California to help finance the Union cause during the Civil War, and silver made Nevada a state of the Union in violation of the Northwest Ordinance's requirement for 60,000 residents as a condition of

Having chopped away the thick, fire-resistant bark, two loggers perch atop their springboards to fell a redwood, with a crosscut saw aptly termed "misery fiddle." A tree this size might take three or more days to bring crashing to earth.
— A.W. Ericson — Calif. Redwood Association

statehood. This happened because its electoral votes were vital to the re-election of Abraham Lincoln in 1864 and its Congressional votes were necessary to pass the Thirteenth Amendment outlawing slavery. The basic lode or vein mining laws of the United States were born out of the Comstock experience, and the first miners' union in the West, the Miner's Protective Association, was formed at Virginia City in 1863. It endured throughout the productive life of the Comstock, which ended in 1880, and set an example for the formation of miners' unions throughout the mining West. The Comstock also gave Mark Twain his first lessons in roughing it and in western humor.

By its physical geography, the Comstock was in the Great Basin. By its political boundaries, it was in the sovereign state of sagebrush and silver, Nevada. Financially, commercially, and politically, it belonged to California, simply because it was owned, developed, and exploited by California. A veritable torrent of silver poured over the Sierra to snap the state out of the economic doldrums that had followed the collapse of 1855, and sent it on its way with increased and expanded developmental velocity. Socially, it produced the "Silver Kings" whose wives and offspring competed with those of the Big Four atop San Francisco's Nob Hill, called "Snob" Hill by the irreverent.

The Comstock was responsible for the creation of California's first stock exchange, making Montgomery Street in San Francisco the financial heart of the Far West. It has been said that more money was made and lost speculating in Comstock mining shares than ever was taken out of the bowels of Mount Davidson. Out of the thousand and more claims that were staked on the Comstock Lode, only about one hundred ever developed into working mines. But the clouds of paper shares in both claims and mines provided the materials for feverish speculation for twenty years. It was a collapse in the value of these shares that gave great impetus to the financial collapse of 1875, the most traumatic event in the state's nineteenth century economic history. Besides its effect upon California, this collapse almost wiped out numerous mining companies in Idaho, which had been financed by California capital, thus indicating the financial influence California had upon the intermountain states and their economies.

The Comstock generated a tremendous demand for mining machinery of all kinds; the depths to which its shafts probed into the heart of the mountain required better, stronger, and more efficient hoisting and steam-generating equipment. California's heavy industry, experienced from meeting the state's own needs, met this demand and grew accordingly. By 1864, San Francisco's foundries had produced a 300-horsepower, high-pressure steam engine for the Comstock, with a drive shaft as "thick as an ordinary man's body." A river steamer carried this formidable mass of metal to Sacramento, whence the "whoa-haw" freighters trundled it to its destination. They were a hardy breed, these long-haul teamsters, and they claimed that if they could

CLIPPER RESTAURANT

Nos. 311 and 313 Pacific Street.
GEORGE W. DETTNER
PROPRIETOR & MANAGER

BREAKFAST AND SUPPER.

COOKED TO ORDER.

Porterhouse Steak........20	Tenderloin Steak..........20	Fried Liver with Pork....10
Sirloin Steak..............15	Veal Cutlets, plain or	Pig's Feet in batter.......10
Rib Steak..................15	breaded..................10	Mackerel, boiled or
Beefsteak, Spanish style.10	Ham, fried or broiled...10	broiled..................10
Beefsteak, plain..........10	Bacon......................10	Tripe in batter............10
Pork Chops 10	Tripe, stewed............10	Salmon, fried or broiled.10
Mutton Chops.........10	Domestic Sausages 10	Hamburg Beefsteak....10
Stewed Beef and Onions.10	Cold Meats..................10	Pig's Feet, soused........10
Stewed Veal................10	Corn Beef Hash........ 10	Stewed Mutton............10
Fish Stew...................10	Cold Boiled Ham..........10	....

EGGS AND OYSTERS.

3 Fried Eggs.............15	Omelette, 3 Eggs..........15	Oyster Stew..............20
3 Boiled Eggs............15	Ham and 2 Eggs..........15	
3 Scrambled Eggs........15	Bacon and 2 Eggs.........15	....

HOT CAKES.

German Pan Cakes..15
Dry Toast..5
Milk, or Boston Cream Toast......................................10
Bowl of Milk, with Mush or Bread................................10
Black Tea, Coffee or Glass of Milk................................5
Hot Cakes, Flannel Cakes and Corn Batter....................5
Chocolate...10

DINNER.
SOUPS.

Chicken...............................5 | Potato......................................5

All 15 Cent Orders and upwards will be served with Butter free of charge. Bread and Potatoes with Meats and Fish free of charge. All single 5 Cent dishes, 10 Cents.

FISH.

Salt Codfish, Family......10	Salmon, baked or fried..10	Fried Tomcods.............10
Bass, baked or fried......10	Mackerel....................10	Fried Smelts 10

BOILED.

Mutton, Mint Sauce......10	Corn Beef and Cabbage...10	Calf Tongue.................10
Pig's Head................10	Corned Pork 10	Boiled Beef..................10
Calf's " Pickle Sauce.10	Ham........................10	

ROASTS.

Beef, stuffed or plain.....10	Mutton...................10	Roast Mutton,MintSauce10
Veal.........................10	Pork.......................10	Chicken.................20

ENTREES.

Roast Pork and Sauer-	Veal Pot Pie.............10	Beef, Spanish style.....10
kraut.....................10	Beefsteak Pie.............10	Stewed Kidney...........10
Sour Beef................10	Lamb Chops.............10	Beef a la Mode..........10

Special today Calves Head Sousle 10¢
" Fried Herring in Batter 10¢
" Assorted Cold Meats - 15¢
1 Veal Chops in Batter - 10¢

PUDDINGS.	PIES.	CAKES.
Corn Starch................5	Apple......................5	Doughnuts......... 5
Rice.........................5	Peach.....................5	Pound Cake................5
Tapioca....................5	Cranberry 5	
Sago........................5		

WINES AND LIQUORS.

California Claret..........20	White Wine.............25	**Glass of Beer**...........5
Half Bottle................10	Ale and Porter, bottle....15	

Dispute with waiter or dissatisfaction must be settled at the Bar.

Credit in all Cases Positively Declined.

10 Cent Dishes with Butter, 15 Cents.

ROOMS TO LET—SINGLE ROOMS PER WEEK, $1.00.

DAVIS PRINT, 536 CLAY ST.
Dettners Printing House, Inc., 835 Howard St., San Francisco

The menu of this San Francisco restaurant during the Comstock Lode heyday, as well as the fact that $1.00 per week would rent a single room, indicates that the living was easy for those who could pungle up the necessary cash.
— *History Room, Wells Fargo Bank*

hook their teams to just one small corner of Hell, they could pull it up by the roots!

As was noted earlier, the Comstock devoured whole forests around Lake Tahoe, and when the railroad finally crossed the Sierra, the forested slopes adjacent to the Truckee River were fed into the mine mouths to shore up the workings underground. By the end of the Big Bonanza in 1880, these workings totalled almost 200 miles in length. The underground formations of the Comstock were unstable, and the famous "Diedsheimer square-set" method of timbering — using timbers that were just squared tree trunks — was evolved to solve the problem. Millions of board feet of lumber and timbers were devoured by the Comstock's workings, and its fuel needs demanded more than three hundred cords of wood each day; each cord being a tightly ricked unit measuring 4 feet x 4 feet x 8 feet.

As the shafts thrust deeper and deeper into the earth, the temperature went up appreciably below 1,000' so that at 2,500 feet, temperatures up to 150° were encountered. The water in the workings was so hot that it could and did scald unwary miners who stepped into it over the boot-tops. Ice cakes had to be used to cool these workings, but even so, men could only work 15 minutes at the "face" of a drift or stope or winze, and then spend thrice this long in "cooling" chambers.

The Comstock provided a new and enormous market for California's agriculture and animal husbandry. The general route of today's U.S. Highway 50 from Placerville east was the principal artery of communication before the Dutch Flat & Donner Lake Wagon Road preceded the railroad across Donner Summit. Three hundred tons of freight a day left Placerville for the Comstock at rates as high as six cents per pound. Six Concord coaches daily provided "express" service to the Comstock, and the Pioneer Stage Line carried 20,000 passengers annually at a oneway fare of $27 *gold*. The magnitude of travel between Placerville and the Comstock may be gauged by the recorded traffic that passed through one toll station in a three-month period in 1864; 6,667 foot travelers; 833 on horseback; 3,164 by stage; 5,000 pack animals; 2,564 four-horse teams, and 4,649 head of cattle. The volume and consistency of this traffic gave the Big Four the courage to undertake building a railroad across the Sierra, inasmuch as it would give their railroad a source of revenue regardless of what the "transcontinental" traffic might become.

Comstock profits gave George Hearst the beginnings of his financial empire. The famous Homestake Mine at Lead, South Dakota — the nation's leading gold producer today — was acquired by Hearst with Comstock gains. Thus it can be said that "Hearst's Castle" at San Simeon, today operated by the Division of Parks and Recreation for the people of California, has its roots well-planted in the workings of the Comstock. The world-famous copper mines in Montana were financed initially by California capitalists with Comstock profits. Other Comstock profits went into other ventures, of which Tevis and Haggin's vast grasslands empire in the Southwest was an example.

Perched literally atop the Comstock Lode, Virginia City became the most cosmopolitan community between St. Louis and San Francisco — the beautiful, bibulous Babylon of the mining West. The Piper Opera House presented the greatest thespians of the day; and the beauteous Julia Bulette, most famous courtesan of her time and place, set the standard of elegance for the Comstock's legion of *filles de joie*. It was a town that learned to live with, and laugh at, the constant winds, dubbed "Washoe Zephyrs," which were alleged to blow laden pack mules off the street with only a minor gust. It was a town, too, that could entertain the notion of blasting a tunnel clear through Mount Davidson below its crest to catch the westering sun in a system of reflecting mirrors that would not only illuminate the streets but melt

Virginia City, Nevada — for twenty years the "beautiful, bibulous Babylon of the mining West," and the largest city between Saint Louis and San Francisco.   — *The Bancroft Library*

the ice and snow that clogged them for many months each year.

The writer was in Virginia City in the 1920's, during a major and fruit-less attempt to re-open the Comstock's remaining workings; after World War II the late Lucius Beebe rediscovered the town and transformed it into one of the greatest tourist traps in the Far West. Today's prices of precious metals brought the Comstock a re-examination by a Texas-based oil and minerals company, but the re-opening of the mines remains in doubt. Still and all, it must be remembered that the original mining on the Comstock Lode left a vast amount of low grade ore that was not worth hoisting out of the hole at the then prices per ounce of gold and silver.

The discovery of the Comstock stimulated the development of real mines and the promotion of imaginary ones all along the eastern slope of the Sierra as well as in adjacent portions of Nevada. What he saw and learned on the Comstock and its environs gave Mark Twain his famous axiom: "A mine is a hole in the ground owned by a liar." The finds at Austin, Aurora, and Bodie (allegedly the toughest town of them all) fanned the speculative fever and benefited California in the process. One of the legacies to California from this mining activity east of the Sierra summit is its smallest county today, Alpine, with perhaps 1,100 permanent residents.

VERTICAL SECTION OF THE COMSTOCK LODE
SHOWING PRINCIPAL MINES AND ORE BODIES WITH DATES OF DISCOVERY

From this chart, it is easy to see why Mark Twain described a Mine as "A hole in the ground owned by a liar!" Even so, such non-producers as Alpha, Exchequer, Bullion-Ward sold thousands of shares on the San Francisco Mining Exchange.
— *The Bancroft Library*

Other mining activity farther south along and opposite the Sierra's eastern wall, at Panamint and Ballarat, and particularly at Cerro Gordo, east of Inyo-Kern, gave Los Angeles a much smaller version of the financial stimulus that the Comstock had given San Francisco. Between 1868 and 1877, some $28,000,000 dollars flowed out of Cerro Gordo alone, and steamers plied Owens Lake carrying 83-pound bars of silver from the smelter to Remi Nadeau's freight teams, which hauled them across the Mojave Desert to Los Angeles. Lead was a by-product of the Cerro Gordo silver mines, and its occurrence here served to lessen the state's dependence upon importations of this base metal from overseas. The stimulus given to Los Angeles by Cerro Gordo was augmented by the expansion of mining interests into Arizona. The most famous of the Arizona strikes was Ed Scheifflen's find at Tombstone; famous perhaps because of the later gunfight near the OK corral.

Two of California's present banking chains trace their origins to the Gold Rush and the Comstock Lode. Wells Fargo, which uses the stagecoach symbol in its advertising, evolved out of the express business of the Gold Rush — a business in which the eastern-born firm of Wells, Fargo & Company became supreme in California after the financial collapse of 1855. The Bank of California, on the other hand, grew out of mercantile profits amassed during the Gold Rush and combined by San Franciscans to handle the banking business of the Comstock Lode, which the bank's founders controlled for many years.

As we have seen, the rudiments of a banking system in California began with the extension of credit by resident merchants of the hide-and-tallow days. Merchants and mercantile firms were the first bankers of the Gold Rush, primarily because they were the only ones who had reasonably fireproof quarters and reasonably theft-proof safes to hold dust and nuggets. Too, their connections with suppliers in the East afforded the first handy means for funneling California gold into eastern coffers.

Banking in California was a business of private banks and bankers for many years after the Rush. Personal character and integrity, plus the durability of premises and resistant qualities of safes, were the basic yardsticks by which a customer could measure the probably security of his funds. The men who wrote the first state constitution prohibited state-chartered banks and prohibited private banks from issuing paper currency. Thus, these first banks were banks of deposit and exchange, not banks of issue. There were no state regulations governing banking practices until the Board of Bank Commissioners was established in 1878. This was not an effective agency of government because its powers extended only to state-chartered banks, which had been made possible by law in 1862, and not to private banks. These came under the commissioners' purview in 1886, but state regulation of banking did not become truly effective until 1909.

The express companies entered the banking business because of the exigencies of life in the mines and the needs of the miners for safety and service. A miner lost valuable time from digging while taking his gleanings down to San Francisco, or even to the valley supply towns. The express business followed the miners into every gulch, canyon, and river bend that attracted them. So did peripatetic merchants, who acted as agents for the express companies until the companies established their own offices and buildings, which they did only in the more stable camps. A miner could deposit his raw gold at one of these agencies or offices and receive a certificate of deposit, for which the issuing office charged a small percentage of the gross amount involved. These certificates could be cashed for their face value at any other office or agency of the issuing company, and often circulated as currency in a land that lacked it.

Thus, it can be said that the express companies pioneered a form of branch banking in California. Many years later, Amadeo Peter Giannini made branch banking and service to small depositors the keystone in the growth of his Bank of America (at first called the Bank of Italy) to its present stature as the second largest bank in the world.

The express companies rendered another vital service to miner and businessman and merchant alike. It was hazardous, as well as uncomfortable, to make the long journey back to the States with one's fortune encased in a money belt strapped around the waist beneath whatever underwear was worn. By depositing funds, be they in coin or dust or nuggets, with the express company in San Francisco or elsewhere, a traveler could get a "bill of exchange" drawn on one of that company's correspondent bankers in almost any of the larger eastern cities, which could be cashed on arrival. Again, the express companies charged a percentage of the gross amount of taking care of a man's actual treasure and transporting it east.

The bills of exchange were payable in gold at destination, and the charges for securing such a convenient slip of paper often were more than offset when the holder could get a premium of sometimes as much as 10% back East for taking the face value of his bill of exchange in paper currency instead of gold. This paper premium for gold probably reflected the then ingrained distrust of Americans for the pieces of paper currency they derisively called "shinplasters." In August, 1864, the Union's inflated paper money could be purchased in San Francisco at the rate of thirty-seven cents gold per paper dollar. California merchants and bankers and others, who could buy in the East in depreciated paper and sell what they bought for good yellow gold in California, increased the state's accumulation of surplus capital for investment.

The necessity for coin or credit is basic to the progress of any frontier or underdeveloped land. California's supply of both gold and silver gave it the means to finance the development of the state, as well as much of the Pacific Northwest and interior far western states. The need for coin or credit was illustrated in Southern California, where the lack of both is said to have

De Luxe travel to the Comstock, via ferry to and from Vallejo, and the Virginia & Truckee RR from
Reno to Virginia City, was the message of this flamboyant advertisement. The "Only One Transfer"
was necessitated by the fact that the V & T was narrow gauge, while the Central Pacific was standard
gauge. — *History Room, Wells Fargo Bank*

been a major factor in that region's slow growth rate for more than thirty years after the Rush. When money could be borrowed in San Francisco for, say, 9 or 10 percent per annum, it commanded 1½ to 5 *percent per month* in Los Angeles and contiguous territory.

Los Angeles' first bank was an outgrowth of Isaias W. Hellman's successful mercantile business. A second bank there was founded by Francisco Temple and William Workman in 1871, but succumbed to the financial panic of 1875. The first means of contributing adequately to the growth of Los Angeles seems to have been based upon men of integrity and collateral who borrowed money at "wholesale" in San Francisco and lent it at "retail" in the Southland. Even so today, savings and loan associations may borrow in large amounts at the prime rate from the major commercial "full service" banks, and lend in smaller amounts at higher rates to individual borrowers.

In the days before government regulation of banking and government insurance of deposits, the rumor that a bank was unable to meet its obligations triggered a "run" on it to get one's deposit before it ran out of the hard coin to which a depositor was entitled. Often the rumor that any one bank was in trouble caused a stampede to withdraw deposits from all banking firms. Scenes of indescribable confusion and human anguish were registered in such instances, and nineteenth century California survived three major financial "panics," a more bluntly expressive term than either "depression" or "recession."

The first of these in 1855 made Wells Fargo, which survived and capitalized upon it, preeminent in express and banking for many years. It also gave an economic fillip to the existing social and political conditions in San Francisco, which resulted in that city's second Committee of Vigilance in 1856.

Twenty years later, the "Panic of '75" literally shattered the state's banking businesses — the Bank of California among them — for many weeks. Many of them never reopened their doors. It was this second panic that led to the beginnings of state regulation of banking. Coupled with a severe drought in 1876-77, which played havoc with the state's sheep industry, this financial collapse stimulated both agrarian and urban discontent. The result was the state's second, or "New" Constitution of 1879, under which, with all too numerous and confusing amendments, emendations, initiative and referendum measures, the state operates today. A slow resurgence of the world's markets for California's agricultural products finally overcame the cloying effects of 1875's economic slowdown.

The third financial convulsion occurred in 1893, and was precipitated by a gold problem in the national treasury very similar to that which confronts the nation today. It was not as sharply "panicky" as its predecessors, but it fanned the fires of Populism in the state which the Democrats used to capture the governorship for one of the few times since the Civil War. The long-lasting effects of the "Panic of '93" in California were alleviated by the rise of petroleum which is discussed in a separate chapter.

Insurance as an economic force affecting growth is another instance in which California benefited from an internally generated source of capital. When *you have* the funds with which to insure against risks those who have not, the profits flow to you, and employment and subsidiary investments are promoted thereby. This is another prime reason for San Francisco's rise to financial dominance in the Far West. The emergence of Los Angeles as a financial center since World War II cannot better be symbolized than through the selection of that city by the Prudential Insurance Company for its main offices for the Far West.

Marine insurance was the first type of risk covered in California, which is quite natural in view of the maritime trade that was so essential to the Gold Rush. Along with the later "inland marine" insurance, it was written either by foreign (largely British) companies or by eastern firms that had established agencies in California. These firms dominated the state's insurance business up to the advent of the Comstock Lode, and the profits from their underwritings flowed east or abroad. Also, their distance from the scene lent a certain detachment to the manner in which they viewed their insureds' losses.

When "The Earth Shook and the Sky Burned" — San Francisco, April 18, 1906.
— *W.E. Worden* — *History Room, Wells Fargo Bank*

Fire insurance was too risky for even the well-established firms to underwrite during the Rush — a most understandable conclusion, given the combustible nature of the building materials used. In fact, San Francisco experienced six disastrous fires in its first two years of Gold Rush life.

Cast-iron buildings were imported to make fireproof premises for businesses, but there were viewed with disfavor after five men were almost roasted to death inside one during the so-called "Great Fire" that swept San Francisco in May 1851. The use of locally made brick, much of it from the prison kilns at San Quentin, and of stone quarried at Angel Island and Benicia, some even imported from China, later reduced the fire hazard. So did the use of iron doors and window shutters, which precluded, or were hoped to preclude, the fire-feeding drafts from these apertures. Mother Lode buildings that still boast such appurtenances are a favorite camera target for today's tourists.

Equally as important as non-flammable building materials in reducing fire's ravages were the volunteer fire companies, which preceded paid municipal fire departments. These organizations performed incredible feats of fire supression with their primitive equipment — hand-drawn hose wagons, hand-pumped water-wagons, and bucket brigades equipped with leather or canvas buckets. Membership in one of these groups was a mark of social distinction, and their Grand Balls and other functions made the outstanding social events of smaller communities for many years.

Profits from the Comstock Lode, both direct and indirect, apparently were the key to the formation of successful California-owned insurance companies that could offer a full line of policies, including life insurance, against all major risks. They were formed, in the main, during the period 1862-70, and the protection against disaster that they afforded was a contributing factor to California's growth. This was clearly demonstrated in the rebuilding of San Francisco after that April day in 1906 when "The Earth Shook and the Sky Burned." The investment and mortgage capital that their profits made available to other California enterprises, and the employment they provided, were other contributing factors to the state's progress. Opposition by the insurance companies to the use of petroleum as a fuel in urban areas was a factor in the state's slow utilization of that tremendous natural resource.

Lakeview No. 1 blew in with a roar in 1910; chewed the derrick to splinters; ground up the casing and spit it out of the hole, and gushed 9,000,000 barrels in 18 months before it was controlled.
— *Courtesy William Rintoul, Bakersfield*

CHAPTER TWELVE

BLACK GOLD'S PROPULSIVE ENERGY

History can be defined and defined well as the story of mankind's control of energy. Within this context, it is virtually impossible to overstate the impact of petroleum upon California's growth and development. The products released from crude oil by today's refining processes affect every facet of our daily lives from home hearth to national defense. Petroleum has been mankind's most flexible source of energy in all recorded history, and the ability to use it has transformed human life — from the kerosene lamp, which was a powerful weapon against the terrors of darkness, down to today's air pollution by the internal, some say infernal, combustion engine. The adaptation of petroleum to transportation wreaked havoc with established systems, both afloat and ashore, and gave us the Jet Age, which ties the world together with an immediacy unknown before.

America's petroleum age began in 1859 with the "Drake Well' at Titusville, Pennsylvania. It came to California in fledging form shortly thereafter, and the later location of its first truly commercial fields in Southern California gave that region an economic boom equivalent to that of the Gold Rush in Northern California. One result was to make Los Angeles the first modern megalopolis to be based upon the flexibility and utility of automotive transportation.

The existence of this fossil fuel first was recorded in 1542, when Cabrillo observed the Chumash of the Santa Barbara Channel using "pitch," meaning asphaltic tar, to caulk their plank canoes. They used it as well to fasten arrowheads to shafts and to seal their water containers. Notations about asphalt beds and oil springs appear in the journals and diaries of the early Spanish explorers and of the Franciscans at the missions. Sailing down the coast in 1792-93, Captain George Vancouver, Royal Navy, recorded the great oil slick that gave iridescent hues to the ocean off Santa Barbara. This phenomenon was caused by crude oil escaping from natural fissures in the geologic formations underwater and was recorded again in fulsome fashion by Professor Benjamin Stilliman, Jr., of Yale University, enroute to Santa Barbara in the steamer *Senator* in June 1864:

> Often for hundreds of acres square at one view . . . the sea boils
> like effervescing soda water, with the escaping gas which ac-
> companies the oil, and great globules of pure oil rising with the gas
> flash out on the surface of the water, tossing it up in jets, and then

Early offshore drilling — the Summerland Oil Field, near Santa Barbara in 1904.

— Courtesy Calif. Historical Society — T.I.T. Collection

An offshore platform today can be located in more than 600' of water.

— Courtesy Standard Oil Co. of California

breaking into films of rainbow hues, like the tints of a dying dolphin [*sic*]. The effect is wonderfully beautiful and exciting.

This faulted, fractured, fissured formation poses a problem to offshore drilling today and escaping crude oil from those operations clotted Santa Barbara's beaches in 1969. In more than thirty years and 26,000 wells drilled offshore, this remains the only major oil spill in American operations. Crude oil is messy as Hell on a beach, but it *is biodegradable*, given time, by sun and wind and wave. This process can be helped along considerably by the use of oil-eating micro-organisms. More than forty billions of dollars accrued to the federal government between 1953-1980 from offshore leases and bonus payments paid by oil companies for the privilege of finding out whether what they had leased contained any oil, and from royalties paid on oil that they did find.

While on the subject of offshore drilling, it is pertinent to note the conflict between California and the federal government over *who* controlled drilling rights to the offshore "tidelands." In one of many efforts to boost oil production during World War II, California leased drilling rights within the three-mile limit offshore to various companies for a healthy royalty to the state. After the war, the federal government asserted the power to control the leasing of rights within the territorial waters of the nation. California resisted by all legal means possible until the Supreme Court in 1947 held that the federal right was pre-eminent. California then joined with Texas and Louisiana, which were having the same squabble with Washington, and lobbied Congress for a bill that would return the offshore leasing rights and royalties to the states. Such a bill finally was passed by Congress but President Truman vetoed it; the following year, a similar bill was passed and newly inaugurated President Eisenhower signed it into law in 1953. A healthy sum accrues annually to the state as a result.

Reverting to earlier oil history, there is a claim that Andres Pico distilled petroleum into illuminating oil at Mission San Fernando as early as 1854-55. Extensive research into the beginnings of the oil industry in California does not confirm this story, and it seems best to consign it to the realm of folklore. It also is fair to say that little use was made of the available surface sources of petroleum during the entire Hispanic regime in California.

As early as 1853-55 some of San Francisco's streets and roofs used asphalt for paving and coating. The asphalt was mined, quite literally, from deposits at Goleta and Carpinteria, near Santa Barbara. Oil that floated atop water springs in parts of Humboldt County was skimmed off during the latter 1850s to make a crude lubricant for the "chutes" by which gigantic redwood logs were skidded to the mills. In 1854, San Francisco became the first city west of St. Louis, Missouri to light its streets by gas, but this gas was distilled from imported coal.

Illuminating oils imported from the East, including coal oil and the

Not all wells came in like a lamb! This one burned for two weeks before a combination of steam and dynamite and courage extinguished the flames long enough to get it capped and its flow saved for use. — *Courtesy of William Rintoul*

newly developed kerosene, were exported by San Francisco firms to the rest of the Pacific Basin. Prominent among the exporters was the firm of Leland Stanford and his brothers, which had branches in Lima, Peru and elsewhere around the rim of the Pacific. The disruption of imported illuminants by the Civil War not only brought California its turpentine boom, it triggered the state's first oil "boomlets," which did not qualify as true "booms," no matter what those involved believed.

The honor of being the first oil well drilled in California generally is accorded the "Davis Well," which was put down in 1861 near Petrolia, Humboldt County. Other candidates for the title were near Martinez, Contra Costa County, and Ventura. The first boomlet, more speculative than productive, saw its major production coming from tunnels driven by Stanford Brothers into the slopes of Sulphur Mountain near Ventura. The state's first well to be drilled by steam power was put down near Rancho Camulos in May 1865. The state's first gusher and a short-lived one at that was "Ojai No. 6," drilled in 1867 by Thomas R. Bard for a syndicate of hopeful investors from Pennsylvania. This first excitement died rapidly thereafter.

Even if oil had been struck in paying quantities during this boomlet, it is *doubtful* that it would have affected California in any major way. The state's crude oil was much harder to refine than the Pennsylvania crude that began our Petroleum Age. This was due to its greater amount of carbon, which resulted from an asphaltum base rather than a paraffine base, and it contained more sulphur. This base makes it much heavier than eastern crude, a fact reflected in the remark of a later Californian oilman when he was congratulated for bringing in a producing well. "Thank God it wasn't a gusher," said he, "or we'd be shoveling the stuff down out of the trees." The qualities of the heavy, "sour" California crude directly affect the state today. In modern refining processes, the "first cut" gasoline — that produced most quickly and with the least processing — yields 37% from light, "sweet" Indonesian or Saudi Arabian crude; 20% from the heavier Alaskan crude, and a measly 4% from San Joaquin Valley crude. More gasoline is extracted by additional refining processes but this increases cost appreciably.

Kerosene was the chief product derived from petroleum for many years, and it dominated the profit picture in the product-mix of that day's refineries. A major problem facing California's infant oil industry until 1910-12 was how to refine California crude to get a reasonably nonexplosive kerosene, and one that did not char the lampwicks, smoke the chimneys, and stink like an overripe outhouse as it burned.

Another problem was developing a burner that could use the heavy California crude as a fuel that would compete with imported coal. Four and one-half barrels of crude gave the thermal energy equivalent of one ton of imported coal; oil had manifest advantages in its lack of ashes and the reduced storage space required. But until improved oil burners were designed and adapted to handle California crude, imported coal remained the state's

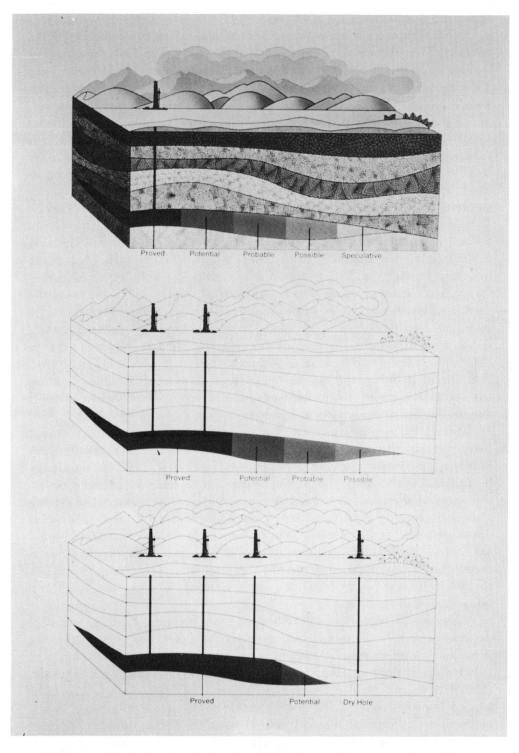

The one sure way to determine the size of a field is with the drill, and this may mean drilling "dusters" to mark its limits.　　　　　　　　　　　　　　　　　*— Standard Oil Co. of Calif.*

basic energy source.

The technological improvements in refining have been continued down to today's petrochemical industry and its marvels. The first gasoline produced in California was marketed for paint thinner, and then for kitchen cooking in places such as Los Angeles, where other fuel was scarce or expensive. It found a market, too, in the Great Valley, where high summer temperatures made a relatively long-lasting wood or coal fire unbearable, for the housewife who could afford the initial investment required by a fast-starting, easily extinguishable, ashless gasoline stove. When Lindberg landed at New York in 1927 to refuel for his epic flight across the Atlantic, his "Spirit of St. Louis," built in San Diego, was loaded with 330 gallons of Red Crown gasoline, refined in California from California crude.

Technological improvements in petroleum production, primarily in drilling equipment and techniques, make a story all their own. The first drilling equipment was the "spring-pole," a limber sapling bent over a rock or stump for fulcrum, and anchored at one end. The iron drilling bit, hand-forged and chisel-shaped, together with weights to give it impact, made the "string of tools." This was suspended from the free end of the sapling by rope, and a stirrup on each side of the rope enabled men to use their feet to "kick down" the hole. The spring of the sapling lifted the "string" back up for another downward kick. This technique apparently is as old as Chinese civilization. It limited drilling to relatively shallow depths, simply because the spring-pole could not provide adequate lift against the weight of tools and drilling line at deeper levels.

Steam came into use thereafter, utilizing a wooden derrick, perhaps forty feet tall, for which California's forests provided the raw material. A boiler-engine system powered a Pittman rod, which actuated the "walking-beam," and the up-and-down action of the walking-beam lifted and dropped the string of tools, which became much heavier in this method. The drilling rope was generally a two-inch hawser-laid Manila line. With these up-and-down cable-tool rigs, still using a chisel-shaped bit, which was rotated by the twist of the rope to get a reasonably round hole, maximum depth approximated 5,000 feet. Below this depth, the stretch in the drilling rope offset the ability of the beam to lift the string of tools high enough to get any downward drilling impact.

The use of wire rope, larger boilers, more powerful engines, and steel derricks gave the cable-tool rigs an extension of life. The next evolution was the diesel-powered rotary drill, using alloy-faced bits. Drilling mud was pumped down the hole to prevent undue wear on the rapidly revolving bit. (Muroc Dry Lake yielded an earth that was admirably suited to this technique.) The modern rotary-rig made possible the technique known as "slant" or "whipstock" drilling, whereby several holes can be put down in different directions from the same drilling platform, and it greatly speeded up the process of "making hole." Rotary-rigs are those used today on offshore drilling platforms, supplied by helicopter and boat, as well as in vessels designed for oil-drilling operations father offshore.

Without the continued improvements in the rotary bit and other drilling equipment, it would be impossible to probe deeper and deeper into the earth in search of oil. This search becomes more urgent in view of the fact that California *consumes* about 500,000 barrels of oil per day *more* than it produces. This shortage is made up by oil from Alaska and to a lesser degree from Indonesia. The recent (1982) discovery of a new field offshore from Pt. Arguello promises to reduce the state's dependence upon imported crude.

The deeper the well, or "hole" in oilfield parlance, the more costly it becomes. Of the more than 100,000 oil and gas wells that have been drilled in the state since 1865, the deepest yet went 22,711 feet in 1975, at a cost of $3,250,000 and it was a "duster," which simply means a dry hole, which means *no oil*! Another "deep test" in the Ventura River canyon went 21,600 feet, at a cost of more than $3,000,000 before the seekers threw in the sponge. It was dry too! By way of comparison, two dusters drilled by a California company on Alaska's North Slope cost slightly more than 34 million dollars. The depths and the costs today are a far cry from the spring pole drillers of the industry's beginnings, and so is the market for petroleum products.

Water flooding — pumping water into oil well holes to force out the oil when gas pressure is insufficient — has increased the productive life of many wells. Steam flooding, which uses live steam in place of water, has been effective in releasing additional amounts of California's heavy crude from older wells. Federal deregulation of price controls on "old" oil has led to increased thermal injection in wells in Kern County and this contributed to the state's increased oil production between 1980-82. A special electrode is being used in Kern County in the hopes of freeing some billions of barrels of tar-like crude which resist other recovery methods. Research is going forward on developing micro-organisms that can be utilized to improve recovery ratios in heavy crude deposits, while other micro-organisms have been used and are still being perfected to clean up oil spill accidents in both ocean and inland waters.

Petroleum transportation, too, has a story all its own. Cans, barrels, casks, buckets, and firkins were the receptacles first used to get crude oil from wellhead to primitive refinery. Then came the forerunners of today's railroad tank cars, and then metal tanks inserted into the holds of wooden-hulled coastwise steamers. The first vessel designed specifically for bulk oil transportation was the steamer *W.L. Hardison* built in San Francisco for the Union Oil Company. This vessel also boasted the distinction of being the first Pacific Coast vessel to be lighted by electricity. She made several voyages before one of her officers, seeking to determine the level of the oil being pumped into her tanks at Ventura, lowered a kerosene lantern into the hold, and she burned to the water's edge.

The first true tanker, in that her hull or "skin" formed the outer wall of her tankage, was the *George Loomis*, which was built in San Francisco for the Standard Oil Company of California in 1895. Her capacity was 6,000 barrels. The feasibility of transporting petroleum in bulk by sea gave birth to the "Oil Coast" along an arm of San Francisco Bay between Richmond and Antioch. Here major refineries are supplied with crude from all the world by supertankers, which in turn carry the refined petroleum products to the world's markets.

California's first oil pipeline in 1879 was all of two inches in diameter and stretched all of seven miles from Pico Canyon to Newhall; thereafter, it was extended from Newhall to tidewater at Ventura. Fires had to be lighted along it in the colder months to keep the viscous crude in motion, and irate farmers tore it up when it sprang leaks in their bean fields and orange groves.

Both steam and water flooding are used to force oil out of wells where lack of natural pressure has shut off their flow.
— *Standard Oil Co. of California*

Despite such drawbacks, this first pipeline possessed notable economic advantages: oil piped to Ventura could be shipped by sea from there to San Francisco for only $0.56 per barrel, whereas the Espee charged $1.10 per barrel by tank car from Newhall to San Francisco.

A larger pipeline from the Kern River Field to a refinery at Richmond on San Francisco Bay encountered its own problems when oil first began to be pumped through it. Unseasonably cold weather virtually solidified the viscous crude and the line had to be tapped every few miles to let some oil ooze out. This was ignited and the resultant heat "unfroze" the crude in the line and let it creep a bit farther along. Four months were consumed in the journey!

The deck of a modern tanker is no place to practice Frisbee games.　　　— *Standard Oil of California*

Today's pipelines criss-cross the state beneath its surface, moving prodigious quantities of crude oil, refined products, and natural gas. Interstate pipelines bring natural gas from Texas and New Mexico, while international lines bring it from Canada and Mexico. These importations account for almost 80% of the state's natural gas consumption, while nearly one-half of the state's non-transportation energy needs are met by natural gas. Nationally, natural gas meets only about 35% of such non-transportation needs.

Natural gas was "flared," (burned) in the early days when it was the orphan of the oil industry and a tremendous hazard to the drilling crew. Wher a well came in as a "gusher," the oil being forced out of the bowels of the earth by tremendous gas pressure, a chance spark from the rock fragments that accompanied the flow could ignite the gas into a torch that seared every living thing for hundreds of yards around. It might take ten days or more before the "wildfire well" could be extinguished by the use of steam, dynamite, and raw guts on the part of the men who subdued it.

Before 1900, gas for street and home lighting was derived largely from imported coal; after the Los Angeles City field came in, petroleum was processed to make the gas until 1913, when natural gas in quantity became available from California's fields. Until 1947, the state produced all its natural gas needs from its own fields, the first of which was discovered by accident in 1864 when a water well was dug to supply the San Joaquin County courthouse in Stockton. Not until 1983 was this field used commercially. For comparative purposes, it might be remembered that 1,000 cubic feet (Mcf) of gas = 1,053,000 British Thermal Units (BTU) and that the typical home's annual heating needs are 60,000,000 BTU, which requires 57 Mcf of gas or 430 gallons of oil or 5,500 pounds of coal. And gas is infinitely cleaner than either oil or coal.

The marketing of petroleum products has come a very long way from the days when the occasional motorist was a venturesome daredevil; a beggoggled and often reviled curiosity in a long linen duster and a Barney Oldfield cap. A sack of oatmeal was carried to clog radiator leaks, because of the swelling properties, and the motorist expected to get one flat tire for every twenty miles travelled. The Reeves Octo Auto sought to beat the blowout problem in high pressure tires by having four wheels on a side. This meant that sooner or later, there were eight tires to change!

Gasoline flowed to the carburetor by gravity, and on a steep hill, the wise motorist turned around and backed up it. If the grade was too long, the back main bearing burned out in a day of splash lubrication only. A carbide drip-generator made acetylene gas for lights, but the stench that went with it made night motoring unpleasant. In those days, gasoline was poured into the tank of the "horseless carriage" from a can in the hands of the general store owner, who carried it as a sideline to his kerosene business. A chamois cloth to filter it first was standard motoring equipment. Even though there are thousands less service stations than there were before the oil crisis of

1973-74 and their numbers are still declining, those that remain with their restrooms, snack machines, soft-drink dispensers and service bays are a far cry from the few haphazard facilities of the early roadside supply points.

Application of petroleum to industrial use was slow to come about because of the difficult refining properties of the crude, the inefficiency of the first oil burners, and the opposition of the insurance companies. Breweries, ice plants, iron foundries, and isolated mining camps in Southern California's deserts were among its pioneering users. For a quarter-century after California's first oil boom collapsed in 1867, the state's petroleum industry progressed at a snail's pace.

An artist's drawing of an early "service" station. — *Standard Oil Co. of California*

The Pacific Coast Oil Company, an ancestor of today's Standard Oil Company of California, operated in that slack period in the Newhall Basin. One of its drillers, C.A. "Alex" Mentry, brought in the state's first truly commercial well in nearby Pico Canyon in September 1875. This well's production, together with the company's other output, was sent to a refinery at Alameda — an indication that the state's principal market then was the San Francisco Bay Area. Exploration and development, as the terms are used today, were unknown; production grew only as demand increased. By and large, the Pacific Coast Oil Company was the mainstay of the state's oil industry well into the 1880's.

Its first real competition was provided when three small companies operating in Ventura County combined to form the Union Oil Company in 1890. Here again, production was determined by what the slowly expanding market could absorb at prices that permitted a profit to the oil men. The same limitation applied to Lacey & Rowland, which operated in the Puente Hills Field east of Los Angeles. Refining was a hit-and-miss proposition, and fuel oil was sold just as it came from the well; sometimes being mixed with the inferior California kerosene to reduce its viscosity and improve its thermal properties.

The real breakthrough in petroleum stemmed from a well put down on West Second Street in Los Angeles by a wandering, down-on-his-luck prospector, who sank it by the shaft technique he had learned in mining for a flow of 7 barrels a day. It burgeoned into the 300 wells of Los Angeles City Field between 1892 and 1894 and turned West Second Street into a raucous, oil-soaked little gulch, which created demands from nearby citizens that the state's attorney-general abate the nuisance. This field laid the foundation of the wandering prospector's enormous fortune, his name being E.L. Doheny, and it marked a watershed in the state's production and use of petroleum and its products. Seventy-five years later, a new multi-million-barrel "pool" was discovered beneath downtown Los Angeles. Drilling operations using a tastefully camouflaged and noiseless derrick, and the "whip-stock" or "slant drilling" technique, probed beneath the city's sprawling municipal complex to tap this pool.

In 1891 the state's total crude production had been 326,600 barrels; in 1895, with the Los Angeles City Field in full flow, it was 1,208,482 barrels. This plenitude of oil forced the price from $1.25 per barrel at the wellhead to but $0.29. At this time, coal was selling in Los Angeles for $5.00 to $7.00 per ton. Given the ratio of 4.5 barrels of oil to one ton of coal, users could get the same energy from oil for only $1.31. The economics of this equation literally forced the state's railroads to take advantage of it.

Petroleum had been used to fire locomotives in Russia and in Peru before it was tried in this country. The Pennsylvania Railroad had used it successfully in 1887, between Altoona and Pittsburgh, but coal still was cheaper for the Pennsylvania's operations. Then, in October 1894, a Santa

Palm trees and oil wells — The Los Angeles City Field.

— *L.A. County Museum*

Fe locomotive burned oil in trial runs over the Espee tracks between Santa Paula and Ventura, with a burner adapted for moving use by the knowhow of Union Oil's mechanical staff at its Santa Paula headquarters. Before the year was out, the Santa Fe was using oil successfully over Cajon Pass, at a substantial saving over coal. Within two years, the Espee had followed the Santa Fe in a major conversion from coal to oil, and the industrial market expanded accordingly. Today's diesel locomotives, of course, use petroleum products for their application of increased adhesive efficiency to tractive effort.

The first adaptation of petroleum for maritime fuel was either in the aforementioned *W.L. Hardison* or in a coastwise lumber carrier, the *Pasadena*, operated by Kerckhoff & Cuzner of Los Angeles, one of the largest lumber firms in the Southland. Petroleum utilization in the transpacific trade eliminated the danger of running out of fuel at sea during adverse weather — a problem that had plagued the coal-burners. A concomitant of increased maritime use was the development of San Pedro Harbor by construction of a breakwater there between 1893 and 1903. San Franciscans referred to it as an "irrigated port," which did not affect its growth in the least.

The availability of cheap fuel at San Pedro provided the initial push that made the present harbor complex there probably the top ranked tonnage-handling port on the Pacific Coast. The opening of the Panama Canal in 1914 also helped. The lands and islands of the Pacific Basin made another growing market for California's petroleum products, and the growth of Southern California was due primarily to the availability of cheap energy in the form of petroleum and its by-products. As this supply of cheap energy gets more and more expensive and less and less available, the state faces some urgent questions that do not concern continued growth so much as they do survival.

After the Los Angeles City Field had sparked the major industrial breakthrough for petroleum use, other fields made a steady stream of new discoveries. Kern River, McKittrick, and Coalinga came in on the antelope and jackrabbit lands of the San Joaquin Valley, and production reached 77,000,000 barrels in 1910, two hundred and fifty times what it had been in 1890. The price of oil at the wellhead went to $0.12 per barrel on occasion. Then came fields at Santa Maria, Kettleman Hills, Santa Fe Springs, Huntington Beach, Midway/Sunset, and Signal Hill, the greatest of them all. Great gushers ran wild, spewing thousands of barrels of oil into the surrounding countryside, excavating holes large enough to swallow a county, it seemed, and sometimes catching fire, as noted earlier. These and other fields made California the nation's largest oil producing state until 1936 and it held second place in this category until 1958. Today it ranks fourth, behind Texas, Louisiana, and Alaska, despite setting an annual production record in 1981.

The woman at the wheel of this 1908 "Tourist" has just negotiated the waters of Eastlake Park, now Lincoln Park, in Los Angeles. — *Calif. Historical Society — T.I.T. Collection*

The plank road across the sandy desert west of Yuma, Arizona, where the "jackass Mail" got its name. — *Westways — Auto Club of Southern California*

California's distances and generally easy gradients made the automobile particularly suitable for individual transportation; its climate permitted a much greater year-round automobile activity for personal enjoyment, business, and recreation, and its winters lacked the prolonged harshness of other sections of the nation which made for easier starting and obviated the necessity for fine tuning and servicing. In 1908, the Los Angeles *Times* called a road race between Los Angeles and Phoenix, via Blythe, the *"most hazardous"* ever undertaken. It was won by a Stanley Steamer with a running time of thirty hours for the 455 miles. In the years before foreign manufacturers carved out a large slice of the American market, Los Angeles assembled more automobiles than Detroit and baked more tires than Akron, Ohio.

The California State Automobile Association and the Automobile Club of Southern California, the latter now the largest automobile club in the world, were founded in 1900. It was largely their influence, or pressure if you prefer, that prompted Governor Pardee (1903-07) to advocate a state highway system, and their continued efforts caused the legislature to authorize multi-million dollar bond issues for highway construction in 1910, 1916, and 1919.

In this last year, which was the year of the first automobile self-starter and the first sedan-type body, the state passed its first Vehicle Fuel License Law, or gasoline tax, which perhaps was unconstitutional but was too lucrative to overlook. This tax went directly to highway construction without review by the legislature and was augmented immensely in 1921 when Congress passed the federal highway act which provided the states with dollar-matching grants for the interstate highway system. This has resulted in more than one mile of road for every square mile in the state and the most ambitious freeway network of any state in the nation of more than 3,000 miles. Asphalt, which the oil fields supplied in quantity, was used for road paving, with the process invented by the Scotsman, MacAdam, and then concrete for which the state had ample supplies of raw material.

By 1924, when England, the most motorized of all European countries, had one automobile for every 100 persons, and the United States as a whole had one for every seven, California had one automobile for every four, with the bulk of these owned in Southern California. Today the state boasts one automobile for every two persons and in Southern California, the ratio is one to every 1.3, which is about the ratio of individual to epidermis. More than 80% of all Southern California households boast one vehicle, while 900,000 of them have two or more.

These growth figures make it easy to understand why automobile assembly plants became located in California, as were tire and accessory manufacturers. They in turn attracted more people, spawning service industries as they did so, and the cycle has kept feeding upon itself, albeit at a slower pace since 1975. In just one year, Californians travel *24,000,000,000* miles on one-day recreational junkets, and billions more on weekend and

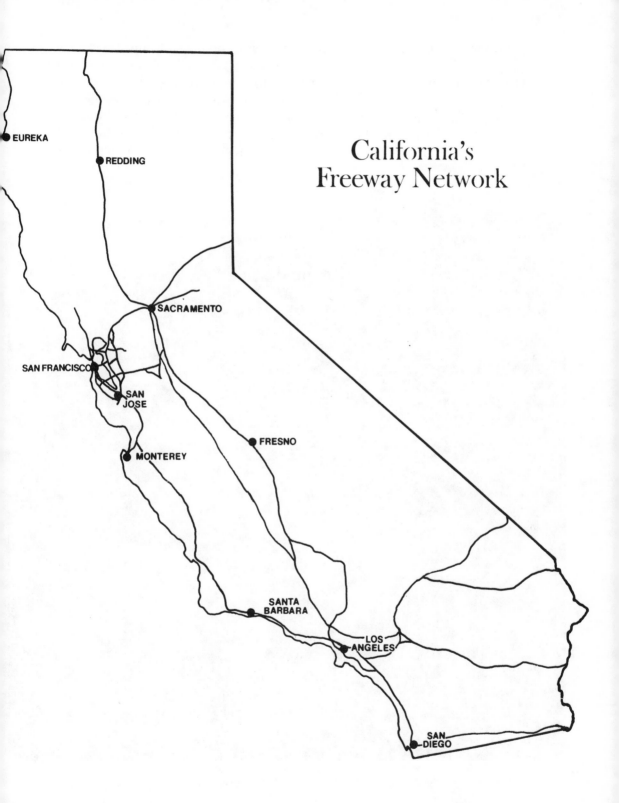

California's Freeway Network

vacation travels. In addition, the state receives millions of out-of-state visitors annually, of whom 70% or more arrive by automobile. The cash return to a community of just 24 overnight visitors is the equivalent of an annual payroll of $100,000, while tourism generates 450,000 jobs statewide and produces upwards of $15,000,000 in gross revenues each year. Until uncertainty about the world's petroleum prices became a factor, it was estimated that tourism would be the largest employer in the state by 2000 A.D.

The state's most beautiful roadside rest where 1-5 crosses the Klamath River.
— *Calif. Dept. of Transportation*

When winter comes to Donner Pass, the plows work overtime to keep it open.
— *Calif. Dept. of Transportation*

The more noxious side effects of the "infernal" combustion engine are more than obvious to residents of California's urban areas, and they have caused the most stringent anti-pollution measures affecting automobiles in the nation to be enacted by the legislature. Almost 40% of *all* crude oil consumed in the nation goes for gasoline production — the percentage is higher in California — and federal clean air standards requiring the use of unleaded gas in all automobiles produced from 1975 onward will increase this proportion, until urban mass transit systems become infinitely better and safer than they are today. This stems from the hard fact that the production of one gallon of unleaded gasoline requires up to 10% *more* crude oil to produce than does a gallon of leaded gasoline.

A final note to the petroleum story is its connection with the citrus fruit industry by providing the most effective fuel to "smudge" against frost. There have been times in the days before "smog" became a dirty word, when the whole of Southern California was smudge-bound for days on end by the outpourings from thousands of oil-burning orchard heaters. Improved versions of these heaters still are used, and in almond orchards as well, where air pollution regulations permit.

California's dependence upon the petroleum-natural gas energy complex is an accentuation of the nation's similar dependence, which today requires the importation of almost 40% of our total petroleum needs. These represent about 30% of the world's total consumption. The 1973-74 embargo by the oil exporting nations of the Middle East stimulated energy

Artist's conception of the Liquified Natural Gas terminal proposal for Little Cojo Bay near Pt. Conception. This is now in abeyance until needed. — *Pacific Lighting Corp.*

The nuclear power plant at Diablo Canyon, near San Luis Obispo, was scheduled to begin generating electricity in 1979, but has aroused determined opposition from anti-nuclear groups that have delayed and may completely prevent its operation.   — *Pacific Gas and Electric Co.*

conservation measures which have received added impetus from growing awareness of the hard and inescapable fact that the *days of cheap energy are gone forever*. A major contributing factor to this disappearance is the steadily increasing population in both California and the nation. California and the nation have changed energy forms before — from wood to coal to oil to natural gas — and each change has been accompanied by a new burst of investment, innovation, employment and prosperity. Whether California will lead the nation in innovative energy changes depends upon the will of its citizens to encourage innovative experiment that will free petroleum and natural gas for those uses, such as agriculture, where it cannot be replaced without exorbitant costs.

A small nuclear plant near Livermore received License No. 1 from the Atomic Energy Commission in 1957, and came to its end twenty years later, when it was producing only industrial and medical neutrons. The next nuclear plant in the state began generating electricity in 1963 on Humboldt Bay, near Eureka, and operated safely and successfully until July 1976. Its capacity was 63 megawatts (Mew) which now require 700,390 barrels of oil per year to produce. A larger plant at San Onofre, near San Clemente, began operation in 1968 and generates 436 Mew, which would require 4,800,000 barrels of oil per year to replace. A second unit is being installed at this plant to double its capacity and a third unit is under consideration. An even larger plant owned by the Sacramento Municipal Utility District (SMUD) generates 913 Mew, the equivalent of more than 10,000,000 barrels of oil per year. An even larger nuclear plant is still awaiting approval in 1984 to begin generating electricity at Diablo Canyon, near San Luis Obispo. At its designed peak capacity it will generate electricity that would require 20,000,000 barrels of oil per year to produce.

Accentuated by its proximity to the San Andreas Fault, this plant has become the focal point of increasingly strenuous opposition to the utilization of nuclear power in the state. The mere mention of the word *nuclear*, or "nuke" in opponents' parlance, produces vivid mental images of a towering mushroom-shaped cloud that would obliterate all life for hundreds of miles around and affect unborn generations for years and years to come. It seems advisable to note that nuclear reactors use low-grade (3% enriched) uranium which cannot be used for explosives; these require 90% enriched uranium. Thus, a nuclear blow-up of a plant using low-grade uranium is unlikely. That there are formidable hazards to the use of nuclear energy, including disposal of the radioactive waste material, is beyond question, as the accident at Three Mile Island in 1979 showed conclusively. What needs to be remembered in light of the statement that began this chapter, is that if we insist on absolutely risk-free sources of energy, we are insisting on the impossible, for there is no source of energy that is without risk of some degree. Southern California Edison has avoided in-state protests by the expedient of investing in a nuclear plant being built in Arizona.

The best statement about the approach to nuclear energy that has come to this writer's attention is by James K. Page, Jr. (*Smithsonian, June, 1979*):

> Let us have no more games played about perfect safety and engineering wizardry. Let us have no more foolishness about shutting down all reactors until the protestors can keep my refrigerator running by some other means. Let us all grow up and think about the unthinkable, rationally and carefully together. Let the industry and the government share the facts with us . . . educable, ultimately wise citizens and we can probably help out. In fact, we will decide. That's what we've been doing in this country, after all, for years with pretty creditable success.

Garbage is one of the many types of biomass capable of providing fuel to power generation, thus supplementing fossil or nuclear fuels.
— *Pacific Gas & Electric Co.*

The use of biomass is another alternative source of energy, and biomass is a collective term applied to plant and animal material, including garbage. Wood is the most popular form of biomass energy and California's timberlands are capable of yielding prodigious amounts of oak and other species that are unsuitable for commercial lumber. A poultry cooperative in Arkansas is recycling 100 tons of chicken manure daily to produce methane gas which can be burned in engines converted for the purpose; the yield is the equivalent of 12,000 gallons of gasoline. Given California's enormous egg-and-broiler factories, one of which near St. Helena has 300,000 hens, there would appear to be more to the poultry business than fowl play. The state's dairies, too, produce biomass in the form of "cow pies" that can produce methane gas and already is being produced in at least one commercial dairy. Sacramento is burning urban garbage to generate electricity and California can supply biomass in many forms: grain and hay straws, livestock manure, cottonseed hulls, nut shells, cull fruits and vegetables, as well as crop surpluses when available. Many technical procedures for converting biomass to energy are known; their commercial applications have to become economically feasible. Whenever we quit living in the Fool's Paradise of petroleum dependency, biomass will become economically feasible.

Another energy saving method, co-generation, has found favor in industrial plants where it is applicable. This method uses fuel more efficiently by burning it only once to get two or more uses. For example: a pulp mill must create steam for its processes. Once the steam has served this purpose, it is used to turn a turbine which generates electricity that is either used in the plant itself or sold to the nearest public utility.

Interstate 580 uses Altamont Pass, one of several "wind gaps" in the Coast Range folds, and if Don Quixote were to ride that way today, he would find windmills at which to tilt of a size beyond his wildest imaginings. Perched on spindly steel stalks, these windfarm-mills use the wind that makes the Pass notorious to generate electricity that is sold to Pacific Gas & Electric Company. Three companies now are operating such windmill farms in the Altamont Pass area and have plans to enlarge them as funds permit. P G & E has completed installation of a monster windmill on a low hill between Vallejo and Fairfield. Sitting atop a 200-foot tower, a blade 300' from tip to tip will start up at a wind speed of 15mph, reach designed generating capacity with a wind speed of 27mph, and "feather" its blades to a standstill at wind speeds of 60mph or more. A year's output from this giant at designed wind speed will generate enough electricity to supply the yearly requirements of more than 1,000 two-bedroom homes.

Southern California, too, has windmill farms operating in the Tehachapi Mountains and in San Diego County, as well as a "David and Goliath" set of generating windmills near Palm Springs. Other prospective windmill farm locations are in the Warner Mountains of Modoc County; the Diamond Mountains in Plumas and Lassen counties; in San Gorgonio Pass east of

Banning on Interstate 10, and in Pacheco Pass east of Gilroy. If, and please note the word, all these sites were developed to their *estimated* capacity, they would generate 5,600 Mew, replacing millions of barrels of oil. This estimate, however, seems to ignore the fact that the wind is a fickle servant. Still, whatever can be generated thereby is a gain.

Ten years ago the use of solar energy was regarded as a science-fiction fantasy. What has happened to oil supplies and prices in the past ten years has made solar energy much more attractive. Passionate advocates of solar energy say that just two weeks of sunshine contain as much potential energy as *ALL* the known global reserves of *ALL* fossil fuels. Whether this is an exaggeration or not is beside the point that all manner of solar devices for home heating, power generation and the like can be fabricated today; the question is whether they can be produced at affordable prices. The conventional "passive" thermal units that sit atop a house and heat water for home use cost about $2,000 and require about 20 years to recover this initial cost through their savings; photovoltaic cells, which are an "active" system, convert the sun's rays directly into electricity through silicon-crystal panels. Hopefully the costs of applying photovoltaic cells to handle all the energy needs of a single-family home can be brought down to about $10,000 within the next decade.

A commercial-type plant using 1,800 heliostats (solar panel collectors) directed by a computer is operated by Southern California Edison on the Mojave Desert near Daggett, where there is plenty of sunshine, as any "desert rat" knows full well. These heliostats rotate with the sun and focus the rays on a steam boiler linked to a turbine generator. It produces 10 megawatts, enough for 1,000 two-bedroom homes, and cost approximately $116,000,000. Using state, federal, and its own funds, SMUD is building the first 1-Mew phase of a photovoltaic solar generating plant, which converts the sun's energy directly into electricity using hundreds of solar panels. This first phase of what may become the world's largest solar generating plant is located next to SMUD's existing nuclear generator in the Sacramento Valley. If state and federal funds continue to be available in the requisite amounts, this plant will grow to a 100-Mew facility. The availability of federal funds also affects plans by the Los Angeles Department of Water and Power to construct a photovoltaic plant in the adjacent desert region. Barring a major technological breakthrough in the near future solar energy probably can provide no more than 10% of the nation's energy needs by the year 2000. In a time when the availability of petroleum is the tripwire in all energy planning, every little bit helps, and in time the potentials of both active and passive solar energy systems undoubtedly will be realized. They have to be!

To stop-gap the energy problem until the alternative sources mentioned above can contribute appreciably to the state's energy needs, use is being made of the old, reliable fossil fuel — coal. In 1979, the California Energy Commission estimated that 12% or more of the state's non-transportation energy needs could be met by 1990 from coal-fired generating plants *inside the state*, using coal imported via the existing interstate rail network. This estimate bumped head on into the hard fact that *coal* is almost as dirty a word as is *nuclear* to the state's dedicated environmentalists. However, about 6% of the state's energy needs already are being met from coal-fired generating plants located in Arizona and Nevada. Another route to coal usage for electricity generation, a 100 Mew plant, is underway in the desert near Barstow, where Southern California Edison and Texaco are converting low sulfur coal from Utah into gas.

What was originally designed to be the world's largest coal-fired generating plant is under construction near Lyndyll, Utah. If, and note the word, it is completed as designed, it will sprawl over *seven square miles*, consume more than 9,000,000 *tons* of coal annually and generate 3,044 Mew, which would require almost 34,000,000 barrels of oil to duplicate. Almost 60% of the designed capacity would be supplied to six areas of Los Angeles. Whether the plant ever is completed to maximum capacity, due to burgeoning construction costs, it appears certain that at least two units, capable of generating 1,500 Mew, will be completed to offset two aging generating plants of the Los Angeles Department of Water & Power. From the foregoing, it would appear that Californians have no qualms about using electricity produced by coal-fired plants in other states. Neither do they seem to realize that all the cement produced in the state utilizes coal in its production.

Another possibility of meeting the state's energy needs is the importation of natural gas from Indonesia, chilled to the point where it liquefies and can be transported by tankers. This liquefied natural gas (LNG) would be unloaded at a terminal near Point Concepcion, where it would be returned to gaseous form and fed into the state's existing network of gas transmission lines. While the state has no deposits of oil-bearing shale, the Union Oil Company has pioneered in the successful extraction of oil from shale deposits in Colorado. The potential of these deposits is enormous but costs of extraction have not yet become competitive with imported petroleum, even at present-day world prices.

The extreme advocates of solar, geothermal, wind, small hydro-generating plants and other alternative energy sources maintain that these can supply all our energy needs by 2000 A.D. This would be a society independent of centralized energy sources of any type and with a per capita energy use similar to that of the early years of this century. Admirable though this may seem to those increasingly uneasy about the mass and impersonalness of urban living, this approach simply ignores California's need for energy in quantities far higher than these sources seem able to produce. This energy need stems not from a need to grow at the rate experienced since 1848, but from the need to maintain such levels of productivity, of personal income and of personal employment as will make the state habitable and enjoyable by future generations. This need demands that the state have a diversified supply of energy from any and every source, including nuclear until it can be phased out over time. If such a supply is not developed and that speedily, California in common with the rest of the world will remain at the mercy of the major oil producing nations of the Middle East, Latin America and Indonesia.

Just enough diamonds were found in the hydraulic workings near Oroville in Butte County to enable that fact to be briefly noted here. More importantly, California was blessed with other mineral resources that lacked the impact of oil but which have played and continued to play a considerable role in the state's prosperity.

The enduring vermillion with which the California Indians colored their rock carvings was derived from cinnabar, the raw ore of quicksilver, and one of the world's few substantial sources of this shimmering, restless metal was found in California. The first important discovery was at New Almaden, near San Jose, while the other major find was at New Idria, in San Benito County. Smaller deposits were found and worked in the Coast Range folds of Lake County. The New Almaden deposits were uncovered just prior to the American acquisition of California, and their production was of great value to the extractive processes for gold and silver that followed.

As fulminate of mercury, quicksilver ignited the small arms cartridges of the nineteenth century; contributing to the Union's victory in the Civil War., to the slaughter of buffalo on the Great Plains, and to the subjugation of the horse-riding Plains Indians, "the finest light cavalry the sun ever shone on." It also increased the powder-smoke fog that shrouds the deeds of the gunfighters within and without the law in the Old West. Fulminate caps also fired the dynamite produced by the state's explosives industry, and thus served to advance the pace of mining and heavy construction.

The "twenty-mule team" of Death Valley fame looms larger in the popular fancy than the borax it hauled. Borax is overshadowed by the numerous borate compounds that today come out of the state's southeastern Basin and Range province. Modern society hardly could exist without the products that these compounds make possible. Before the state's borax riches were unlocked, the bulk of the world's supply came from Tibet and from Tuscany in Italy; today California produces about 90% of the Free World's needs.

The center of the state's borates production today is the great dry lake that John Searles discovered in 1862. Once the Espee rails came within hauling distance of Searles Lake, a company was formed to work its deposits in competition with the more publicized operations in Death Valley. It was not until this century that our level of technology was able to tap all the riches contained in and below the saline crust, ten feet thick, of the lake bed.

Among these are gasoline additives and additives for glass and glazes; cleansing agents for detergents; components of weed and insect killers; fire-extinguishing compounds for home and industry, and for forest fire fighting by "borate bombers." Other compounds are used for alloying steel and for giving the grit to abrasives, of which boron carbide is one of the hardest known. As if this roster was not enough, they also yield gypsum for plasterboard, and "Bristol Salt" for softening the Colorado River water supplied to Southern California by the Metropolitan Water District. Air-conditioning enables the desert towns to remain oases of production when the white hell of summer descends upon their Mojave Desert locale.

The widely distributed supply of raw materials for cement spans the length and breadth of the state, including shells dredged from San Francisco Bay, where long ago the *Costanoan* and *Miwok* tribelets depended upon shellfish as their granary. The utility of cement, its availability, statewide

Just as wet and just as powerful as the ditches that brought water to the hydraulic "monitors," this ditch carries 4,000 gallons a second to a modern powerfhouse.   — *Pacific Gas and Electric Co.*

distribution, and relative cheapness have made it a powerful factor in California's ability to construct not only highways but also the dams, aqueducts, and canals of its major water distribution and storage system. Further use in irrigation pipe and systems, and in industrial and residential construction makes cement one of the state's most valuable natural assets.

Available hand in hand with cement are rock, sand, and gravel — aggregates — which cement binds together by criss-crossing interlocking crystals as the liquid mass sets into concrete. The role of gold-dredging debris in constructing Oroville Dam is a dramatic example of this correlation of assets, while the rotating "ready-mix" truck that delivers the makings of a new patio relates it directly to the individual Californian.

California's clay products and ceramic tile industries utilize clays that the California Indians were unable to transform into pottery. Millions upon multiplied millions of single-celled sea plants called "diatoms" were laid down on California's coastal lands as they subsided and emerged with the rhythms of geologic time. California leads today in the world's production of diatomaceous earth, which is essential to industrial filtration processes and to the swimming pools that are so much a part of the "outdoor syndrome" in California living. The state's purest deposits of this earth are worked near Lompoc.

Iron ore from Eagle Mountain enabled the Kaiser interests to build the state's first integrated steel complex near Fontana during World War II. Tungsten and vanadium mines perch high on the eastern reaches of the High Sierra, and copper gave its name to Copperopolis on the Mother Lode. Other copper deposits were worked in Shasta County and in the intramontane reaches of Plumas County, though copper was never a major item in California's cornucopia of natural resources. It did not need to be.

Riding the Mount Lowe Incline Railway, near Pasadena, was not for the faint hearted.
— *Courtesy L.A. County Museum*

CHAPTER THIRTEEN

SUN-SEEKERS

California' tourism, health industry, Hollywood, aircraft manufacture, and space-age technology — each of these seemingly disparate elements in the state's social and economic life owes its beginning to the beneficent qualities of the climate. In this way, they accentuate the opening portion of this narrative, which was devoted to the state's physical geography.

The therapeutic qualities of California's climate received their first boost from Sebastian Vizcaino, the Basque mariner who rediscovered California for Spain in 1602. At San Diego he saw an Indian woman with a navel that "protruded like a gourd," while the wrinkles in her stomach resembled those of a "blacksmith's bellows." These were marks of great age to Vizcaino, and he attributed the woman's longevity to the salubriousness of the climate in which she lived.

Early travelers and explorers wrote glowingly of this same climate and, as noted earlier, it was John Marsh's reports on the climate of northern California that encouraged the first agricultural party of overland emigrants to quit Missouri's chills and fevers. The gospel of the climate was spread by returning gold-seekers, but until the overland rail link was forged, travel remained too difficult for significant numbers of simple health-seekers or sun-lovers to make the journey. The railroad promoted the travels of journalists, such as Charles Nordhoff, and their accounts in books and magazines encouraged health-seeking tourism in the 1870's. Southern California, the "Italy of America" — where the plaster-and-lath beach community of Venice sought to recreate its Italian counterpart, complete with Grand Canal — was the beneficiary of most of this eastern publicity.

The town of Ojai, in Ventura County, once an exotic haven for Theosophists and long an exclusive residential community, got its start as a health resort named Nordhoff. Other Southern California communities were similarly favored by doctors who prescribed the mild, sea-tempered climate for patients suffering from various ailments. Mineral springs throughout the state, such as Warner Hot Springs behind San Diego, were added attractions for health-seekers, as this was the heyday of balneology, the science of the therapeutic use of baths, which has had a re-birth in the use of "hot tubs" today. The direct rail connection of Southern California with the East in the 1880's gave further impetus to this traffic, and it continued in a floodtide well into the period of World War I. California's natural wonders, such as the

Redondo Beach Hotel in its glory days, ca. 1898. — *Calif. Historical Society — T.I.T. Collection*

Tent City with Hotel del Coronado — Fun in the sun and the surf in a leisurely time.
— *San Diego Historical Society — T.I.T. Collection*

Big Trees, the Redwood Groves, Yosemite, Lake Tahoe, and all the rest, became sightseeing and honeymoon havens with the advent of improved external and internal communications.

The mild winter climate, which often fills the northern and central coast of california with sunshine, in contrast to the fog-shrouded summers there, spawned the stately pleasure domes of the Hotel Del Monte near Monterey, the Hotel Del Coronado near San Diego, and the Potter Hotel at Santa Barbara. These, admittedly, were not for lower-income visitors. Most had an array of spur tracks for the private-railroad-car trade, and beginning at the turn of the century, they competed successfully with Florida as the winter resorts for such monied easterners as the Rockefellers, du Ponts, Cudahays, and their ilk.

Southern California attracted hosts of less affluent citizenry from

When visiting the Big Trees was an adventure.
— *L.L. Davis* — *U.S. Forest Service*

Potter Hotel in Santa Barbara, ca. 1905, when it was a stately pleasure dome of the winter resort trade. — *Author's Collection*

the East and Middle West who came to bask in the sun and avoid the rigors of severe winters. In fact, San Diego attracted so many of the elderly infirm that it was known at one time as the "city of suicides." One of Southern California's largest annual gatherings was the picnic of former Iowans at Long Beach; and Lodi, near Stockton, became a favored winter rendezvous for South Dakotans.

California long has been a favorite spot for summer tourists, as the number of out-of-state licenses on the freeways inescapably attests. Yosemite Valley entertains "wall-to-wall" people all through the season to the traditional Labor Day weekend. Such widely publicized attractions as Disneyland and Marineland-of-the-Pacific and their imitators exert a powerful pull among peoples of all the world, and they benefit from the low construction costs and the greater number of operating days per year made possible by the climate.

San Diego's double-decker street cars, 1905.
— Calif. Historical Society — T.I.T. Coll.

The Sierra Nevada, where the Donners perished, where Snowshoe Thompson did his deeds, gives California a tremendous winter sports region for devotees of "*skeeing*" or "*sheeing*," as you prefer. California's first organized ski races were staged at La Porte, once known as Rabbitt Creek, in the 1850's, and outsiders were invited to compete in these events for the first time in 1860. Snowshoe Thompson is said to have cost his backers $500 by losing to the La Porte racers, when the latter invited his participation. Today, the roads into the ski country are as thronged on winter weekends as ever they were in the days of traffic to the Comstock Lode. And today, whenever the winter storms do not perform as they should, ski resorts use thousands of gallons of water per night to make artificial snow for the enjoyment of skiers and snow-bunnies.

California's coast lacks the great combers of the "Banzai Tube" on the windward side of Oahu, but the cry of "Surf's up!" attracts thousands of devotees at all seasons of the year — even when, to this thin-blooded, over thirty writer, the water would make an Antarctic-born penguin demand a battery-heated wet suit. The first surfboard used by the famous Duke Kahanamoku was fabricated from California redwood; today, California leads the nation in the manufacture of light, be-ruddered polyurethane surfboards. Surfing has become a virtual way of life for its fanatics, and this has given rise to the cry, "Would you want your daughter to marry a surfer?" among those who seek to disparage all things Southern Californian.

Far less strenuous recreation than surfing or skiing, and one perhaps more aesthetically rewarding than watching those who do, is to be found in awaiting the return each year of the swallows to San Juan Capistrano. These birds find their counterparts in the insect world in the hosts of monarch butterflies (*Amosaie plexipus*) that migrate each autumn from east of the Rocky Mountains to warm themselves through the mild coastal winter by clustering on two tall pines at Asilomar, near Pacific Grove. These are the only members of the order *Lepidoptera* known to make annual migrations; and they have the singular status, so far as it is known to this writer, of being the only insect protected by a municipal ordinance.

The camera work of Edweard Muybridge — there are those who accent the last syllable of his surname — in capturing the action of a running horse on Leland Stanford's farm near Palo Alto is held by some to be the birth of the motion picture. The initial recorded showing of "pictures that moved," using examples of Muybridge's work, was held in San Francisco in 1880. Other sources maintain, apparently with more reason, that modern cinematography stems from pioneering work by French inventors.

America's pioneer picture-makers moved from the East Coast to California shortly after the turn of the century. One view is that they did so to escape their creditors. A stronger reason for the move seems inherent in the climate, which afforded more shooting days outdoors and thus reduced studio-use expense, and in the varied terrain and scenery which reduced expensive indoor set construction. Too, the cost of building studios was much

Sausalito and Richardson's Bay, ca. 1916, with Belevedere Island in right background.
— *Pacific Gas & Electric Co.*

Passion and tragedy before the camera, ca. World War I.　　　　　　　*— Calif. Historical Society*

lower in a climate that did not require, for example, steam heating or the burying of water pipes three feet below ground level to prevent freezing.

One of the first major sites for movie-making in California was at Niles Canyon, now a part of Fremont, where Essanay Studios cranked out hundreds of the "Bronco Billy" Anderson one- and two-reel "westerns," for the nickelodeon trade, and the "western" has remained staple film fare ever since. The California Motion Picture Company, financed by San Francisco entrepreneurs, had a studio near San Rafael, where it made a dozen or more films, most of which starred Beatriz Michelena, including the daring and highly acclaimed "The Unwritten Law." Between 1910-14, however, the industry became concentrated in a Southern California community that had been founded in 1887 as a temperance colony. When the film makers discovered Hollywood, it had fewer than 5,000 people and boasted a civic ordinance prohibiting the driving of more than 2,000 sheep at a time down what became Hollywood Boulevard. The big event of its daily life was the arrival of the stage from Los Angeles to Toluca Lake.

Why the film industry left the sophisticated and cosmopolitan mileu of the San Francisco region for the more rigidly conventional, evangelical atmosphere then enveloping the City of the Angels and its suburbs seems best explained by the latter's superior scenic and climatic conditions in the pre-smog days. An added inducement may have been the proximity of the Mexican border, which then offered swift sanctuary via automobile from creditors and strict interpretationists of other statutes.

The rise of the motion picture industry was sparked by the "feature" film, meaning one of more than two reels, and its development of the "star" system turned Gladys Smith into Mary Pickford at $10,000 per week. The impact of these developments upon the American public made Los Angeles a news source rivaling the world's greatest cities. Even such grubby stories as the "Fatty" Arbuckle scandal, or Wally Reid's destruction by hard drugs, made news for America and the world at large. And publicity was publicity, for the industry and for California, following the old maxim, "I don't care what they say about me, as long as they spell my name correctly!" By 1946, weekly "movie" attendance reached 90,000,000 persons nationally.

Hollywood and its environs became a tourist attraction *par excellence*; more importantly, it became the entertainment capital of America, and it largely has retained this position as the industry moved away from movies into radio and then into television. Today, most feature films and perhaps 25% of *all* the films made in America come from the producing center known loosely as Hollywood. (These figures are accurate when written, they may not be when read, so swiftly does change affect the cinema-television production matrix.) The effects of this industry on California's economy cannot be measured accurately but they have been most substantial and prolonged.

A by-product of the movie industry in the "Home of the Stars" has been to give a most prosperous boost to the fashion world, or garment trade, if you prefer. Los Angeles now is second only to New York City in clothing production. Another by-product was the rise of a cosmetics industry out of the wizardry of the Max Factors and Perc Westmores who prepared filmdom's greats for their celluloidal roles. Technologically speaking the foundation laid down by this variegated industry also contributed to the rise of the electronics industry which today is so important to California.

The aircraft industry has progressed immeasureably from the days when the correct way to determine whether a biplane was rigged to airworthiness was to release a sparrow between its wings: if the bird escaped, you needed

Miss Scott at Dominguez Field air meet. If there is a safety belt it is hard to see.
— Calif. Historical Society — T.I.T. Collection

more wire! The full measure of its growth has been due in great part to California's climate, which provided more flying days per year in the days before sophisticated instrumentation, and much lower plant construction costs.

Frederick Marriott, a transplanted Englishman with a passion for aerial navigation, raised enough money in Northern California to form the Aerial Steam Navigation Company in 1866. Its only product was finished in mid-1869; a blimp-type craft that was 37 feet long by 14 feet wide, with a cloth-covered wing on each side at the end of which was a propellor driven by a small, brass alcohol steam engine. On July 2, 1869, she made the first lighter-than-air flight in the United States, staying in the air for more than ten minutes and attaining a speed of five mph. In that same year, the rails were joined in Utah and the need for speedy communication with the East had been resolved.

More significant to the science of aerodynamics was the work of John Joseph Montgomery. Twenty years before the Wright brothers got off the ground, he made a heavier-than-air glider flight off Otay Mesa near San Diego on August 28, 1883. Montgomery has been dubbed the "Father of Basic Flying," because of his discovery of the lifting principle of an airfoil, which was the vacuum above it. He was killed in 1911 during another glider experiment at what is now Montgomery Hill in the community of Santa Clara.

Bewhiskered and eccentric, Lyman Gilmore is another Californian accorded stature as a pre-Wright brothers pioneer. Born in Cowlitz, Washington in 1874, Gilmore is said to have made a heavier-than-air flight in a glider he designed and built himself in 1891, when a precocious seventeen years of age. In May 1902, at the Big Meadows, now Lake Almanor, in the knuckle of the Sierra-Cascade ranges, Gilmore claimed to have made a truly significant heavier-than-air flight of two minutes duration. The plane was of his own design and construction, powered by a steam engine, and launched into the air down a chute. In 1908, he did build the world's first cabin monoplane, which did not fly, and another smaller plane that did. When his planes and hangar at Grass Valley were destroyed by fire in 1935, he abandoned his interest in aeronautics.

The state's commercial aircraft industry had its humble beginnings between 1906-09 in an abandoned church in downtown Santa Ana, when Glenn L. Martin, one of aviation's great pioneers, began building planes there. Both he and Glenn Curtiss, another aviation great, were emigres from the hazards and expenses of eastern weather, and Curtiss founded the first flying school in the state at North Island in San Diego. The first air meet in the United States was held at Dominguez Hill, between Compton and Long Beach, January 10-20, 1910, and Curtiss set a new world's speed record of *sixty miles per hour*! At this same meet, Louis Paulhan, a French aviator, set an altitude record of 4,149 feet in a Farman biplane and delivered a passenger safely to Redondo Beach, 20 miles away. Later this same year, another air meet was held at Tanforan Race Track, near San Francisco, and in 1911, Eugene Ely made the first carrier-type landing by setting his Curtiss "pusher" biplane down on the deck of the *USS Pennsylvania* in San Francisco Bay. On May 10, 1912, Glenn Martin made the world's first water-to-water flight, which also was the longest and fastest overwater flight to that time, when he flew a hydroplane from Balboa to Avalon Bay at Catalina Island.

World War I, of course, gave a tremendous boost to aviation use and development, and between the two world wars, Southern California blossomed as the home of the nation's most noted aircraft. The first planes to fly around the world were the products of Donald Douglas' talents, which he

A Wright Brothers "Model B" at Dominguez Field air meet.
— *Calif. Historical Society — T.I.T. Collection*

An intrepid airman, probably Richard S. Ely, pioneers sea-going flight from the crude flight deck of *USS Pennsylvania* in San Francisco Bay, ca 1911. — *The Bancroft Library*

had developed as chief designer for Glenn Martin, before breaking away to start his own firm in the back room of a barber shop on Pico Boulevard in Los Angeles, which he later moved to Santa Monica.

In the between-wars period, too, the Navy established its Pacific aviation headquarters at North Island in San Diego Bay. Alan and Malcolm Lougheed moved their manufacturing plant from a garage in Santa Barbara to Burbank in 1920 and became the Lockheed company. T. Claude Ryan established the first regularly scheduled airline service in the state with daily flights from San Diego to Los Angeles in 1922, and the next year, he founded the San Diego company that built the "Spirit of St. Louis" in which Lindbergh made his epic transatlantic flight in 1927. In this same year, Maitland and Hegenberger won the disastrous Dole transpacific air race to Hawaii from Oakland, and the first airmail was flown from California to New York. The mail flight began at a forgotten field near Concord, east of San Francisco, and required almost 33 hours and 15 stops for its completion. The fare was $404 per passenger. Finally, in 1928, a wealthy resident of Los Angeles, Captain G. Allan Hancock, financed the 7,800-mile flight between California and Australia that brought its Australian pilot a knighthood and made the names of Sir Charles Kingsford-Smith and the "Southern Cross" world famous.

These examples point the premise that the productive heart of the nation's aircraft manufacturing capacity was beating in Southern California between the wars. During World War II, its pulsing heart beats made the difference between Allied air supremacy and defeat, a matter exemplified by the aircraft industry's jump from 20,000 employees in California in 1939 to 243,000 in 1943. Together with its offshoots, the aircraft industry created a reservoir of skilled engineers and technicians who could and did adapt to the needs of space-age contracting and production.

The airplane is ubiquitous in California's daily life. Its use for seeding, fertilizing, and insecticide application in agriculture has been noted; so has its use in forest-fire fighting. It is also used for pest control and reforestation in this vital industry; for aerial surveying and mapping, and for swift patrol of long-distance electrical transmission and telephone lines. Few radio disc jockeys could earn their salt without a traffic-spotting helicopter to keep their audiences abreast of what is happening during the rush hours on the state's assorted freeways and other urban "dodge-em" arenas.

Muroc Dry Lake is a testing ground for supersonic aircraft, and Edwards Air Force Base encompasses 300,000 acres and boasts 350 good flying days per year. It also provides the basic landing site for the space shuttle craft, while another space shuttle landing field is slated for Vandenberg Air Force Base near Santa Maria. The Mojave Desert community of Palmdale has mushroomed because of the space and flying days it offered the aircraft and space-age industries of the Los Angeles Lowlands. The vast air terminals are an integral part of (and annoyance to) the state's great urban centers, but

Glenn Martin's great flying boat "China Clipper" throbs over the San Francisco waterfront on the start of its historic air mail flight to Manila, November 22, 1935. Flying time was 59 hours, 49 minutes, with overnight stops at Honolulu, Midway, Wake Island and Guam. Flying time today is less than 16 hours with no overnight stops. — *Pan American World Airways*

without such terminal facilities, these urban centers would not have the interstate transportation facilities the railroads once provided, to say nothing of international flights.

The climate and terrain of California add one soothing factor in the air age: the sport of gliding. The best sailplane currents in the world, it is said, are found on the east side of the Sierra in the Owens Valley region; there the "Sierra Wave" permits superlative soaring. From the White Mountains, across Owens Valley from Mt. Whitney, a hang gliding flight of four hours and 67 miles to Mina, Nevada, set a local record. Less spectacular but equally soul-satisfying gliding can be done virtually throughout the state. The first *man-powered* heavier-than-air flight was made in 1977 over a course in Kern County with Bryan Allen doing the pedalling in a machine designed by Paul MacReady of Pasadena. Allen pedalled another MacReady creation, the *Gossamer Albatross*, across the English Channel from England to France, while MacReady, incidentally, in 1956, became the first international soaring champion from the United States.

It was because of the climate that pure science, which is here defined as the pursuit of scientific knowledge for its own sake, first came to California. Astronomical observatories, such as those at Mount Wilson, Mount Hamilton, and Palomar Mountain, were so located because the clarity of the atmosphere made observations clearer and longer than elsewhere; and here again, the climate reduced construction costs far below those where the winters were more severe. Palomar holds the world's second largest *optical* telescope, which is exceeded only by one of 236 inches in Russia. What these began, today produces space probes fired from the Vandenberg Missile Range that have lighted up the evening sky upon occasion as far north as San Francisco, and clogged police department switchboards with queries.

The human link between past and present explorations of space in California seems personified in the bewhiskered, shrewd, and crafty realist named James Lick. A piano-maker from Pennsylvania, Lick came to California by way of South America, where he had prospered, and arrived in San Francisco in 1847 with perhaps $30,000 in his possession. He eschewed the Gold Rush and its attendant mercantile pursuits, and concentrated his energies in real estate investment. He was reputedly worth some $4,000,000 by the early 1870's, when Professor George Davidson, then president of the California Academy of Sciences, introduced him to star-gazing through a homemade telescope atop one of San Francisco's famous hills. For whatever reasons — perhaps because their lonely, pristine beauty stirred his soul — James Lick fell in love with the stars. At his death in 1876, he bequeathed $700,000 (a colossal sum in those days) to build an observatory for the advancement of science. Mount Hamilton, 4,261 feet above sea level, was selected as the site, and Lick Observatory atop its crest was completed in 1888. The first true study of the nebulae was made there.

Intertwined with the advent of science has been the growth of what properly can be called technological "knowledge centers." By this is meant such institutions as California Institute of Technology, whose evolution from Amos "Father" Throop's private school for boys and girls was stimulated by the first solar research conducted atop Mount Wilson, high above the then smog-free and orange-grove dotted residential community of Pasadena. Not to be overlooked are such other assets as the major scientific research centers at Stanford University, the University of California at Berkeley, and UCLA. Ernest O. Lawrence built the world's first cyclotron at Berkeley in 1929, which made possible the experiments that led to plutonium production and the first nuclear fission explosion in history. The Stanford Linear Accelerator, the world's longest, serves as a testing station for both pure and applied research in many fields, including medicine. At Cal Tech, Theodore von Karman promoted research into both aerodynamics and jet propulsion which led to creation of that university's world-famous Jet Propulsion Laboratory,

From biplanes to Space Age vehicles, California has played a leading role towards a future beyond imagination.
— *The Bancroft Library*

and later spawned Aerojet General, the first private rocket building firm in the nation. All these bear witness to the cross-fertilizing effects of the growth of scientific activity and its translation into applied technology by the reservoir of talents such institutions have made possible.

The Gold Rushers have been criticized for not paying much attention to public education. Considering that they were predominantly bachelors who intended to make a "pile" and take it back home, this is understandable, even though the criticism overlooks the fact that the first state constitution called for a free public grammar school in each district within the state, with such to be held for *at least three months each year*. San Francisco got its first public high school in 1856, well after higher education had been served by sectarian zeal. University (then College) of the Pacific opened its doors at San Jose in 1851 in testimony to Methodist energy, while the College (now University) of Santa Clara arose this same year in Catholic counterpoint. The first woman's college established west of the Rocky Mountains began in 1851 as a seminary in Benicia, which was bought by Cyrus and Susan Mills to become Mills College in the Oakland foothills. The College of California in Oakland was absorbed by the University of California in 1869, which then moved to the nucleus of its present Berkeley campus and graduated its first class of twelve in 1873.

The University of California system now boasts eight campuses, while the State University system, which arose out of the state's first teacher training institutions, or Normal Schools, has nineteen campuses throughout the state. California has pioneered in the development of the "Community college" concept ever since the city of Fresno established the state's first public junior college in 1910. Commitment to quality public education has been of incalculable value in maintaining and stimulating the state's growth and the quality of its intellectual life. The importance of this educational commitment is accentuated by the wave of emigrants, both legal and "undocumented," from Latin America and Asia. In San Francisco, enrollment in the public schools due to this influx grew at a rate during 1981-82 faster than any other of the nation's fifty largest school systems. This at a time when enrollments are dropping in most school districts. The expansion of this commitment at every level is the *sine qua non* in keeping California a place for those who seek to better their condition in life in the "Golden Shore by the Sundown Sea."

Today's electronics industry had its beginnings on what had been Leland Stanford's favorite farm. In 1912 at Stanford University, Lee de Forrest began his experiments that made him the inventor of the oscillating vacuum tube, the precursor of the wonders of solid-state and miniaturized electronics, not to mention whatever major advances may be made after these lines are written. De Forrest also developed experimental sound films that became the ancestors of the "talkies" in the late 1920's.

Concurrently with de Forrest's experiments, Charles Herold's "wireless" laboratories at San Jose made the first radio station broadcast — using a "carpet" antenna comprised of *11,000 feet* of wire strung back and forth between two tall buildings. This evolved into radio station KQW, which secured the first federal license for radio telephony, and then into station KFRC, which originated the first audience show in radio history with Al Pearce's "Blue Monday Jamboree." Radio's first dynamic speaker, the Magnavox, was produced at Oakland in 1922, and the first radio drama — the ineffably soapy "One Man's Family" — began its generation spanning run over KGO, San Francisco, in 1932.

All of the scientific skills and technological knowhow that had been accumulated through the cinema, communications and aircraft industries was put to good use even before Pearl Harbor. Then the advent of World War II became more significant to present-day California than any of the strands that had been weaving and interweaving since the Gold Rush ended. Conscious of it or not, California became not the end of the rainbow in the West, but the nation's window upon the Pacific. In this sense, California came again to what she had known under Spain and Mexico — the sea beyond the sundown shore tempted her with possibilities and plunged her into dangers out of the old, well-known Atlantic World.

Expanding a process that had begun before the nation was involved directly as a belligerent, the Army built huge training camps near Monterey, Paso Robles, San Luis Obispo and Santa Maria. The Marine Corps established a West Coast equivalent of its Quantico, Virginia, base near Oceanside, and the Air Force laid down major training centers at Victorville, Merced, Santa Ana and Chico. The Navy, too, enlarged and improved its facilities at Mare Island and San Diego; acquired Treasure Island in San Francisco Bay; took over Terminal Island in Los Angeles Harbor and developed Port Hueneme as a true deep-water port, as well as the headquarters for its famous Construction Battalions, or Seabees. These massive installations, coupled with government spending for military goods and services and other aspects of national defense, poured $35,000,000,000 into the state between 1942-46, a yearly average nearly twice the average value of all California production in the pre-war years.

Unencumbered by commitments to outmoded products and systems of production, California leaped ahead of the nation in every way. Shipyards went in at Eureka, San Francisco, Sausalito, Richmond, Oakland, Alameda, San Pedro and San Diego, and these produced more than one-third of all the Liberty ships produced in the nation. The integrated steel plant at Fontana, the first such west of the Rockies, was a wartime product; oil production went from 226,000,000 barrels per year to 378,000,000, a figure exceeded only rarely since those years, textiles, machinery of all kinds, chemicals, electronic gear, and agriculture more than doubled in production, with the result that the state crammed twenty or more years of industrial development into just five.

This tremendous expansion created an equally enormous demand for man-power, which was aggravated by the fact that more than 700,000 Californians were transferred from the labor pool into the armed forces and the Japanese segment of the labor force was interned. Unemployment in California dropped from 380,000 in 1940 to just 25,000 by the end of 1943 and the wartime industries went out and recruited workers all over the nation, particularly in the South where farm mechanization had left thousands of Negroes out of work. The *bracero* program was instituted to bring in farm labor from Mexico to meet the needs of California agriculture, and the legal emigration from Mexico, in which the *braceros* were not counted, more than doubled during the war years. Workers in manufacturing jumped from 461,000 to 1,186,000 during these years and the total labor force went from 2,703,000 to 3,854,000. On top of these increases were the hundreds of thousands of service personnel, either stationed in California, or in staging areas awaiting shipment overseas. During the war, California gained 1,315 new residents each and every day for more than five years.

This influx continued after the war was over. Service personnel who had discovered California during the war descended upon the state after their discharge. This influx came from all sections of the nation and added a younger and a better educated element to the population than any of the preceding waves of population, except the Gold Rush. The influx of Mexicans, both legal and illegal, increased and these began to refer to themselves as Chicanos, from *Mexicano*, the "x" having a "ch" sound in Nahuatl, the language of the Aztec. An excellent work on these peoples is *The Chicanos: A History of the Mexican Americans* by Matt S. Meier and Feliciano Rivera. From 1940-70, the state gained 13,000,000 in population, which works out to 49 per hour for each of these thirty years.

California's economy had a sustained impetus during these years from continued federal spending for national defense, particularly in the aircraft and aerospace industries, as the Korean War was followed by the Cold War years and then by the nation's involvement in Southeast Asia. Before the National Aeronautics & Space Administration (NASA) was located at Houston, Texas (through, it would appear, political divination during Lyndon Johhnson's tenure in the White House), California far outstripped the rest of the nation in the value of federal "prime contracts" for space-age research and development. The slowdown in the value of such contracts and its effect upon the state can be seen in the slowing of California's growth rate in the early 1970's. Such space-age contracts again are increasing.

The reservoir of both pure and applied science that the state possesses are of maximum importance and this nowhere is better illustrated than in what has come to be known as "Silicon Valley." Stretching north from San Jose for twenty-five miles, in what once was the "Prune Capital" of the world, it holds perhaps the greatest concentration of brain power in the nation, if not the world. This is home to some 600-800 companies, no one knows how many at any given time, because if they "mass produce millionaires," as *Fortune* says, they also mass produce mergers, dissolutions, and failure, so intense is the competition. The area takes its name from the ubiquitous semi-conductors, engraved wafers of silicon about one-quarter-inch square, which enable a mini-computer today to do the calculating that would have cost $1,000,000 twenty years ago. These have taken the space probe to Jupiter, revolutionized the computer industry, and, in the process created what has been called the "world's largest job market," from specialized scientific and engineering skills to custodians.

Silicon Valley exemplifies what the post-war years have brought the state because of its accumulated reservoir of talents and skills; and what Californians have been doing since the Gold Rush: *"performing difficult tasks for substantial rewards at considerable risk."*

CHAPTER FOURTEEN

FROM YANG-NA TO IMPERIAL CITY

The shape of the future is said to be the "megalopolis," the overpowering urban concentration that will make today's greatest cities seem no more than the rustic villages of a bygone time. Three of these are foreseen for California: one will cover the southern coast with a solid mass of humanity from San Diego to San Luis Obispo; another will dominate the Great Valley from above Sacramento to Bakersfield; and the third will engulf the San Francisco Bay region from San Rafael to Salinas-Monterey.

It is in this megalopolitan context that the rise of Los Angeles has been the most significant California development of the twentieth century. Reapportionment of the state legislature has given political domination of the state to Southern California, with the key being held by the City and County of Los Angeles. This allocation of political power was justified on the grounds that it provided the greatest good for the greatest number, which is a modern way of expressing the old saying that "might makes right." It has been justified as well on the grounds that approximately 70% of the state's total tax revenues are derived from Southern California. This tax base reflects the status of Los Angeles as an economic power within the state, surpassing the long-established eminence of San Francisco in this respect.

History reveals a pendulum-like swing between power centers in the state. During the Mexican period, 1822-46, Southern California held the edge, both in people and property. The Gold Rush swung the power center to San Francisco and north-central California. The rise of Los Angeles returned it to the southland, where it seems destined to remain; unless, of course, everything west of the San Andreas Fault suddenly cracks off and disappears beneath the sea, which would be the ultimate expression of "The Westward Tilt." It should be noted that 97% of Los Angeles' population has come there since 1900. Before that date, the evolution of Indian village into *pueblo* into city had proceeded with almost glacial rapidity.

In 1781 the *Gabrieleno* village of *Yang-Na* provided the site of the second true *pueblo* established by Spain in California. Its first settlers, eleven *pobladores* and their families, had made the overland trek from Sinaloa; they were the Indian, Negro and *mestizo* admixture of Spain's northern frontier. By 1797, the village had grown to perhaps 300 persons, who still dwelled in brush-and-tule habitations, because they were kept too busy farming to feed themselves to spare time for building proper *adobe* abodes.

Where to play Russian Roulette in rush hour traffic   — *Calif. Dept. of Transportation*

The settlement did not get *ciudad* (city) status from Mexico until 1835, after secularization of the missions, when the American forces occupied it in 1846, it had a population of perhaps 3,000 *poco mas o menos*. Even after the Gold Rush brought a fleeting prosperity to the great *ranchero* families, it slumbered on. As T.H. Watkins has said so well:

> When compared to the simple vigor of San Francisco and Sacramento, the towns of the south seemed preserved in aspic for a generation, gelid in their development and more than a little primitive in their social structure. San Diego and Santa Barbara had risen barely above village status by 1860 and the region's leading metropolis, Los Angeles, could be described in that year as a "city of some 3,500 or 4,000 inhabitants, a regular old Spanish-Mexican town, where fifty to sixty murders per year have been common."

No wonder it won the name of *El Pueblo de los Diablos*!

In 1860, Los Angeles held less than 2% of the state's total assessed valuation of $147,104,955 in real and personal property. Its first "boomlet" occurred in the decade of the 1860's and was due to two things: the growing scarcity of land at reasonable prices in the northern part of the state and the climate of the southland. Agricultural colonies flourished — Etiwanda, Ontario, Riverside, Compton, and Pasadena, plus the German colony at

Passengers and train crew pose after arrival in Los Angeles during the "Boom of the Eighties."
— *Calif. Historical Society — T.I.T. Collection*

"We're giving the land away; it's the climate we're selling" — "Lucky" Baldwin, 1890.
— Calif. Historical Society — T.I.T. Collection

Anaheim. By 1870, cultivated land in Los Angeles County alone had increased from 5,000 acres to nearly 40,000, and the city had almost 17,000 residents, two *genuine* banks, and a railroad to its harbor at San Pedro. The financial crises and drought of the 1870's saw Los Angeles shrink to less than 12,000 inhabitants by 1880.

It was helped out of this slough of despond by the silver discoveries at Cerro Gordo (Fat Mountain) two miles above sea level in the Inyo Range, which some enthusiasts say produced $28,000,000 in silver and lead over a ten-year period. Whatever these mines produced was a veritable bonanza to Los Angeles, and Remi Nadeau's great freight teams that supplied the mines and hauled back the silver made an enormous market for hay and grain to fuel his motive power. The real growth of the southland began when it gained a railroad connection with the rest of the nation, and this growth exploded when it got two such connections.

The Espee and the Santa Fe met at Deming, New Mexico in 1881 for the first link; arrival of the Santa Fe via Needles and Barstow in 1885 was the second. These gave Los Angeles a much larger trading area in the Southwest than it had enjoyed before, and expanded its position as a distribution and investment center. The Santa Fe planned a great oceanside terminal at Redondo Beach, while the Espee had similar ideas for Santa Monica. More than this localized rivalry, the two railroads set in motion the first great "boom" in Southern California's history.

On the morning of March 6, 1887, the two roads went to the mat on one-way fares from Kansas City to Los Angeles. That morning they opened even at $12 per passenger; the Santa Fe dropped to $10 and the Espee met that and dropped to $6, the Santa Fe met that and dropped even more. By early afternoon, the one-way fare had reached the ridiculous figure of exactly $1. The rates quickly bounced back from this low but never to what they had been before the scrimmage began. The Espee alone brought

The Big Red Cars served all of Los Angeles and served it well.
— *Calif. Historical Society* — *T.I.T. Collection*

120,000 immigrants to California in the year that followed this fare fight, and people of all ages, conditions and economic assets swarmed into Southern California in a lemming-like display unseen since the Gold Rush. Towns were laid out in the dry bed of the Los Angeles River, and on the ridge-ribs of the adjacent mountains where only a mountain goat or a hot-air balloon could provide transportation. Town site promoters had their agents meet trains at the California border with sales pitches that would make a carnival barker blush with shame. The "Boom of the Eighties" fizzled out, as all such do, but its enduring impact is shown by the population growth of Los Angeles and Orange counties from 33,400 in 1880 to 190,000 in 1900.

This growth was aided by the upsurge in petroleum production brought about by the Los Angeles City Field. It was given another boost by the successful struggle to build a good harbor with federal funds at San Pedro, the "hellhole" of the coast in the hide-and-tallow days, rather than at Santa Monica where the Espee controlled the waterfront acreage. Another shot in the arm, so to speak, came with its third transcontinental rail link in 1906, when the present Union Pacific line was completed from Salt Lake City. By 1910 Los Angeles boasted 310,000 people and was the hub of what soon became the largest rapid transit system in the world — the "Big Red Cars" of the Pacific Electric Railway system, the true creator of the urban sprawl that the automobile carried to excess. Los Angeles also had a problem — a thirst for water that was not due to its temperance tendencies.

From the time of its founding, Los Angeles had the right under Spanish law to *ALL* the water of the Los Angeles River. This sensible notion that defined a city by its watershed brought complications when new towns appeared upstream after the Civil War. It required several hundred lawsuits after 1880 to establish the city's right to its *pueblo* water heritage that was being used in Glendale and elsewhere. The same principle applied to San Diego, although it was much later in coming to a legal victory because the growth pressure there was long delayed. In large measure this delay was due to Los Angeles' growth. Today, however, San Diego is the second largest city in the state, thus relegating San Francisco to third.

Los Angeles' growth was made possible, after the Los Angeles River had been tapped for all it could supply, largely by the foresight, energy, and determination of William Mulholland, chief engineer of the city's municipally owned water company, who had emigrated from his native Ireland to become a ditch tender on the old *zanja madre*. His solution to the city's water problem, without which it could not have grown much beyond its 1910 figure, was the waters flowing down the eastern slope of the High Sierra into Owens Valley. To bring this water to Los Angeles would require crossing a desert as large as the state of Massachusetts, with a system of aqueducts, tunnels, siphons, and dams more than 200 miles long. It also would require purchasing lands in Owens Valley that held the water rights necessary to Mulholland's plan.

Wm. Mulholland did not waste words. "There it is," he said, "Take it!" as the first water from Owens Valley gushed into the San Fernando Reservoir.　　　　　　　　　　　　　　　　*— L.A. County Museum*

Working secretly but offering fair prices, the city's agents committed it to more than $1,000,000 in land costs alone. President Theodore Roosevelt was persuaded to abandon plans for a Bureau of Reclamation dam in Owens Valley, and the city then passed a $23,000,000 bond issue, the largest ever undertaken by any municipality anywhere at that time, to finance construction which began in 1906. Rumors went around and persist today that wealthy *Angelenos*, such as Harrison Gray Otis, owner of the *Los Angeles Times*, had financed the successful bond issue campaign because they owned land in the San Fernando Valley that would acquire irrigation water from Owens Valley. The truth of the matter is that Otis and others *had* acquired San Fernando Valley land *before* the bond issue had been proposed and they had done this because they knew that Henry E. Huntington was going to extend his Big Red Cars into the valley and their grain fields would appreciate in value thereby.

After seven years of arduous labor, the first large-scale water supply system in the West was finished. More than 15,000 spectators gathered at the northeast corner of San Fernando Valley on November 5, 1913 to watch the first surge of water tumble down into the reservoir. By 1915, Los Angeles had annexed most of San Fernando Valley and by 1920 it had grown to

(Above) Answering the alarm! Fifth and Hill Streets, 1900. (Below) Los Angeles mounted police, May, 1904, on Broadway.
— *Calif. Historical Society — T.I.T. Collection*

576,000, surpassing San Francisco for the first time.

Among the many features of the Owens Valley aqueduct was the San Francisquito Dam above the Newhall Basin, which was designed to ensure a year's supply of water for the city should anything happen to the system that supplied it. It fulfilled this purpose between 1924-27 and then, in the early morning darkness of March 12, 1928, it simply and suddenly collapsed. A wall of water roared down the canyon into the Newhall Basin and funnelled down the Santa Clara River to the sea below Ventura, traveling 54 miles in less than six hours, and claiming more than 400 lives and wiping out millions upon millions in property damage. It remains the *largest man-made disaster* in California's history to date. Even though it appears that what today are known as the "earth sciences" were not sufficiently developed then to give Mulholland the geological data necessary to have precluded the dam's location where he placed it, he stood up and took the blame for the faulty engineering that had caused his masterpiece to crumble. Despite this manly stand, a rumor gained credence that sabotage, not Mulholland's engineering, broke the dam asunder.

This rumor had its source in the war of sabotage that Owens Valley residents began against the aqueduct in 1924. This first great water war in the West erupted because Los Angeles was using almost all the water to which it was entitled by its original purchases in Owens Valley. The city's agents began efforts to buy more land with attached water rights in 1923, but the prices asked were deemed outrageous. The impasse then was punctuated by the dynamiting of portions of the aqueduct no less than nine times between 1924-27. In the end, Los Angeles paid more than $12,000,000 for the land it needed, and "The Rape of Owens Valley" was completed. The aqueduct system was thrust north into the Mono Lake drainage in 1940, and Crowley Lake was constructed to store more water for Los Angeles. It is a favorite recreation area for southland residents today, and Owens Valley numbers more permanent residents than it did before Los Angeles slaked its first great thirst for water. This thirst today threatens the destruction of Mono Lake, which Mark Twain dubbed "The Dead Sea of the West," and its destruction would mean the loss of a unique natural wonder.

An outgrowth of the Owens Valley water supply was the need to pay for its cost, at least in part, by selling the electric power it could generate. This put Los Angeles into the public power business, a paradox in what was an adamantly "open shop" city. This militant anti-unionism was helped by the continued flow of inmigrants, which kept the labor pool filled with people eager to take any kind of work to get their start on a new life in sunny Southern California. Trade union efforts in 1910 to organize the city's skilled crafts met violent opposition from employers, supported by the *Los Angeles Times*. This culminated in the dynamiting of the newspaper's building on October 1 in which 20 employees were killed and 17 injured. This cost Job Harriman, the Socialist candidate for mayor, his chance for election,

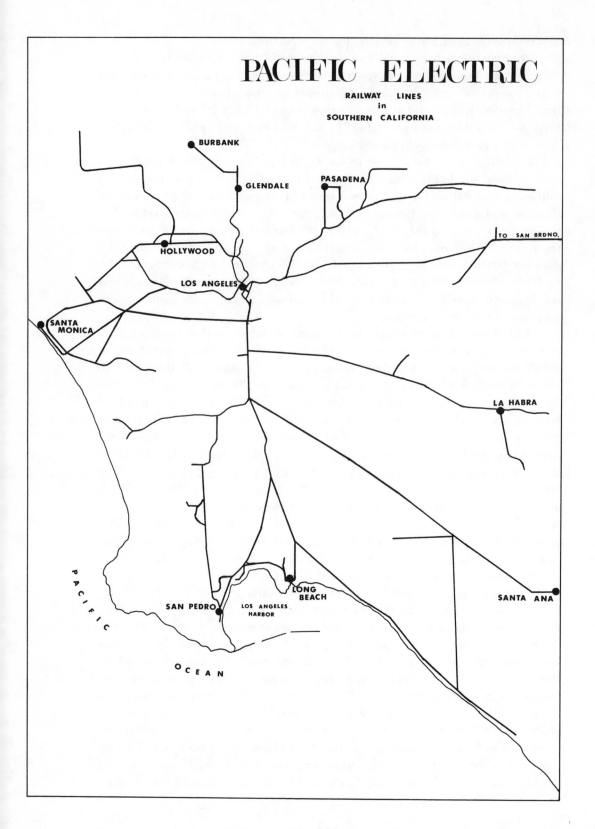

PACIFIC ELECTRIC

RAILWAY LINES
in
SOUTHERN CALIFORNIA

BURBANK

GLENDALE

PASADENA

TO SAN BRDNO.

HOLLYWOOD

LOS ANGELES

SANTA MONICA

LA HABRA

PACIFIC

SAN PEDRO

LOS ANGELES HARBOR

LONG BEACH

SANTA ANA

OCEAN

and gave organized labor in Los Angeles a setback that lasted until the maritime unions flexed their collective muscle in 1932-36.

The need for more electric power led to another imperial expansion northwards, when the Southern California Edison Company reached across the Tehachapi Range to develop hydroelectric power on the west side of the Sierra near Huntington Lake. The city's public power proponents, led by the reformers who would spearhead its political cleansing, succeeded in forcing the utility company to sell its facilities inside the city limits to the Los Angeles Department of Water and Power which, with other acquisitions, became one of the largest municipally-owned systems in the world. A 500,000 volt transmission line from John Day Dam on the Columbia River — a part of the federally owned Bonneville Power Administration — has been built into the Great Valley near Redding, where it feeds into the system that carries additional power to the south land when such is needed and available.

While the city operates its own water and electric systems, Pacific Lighting Corporation still supplies its natural gas with more than 36,000 *miles* of transmission and distribution lines. These serve more than 3,600,000 gas connections, one out of every 12 gas customers in the nation, more than any other gas distributor in the nation, and with the cities of Long Beach and San Diego as wholesale customers, serve 600,000 more connections. More than 95% of the natural gas consumed in Southern California comes from outside the state, primarily from the American Southwest. A growing uncertainty as to the future of these sources of supply, and the need to import supplies from Indonesia and Alaska in the form of liquified natural gas (LNG), explains the company's plans to construct an unloading terminal at Little Cojo Bay, near Point Concepcion, which has brought pronounced opposition from environmentalists and Indian groups. Despite this opposition, the proposal has cleared the major regulatory hurdles but has been shelved until future needs make it necessary.

Fundamental to Los Angeles' northward expansion was the "good roads" program it boosted so ardently. The old road between Los Angeles and the San Joaquin Valley meandered across the Mojave Desert and Tehachapi Pass. This was replaced in 1915 by the Ridge Route motor highway (the "Grapevine" of infamous memory), which boasted a curvature equal to 110 full circles in its forty-eight miles. With this artery across the Tehachapi "knot," Los Angeles began to function as a magnet pulling the upper San Joaquin Valley southward. This effect has been reinforced and increased by successive highway improvements, U.S. 99 in 1933, and more recently Interstate 5. Good roads and San Pedro Harbor also determined Los Angeles' ability to dominate the trade of the Imperial and Coachella valleys as they developed under irrigation, a trade which San Diego had anticipated would be hers. The overpowering growth of "automobility" in the Southland now sends 400-500,000 vehicles per day past a single point near the Los Angeles Civic Center. Instead of creating "autopia," this has spawned a new definition of Los Angeles as "1,000 miles of freeways and 10,000 miles of cars."

Westlake Park in 1889.

Los Angeles — The Improbable City.

The possession of an adequate water supply was vital to the growth of the aircraft and cinema industries before and after World War I, and without it the tourist trade would not have kept on growing. Fish canning and women's apparel added new economic muscle, while automobile assembly plants, tire manufacturing factories, oil refineries, and salt-evaporating ponds grew apace. These attracted people, and people stimulated construction, and service industries multiplied to meet the needs of multiplying urban residents.

Between 1920-30, California added 2,251,000 people; of this number, 1,900,000 were out-of-state immigrants, and of these 1,368,000 settled in Southern California. It was an influx that exceeded the decade of the Gold Rush! By 1930, Los Angeles had 72,933 Illinoisans, 49,500 Missourians, 49,337 New Yorkers, 42,212 Ohioans, and 41,352 Iowans.It also had varieties of motor cars that were filling in the open spaces between communities already served by the Big Red Cars. The automobile, as it came to be known, eventually killed the Pacific Electric's interurban network, and even after the Arab oil embargo, Los Angeles' voters turned down a 1976 proposal to build a 232-mile mass-transit system. A subsequent proposal calls for a subway system from downtown Los Angeles under Wilshire Boulevard as far west as La Brea at an initial cost of more than $1,000,000,000, which undoubtedly will be much more due to unchecked inflation. Former governor "Jerry" Brown, proposed an even more costly mass-transit system that would utilize buses in the main.

The Great Depression, so it is remembered by this writer's generation, marks the first time that California had experienced the full effects of a national economic debacle. Although it suffered proportionately far less than the heavily industrialized population centers of the East and Mid-West, it was worse in Southern California than elsewhere in the state. By 1934, there were 1,250,000 people on the state's relief rolls, about 20% of the population. The great majority of these were clustered in Southern California, which led the nation in the number of bankrupticies, and seventy-nine persons leaped to their deaths from the Arroyo Seco bridge near Pasadena.

Still the lure of California, building in the national consciousness since the Gold Rush, exercised its appeal and thousands upon thousands flocked westward in the belief that it could not be any worse there than where they were, and certainly the climate would be milder. The state's growth rate slowed to its lowest level since 1850, but even so, it was a rate three times as large as that for the nation as a whole. The legislature reacted to this influx by passing an unconstitutional measure that closed the state's borders to "undesirables," an echo from the anti-Oriental agitation of the nineteenth century.

Together with the "Okies" and "Arkies" from the Dust Bowl regions, thousands of Negroes left the Deep South because of the depression and farm mechanization. The state's Black population increased by more than 50% in these years and a substantial number of them settled in Los Angeles, where, interestingly enough, one of the early streets of the Hispanic *pueblo* was called *Calle de los Negros*. By 1970, there were more Black people in California, than in any of the southern states except Texas. Approximately one-half this number lived in Los Angeles and of these about 90% lived in the south-central section of the city, where the chief sub-community was Watts. Los Angeles today has the largest proportion of blacks of any city in the nation after Washington, D.C.

Legal emigration from Mexico dropped sharply after 1930 and illegal emigration probably did so as well. In both cases, the reason was the same: no economic incentive to make the jump to a foreign land. Also, there were no great population pressures, such as exist today, or political upheavals in Mexico to force them out. Los Angeles had almost one-half the total Mexican population of 300,000 in California when the Depression hit, and had about this same proportion when the labor shortages of World War II triggered another movement out of Mexico towards the land of greater economic opportunity. This movement has continued ever since and Los Angeles today is the second largest Mexican center in the world and 30% or more of its population is Chicano. Their children have made both whites and blacks minority groups in the city's schools and the Mexican-American, legal, illegal or "undocumented" as the bureaucratic euphemism has it, has become the nation's largest ethnic minority, with California holding 30% of the total.

This has come about for the same reason that California always has attracted those seeking to better their condition in life. Each year, almost 1,000,000 Mexicans enter the job market there and available data indicates that one-half the labor force in Mexico is partially or wholly unemployed and that unemployment is growing. These predominantly are young males and Mexico today has twice as many people under the age of 15 as she had *total* population in 1950. Until Mexico's wealth in petroleum and natural gas can be utilized to improve and expand the socio-economic opportunities for her citizens, the United States in general and Southern California in particular will be the "safety valve" for her economically disadvantaged. A Chicano who knew both countries well summed up the difference during a class discussion in these words: "If you can be rich, be rich in Mexico; if you must be poor, be poor in the United States."

Amidst the depression gloom, construction of Hoover Dam on the Colorado River gave Los Angeles a ray of sunshine, not because it eliminated unemployment there but because it ensured the city's future. As early as 1920, William Mulholland had foreseen that Los Angeles would outgrow its water supply from Owens Valley. The only other major source was the silt-laden waters of the mighty Colorado, which was both an interstate and an international stream — draining parts of six other states and flowing into the Gulf of California. This problem would have to be resolved before a dam of the necessary magnitude could be built to store its water and generate power.

The first problem was solved in 1922, when Herbert Hoover, then Secretary of Commerce, convened a meeting of representatives from the seven affected states in Santa Fe, New Mexico. After days of heated arguments, it was agreed to allocate 15,000,000 acre feet per annum of the river's flow equally between the Upper Basin states — Wyoming, Colorado, Utah, New Mexico — and the Lower Basin states — Nevada, California, Arizona. Whenever a treaty was signed with Mexico regarding her share of the river's flow, it would be taken from the excess above that which had already been allocated to the seven states. The state representatives then signed the Colorado River Compact and sent it home for ratification. All did so except Arizona, which wanted her own dam on the river and regarded California as an ever-thirsty, water monster. For the next 40 years, the two states would bicker over their respective allocations and Arizona upon occasion would call out her National Guard in an effort to thwart California's evil designs.

In addition to the urban southland's future water needs, there was an agricultural need in the Imperial and Coachella valleys. A major dam on the Colorado was necessary to prevent another disaster such as that of 1905, when the river overflowed its banks and created the Salton Sea, while wiping out most of the painfully created irrigated farmland. Furthermore, a better irrigation system, one that would guarantee a certain and adequate supply of water, was needed to replace the existing one that wandered from its diversion point below Yuma into and across Mexico for sixty miles before turning back into the Imperial Valley where its water was used. What became known as the All-American Canal became part of congressional efforts to pass a measure authorizing the federal government to construct facilities on the Colorado River.

Passage of such legislation was stalled for many years by opposition from Arizona and from private utility companies, to whom the idea of the government entering the power generating business was worse than communism. Appropriate legislation finally was passed in 1928 and signed into law by President Coolidge. In the meantime, Los Angeles had realized that the cost of bringing the water from the Colorado was beyond her ability to pay. Many of the other cities in the southland, however, also could foresee the day of the "dry faucet," and ten of them joined with Los Angeles to form the Metropolitan Water District (MWD), which is *the* water power in Southern California today. The MWD promptly contracted for 1,212,000 acre-feet per annum of California's share and, in 1931, the voters approved a $220,000,000 bond issue to build Parker Dam, downstream from Hoover Dam. Here MWD would divert water through 242 miles of aqueducts and tunnels, lifting it 1,617 feet in the process, to a storage reservoir near Riverside, whence it would be distributed throughout MWD's service area. Without this water, Los Angeles could not have grown to its position of dominance in the state's affairs today. As a by-product of the MWD's construction, Lake Havasu behind Parker Dam is one of the fastest growing recreation areas in the Southwest today.

Spring Street, Los Angeles, throbbing with street cars, tin lizzies, and the 43rd annual session of the U.O.A. Druids in 1907. — *L.A. County Museum*

Let it not be imagined that Hoover Dam ended Arizona's bickering with California over which one got how much water from the Colorado. In 1952, Arizona sued for what she claimed was her fair share. The case went to the United States Supreme Court, which appointed a Special Master to take the evidence in the matter. After six years and 22,593 pages of testimony, he made his decision in favor of Arizona and this was upheld by the Supreme Court by a 5:3 vote in June 1963. California' share was reduced by more than 600,000 acre-feet per annum, but this reduction will not take effect until Arizona can use it, probably by 1985, when the Central Arizona Project is scheduled to begin delivery of water to the Phoenix-Tucson metropolitan area.

Just the prospect that the Supreme Court might rule in Arizona's favor was enough to ensure Southern California's support for the 1960 state bond issue that provided initial financing for the Feather River Project, of which Oroville Dam, completed in 1969, is the keystone in the largest water-moving project in the history of western civilization. Oroville Dam also has the distinction of being the tallest dam in the nation, at 770 feet, and is nearly one mile thick at the bottom, with a two-lane roadway along its 5,600-foot crest. It has become a major recreation area for interior Northern California, and the City of Oroville may be excused for feeling that it is, indeed, California's best town by a dam site.

Southern California now is regarded by enthusiastic boosters as encompassing everything as far north as Fresno in the Great Valley and San Luis Obispo on the coast. Whatever its extent, it is regarded as an ever-thirsty menace by central and northern California, and by other western states as well, where candidates have been known to campaign on the promise to empty the 300,000 [sic] swimming pools in Southern California that are filled with Colorado River water. No matter what others may think of it, there is no denying the throbbing vitality, as palpable as smog, that emanates from Los Angeles.

It constitutes the largest consumer marketing area west of the Mississippi River; it has the most bankruptcies in the nation and is a national leader in fashions — both in clothing styles and in ways of outdoor living. It is at once a showcase for the superficial and has surpassed the San Francisco Bay area as a financial, cultural, and educational center. It boasts the wealthiest community per capita in California, Rolling Hills, and the poorest, Hawaiian Gardens, while neighboring Orange County has the highest per capita average income in Southern California. It is truly New York-on-the-Pacific, an imperial city of worldwide influence.

Nestled amidst the Sierra granite, Hetch Hetchy Reservoir stores water for San Francisco 149 miles away.
— *San Francisco Public Utilities Commission*

CHAPTER FIFTEEN

THE WATER OF LIFE ITSELF

This interpretation of "the world of California" must end very much as it began — with the realization that the natural forces of California's creation will continue to effect, perhaps even control, its future, just as they have dominated its past.

Homo Sapiens (the thinking creature) is subaerial, living between water and air and needing both to sustain life. Despite the upsurge in emphysema, lung cancer and other nastinesses from air pollution, these will not kill us as quickly, nor limit the state's chances for survival, as surely as will the lack of water. This must be borne in mind in reading what follows.

It is well to remember, also, that among all the variable things on this spinning cinder we inhabit, perhaps the most variable are data pertaining to California's water supply, both present and foreseeable. The figures presented hereinafter are those that seem most reasonable to the author, but there is no denying that whatever figures are used, other figures will be used to dispute them. Another point to remember well when it comes to water in California is the basic maldistribution that made possible the career of Charles Mallory Hatfield, known as "The Rainmaker" in his time.

Mallory practised what he called

The Wind Gap pumping plant lifts water from the north 2,000 feet over the Tehachapi Mountains for the thirsty southland.
— *Dept. of Water Resources*

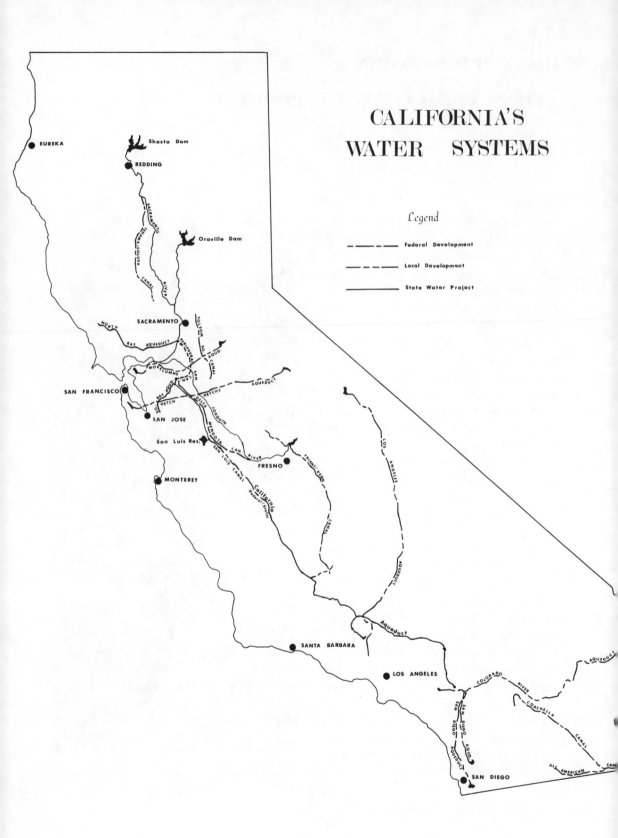

CALIFORNIA'S
WATER   SYSTEMS

"pluviculture" in the watershort lands of Southern California. In 1903, he signed a contract with a Los Angeles farmer to produce rain. He installed several evaporating tanks on the farmer's land that were filled with chemicals, "the character of which must necessarily remain secret," so he told the worried farmer. It then proceeded to rain more than one inch during the next five days. The delighted farmer paid him the sum of fifty, large, round dollars, which were silver in those days.

Upon another occasion, his apparatus apparently brought eleven inches of rainfall to the watershed of the Lake Hemet Land and Water Company, and in another year brought eighteen inches in four months for the City of Los Angeles. In 1916, he not only filled San Diego's reservoirs but caused a major flood; the city then refused payment on the grounds that he had made *too much rain*!

Hatfield was not a magician and his "secret" chemicals are questionable. What he was, however, was a careful analog student of weather patterns. He never offered his services except at the end of a long, dry spell, when past rainfall records indicated that the odds were in his favor. In this he did much the same thing as did the Hopi and Zuni elders when they held their tribal rain dances in the summer months when thunderstorms were most likely. Hatfield was put out of business by the great water storage and transporting projects that have made California what it is today.

The first of these were the systems that delivered water to the hydraulic monitors, as the days of "poor man's diggings" on the Mother Lode came to an end. Then came the mutually-owned water districts, made possible by the Wright Act of 1887, that were basic to the rise of irrigated agriculture and still are important today. These were followed by the great municipal quests for water — such as San Francisco's Hetch Hetchy Project, which provoked a bitter fight with San Joaquin Valley farmers, who feared loss of irrigation water from the Tuolumne River, and with the Sierra Club, which wanted to preserve the unspoiled beauty of Hetch Hetchy Valley as an integral part of Yosemite National Park; Oakland's Pardee Dam on the Mokelumne River and, as mentioned earlier, Los Angeles' Owens Valley and Colorado River projects. Overshadowing these came the gigantic systems of the federal and state governments.

Today's federally constructed and operated Central Valley Project (CVP) first was envisioned as a state project to store and transfer surplus water from the Sacramento River drainage to water-deficient areas of the state, particularly the San Joaquin Valley. The 1930's depression ended the state's involvement in this project and it became a federal operation of the Bureau of Reclamation (BuRec). Its key feature is Shasta Dam, completed in 1935, and the great lake it created at the junction of the Sacramento, McCloud and Pit rivers. During the next twenty years, Friant Dam was completed, as were the Madera and Friant-Kern Canals and the 120-mile long Delta-Mendota Canal, which delivers water pumped from the so-called Delta

Mighty Oroville Dam, keystone in the state's master water plan for slaking the thirst of the trans-Tehachapi region and providing irrigation water to the arid upper San Joaquin Valley.

— *Department of Water Resources*

Pool at Tracy to the San Joaquin Valley. Still later, BuRec completed the Trinity-Whiskeytown complex on the upper Sacramento River watershed and joined with the state's California Water Project (CWP) in building the San Luis Dam and a portion of the man-made river that transports CWP water southward.

Preliminary work on CWP facilities near Oroville began in 1957 but it was not until 1960 that initial financing was made certain when the voters approved what then was the largest bond issue ever contemplated by any political subdivision of the United States, a matter in which Governor Edmund G. "Pat" Brown played an important role and which was passed by Los Angeles' fears of losing some Colorado River water. Its key feature is Oroville Dam and CWP facilities now comprise 23 dams and reservoirs, 16 pumping plants, 5 power plants and the 444-mile long main line of the California Acqueduct, plus its branches to the San Francisco Bay Area. An integral part of the CWP is a trans-Delta water transportation system, of which the so-called Peripheral Canal is but one manifestation of a long drawn out conflict.

Another federal agency, the U.S. Army Corps of Engineers (CE) is involved in California's water resources from the standpoint of flood control and improvement of navigation. Principal flood control projects include Pine Flat and Isabella Reservoirs in the Tulare Basin, Folsom Dam on the American River, and Lake Mendocino on the Russian River. Other projects include dams in Nevada County and on the Mojave River; the New Melones Dam on the Stanislaus; Warm Springs Dam on the Russian River; Hidden Dam on the Fresno River, and Buchanan Dam on the Chowchilla River. Operation of Folsom and New Melones dams and their power generating capacity was turned over to BuRec once completed by the Engineers.

The man-made river of the California Acqueduct snakes its way down the San Joaquin Valley.
— *Dept. of Water Resources*

With all these facilities, the question logically can be raised: What is the water outlook for California's future? The answer must be — *unclear and uncertain*. To understand what follows, it will be well to grasp again the meaning of an acre-foot of water, the standard measurement unit for water resources. One acre-foot of water equals 325,700 gallons, which one of the state's Director of Water Resources was quoted as saying would supply four persons with their average annual water needs. This works out to a daily consumption per person of 225 gallons, which may seem high before you take into account swimming pools, hot tubs, saunas, spas, lawn and garden sprinkling, the weekly ritual of washing the family car, showers, shampoos, washing machines and drinking, either straight or mixed. Remember, too, that it takes 100,000 gallons to process one ton of steel and 2,000 gallons to refine one barrel of petroleum.

The following tables in acre-foot amounts approximate the state's basic water picture.

GROSS WATER SUPPLY

Annual precipitation	200,000,000
Inflow from Oregon	1,400,000
Imports from Colo. River	4,400,000
Groundwater overdraft	2,200,000
TOTALS	208,000,000

GROSS WATER DISPOSITION

130,200,000	Evaporation and Transpiration
1,200,000	Runoff to Nevada
3,400,000	Salt repulsion in Delta
45,100,000	Runoff to ocean
** 27,100,000	Depletion of applied water
207,000,000	

**USES OF APPLIED WATER

31,700,000	Agriculture
5,100,000	Municipal and Industrial
600,000	Fish, wildlife, recreation
37,400,000	
Less (10,300,000)	Re-used after original application
27,100,000	Net depletion of applied water

From the above, it would appear that the state has an annual water surplus of 1,000,000 acre feet. Appearances can be deceiving.

The state's annual gross water supply includes 2,200,000 acre feet of ground-water *overdraft*, which means that more water is being pumped from underground aquifers than is being replenished by rainfall, irrigation percolation, stream flooding and other replacement sources. Overdraft pumping has caused some 4,300 square miles of the San Joaquin Valley to sink, and continued overdraft pumping from ever-deepening wells consumes more energy and costs more. Without this ground- water overdraft, the state's annual *water deficit* would be 1,200,000 acre feet, or enough to leave 4,800,000 human beings unwashed and thirsty. To continue to depend upon ground-water overdraft is to live in a Fool's Paradise.

Allocation of Colorado River water under the seven-state compact in 1922 divided 15,000,000 acre feet per annum equally between the Upper and Lower Basin states. In the latter category, California finally received 4,400,000 acre feet, Arizona 2,800,000, and Nevada 300,000. By treaty with Mexico in 1944, the United States guaranteed her sister Republic 1,500,000 acre feet annually of water suitable for irrigation. Thus the total allocations come to 16,500,000 feet, which would not be a matter of concern *if* the river's available water was the 18-20,000,000 acre feet per annum it was thought to be in 1922. Unfortunately, the annual average water available for the past forty-five years has been only 13,900,000 acre feet. Sometime in the foreseeable future, California, which means Southern California in this instance, can expect a substantial reduction in the amount of water available to it from the Colorado River.

It was believed that the CWP's Feather River-San Luis Project would be able to offset reduced supplies from the Colorado River whenever they finally occurred. The MWD and water agencies in the San Joaquin Valley signed contracts with CWP to deliver them 4,000,000 acre feet per annum when the project was completed. CWP signed additional contracts with counties in the San Francisco Bay Area and with Santa Barbara County to deliver them some 200,000 acre feet per annum when the project was completed and they needed it. The South Bay Aqueduct already delivers 132,000 acre feet to Alameda and Santa Clara counties, while the North Bay Aqueduct to deliver 30,000 acre feet annually to Napa and Solano counties will be completed in 1984 if all goes well.

After spending $5,000,000 to keep their contract option open since 1961, Santa Barbara's voters in 1979 cancelled their contract with CWP in the belief that they could not get any water from it, no matter how long they waited or what the cost. Their belief stemmed from the hard fact that CWP contracts today call for delivery of 4,000,000+ acre feet per annum by 1990, while its firm yield is but 2,300,000 acre feet in *normal* years. In the drought years of 1975-77, its firm yield dropped well below the normal figure.

Sierra snowpack measurements throughout the winter indicate how much water will be available for power and irrigation the following summer.

— *Pacific Gas & Electric Co.*

As if this shortage were not enough, there is the problem of salt build-up in the irrigated lands of the San Joaquin Valley. Each time water is used for irrigation, salts are left behind as crops soak up moisture through their roots, and this salty residue normally enters the sub-surface return flow into rivers and streams or percolates into the groundwater. In these cases, the salt content is diluted to a point where it is not injurious to most plant life. In sections of the San Joaquin Valley, however, shallow layers of impermeable clay act as natural obstacles to prevent subsurface flow and cause brackish water to back up within five feet of the surface. This is injurious to crops, even those that are salt resistant, and some 400,000 acres already are almost unusable for productive agriculture.

The long-range solution to this problem is a massive underground drainage system extending from Bakersfield north for almost 300 miles, which would flush the saline build-up into Suisun Bay. This would require tremendous additional water supplies and raises serious questions as to the effect of this saline discharge upon the waters of the Delta and San Francisco Bay. It also raises grave questions as to the ability of agriculturalists to pay for the costs of both flushing water and incoming irrigation water.

Many and varied solutions to the state's water problems have been proposed, and among them "sky farming" makes a modern reminder of "Hatfield, the Rainmaker." Essentially, this calls for the use of radar to track incoming cold Pacific storms, and the seeding of these storms over the Sierra by silver iodide particles, distributed both by aircraft and from propane-burning ground generators at high elevations. The cloud physics are clear enough but the results of a five-year test by BuRec are not conclusive as to the additional rainfall benefits derived from this technique. Furthermore, how would California contend against legal action by Nevada and Arizona, for example, for milking their share of moisture out of passing storms?

A proposal that has received lip service support from the Colorado River Compact states calls for the federal government to construct facilities to divert several million acre feet of water annually from the Snake River in Idaho, the last water-surplus river of any magnitude in the Far West, into the drainage system of the Colorado River. This plan has bumped head-on into an impregnable adverse legal position maintained by Idaho, Oregon, and Washington. Tourists with California license plates should not discuss this proposal loudly, if at all, in the three states mentioned.

A different proposal would eliminate interstate friction over the Snake River's waters. This calls for a massive pipeline system to be laid on the ocean floor from the mouth of the Columbia River to Southern California. Inasmuch as the Snake drains into the Columbia, this pipeline would transport fresh water that was not being used upstream, otherwise it would not reach the mouth of the Columbia, and thus prevent unseemly squabbling. This may sound far-fetched, even "far out," but it is indicative of the magnitude of the state's water problem. Equally indicative is the proposal to tow

Brawley's Main Street before Colorado River water came. — *San Diego Historical Society—T.I.T. Col.*

gigantic icebergs from the Arctic or Antarctic oceans to melting terminals on the Southern California coast. If this should be done, the 'bergs from the Antarctic probably would be used because of their higher fresh water content. To use them, however, would require international agreements and would raise questions as to the effect of iceberg removal upon the Antarctic ecology.

In 1969, the use of nuclear energy to desalinate ocean water for urban needs, thus freeing CVP and CWP water for agricultural use, was heralded as the solution to California's water problem. Enthusiasts envisioned multi-purpose nuclear plants that would produce 1,000,000 kilowatts and and a daily water supply of 400,000,000 gallons for domestic and industrial use at affordable costs. In addition, these plants would process the salt water residue to extract 2,000 tons of ammonia and 360 tons of phosphorous daily. One such plant, it was claimed, would produce enough fertilizer to serve 200,000 acres, which in turn would yield enough grain to feed almost 2,500,000 people at the level of 2,400 calories daily. Moreover, such a plant could export enough fertilizer annually to underdeveloped countries to cultivate another 10,000,000 acres. In this view, California's water problem and the world's hunger were capable of solution, and the length of California's coastline afforded numerous sites for such multi-purpose plants.

Today very serious questions can be raised as to the effect such large-scale intrusions would have upon the ecology of the sea. Would they so affect the state's normal weather patterns that even desalination gains could

The Sierra streams were the initial sources of California's water of life.   — *Pacific Gas & Electric Co.*

— 317 —

not offset the resultant loss of water storage in the Sierra Nevada? What effect would they have upon the whole web of life in California that radiates from its sea-born climate? Until these questions can be answered with substantial accuracy, if indeed they ever can, California must look inward for the water of its future life.

It should be obvious from the foregoing that the state faces a major problem in securing enough water on a sustained basis simply to maintain its present population and productivity. This present problem looms ever more menacing when demographic projections envision both the Los Angeles and Bay Area conurbations *doubling in size* by the year 2000. Where then can the state procure the water supply to permit unborn generations to have an opportunity in life for something besides the destruction of self-respect that comes with unemployment and government handouts? This is a matter of the utmost concern, or should be, for ethnic minorities; indeed for all those who for whatever reason have to claw their way up from the bottom rung of the economic ladder.

One course of more water is the reprocessing of sewage. Los Angeles, for example, discharges sewage into the ocean each day in the same amount roughly that it receives from Owens Valley, despite reclaiming additional amounts at its Whittier Narrows plant for industrial use. The University of California at Irvine uses reclaimed sewage water to irrigate its grounds, while Orange County injects treated effluent into wells along its coastline to form a barrier against sea water intrusion into its underground aquifier. The theoretical chemistry exists to make sewage water as potable as that from a mountain spring, but there are serious concerns that carcinogenic substances may exist in such treated water under present processing systems, and that suitable biological quality control still is open to question when it comes to large-scale treatment of sewage for domestic re-use. It probably is "somewhere down the road" before this source makes a major contribution to the state's water supply.

The foreseeable major contributions to htis supply will be, as they have been since 1935, a combination of federal and state projects. Among the CE projects is the recently completed New Melones Dam on the Stanislaus River, which will supply 210,000 acre feet annually for agricultural use and generate enough electricity to replace 513,000 barrels of oil per year if filled to capacity. It also will flood a stretch of river where white-water rafting had become a popular pastime and a profitable business, thanks to the water discharge from existing power generating plants upstream. A BuRec project is the Auburn Dam on the American River, now being redesigned because of earthquake considerations. Hopefully by 2000, this dam will contribute 320,000 acre feet annually for agricultural use and generate electricity equivalent to that produced by 661,000 barrels of oil. Two CE dams are proposed for Cottonwood Creek, a tributary of the Sacramento River below Redding, that should yield 500,000 acre feet annually with concomitant generating capacity. The most favorable completion date for this federal project is 1995, while the probability is that it will be much later.

The state has plans to build a storage reservoir in western Glenn and Tehama counties which would increase the yield of the integrated CWP/CVP water supplies. This reservoir would receive excess Sacramento River water during the winter and spring surplus flows by pumping and would release this water during the dry season, thereby generating "pay back" electricity for that consumed in pumping. Another proposed CWP project is the Los Vaqueros Reservoir in the hills of eastern Contra Costa County, a few miles west of the Delta. This reservoir would be used on an annual fill-withdrawal cycle, storing surplus winter water and releasing it when needed, and would have some excess power generating capacity over that required by the pump lift from the Delta. These proposals now are in abeyance, pending a long range solution to the trans-Delta water transport squabble.

The Delta makes a triangular stage — Sacramento, Stockton, Antioch — for a major controversy over the water it receives from the San Joaquin and Sacramento rivers on their conjoined way to the sea through Carinquinez Strait and San Francisco Bay. The controversy gained intensity in recent years from the proposed Peripheral Canal, which in some form has been a part of CWP since its inception. This called for the diversion of both CVP and CWP water from the Sacramento River near Hood and moving it via a 43-mile long, 500-foot wide canal around the southeastern edge of the Delta to pumping plants near Tracy that would lift the water into the existing southward-flowing aqueducts of both CVP and CWP.

Proponents of the Canal said it would save 1,000,000 acre feet annually, thus adding this amount to the state's water supply; an amount roughly equal to the Colorado River water expected to be lost by Southern California. At the same time, proponents said that the Canal would not appreciably diminish the existing water quality in the delta. Opponents of the Canal said that such claims are so much clotted nonsense! In their view, the Canal would deal a death blow to Delta water quality. Stripped of the rhetoric from both sides, the Peripheral Canal controversy, which was the latest manifestation of the whole idea of some form of trans-Delta water transportation system, boils down to a competition between water users south of the Delta and Delta water interests. Powerful agricultural, urban, and environmental interests are involved on both sides.

The Canal was a pet project of Governor "Jerry" Brown, just as the CWP was a pet project of Governor "Pat" Brown, his father. Even though the Peripheral Canal proposal was soundly defeated by the voters in 1982, including a 39% vote against it in Southern California, the fact remains that authorization for a trans-Delta water transportation system was included in the Burns-Porter Act of 1960 and still applies. Thus, the conflict over the Delta seems destined to be a part of the state's "politics of water" for some

The Delta — artery of commerce, houseboater's paradise, productive agricultural region, scene of continuing controversy.
                                                                    — *Dept. of Water Resources*

PROPOSED DELTA FACILITIES

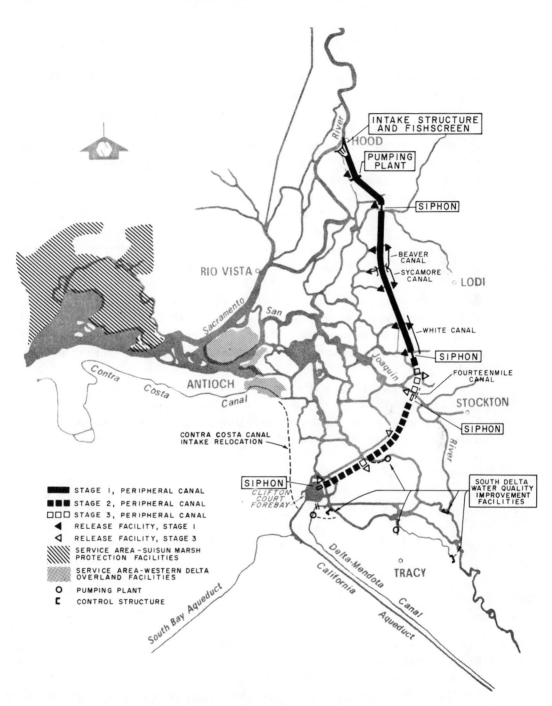

Map of the Delta showing the proposed and controversial Peripheral Canal.
— *Courtesy Dept. of Water Resources*

years to come. Should another dry year or two come along, to say nothing of a drought like that of 1924-29, the 1,000,000 acre feet allegedly available by constructing the Canal would be very, very appealing to voters with dry faucets. Of course, waiting for a drought to affect the state might be a case of too little, too late.

Another controversial source of more water is that stored in the underground aquifiers of the Sacramento Valley between Red Bluff and Sacramento. This has not yet generated as much emotional voltage as did the Peripheral Canal, simply because those most affected by it, the valley agriculturalists, are not as numerous or as organized as are protectors of the Delta environment. These aquifiers supply irrigation water to many users but they have not been overdrafted, as have the aquifiers of the San Joaquin Valley. Thus, it is *alleged* that millions of acre feet annually could be pumped from these aquifiers for *export* southwards via the Sacramento River and the Delta without damaging the present users. Valley farmers assert that it would confiscate their property rights to sub-surface water; rights which traditionally and legally have accompanied purchase of the land above it. They also assert with good reason that their wells would deepen, their land would subside, and their costs would increase beyond their capacity to pay if the export of underground water became a reality. Given the nature of California's water problem, it is safe to say that sooner or later, and probably sooner, there will be a major overhaul of the whole system of water rights in the state by legislative action. This has been foreshadowed by the 1979 "Report of the Governor's Commission to Review California Water Rights Law."

A major source of extra water for California — a source that is the *most* controversial of them all — is to be found in the rivers of the state's North Coastal Region. This was touched upon in the opening chapter of this work and is presented in more detail here. The annual run-off of these rivers that flows unused and virtually unchecked into the sea is in the following amounts:

Klamath River	12,000,000 acre feet
Eel & Van Duzen rivers	6,300,000 acre feet
Smith River	3,000,000 acre feet
Mad River	1,000,000 acre feet

The Mattole River sends another 1,000,000 acre feet of run-off into the sea, but is excluded from the above table because of apparently insurmountable construction problems in utilizing this flow.

In 1972, with apparently plenty of water in the state and with the environmentalists and land developers of this region in a strange alliance, the legislature designated all these as Wild Rivers, with one exception, thus barring them from any incorporation into the CWP. The exception was the Middle Fork of Eel River, on which it was proposed to build the Dos Rios Project. This would impound enough water to send 900,000 acre feet annually through the Coast Range folds into the Sacramento River for utilization elsewhere via the state's gigantic water transfer system. This amount would more than offset Southern California's loss of Colorado River water, should the Peripheral Canal idea or a similar trans-Delta facility be abandoned. To do this, however, would require flooding Round Valley, which contains the town of Covelo and an Indian Reservation on which reside friction-prone and faction-ridden fragments of various California tribelets. Opposition to the Dos Rios Project in the early 1970's caused it to be postponed for further consideration until 1984, at which time there is no surety that it will be reconsidered.

Another major source of additional water and the one most appealing to this writer involves the existing storage complex at Shasta Dam. By enlarging this dam, or building another smaller one below it, while, at the same time, building small dams on the rivers that feed into Shasta Lake — the Pit, McCloud, Sacramento — to store surplus winter and spring run-off *before* that run-off reaches the main lake, it is alleged that as much as 14,000,000 acre feet per annum could be added to the state's water supply *without* in any way impairing the existing storage facilities at Shasta Dam or downstream water quality in the Delta or elsewhere. It also would avoid the bitter fight certain to erupt over any plans to tap the North Coast rivers for their wasted run-off. However, the cost of this enlarged Shasta Dam — Lake complex and the time required to make it operable preclude its consideration in surveying the state's water needs for the remainder of this century.

In the following forecast of California's additional water needs and supplies by the year 2000, the North Coastal rivers and the Dos Rios Project have been excluded because of their controversial nature. Given all the practical sources of new water supplies mentioned in this chapter, including groundwater export from the Sacramento Valley and a trans-Delta facility of some type, it appears unlikely that the state will obtain more than a per annum acre footage of 3,500,000, while the projected demand for additional water is for more than 5,000,000 acre feet per annum; a per annum shortfall of 1,500,000 acre feet, in addition to the present overuse of groundwater in the San Joaquin Valley.

With this shortfall in mind, it is appropriate to close this interpretation of "the world of California" with the late Arnold Toynbee's definition of history as being the study down the ages of mankind's response to challenge. California has met and overcome many challenges in its past. Its water problem today, regardless of what figures are used to support one position or another, presents one of the two greatest challenges to its future — the other being energy. How the state and its peoples meet these challenges will determine whether The Golden Shore by the Sundown Sea will remain what it has been since 1841 — the Mecca for those who seek to better their condition in life with all the risks that such a quest entails.

There is a feeling of confidence in California's political, industrial, social and commercial worlds that California's location on the so-called Pacific Rim, or Pacific Basin if you prefer, will enable it to influence effectively, if not dictate, the future direction of the United States. This will come about simply because the balance of power has shifted from the old Atlantic seaboard states to the Pacific Coast states, among which California is the dominant member. In essence, this is what Garrett Mattingly foresaw at Harvard before World War II — that the history of the United States was the history of a nation in transition from an Atlantic to a Pacific world.

In the days when it was possible to travel from Sonoma to San Diego without purse or horse through the courtesy of the ranches and the missions, the traveller was expected to give courteous thanks for hospitality received. In turn, the host expressed the wish that the wayfarer would have good of what had been extended. That wish is here expressed in the olden phrase:

Buen Provecho!

CALIFORNIA'S GROWTH

	Calif. Population	Growth Rates Calif.	Nation	Remarks
1820	3,720 est.—		—	Includes perhaps 13 "foreigners"
1846	9,000 est.—		—	Includes perhaps 900 "foreigners"
1852	264,435	—	35.9%	First accurate state census
1860	379,994	70.0%	35.6%	Golden Dream in full bloom
1870	560,247	47.4%	26.6%	Railroad completed 1869
1880	864,694	54.3%	26.0%	Depression 1873-1877
1890	1,213,398	40.3%	25.5%	Santa Fe RR reaches L.A. 1885
1900	1,485,053	22.4%	20.7%	Depression 1893-1897
1910	2,377,549	60.1%	21.0%	Boom resumes in So. California
1920	3,426,861	44.1%	14.9%	WW I affected national rate
1930	5,677,251	65.7%	16.1%	Post-WWI boom in S. California
1940	6,907,387	21.7%	7.2%	Great Depression of the 1930s
1950	10,586,223	55.3%	14.5%	WW II and aftermath hit California
1960	15,717,204	48.5%	18.5%	Post-war boom continues in California
1970	19,971,069	27.0%	13.5%	Post-war boom slackens
1980	23,667,902	18.5%	11.4%	Lowest increase since 1852.
1990	**27,905,000**	**State Department of Finance projection**		

From the above table, it can be seen that the state's population virtually has doubled every twenty years between 1860-1970. Net in-migration averaged 300,000+ annually, 1955-1964, accounting for almost 60% of the net population increase in these years. A *slowdown* in the annual rate of growth began in 1964, dropping from 3.4% annually to virtually nothing in 1970. In this latter year, one of the state's leading bank's senior economists believes that the state suffered, or enjoyed as you prefer, a net *OUT-migration* of 27,000$^{\pm}$, due probably to a drastic decline in the aerospace industry stemming from a marked reduction in the amount of government prime and sub-contracts. The continuing "steady state" of the annual growth rate, 1970-1980, probably is due primarily to increased economic opportunities in the southern "Sun Belt" states from Florida to Arizona.

SIGNIFICANT POPULATION SHIFTS

(By Major Economic Areas)

or

FIGURE-HAPPY HISTORY

	1860	1880	1900	1920	1940	1960	1970	1980
CALIFORNIA TOTAL	380,000	864,700	1,485,100	3,426,900	6,907,400	15,517,200	19,971,069	23,667,902
Bay Counties (6)	84,300	348,000	543,000	1,009,500	1,462,000	2,783,400	3,281,238	3,485,833
Santa Clara Co.	11,900	35,040	60,200	100,700	175,000	642,315	1,065,313	1,295,071
Napa & Sonoma	17,400	39,160	55,000	72,800	97,500	213,300	284,025	398,880
L.A. & Orange	11,330	33,400	190,000	998,000	2,916,400	6,742,700	8,463,213	9,410,212
San Diego Co.	4,320	8,600	35,090	112,248	289,350	1,033,011	1,357,854	1,861,846
San Bernardino Co.	5,551	7,800	27,401	73,401	161,100	503,600	682,233	895,016
Santa Barbara & Ventura	3,540	14,586	33,300	69,800	140,240	368,100	642,821	827,868
Imperial & Riverside	—	—	17,900	93,750	165,260	318,300	531,408	755,276
Mother Lode & Northern Mountain Co. (17)	132,840	133,010	144,740	124,500	203,700	298,300	378,289	585,322
Sacramento Co.	24,142	34,400	45,900	91,030	170,350	502,800	634,373	783,381
San Joaquin Co.	9,435	24,350	35,450	79,900	134,200	250,000	291,073	347,342
Fresno Co.	4,605	9,500	37,860	128,800	178,600	366,000	413,329	514,621
North Coast (4)	10,457	37,500	56,000	69,700	86,500	187,500	184,921	229,835
Central Coast (4)	11,465	38,830	64,160	85,135	162,730	379,000	495,156	659,025
Sacramento Valley (7)	40,200	69,360	68,750	101,650	142,100	269,600	339,896	432,233
Merced & Stanislaus	3,380	14,400	18,800	68,135	121,850	247,750	299,135	480,460
Upper San Joaquin (4)	4,638	16,900	51,100	148,100	300,760	510,800	626,792	785,681

Two major shifts should be visible in the above tabulation; one is the concentration of population in urban centers after the Gold Rush waned, and the other, and most important to the state's present and future, is the rise of Southern California to dominance in population and economic importance thereby. The explosion of Santa Clara County between 1940–1980 should be noted. To what can this be attributed? The almost 200% increase in the Mother Lode and Mountain counties between 1940–1980 is due largely to the growth of Eldorado, Nevada, Placer, Amador and Calaveras counties as retirement havens and bedroom communities for Sacramento and Stockton.

THE SPANISH TRIPOD OF SETTLEMENT

THE TWENTY-THREE MISSIONS

San Diego de Alcala, July 16, 1769.

San Carlos Borromeo (Carmel), June 3, 1770.

San Antonio de Padua, July 14, 1771.

San Gabriel Arcangel (*the mother of Los Angeles*), September 8, 1771.

San Luis Obispo de Tolosa,* September 1, 1772.

San Francisco de Asis (Dolores), October 8 (or 9), 1776.

San Juan Capistrano,* November 1, 1776.

Santa Clara, January 12, 1777.

Purisima Concepcion de Maria Santisma, 1780, was located opposite the present city of Yuma, Arizona. Together with its sister mission, San Pedro y San Pablo, 1780, it was destroyed in the Yuma uprising of 1781 that closed the overland route between Alta California and Sonora.

San Buenaventura, March 31, 1782.

Santa Barbara, December 4, 1786.

Purisima Concepcion, December 8, 1787.

Santa Cruz, August 28 (or September 25), 1791.

Nuestra Senora de la Soledad, October 9, 1791.

San Jose de Guadalupe (distinct from the *pueblo* of San Jose), June 11, 1797.

San Juan Bautista, * June 24, 1797.

San Miguel Arcangel, July 25, 1797.

San Fernando Rey de Espana, September 8, 1797.

San Luis Rey de Francia, June 13, 1798.

Santa Ines (or Ynez), September 17, 1804.

San Rafael Arcangel, December 14, 1817.

San Francisco Solano* (Sonoma, the only Mexican-established mission), July 4, 1823.

Pueblo status was granted the civilian communities that grew up around these missions.

Presidios

San Diego, July 16, 1769

Monterey, June 3, 1770

San Francisco, September 17, 1776

Santa Barbara, April 21, 1782

Pueblos

San Jose, November 1777

Los Angeles, September 4, 1781

Branciforte, 1797 (virtually still-born)

Pueblos also grew up around each of the military posts.

THE GOVERNORS OF CALIFORNIA

Spanish Governors

GASPAR DE PORTOLA

Governor of *Las Californias*, residing at Loreto from December 17, 1767, until his departure for Alta California, May 13, 1769. He was the new land's military commander, rather than civil authority, until July 9, 1770.

FELIPE DE BARRI

Governor of *Las Californias*, 1770-1775, residing at Loreto. Pedro Fages and Fernando Rivera y Moncada exercised military command in Alta California during this period. Moncada later was killed in the uprising at the Yuma Crossing that closed the overland route from Sonora and Sinaloa.

FELIPE DE NEVE

Governor of *Las Californias* residing at Loreto until the provinces were separated and thereafter at Monterey, February, 1777 to September, 1782.

PEDRO FAGES

September 1782 to April 1791. His domestic difficulties provided Monterey with its choicest gossip and exacerbated the normal friction between the military and religious factions.

JOSE JOAQUIN DE ARRILLAGA

Interim governor, April 1792 to October 1794.

DIEGO DE BORICA

October 1794 to Jaunary 1800. A Basque, Borica ameliorated the laws that applied to *los Indios*.

JOSE JOAQUIN DE ARRILLAGA

Interim governor, 1800-1804; constitutional governor, 1804-1814. Russian penetration began during his administration.

JOSE DARIO ARGUELLO

Acting-governor, 1814-1815, at Santa Barbara.

PABLO VICENTE SOLA

August 15, 1815 to November 22, 1822, was the last of the Spanish governors; his term carried over into the Mexican period.

Mexican Governors

LUIS ANTONIO ARGUELLO
Acting-governor, 1822-1825, was the first native Californian to hold the post.

JOSE MARIA DE ECHEANDIA
1825-1831, moved the capital to San Diego; the first overland penetration of California by Americans occurred during his administration.

MANUEL VICTORIA
1831-1832, served for about three months.

PIO PICO
1832, served for about three weeks. He represented the *hijos del pais* of Southern California.

JOSE MARIA DE ECHEANDIA
1832-1833, resided in the south.

AGUSTIN VICENTE ZAMORANO
1832-1833, resided in the north. He was the first printer to ply the trade in California. (The turnover of governors between 1831-1833 reflects internal strife ignited by sectionalism and secularization of the missions.)

JOSE FIGUEROA
1833-1835. Had he not died on September 29, 1835, this most capable of the Mexican governors might have alleviated the plight of the ex-mission Indians and have prevented the political turmoil that followed.

JOSE CASTRO
Acting-governor, 1835-1836.

NICOLAS GUTIERREZ
Acting-governor for four months, 1836.

MARIANO CHICO
Served three months, 1836.

NICOLAS GUITERREZ
Returned as acting-governor for another three months later in 1836. Agitation for home rule explains these short administrations.

JUAN BAUTISTA ALVARADO
Revolutionary governor, 1836-1838. Recognized as governor by Mexico, August 8, 1838, he served until 1842. In actuality, Mariano G. Vallejo was co-governor during the period of alleged independence from Mexico.

MANUEL MICHELTORENA
1842-1845, was the last governor appointed by Mexico.

PIO PICO
1845-1846. Jose Castro exercised military command in the north during this time and met Fremont's junketing in that region.

JOSE MARIA FLORES and ANDRES PICO
1846-1847, were provisional governors in Southern California during that section's revolt against United States occupation forces.

United States Military Governors

Commodore John D. Sloat	July 7, 1846
Commodore Robert F. Stockton	July 23, 1846
Captain John C. Fremont	January 19, 1847
General Stephen W. Kearny	March 1, 1847
Colonel Richard B. Mason	May 31, 1847
General Persifor F. Smith	February 28, 1849
General Bennett Riley	April 13, 1849

Governors of the State of California

The original term of office was two years, to begin the first Monday after the first day in January. The term was extended to four years by constitutional amendment in 1862, and was to begin the first Monday after the first day of December. The constitution of 1879 restored the January date for inaguration and limited the term of the first governor serving under this constitution to three years. From 1850 to 1880, California's general elections were held on the first Wednesday in September, with a separate judicial election held thereafter. The new constitution provided for state elections to coincide with national election dates, beginning in 1880.

NAME	BIRTHPLACE	PARTY	INAUGURA-TION
Peter H. Burnett	Tenn., 1807	Ind. Dem.	Dec. 20, 1849 (Resigned Jan. 9, 1851)
John McDougal	Ohio, 1818	Ind. Dem.	Jan. 9, 1851
John Bigler (First two-term governor)	Pa., 1805	Dem.	Jan. 8, 1852
John Neely Johnson (Youngest governor elected)	Ind., 1825	Amer. (Know Nothings)	Jan. 9, 1856
John B. Weller	Ohio, 1812	Dem.	Jan. 8, 1858
Milton S. Latham	Ohio, 1827	Lecompton Dem.	Jan. 9, 1860 (To U.S. Senate)
John G. Downey (Only naturalized governor; first governor from Southern California)	Ireland, 1827	Lecompton Dem.	Jan. 14, 1860
Leland Stanford	N.Y., 1824	Rep.	Jan. 10, 1862
Frederick F. Low (First four-year-term governor)	Maine, 1828	Union	Dec. 10, 1863
Henry H. Haight	N.Y., 1825	Dem.	Dec. 5, 1867
Newton Booth	Ind., 1825	Rep.	Dec. 8, 1871 (To U.S. Senate)

NAME	BIRTHPLACE	PARTY	INAUGURA-TION
Romualdo Pacheco (First native-born state governor)	Calif., 1831	Rep.	Feb. 27, 1875
William Irwin (The new constitution of 1879 made this the longest four-year term)	Ohio, 1827	Dem.	Dec. 9, 1875
George C. Perkins (Only governor elected to a three-year term)	Maine, 1839	Rep.	Jan. 8, 1880
George Stoneman	N.Y., 1822	Dem.	Jan.10, 1883
Washington Bartlett	Ga., 1824	Dem.	Jan. 8, 1887 (Died, Sept. 12, 1887)
Robert W. Waterman	N.Y., 1826	Rep.	Sept.13,1887
Henry H. Markham	N.Y., 1840	Rep.	Jan. 8, 1891
James H. Budd	Wis., 1851	Dem.	Jan.11, 1895
Henry T. Gage	N.Y., 1852	Rep.	Jan. 4, 1899
George C. Pardee	Calif., 1857	Rep.	Jan. 7, 1903
James N. Gillett	Wis., 1860	Rep.	Jan. 9, 1907
Hiram W. Johnson (First four-year governor to be re-elected)	Calif., 1866	Prog. Rep.	Jan. 3, 1911 (To U.S. Senate)
William D. Stephens	Ohio, 1859	Rep.	Mar. 15, 1917
Friend W. Richardson	Mich., 1865	Rep.	Jan. 9, 1923
Clement C. Young	N.H., 1869	Rep.	Jan. 4, 1927
James Rolph, Jr.	Calif., 1869	Rep.	Jan. 6, 1931 (Died, June 2, 1934)
Frank F. Merriam	Iowa, 1865	Rep.	June 2, 1934
Culbert L. Olson	Utah, 1876	Dem.	Jan. 2, 1939

NAME	BIRTHPLACE	PARTY	INAUGURA-TION
Earl F. Warren	Calif., 1891	Rep.	Jan. 4, 1943
(Only three-term governor to date)	(Appointed to Supreme Court, 1953)		
Goodwin F. Knight	Utah, 1896	Rep.	Oct. 5, 1953
Edmund G. Brown	Calif., 1905	Dem.	Jan. 5, 1959
Ronald Reagan	Ill., 1911	Rep.	Jan. 5, 1967
Edmund G. Brown, Jr.	Calif., 1938	Dem.	Jan. 5, 1975
George Deukmejian	N.Y., 1928	Rep.	Jan. 5, 1983

Of the thirty-five governors to date, only seven have been born in California.

THE COUNTIES OF CALIFORNIA

Almost half of the state's fifty-eight counties retain the names if not the size, that they were given in 1850 when the state was first divided into political subdivisions. These "original" counties are: Butte, Calaveras, Colusa, Contra Costa, El Dorado, Los Angeles, Marin, Mariposa, Mendocino, Monterey, Napa, Sacramento, San Diego, San Francisco, San Joaquin, San Luis Obispo, Santa Barbara, Santa Clara, Santa Cruz, Shasta, Solano, Sonoma, Sutter, Trinity, Tuolumne, Yolo, and Yuba.

The "new" counties were created because of economic and population shifts during the years that followed:

Nevada	1851	Lake	1861
Placer	1851	Alpine	1864
Siskiyou	1852	Lassen	1864
Sierra	1852	Inyo	1866
Tulare	1852	Kern	1866
Alameda	1853	Ventura	1872
San Bernardino	1853	San Benito	1874
Humboldt	1853	Modoc	1874
Plumas	1854	Orange	1889
Stanislaus	1854	Glenn	1891
Amador	1854	Madera	1893
Merced	1855	Riverside	1893
Tehama	1856	Kings	1893
Fresno	1856	Imperial	1907
San Mateo	1856	(The standard work on the state's	
Del Norte	1857	counties is Owen C. Coy's *California County Boundaries*).	
Mono	1861		

The transverse ranges, with Tehachapi Pass for datum point, made the traditional northern boundary of Southern California, which thus contained San Diego, Imperial, Riverside, San Bernardino, Orange, Los Angeles, Ventura, and Santa Barbara counties. Water quests and improved communications brought Inyo, Mono, and Kern counties properly within its orbit. Enthusiasts also claim Tulare, Kings, and San Luis Obispo counties for the Southland, while extremists add Fresno County as well.

Today's demands to divide the state into two separate political entities are nothing new. In the Constitutional Convention of 1849, the delegates from the southern section of the state raised the question of division. In 1850, a group of *Angelenos* petitioned Congress to declare the counties south of Monterey along the coast and south of the Tehachapi Mountains a separate entity to be called the Territory of Central California. In 1851, a convention to divide the state was called in Los Angeles but nothing sub-stantative came of it. Finally, in 1859, Andres Pico secured approval of the legislature for the formation of the Territory of Colorado to include every-thing from San Luis Obispo south along the coast and below the Tehachapi Mountains. This measure was assured of the necessary two-thirds affirma-tive vote in the counties affected, but when the matter went to Congress, the sectional schism over the issue of slavery and state's rights kept it from getting congressional approval. The issue was kept alive down the years until the re-apportionment of the legislature along the lines of the Supreme Court's one man—one vote philosophy, which gave the one-time "cow counties" of southern California control of the legislature. The issue is not yet dead but with a reverse twist, as now the northern counties which are the water sources for Southern California utter demands for separatism, claiming that they are under-represented in state government and political influence and that the water they originate should cost Southern California more than it does already. In 1965, State Senators from both parties repre-senting northern California districts supported bills in the legislature which proposed, unsuccessfully, to split the state in two at the Tehachapi Moun-tains. It does not appear to this writer that either section could afford the financial burdens that would occur by becoming two separate states.

Intermittently for more than a century, the counties east of the Sierra summit have protested their inclusion in California, and Nevada has on oc-casion encouraged these outcries for its own purposes. "Geographical inhu-manities" still afflict portions of California, to a diminishing degree, but it is not believed feasible, let alone desirable, to start dismembering the state. A possible exception might be the cession of California's trans-Sierra terri-tory to Nevada, reserving the water potential of Mono and Inyo counties for Los Angeles, in return for an outright grant of Nevada's share of the Colo-rado River water.

HISPANIC LAND GRANTS

In Spain's New World possessions, *all* land belonged to the King of Spain. Not until October 17, 1754 was the Viceroy in Mexico City given authority, as agent of the Crown, to make grants of land. During Spain's tenure in Alta California, possibly 25 grants of land to individuals were made. The bulk of the some 800 land grants finally confirmed by the United States were made during Mexico's tenure in Alta California, and the great majority of these were made between 1834-1846 after secularization of the Missions. Hence the use of the term Hispanic to denote land grants made prior to the state's acquisition by the United States. Under both Spain and Mexico, the basic unit of measure in these grants was the square league of about 4,400 acres, while a lineal league amounted to 2.633 of our statute miles today.

Neither Spain nor Mexico intended the Missions to have title to the lands they operated. These lands were allotted to the respective Missions for the use and benefit of *los Indios*, and the Missions were only Trustees of these lands until the Indians they converted had been brought to such stage of proficiency in agriculture and animal husbandry that they could operate the lands for their own use and benefit. The original thought in 1769 was that ten years from its founding would be sufficient for each Mission to accomplish this end of transforming the Indians into self-sustaining *pueblos* in a Spanish society. What happened to this plan when the Missions finally were secularized is explained in the text chapter regarding the rise of the *rancho* system as the principal socioeconomic unit of Mexican California.

When an individual in Hispanic times wished to obtain some land upon which to support himself and family, he followed what was a relatively simple procedure. Having found the land he wanted, he made a crude map of it and attached it to a petition requesting the land described to El Gobernador in Monterey (*diseno*). The governor forwarded this to the nearest magistrate (*alcalde*), who then reported whether the requested land would or would not conflict with existing ownerships. His report was attached to the original petition and the whole sheaf of papers, now known as an *informe*, was returned to the governor. If the governor found all to be in order, he issued a decree granting the land requested, sending the original to the petitioner and retaining a copy of the decree, together with all its supporting documents, in the governmental files. In theory this was an orderly, sequential procedure, gratifying to the bureaucratic mind. In practice, it was followed more in the breach than the observance, and this lead to great heartache, legal chicanery, and loss when the Americans took over.

After the governor's official grant, the final step was the survey and the owner's confirmation in juridical possession. There were no surveyors as we know them today in Alta California of Hispanic times. The local *alcalde*, together with the local friar and two especially sworn witnesses, accompanied by the petitioner, started at a pre-determined point set forth in the aforementioned *diseno*. One of the witnesses had a tall stake at the bottom of which was fastened a rawhide *riata* or a *cordel* (string) of braided rawhide about thirty-three feet long. He set his stake in the ground from horseback. The other witness took his stake to which was fastened the other end of the rawhide string and galloped away until he reached its end. He then stuck his stake in the ground and the other witness galloped around him and so they went until the measurements were completed. They covered a lot of ground in a short time and their measurements were approximations only. Who cared? Land was so plentiful that another 100 acres, more or less, was of little moment. They set boundary markers as they went, perhaps a cow's skull in a mound of rocks, a thigh bone in a badger den, or used natural features, such as a clump of cacti or a lone oak tree. All these were duly recorded, BUT as the years rolled by, such markers were subject to weather, varmints, old age and the like. In all too many instances, they were not replaced. Land was cheap, and besides everyone knew where HIS land was and so did his fellow land owners. These crude surveys added more confusion and more opportunities for chicanery when it came time to translate them into the rectangular grid survey of the American system.

Another source of confusion and conflict stemmed from the laws pertaining to land grants adopted by Mexico on August 18, 1824, three years after independence from Spain. These set a maximum of 11 square leagues, say 48,800 acres, as the maximum that could be granted to one person — 1 league of irrigable land, 4 leagues of farming land, 6 leagues of pasture land. This maximum was exceeded in several of the grants and none of them known to this writer fulfilled the requirements for the three types of land use. Under Mexican law, NO grants were to be made within 10 lineal leagues, say 26.33 miles, of the seacoast or within 20 linear leagues of any foreign country. Many of the grants made in California violated the law by being located within 26.33 miles of the sea. Only citizens of Mexico could receive land grants; thus, the early foreigners who settled in California had to become naturalized Mexican citizens, a simple process of sworn affirmation, and become ostensible Catholics, which for many of them simply meant leaving their conscience at Cape Horn or at the summit of the Sierra Nevada or at the Yuma Crossing of the turgid Colorado River. Neither Spain nor Mexico conveyed mineral rights with a basic land grant. These were retained by the Crown or the Republic of Mexico, as the case might be. However, the Hispanic land grants that were confirmed by the United States, conveyed mineral rights with title to the land, thus giving the land grant claimant much more than he had been entitled to under the laws that governed making the original grant.

The practices employed in agriculture and animal husbandry during the Hispanic period in California and enduring well into the American period put the BEST lands in California within the Hispanic grants. The impact of this upon the settlers who flocked into California with the Gold Rush wrote an unpleasant chapter in the history of mob violence in the United States.

Solemn pledges in the Treaty of Guadalupe Hidalgo bound the United States to respect and protect all property rights, of which land grants were the most important, acquired by residents of California under the preceding governments of Spain and Mexico. Embroiled in the sectional schism over slavery, Congress had not provided land laws for California, nor had its public domain been surveyed, nor had the *Californios* been confirmed in their land titles before the Gold Rush brought the tidal wave of American emigration. Conditioned to a "farm" in humid, well-watered, woodland regions, the settlers could not grasp the necessity for the vast acreages required to sustain a pastoral society during the virtually rainless season in California between May and November of each year. The settlers "squatted" wherever they damned well chose, without regard to claims of title by the *Californios*, and they put pressure on both state and federal governments to "do something" about these monstrous claims to vast acreages. This pressure, coupled with the fact that there had been cases of fraudulent land grant claims in the Louisiana Purchase, led to the Land Title Act of March 3,1851, by which the United States compromised its treaty pledges aforementioned.

This Act threw the burden upon every claimant to a Hispanic grant to establish solid proof of valid title before the Board of Land Commissioners appointed by the Act. The commissioners' decision could be appealed to the United States District Court and could be carried to the nation's highest tribunal if such could be afforded. It became automatic procedure for the United States to appeal to the district court whenever a grant title was held to be valid. After the court's decision, if favorable to the claimant, an official survey of the grant's exterior boundaries had to be made by the United States Surveyor-General for California. Only after this survey had been approved by the General Land Office in Washington could official United States title be issued that assured the grant's claimant of solid title to his land.

Seventeen years was the average elapsed time required to obtain such assurance of ownership under the procedures outlined above. The long delay clouded title for all this time, enhanced "squatterism," and spawned the costs of prolonged litigation and travel, as the Board and the U.S. District Court both took root in San Francisco which increased the expenses of claimants from the southern section of the state. Through all these years, the claimants to the Hispanic grants bore a more onerous tax burden than did their fellow Californians. Spain and Mexico had taxed only the *produce* of the land, not the land itself. When California became a state, the burden of taxation on real property, meaning land, which had been the basis for the American tax system since the Republic began, fell most heavily upon the grant claimants, because the miners had NO real property to speak of, being nothing more or less than trespassers upon the unsurveyed public domain of the United States. To meet the expenses attendant upon proving title, the *rancheros* borrowed money at ruinous rates of interest from those who had it, such as five per cent *per month* and even higher. If the interest was not paid each month, the unpaid sum was added to the principal and it began drawing interest at the ruinous rates mentioned. *Poco a poco*, even as a mouse might gnaw at a whole wheel of cheese, these interest rates nibbled away at the patrimony of the *Californios*.

It is the combination of all these factors, rather than forcible dispossession of the grant owners, that explains why the great *ranchos* of the Hispanic period passed into other hands. Today only one of the major Hispanic land grants, the *Llano Seco* (Dry Plain) in Butte County, retains its original size.

CALIFORNIA LAND: PAST AND PRESENT

The basic unit of land area in the United States is the acre, which equals 43,560 square feet and is equivalent to slightly more than nine regular-size basketball courts or slightly more than three Olympic-size swimming pools. The other land measurement unit commonly used is the square mile, meaning a block one mile on each side, and this is equivalent to 640 acres. (In the metric system, the common unit of land area is the *hectare*, equal to 2.471 acres.) With these measurements in mind, it will be easier to comprehend the data pertaining to land in California since American acquisition of it in 1848.

Total area of California	=	101,563,500 acres
Deduct inland water area	=	1,356,780 acres
NET LAND AREA	=	100,206,720 acres

Out of this vast expanse, modern methods and techniques in agriculture and animal husbandry find only about 20% suitable for profitable or potentially profitable cultivation. Of this acreage, some 9,300,000 irrigated acres produce the greater part of the state's annual $10,000,000,000 or more in farm products income.

With the methods and techniques prevailing in the 19th century, much less acreage was suitable for profitable agricultural or animal husbandry pursuits, the latter being confined largely to grazing valley grasslands and foothill browse. This scarcity of tillable and profitable acreage accentuated the problem confronting Anglo-American settlers who were imbued with the "free land" tradition that was an integral part of it and a primary motivating force in the American move westward. It must be remembered as well that the "free land" from the Public Domain tradition had been embodied firmly in the nation's laws before the acquisition of California. The following figures are most pertinent to understanding the relative unimportance of the Public Domain as a factor in California's socio-economic development.

CALIFORNIA'S NET LAND AREA		100,206,720 Acres
Confirmed Hispanic Land grants	8,850,000	
Federal land grants to railroads	11,588,000	
SUBTOTAL		- 20,438,000 Acres

Federal Land Grants to State, 1850-1866:

For internal improvements	500,000	
For a Seminary of learning	46,080	
For an A & M College	150,000	
For support of common schools	5,534,000	
For improvement of swamp lands	2,192,875	
SUBTOTAL		8,422,955 Acres

TOTAL PUBLIC DOMAIN	71,345,765 Acres

Acreage in the Public Domain seems arithmetically ample to have provided the standard 160-acre farm for a multitude of families. However, within this acreage were classes of land that long were classified as "barren and desert," "grazing," and "forest and watershed" and totalled more than 65,000,000 acres.

There were other hard facts confronting the land-hungry settler in 19th century California. The Hispanic land grants encompassed the best agricultural lands along the coastal strip from San Francisco Bay to San Diego, and these lands by-and-large passed into the hands of large landowners and speculators. The federal grants to the State and to the railroads, the latter of which became part of the vast Southern Pacific rail network, ate up much of the best land in the Great Valley. The disposition of these lands, especially by the State of California, also tended to concentrate their ownership in a relatively few hands. Added to these patterns of concentration was the fact that fraud in the acquisition of Public Domain lands under the various federal laws pertaining thereto made another concentrating force. By 1870, 22 owners of 70,000 acres or more occupied as much land as did 23,000 owners with 500 acres or less, and the average land holding in the state was 477 acres, much higher than the average in other states, and not much lower than it is today. Bearing these facts in mind, it should be easy to understand the political voltage generated by the cry of "land monopoly" that arose after the Civil War. It was the prevalence of large tracts of land being kept idle, thus avoiding the higher tax rates that applied to "improved," meaning productive land, that produced Henry George's "single tax" theory, perhaps the most important socio-economic theory to have been produced by the California experience to date.

There are three broad categories of land ownership in California today:

Private ownership	51,269,500 Acres
Federal ownership	45,278,000 Acres
State and local government	5,016,000 Acres

It is relevant to note that ownership by various government agencies seriously affects many of the state's fifty-eight counties. Approximately 40% of Fresno, Madera, Monterey, Shasta, and Tulare counties is in federal ownership alone, while more than 50% of Imperial, Lassen, Riverside, Santa Barbara, Sierra, and Ventura fall into this category. The percentage climbs above 60% in Modoc and Siskiyou; reaches 70% or more in Plumas, San Bernardino, Trinity and Tuolumne; soars beyond 80% in Inyo and Mono, counting state ownership as well, while tiny Alpine is 90% owned by the federal government. Strange as it may seem in the densely populated southland of the state, more than one-quarter of Los Angeles and San Diego counties is in federal hands.

Land use in the state overlaps the categories of ownership given above, and the major categories of use may be of value in understanding present usage as a basis for future planning.

Forest and watershed lands	39,000,000 Acres
Grasslands and pasture lands	24,000,000 Acres
Croplands, irrigated and dry farm	11,000,000 Acres
Urban and transport systems	5,700,000 Acres
Rural parks	7,213,000 Acres
Wildlife refuges	188,000 Acres
Defense installations	8,800,000 Acres
Institutional	86,000 Acres

THE MECHANICS OF POLITICS

Party politics American-style came to California with the Gold Rush, and they made a marked change from its politics during the Mexican period. Lacking any tradition of or much practical experience in representative self-government, the *Californios* had coalesced around strong personalities, the *caudillo* pattern long evident throughout Latin America, and the web of family each possessed. (As a passing thought, we seem now to be approaching the old *Californio* pattern with television promoting the cult of personality and special interests and ideologies taking the place of the web of family.) Nineteenth century politics were quite different from those of today and several factors need to be grasped firmly to understand what went on politically from statehood until the election of Hiram W. Johnson as governor in 1910.

In those days, the party platform, which was its statement of principles — those things for which it stood — was more important by-and-large than the party candidates, who were expected to make their campaign on their party platform. It was possible then to distinguish basic differences between the two major parties, and partly loyalty was held next to godliness and cleanliness in the hearts of the party faithful. For most of those sixty years, political parties were regarded as private clubs and were outside the regulation of the state. Parties selected their candidates by their own processes; printed and distributed their own ballots at the polls, and provided their own poll watchers, although the counties did furnish election officials who were appointed by each county's Board of Supervisors.

There was no Great Register of Voters in the counties until 1866, which made it possible for the parties to vote their members early, often, and here and there, as well as voting the passenger lists from passing steamers and stagecoaches, as well as whatever tombstone names they could find and copy before election day. Despite the establishment of the Great Register, voter registration was not efficient until the 1930s. Today, with postcard registration of voters, with absentee ballots, and a sizeable transient student population entitled to vote, we may be trending toward the old days of "early and often," unless a truly master computer registration system is established in Sacramento to make it impossible.

There was no secret ballot until 1891, when the so-called "Australian ballot" was imposed by the state. It took more personal courage then than it does today to walk up to your polling place, or places if you were really dissident, get your ballot from your party representative, mark out any names you did not favor, write in those that you did, and then deposit your ballot in the box provided by your party. To prevent such "ticket splitting," in itself a violation of cherished party regularity, the party organizations went to elaborate lengths to prevent it. Each party printed its ballots in a distinctive color, or several of them, and printed the candidates' names so close together that a would-be "ticket-splitter" had a good chance of running his write-in name into another name on the ballot, which then would be declared invalid when it was counted by the party henchmen when the polls closed. The climax of this type of ballot was reached by Vallejo's Republicans in 1871 when they printed and distributed what became known as "The Tapeworm Ballot" from its size and green stripes. Measuring only 6½" x ¾", it held the names of thirty-one candidates for office, from Governor to Town Constable, plus two Constitutional amendments, all printed on *one side of the ballot*! The state entered the field in 1874 by taking over the ballot printing for all parties, providing a uniform 5" x 12" ballot, with plain black lines separating the candidates and providing room for write-ins.

The grassroots key to partisan political power was the county central committee of each party, the members of which were selected during a caucus of party members in each county. This central committee was reponsible for selecting the party candidates for county elections and it had other important duties as well. Until adoption of the so-called "federal plan" of apportioning the legislature, both houses of the legislature were elected on a population basis. Most counties were combined with other counties or parts of other counties to form joint Assembly, State Senatorial, and Congressional Districts, and it must be remembered that United States Senators were elected by the legislature until 1912. This meant that aspirants for the U.S. Senate took a personal interest in the selection and election of legislators favorable to their cause. This required that they take some interest in the delegates to the district conventions where party candidates were chosen. These delegates were chosen by the county central committee, as were the county delegates to the party's state convention where the party's candidates for state offices were selected. This method of choosing delegates at the discretion of the county central committee was not altered until 1901, when the legislature made delegate elections mandatory in the state's twelve largest cities, leaving the smaller communities and the counties to go their time-honored way. The direct primary method of determining party candidates was not established until 1909, but the central committees still exercised their influence by making pre-primary endorsements of the candidates they favored.

The state conventions were dominated in the main by one urban center, which meant the San Francisco Bay area, until the first decade of this century. For example: in one party's state convention of 830 delegates, an unwieldy number, San Francisco and its satellites sent almost 40%. Inasmcuh as San Francisco was among the most "boss" ridden municipalities in the country for many years, and its bosses were "honest" bosses who would stay bought, this meant a bloc of delegates that had to be reckoned with by anyone interested in getting something out of the convention. The small delegations — Butte 12, Ventura 9, Shasta 8, Amador 5, Lassen 2, Mono 1, for examples — played a not unimportant role. They served as trading material for their local candidates or demands; trading their votes in return for support from whatever "machine" was running the convention. For much of this sixty-year period, the "machine" was run by the Southern Pacific, whenever it felt it necessary to do so. Also, Republican delegates from such unreconstructed and irretrievably Democratic counties as Colusa, Lake, Tulare and Yolo, where no Republican could be elected dog catcher's assistant, still had trading weight value in their party's state convention. The same applied to Democratic delegates from rock-ribbed Republican counties.

At the apex of the party machinery was the State Central Committee which was selected by hook or by crook at the state convention. It appointed the Executive Committee, which managed the statewide campaign for state offices, and its members did not have to be members of the state central committee, which opened the way for shenanigans of diverse kinds. An interesting aspect of these times is that the candidates selected for state and congressional offices were assessed a fee by the Executive Committee which then proceeded to distribute these and other funds collected as it saw fit.

It was in the exercise of the mechanics of this party system that "boss" and "machine" control of the state's political life was effective. Not until political and social reformers learned to exercise similar control of party mechanics were they able to become effective. Having learned how to manage the machinery, the reformers proceeded to dismantle it after 1910. Their actions contributed immensely to the unstable nature of California politics today, a matter of perplexity to political pundits and other soothsayers. Party politics with all its faults had provided the cement that held the political process together on the basis of broad principles, whereas today we seem to have the "packaging" of trendy personalities and causes.

URBAN POLITICAL POWER

Seven counties contained 14,467 or 63% of the state's 22,835 voting precincts in the 1980 general election. These same seven counties contained 64% of the state's eligible voting population and 63% of the state's registered voters who cast 63% of the 8,781,174 votes cast.

COUNTY	PRECINCTS	VOTERS Eligible	Registered	Votes Cast	% Turnout Eligible	Regis-tered
Santa Clara	1,050	860,912	613,758	484,444	56.3	78.9
San Francisco	864	492,546	407,982	268,050	54.4	65.7
Contra Costa	671	449,214	358,881	291,155	64.8	81.1
Alameda	902	787,014	595,292	439,026	54.6	72.2
Los Angeles	6,748	4,994,610	3,262,932	2,498,064	50.0	76.6
San Diego	2,170	1,273,378	948,705	736,246	57.8	77.6
Orange	2,062	1,346,600	1,013,337	791,593	58.8	78.1

Contra Costa County had the highest percentage of votes cast to eligible voters, while the other counties generally followed the statewide pattern of an average 54.9% votes cast to eligible voters. Most of these seven counties approached the statewide average of 77.2% of votes cast to registered voters, only San Francisco and Alameda counties falling markedly short. The highest percentage in the state of votes cast to eligible voters and of votes cast to registered voters belonged respectively to Tuolumne County with 79.6% and San Benito County with 84.9%. When it is considered that 1980 was a Presidential election year, the turnout of voters as a percentage of the total eligible voters is a sorry commentary on the general populace's regard for the right of franchise.

Counties that are urban dominated have a hammerlock on the Legislature since the one man-one vote decision as the following tabulation clearly shows.

COUNTIES	STATE SENATE	ASSEMBLY	CONGRESS
S.F. Bay Area & Santa Clara	8	17	9
Sacramento, San Joaquin, Stanislaus and Yolo	3	6	3
Fresno, Tulare & Kern	3	4	3
Monterey, Santa Cruz, San Luis Obispo, Santa Barbara, Ventura	2	4	2
Los Angeles	14	28	16
Orange	3	6	3
San Diego	3	5	3
Other So. California Counties	2	6	2
Rest of State	2	4	2
Total	40	80	43*

*largest congressional delegation in the nation

The First Congressional District includes fourteen counties, stretching from the Oregon boundary to the lower Sacramento Valley, the largest Congressional District in the nation in area, while the First State Senatorial District includes fifteen counties for an even larger area. These Congressional Districts, as well as the apportionment of seats in the legislature will be redone after the 1982 general election, due to voter disenchantment with the legislature's self-serving, partisan reapportionment of seats after the 1980 census.

From the preceeding tabulation, it should be readily apparent that the urban dominated counties, particularly the megalopolitan ones, have firm control of the legislature. On matters affecting the megalopolitan areas, this should enable the cities to control legislation to correct urban problems. The hitch in this strength is the ability to put together and to maintain a cohesive alliance that will override party, sectional, and local allegiances. The above tabulation also should make clear that Southern California, the derided "cow counties" of the last century, has the votes to control both houses of the legislature. Again, the problem affecting this control is to find a common cause, other than that of obtaining more water from Northern California and anywhere else it can be found, that will bind these legislators together.

While most of the debate, both past and present, over dividing the state has concentrated on the North versus South cleavage, the tabulation of legislative seats leads to another aspect of divisive tendencies. In this aspect the division is not between North and South but between the coastal "strip" from Marin and Sonoma counties to San Diego and the interior "colony" of this coastal dominance. To date this has not produced the rhetoric that the North vs South division has engendered but it is worth remembering for future reference.

It may be useful here to dispose once and for all time of the political folklore that the two U.S. Senate seats always must be divided between Southern California and the rest of the state. Nothing in California's statutes or political tradition mandates such an equal division. There have been many times in the past and will be again, if the voters so decide, when both the U.S. Senators come from the same section of the state. Given the nature of the urban domination of the state, it appears likely that both U.S. Senators will come from Southern California with increasing frequency in future.

Californians have no reason to pat themselves on the back regarding their participation in the electoral process over the past generation. Since 1958, the *eligible* voting population has increased almost 80%, much of which was due to lowering the voting age to 18. However, the percentage of those *eligible* to vote who *actually registered* to vote has *declined* 33% in the same span of time. Even worse is the fact that the percentage of *votes cast* to *actual registered* voters also has shown a decline down these years, although this decline has not been as steep as that of eligible voters to registered voters. This decline, or apathy if you prefer, is accentuated by remembering that the United States is the only country in the world that permits residents to vote who cannot read or write the national language and thus technically are ineligible for citizenship. It has been said that self-governing people get the governments at every level that they deserve. The foregoing lines may offer an explanation why this too often proves to be the case.

HIGHLIGHTS OF CALIFORNIA POLITICS

Politics has been defined as the means of peaceably determining who gets what, how much, from whom and when! It also can be defined as the process by which we manage to curb our most carnivorous instincts in order to live in reasonable amity with our fellow humans. Both these definitions apply to California politics with the added burden of adapting them to the prolonged, intense, and unstabilizing growth that has occurred because of the interaction between restless, self-seeking humans and a bountiful supply of exploitable natural resources. The major efforts to adjust to the changes caused by growth and technology make the highlights summarized in this chapter.

San Francisco in 1851 was a brawling, swirling, masculine collection of 23,000, plus the uncounted thousands going to and returning from the mines in waves of almost tidal regularity. Its residents were intent on the main chance, as indeed were all the gold rush immigrants, and that main chance was to make a "pile" and go back home to enjoy it. Their psychology, their civic mindedness, was that of transient and hopeful seekers with little or no thought of making California their permanent home.

The city had been incorporated in 1850, with duly elected municipal officials and an established court. In 1851 it had seventy-five woefully underpaid constables, perhaps one-third of whom were on duty at any given time, and the caliber of these law officers was not of the best. It also had a well organized political machine, directed by David Broderick, of Irish extraction from New York, where he had learned the art of urban "boss" politics as practised by Tammany Hall. It had, as well, a substantial lawless element built around the "Sydney Ducks," men from the English penal colonies in Australia.

From mid-April, 1850 to mid-May, 1851, the city had seen 184 men committed to trial in the district court for crimes ranging from simple theft through armed robbery to assault and battery and murder. On July 4, 1851, only nine of these were serving sentences in the local jail, with perhaps a half-dozen more incarcerated awaiting trial. All the others had disappeared from custody by one means or another. Added to these elements was the fact that the city had been swept by a series of disastrous fires over the preceding eighteen months with perhaps the most destructive occurring on May 15, 1851. The suspicion that some of these fires had been set deliberately to aid in looting business establishments in the attendant confusion added a measureable dimension to the feeling of uneasiness and helplessness that the city's porous legal system and corrupt politics already had engendered.

A particularly brutal assault and robbery triggered the city's First Committee of Vigilance, an extra-legal association of the leading merchants and

"For the mutual protection of life and property . . ." A certificate of membership in San Francisco's second Committee of Vigilance. Note that the member was No. 3,217 enrolled therein. *— Courtesy The Bancroft Library*

small businessmen, plus clerks and others connected with commercial pursuits, numbering about 500. They were not a mob, but a well-organized, disciplined group, that kept records of its proceedings and was determined to cleanse their city of its worst criminal elements in order that they might go about the business of making their "pile" in reasonable safety. They boarded vessels arriving in the Bay, mostly those from Australia, and questioned their passengers, actually sending seven back to Australia without letting them land. They also held ninety trials in their own court, hanging four men, whipping one, banishing 28, delivering 15 to the regular authorities, and releasing the rest. With this done, the Committee disbanded of its own volition, feeling with some reason that a salutary lesson had been given the city's criminal element. The lesson was short lived.

Conditions contributing to the rise of the city's Second Committee of Vigilance in 1856 were far more complex than those that had brought about its first. A political vacuum occurred when the Whig Party, both nationally and in California, disintegrated as a major force over the issue of chattel slavery. The local vacuum was not filled by the fleeting rise of the Native American (Know Nothing) Party to state prominence in 1855, nor by the infant Republican Party which held its first meeting in the state on April 30, 1856 in Sacramento. This left the Democratic Party as the major cement in the political process and it was split into factions by the personalities and political ambitions of David C. Broderick and William M. Gwin. Gwin at this time was the state's senior U.S. Senator and Broderick would become the junior Senator in 1857; Gwin controlled federal patronage in the state and Broderick's machine controlled San Francisco. John W. Caughey summed up city matters when he wrote:

> Municipal offices fell into the hands of unprincipled persons. Scandals occurred in connection with public-works contracts, local government expenses shot up, and elections were brazenly manipulated. The courts also were notoriously corrupt . . . it was apathy of businessmen and of the people generally that made this sad state of affairs possible.

The apathy that Professor Caughey notes was born of prolonged prosperity which perpetuated the transient psychology mentioned earlier. This was given a nasty shock in 1855 with the state's first financial "panic," a far more expressive term than "depression" or "recession." Gold production had peaked at $81,000,000 in 1852, a tremendous climb from the ten millions of 1849, and then started downward, declining some 30% by 1855. Concurrently, the state became self-sufficient in wheat and flour, thus ruining many merchants who had long-term commitments for imported flour and grain, with resultant unemployment and hardship for their employees. Then the state's leading express and banking house, Adams and Co., failed, dragging other express and banking firms down with it and the shimmering golden bubble of many dreams went "pop." It was a sobering experience for

"Sharpshooters" of the Second Committee of Vigilance. — *The Oakland Museum*

those who got through it, leaving them with lowered expectations about making their "pile" in a hurry and going "home." Home now was to be California and it can be said that the Second Committee of Vigilance, whose 6,000 members hanged two men and scared many others, marks the end of the transient psychology and the beginnings of constructive citizenship in the state's largest city and its financial, commercial, and cultural heart. It also left the city the political legacy of the Peoples Independent Party which exercised a sobering influence on San Francisco's urban politics for some years.

If the split in the Democratic Party had not widened, taking on overtones of pro- and anti-slavery factions, until it culminated in the death of Broderick from a duel fought with David S. Terry, Chief Justice of the state Supreme Court and a partisan of Gwin, the Republican Party would have had a more difficult time getting started than it did. As it was, their meetings were disrupted by hecklers, using overripe eggs, rotten vegetables, and other distractions, while some enthusiasts in Sacramento put up printed posters calling them "traitors" and recommending their hanging! In some communities, the Republicans found it advisable to hold their meetings secretly behind closed doors! The animosity they engendered seems due mainly to their unequivocal opposition to the *expansion* of slavery, not its abolition, which to most Californians seemed to threaten the stability of the federal government without which there could be little chance of the long-hoped for Pacific Railroad to bind them to their countrymen two thousand miles away. They were called "Black Republicans," and "Nigger Lovers," plus choice and unprintable epithets, but even their most rabid opponents admitted that they had good men in their ranks. Among them were the Sacramento merchants — Stanford, Hopkins, Huntington, Crocker — whom the party brought into intimate contact for the first time and who would a few years later undertake the western end of the railroad that linked the nation together.

Their first presidential candidate, John C. Fremont, ran a very poor third in California in 1856, despite his popular image as the hero of the Bear Flag Revolt and despite the fact that his party in California made a determined bid for the support of *all* its minority groups, whether they could vote or not, and Negroes, Indians, and Orientals could not. They did, however, send three members to the State Senate and eleven to the Assembly. They had no luck with their first gubernatorial candidate, Edward Stanly, in 1857, or with Leland Stanford in 1859. Their big chance came with the presidential election of 1860 and they were aided immensely by Broderick's death, as he had supported Stanford for governor in 1859 and the Republicans now claimed him as a martyr to the cause of free men everywhere. Aided and abetted by Union Democrats, mostly Broderick's adherents, they carried the state's four electoral votes for Lincoln but only barely.

With the firing on Fort Sumter, the mood of the state began to swing to support of the federal Union. An oath of loyalty to the Union was required of teachers and attorneys, with no pay for teachers who did not sign it and a $1,000 fine for attorneys who did not. The Republicans made the most of this swing to the Union cause. Leland Stanford won the governorship in 1861 and the Republicans sent the first three of a long line of their party's representatives to Congress. For the next four years, a Unionist fusion of Republicans and anti-slavery, anti-secession Democrats carried the gubernatorial election in 1863 and gave Lincoln a whopping majority in 1864 over George B. McClellan, one of his former generals. With the "Stillness at Appomattox," the Unionist fusion fell apart, as many Democrats returned to their original party, and the Republicans would not be effective at the polls again until 1871, when they elected the governor, three congressmen, and gained control of the Assembly. These gains, interestingly enough, were the result of the party's opposition to unrestrained railroad practices and unrestrained Chinese immigration. With this election, the Republicans were on their way to their long period of dominance in the state's major elections. In this, California reflected what the Civil War had done for the party that had preserved the federal Union, abolished slavery in the Constitution, and settled the question whether the states or the federal government were to be all powerful — transform it from a sectional agrarian party into the national party of the new industrial and increasingly urban and technological America.

California's reaction to this new America produced political actions that affect the state today and the reaction was not long in coming, as historical time is measured. As befitted the changing nature and increased complexity of California life, there were many forces at work in the politics that produced the New Constitution of 1879. These forces found the tangible, visible focus of oppression, without which no protest movement can convince its adherents of the justness of their fight, in the Southern Pacific (Espee) and its subsidiary railroads. The Espee was politically undemocratic and economically oppressive whenever it thought its interests, as it saw them, were threatened. Of this there can be no question. On the other hand, the railroad built far more in California than it ever stifled or destroyed, but this was over the long haul of time, and human nature is hard pressed to see the long-range benefits from something that at the moment seems a menace.

The Espee was the largest landowner, largest employer, and largest taxpayer in the state. Given the unthinking tendency, one quite visible today, of automatically equating *bigness* with *badness*, the railroad was bad beyond a doubt, and its owners were the richest men in the state. It and they were popularly believed to so control the legislature, as well as local governments, that when one of them used pepper the whole state sneezed. That this monolithic control is open to serious question does not alter the popular belief of the times.

The railroad also was accused of introducing the Chinese into the state to build the Central Pacific, which was manifestly wrong, as there were more than 30,000 Chinese in California before the first dirt was moved in that road's construction. It also was held responsible for so manipulating the President and the U.S. Senate that the Burlingame Treaty with China was signed in 1868, which permitted the free and unrestricted immigration of Chinese. This again was wrong, as the Treaty was only a standard commercial treaty between sovereign nations but it did mark the first time that the Emperor of China had authorized his subjects to emigrate freely. This enabled Chinese from provinces close to the seat of imperial power to emigrate, rather than only those from the more remote southern provinces that had been in rebellion against Peking (Beijing), and Chinese immigration into California peaked some years *after* the frenzy of railroad construction had ended. The root of the Chinese/Southern Pacific connection is to be found in the fact that when the transcontinental rails were joined in 1869, some 10-12,000 Chinese construction laborers were thrown onto the general labor market.

Another factor in the anti-railroad feeling stemmed from the short-term impact of linking California with the nation. Isolated on the western edge of the continent, California had developed a remarkable manufacturing capacity, ranging from iron foundries and forges in San Francisco and the major interior cities, to boot and shoe plants, carriage makers, linen and woolen mills, flour mills and the like. With easy, fast, reasonably inexpensive rail connections with the industrial centers of the East, which had grown tremendously as a result of the Civil War's demands, California was flooded with everything she manufactured at prices her home industries could not match. The result was many business failures and resultant unemployment. Another result of rail connection with the East was to make it easier for more and more immigrants to enter the state and the majority of these were those seeking to better their condition in life, which meant competing for jobs and whatever other economic opportunities presented themselves.

Added to these discontents was a deep-rooted farmer unrest over unfair taxation, as they saw it, unfair freight rates, the competition of cheap "coolie" labor, and the evils of grain speculators and water and land monopolists. In the latter category, Henry Miller was in the process of putting together holdings of some 750,000 acres along the San Joaquin and Kern rivers and there were others with holdings as large or larger. In protest against their plight, as they saw it, the farmers around Napa organized the first Grange (Patrons of Husbandry) in the state in 1873 and within a few months there were thirty-three of them in existence around the state with their headquarters in Napa. In 1874, a successful rural drive reversed legislation which required farmers to fence their lands against wnadering livestock and required ranchers to fence their livestock in. Rural Californians in common with farmers across the nation were in the throes of the conflict between traditional agrarian values and those of industralization.

How urgent these festering discontents would have become had California's economic expansion continued unabated must remain a question. What is not a question is what happened. The terrible "Crash of '73" that devastated the financial and industrial centers of the East did not hit California until 1875. In the interim, millions of dollars in gold and silver flowed from California eastwards to alleviate the distress there. In the summer of 1875, the Comstock mines either reduced or omitted their dividends, the Bank of California, the largest and most powerful in the state, failed utterly, dragging other banks down with it, and a general financial panic gripped the state. The price of wheat, the state's major money crop, "went to Hell in a handbasket," as the old saying had it, and a severe drought gripped the state in 1876-77, causing total crop failures and causing sheepmen to lose 40% of their estimated six million head. Then, in January 1877, the famous Consolidated Virginia mine on the Comstock passed its monthly dividend, precipitating another ruinous panic which saw more than 400 businesses fail and some 30,000 men be thrown out of work. Anti-Chinese sentiment erupted throughout the state, finding its center in San Francisco, where vicious anti-Chinese riots took place. William T. Coleman, "The Lion of the Vigilantes of 1856" organized a force of 5,000 men armed with pick handles, to quell outbreaks of violence by the city's lawless element. What was not quelled was the deep-seated sense that the California dream of Canaan-on-earth, the land flowing with milk and honey, had come apart and something had to be done to restore it.

The political spearhead of the restoration movement was the Workingmen's Party, led by Denis Kearney, an Irish teamster in San Francisco, who whipped up enthusiasm at open air meetings on the city's vacant lots by advocating a little "judicious hanging" of capitalists and turned his cry of "The Chinese Must Go!" into a religion. The means of salvation was to write a new state constitution that would correct all the evils that plagued the state. The urban Workingmen's Party found widespread rural support, which was not as rabidly anti-Chinese as the Kearneyites but did want regulation of taxation and railroad rates and fares. The legislature previously had passed a measure calling for the election of delegates to a convention to frame a new constitution and the prospect of having this convention dominated by the Workingmen and the farmers scared substantial segments of the two major parties into a so-called Non-Partisan coalition to prevent it. In this they were successful, gaining 78 delegates to 51 for the Workingmen, with the other 23 split three ways.

The convention met in Sacramento for a little over five months, adjourning on March 3, 1879 with its work completed, a work that people in the East held up to scorn as a horrible example of democracy at work in Western America. As in any reasonable political gathering, its work was the result of many compromises between various extremist positions on various burning issues. Its main accomplishments were:

a)   a State Board to equalize tax valuations among the various counties, thus preventing local favoritism to railroad and other corporate interests;

b)   an elected State Railroad Commission to have jurisdiction over railroad rates and fares within the state;

c)   a specified accountability for directors and stockholders of banks and corporations doing business in the state;

d)   the eight-hour day on all public works in the state;

e)   a vicious, four-section anti-Chinese article that later was declared unconstitutional by the Supreme Court as usurping the power of the federal government, and

f)   reform of the court system by creating a Superior Court in each county.

Other items increased the minimum school year from three months to six; state school funds and taxes were to support only primary and grammar schools, thus hindering the growth of high schools; lobbying was made a felony, which came to be honored more in the breach than the observance; the governor's pardoning power was reduced; the legislature's tight control over the cities' abilities to frame their own laws was curtailed, and appropriations to benefit any religious school or hospital were prohibited.

The completed document ran to 16,000 words and its greatest defect was its endeavor to cover every possible evil that the delegates could envision happening, thus making it a detailed and circumscribing document, rather than a statement of broad policies to guide the elected representatives of the People. When the New Constitution was put to the vote of the people, it was opposed by the major corporations and newspapers in the state. The Workingmen's Party split on the matter of ratification, and only the rural vote pulled it through by a margin of 10,825 votes out of the 145,000 cast. This rural support stemmed largely from the belief that the State Board of Equalization and the State Railroad Commission would resolve their main complaints of unfair taxation and exorbitant railroad rates and fares. It would take the people of California thirty more years to make these regulatory agencies truly effective.

Thirty years may seem far too long to effect needed political changes, particularly to a generation conditioned to expecting its desires to be gratified NOW. Change, of course, can be brought about quite quickly, witness Adolf Hitler, but such totalitarianism is the death of self-government by a free people through the political process. This process in California had to cope with the unstabilizing impacts of sustained growth. In the decade after the New Constitution, the state's population increased by 40%, largely in the Bay Area counties. The nationwide "Panic of 1893" slowed the growth rate to slightly more than 22% between 1890-1900, but between 1900-1910, a tremendous acceleration occurred. The state increased some 60%, with even greater percentage increases in Southern California and the San Joaquin Valley, which became strongholds of the reform movement as this decade came to a close. This decade, too, began the rise of Los Angeles to political power, which in turn caused the polarization of the state's two great urban centers that has marked much of the present century's politics.

The anti-Chinese sentiment expressed in the unconstitutional clause of the New Constitution soon found federal expression, thanks to California's growing political muscle, in abrogation of that part of the Burlingame Treaty that granted the reciprocal right to citizens of either country to emigrate freely to the other. In 1882, Congress passed a ten-year exclusion bill against the Chinese, there being some 75,000 in the country, mostly in California, which was followed by the Scott Act in 1888, which prohibited the re-entry into this country of Chinese laborers who had gone back to China for a visit. In 1892, the Geary Act extended exclusion for another ten years and exclusion was made permanent in 1901. It was not repealed until 1943, when both countries were wartime allies against Japan.

Agrarian hopes that the state agencies established by the New Constitution would bring about effective tax equalization and railroad regulation were not realized. The Espee's alliances with whatever party was in power in Sacramento, plus its working arrangements with San Francisco's procession of "bosses," gave it strong representation on, if not outright control of, the elected four-member Board of Equalization and the three-member Railroad Commission. It also began to take a direct interest in the election of judicial officers, regarding the courts as its last line of defense should it lose control of the regulatory agencies. Generally prosperous conditions in this period, not "boom" times but not hardship years either, contributed to voter apathy, but this general prosperity did not reach the farmer. All through this period, he saw the prices he received at the farm gate decline steadily, and in this he shared the experience of farmers throughout the nation. The farmer, even today, is not a price-fixer but a price taker. This explains why the farmers of California were prominent in the next protest movement, even though its origins and initial strength were urban. This rural-urban fusion was similar to that which had produced the New Constitution, and it should be remembered, both to understand the past and for future guidance, that the basic interests of rural producer and urban consumer are fundamentally opposite. The farmer wants high prices for food produced: the urban resident wants low prices for food consumed.

In 1888, Edward Bellamy's utopian novel *Looking Backward* inspired a socialist, evangelical movement with a strong tinge of spiritualism called Nationalism. It became more prominent in California than elsewhere in the nation, and especially in Southern California. The Nationalists called for government control of transportation and communication, direct election of

U.S. Senators, municipal ownership of utilities, the Australian (secret) ballot, the initiative and referendum to restore political power to the people, and made a nod in the direction of women's suffrage. They and their program became assimilated by the Farmer's Alliance, which also sought to remove corruption in the legislature, and it in turn became swallowed by the Peoples' Party, or Populists, in 1891. This soon became a statewide third party with enough political "clout" to make it and its platform attractive to the Democrats, who saw a chance to gain strength in traditionally Republican strongholds through fusion with the Populists.

The Populists were coy towards the Democratic wooing, possible because the Panic of 1893 gave impetus to their efforts to enlist more urban labor support. This was followed by the nationwide railroad strike of 1894 which added fuel to the Populists' belief that a vigorous farmer-labor party could become the balance wheel in California politics. Although the Populists elected eight Assemblymen in the 1893 election, most of them with Democratic support, the 1894 election was a Republican landslide, save for James H. Budd, who became the last Democratic governor for forty-four years. In 1896, the Populists and the Democrats came together on the issue of making silver coins legal money again and coining it in "free and unlimited" amounts. In actuality, this was a demand for inflation, cheap money, using a precious metal, silver, not the paper currency of today, to accomplish this end. This tolled the death knell of the Populists as an effective third party in California, but they had paved the way for the most successful reform movement in the state's hustory, a movement that saw the Southern Pacific cast as the villainous "Octopus" that was strangling the whole state in its tentacles.

The Espee's role stemmed from the fact that it had been too successful in doing what was and is done by every special-interest group — be they farmers, trade unions, corporations, civil rights activists, environmentalists, or Friends of the Double-Jawed Nutcracker — use the political process to attain its goals and protect its interests. Until 1893, it had operated more-or-less behind the scenes, maintaining a low profile, and working through political personalities, bosses and their machines. Then it established a Political Bureau within its corporate structure under William F. Herrin, a San Francisco lawyer, Democrat and practicing Catholic. He operated the Political Bureau as a business, dispensing favors in return for results. This gave the Espee a high visibility in matters political and Herrin's henchmen had all the delicacy of a butcher cutting meat on his block when it came to applying economic and political pressures to get what they wanted. Coupled with this mistake in the then unknown field of public and community relations was Herrin's failure to recognize the growing power of Southern California in general and Los Angeles especially, which is where the effective cleansing of California politics began.

The Southland's phenomenal growth after 1887 came mainly from mid-

William F. Herrin, head of the Southern Pacific's Political Bureau, which was believed to control the state's politics for its own ends. — *Southern Pacific Co.*

western, conservative Republican origins. They were addicted to temperance measures and equated Democrats with the sinful goings on in San Francisco, a city which no young lady should visit without a chaperone. Los Angeles became the first California city (1902) to adopt the initiative, referendum, and recall in its government, and was the first American city to recall an elected official, a councilman in 1904. A similar "good government" movement (1897) in San Francisco elected James D. Phelan as Mayor, but when his term expired it left a vacuum which was filled promptly by Abraham Ruef, the "Boodling Boss," and his "Musical Mayor," Eugene Schmitz, who raised political graft to the status of a fine and expensive art. Sacramento elected reform mayors in 1900 and 1902, while Oakland elected an anti-Espee Mayor in 1902, George C. Pardee, who as governor (1903-1906) would earn the title of "Father of the State Highway System." These reformers fell into two broad groups — political/moral and social/economic — which blended as well as oil and water. Their pathway to success began with the realization that political democracy had to precede social democracy in order to abolish urban political immorality and the Espee's political apparatus.

The direct result of the Espee's ham-handed conduct of the Republican State Convention at Santa Cruz in 1906 and its equally blunt manipulation of the legislature of 1907 was formation of the Lincoln-Roosevelt League of Republican Clubs at a meeting in Los Angeles, May 21, 1907, with a following meeting in Oakland three months later. This organization operated outside the regular party framework and was composed of conservative anti-railroad Republicans, discontented farmers throughout the state, and the reform elements in the cities mentioned earlier, of which those in Los Angeles and adjacent counties were the most numerous. Its primary purposes were to restore morality to public office and political power to the people, and it was anti-Chinese and anti-organized labor. It quickly gained widespread newspaper support from Republican journals, and it boasted a high proportion of professional men in its membership, which was predominantly middle class, of North European extraction and Protestant. It was born, grew and succeeded in a period of expanding prosperity in California which makes it unusual in the roster of effective protest or reform movements.

By 1909, it had enough strength in the legislature, thanks to the support of anti-railroad Democrats, to secure passage of a law requiring party candidates to be chosen in a primary election, rather than the convention system, and this resulted in 1910 in what still can be regarded as the most significant primary election in California's history. The L-R League was able to get the candidate it wanted in Hiram W. Johnson, a successful attorney who had gained statewide attention through his prosecution of Ruef and his minions for graft in San Francisco's civic affairs. Alden Anderson, then State Superintendent of Banks, was thought to be the Espee's choice,

"YOU ARE A STUFFED JURY; WE HAVE STUFFED YOU. NOW GIVE US OUR VERDICT."

Before election Mayor Phelan made a criminal contract to deliver control of the Police Department to A. M. Lawrence. After election the Mayor sought to evade the payment of the price that had been exacted in his dishonorable bargain. Lawrence had several conferences with him and came to the conclusion that the Mayor intended to give him the "double cross." He then sought Garret W. McEnerney, and with him went to the Mayor to demand that which his Honor had criminally promised and what he sought as a trickster to withhold. At that conference McEnerney used the quoted words and Mayor Phelan kept his ante-election, felonious bond.

California politics never has been a game for those with weak stomachs or thin skins. Here Mayor James D. Phelan of San Francisco is charged with election shenanigans to gain the office.   — *Courtesy The Bancroft Library* and three other Republicans entered the primary field, something that would have been impossible under the convention system. Johnson campaigned tirelessly throughout the state in a red Locomobile touring car, thus showing his independence of the railroad, and he hammered one theme and one theme only, "Kick the Southern Pacific Out of Politics." When the votes were tallied, Johnson took the nomination with 47% of the vote, and this primary vote remains a political curiosity, became more Republican votes were cast in the primary than the party polled in the general election.

His Democratic opponent in the general election, Theodore A. Bell of Napa, was as anti-railroad as Johnson, but his cause suffered when the Espee threw its support to him, as being preferable to "Holy Hiram." Bell's campaign also suffered because of his harping on a wide range of reform issues. Johnson stuck to the tried and true slogan of getting the railroad out of politics and it worked, thus starting Johnson on an unequalled career of thirty-five years as governor and U.S. Senator. Republicans continued their control of the legislature and enough of them were reform-minded to ensure that the progressive element in the party would be dominant. With this election, the Espee's "Octopus" image became a reminder of what did and still can happen whenever the voters let the apathy of affluence and sheer physical laziness permit "boss" or "special interest" rule to come again.

Flushed with victory and convinced of the righteousness of their purposes, the Johnsonians proceeded to stand California on its political head and shake it vigorously. They made the only massive revision of the New Constitution of 1879 and of the state's statutes that has come about to date, and certain of the things they did still affect us today. Among these were putting teeth in the State Board of Equalization and the Railroad Commission, the latter becoming today's Public Utilities Commission. A workmen's compensation law was enacted and the doctrine of employer's liability became law, as did the eight-hour day for women workers. Political patronage was removed from most state jobs by the adoption of civil service legislation; the first state budget was adopted, indeed the first such for any state, and a State Conservation Commission was established. In addition to these worthy measures were those that virtually gutted the traditional party structure and gave the state ample opportunities to indluge in the politics of confusion that have puzzled political pundits ever since.

The election of judges and state educational officers was made non-partisan and this was extended later to ALL city and county offices, thus cutting off grass-roots support for party programs and party regularity. Party endorsement of candidates in primary elections was prohibited, which was another blow to party solidarity and support. To re-establish grassroots support and provide a means of developing good young candidates, unofficial party organizations arose which did make pre-primary endorsements and performed many of the tasks that the official party structures once had done. These were the California Republican Assembly (1934) and the

California Democratic Council (1953), while the two most prominent names to come out of these groups to date have been Earl Warren and Alan Cranston.

To restore political power to the people, the initiative, referendum, and recall were adopted, thus providing the voters with the means of initiating legislation, repealing legislation, and removing elected officials from office for due cause. These had the unforeseen effect, as the years rolled by, of enabling the legislature to "get off the hook" of taking a stand on legislation that might affect their political future. A good example of this was Proposition 13 (1976) which was voter reaction to the legislature's shilly-shallying and dilly-dallying over tax-reduction measures. Careful personal attention to the measures presented to the voters at both statewide and local elections will ensure that the initiative process is not used to bypass duly elected legislative and governing bodies on behalf of some special cause of interest. The recall provision especially irritated conservative Republicans who had supported Johnson because of his and their anti-railroad stand. This irritation became alienation when Johnson became Theodore Roosevelt's vice presidential running mate on the Progressive Party ticket in 1912, and "Holy Hiram" saw the writing on the wall.

He bulled a measure through the legislature enabling candidates to file on any and every party ticket that they wished in the primary election, without showing their party affiliation on any ballot. Johnson intended to be re-elected governor in 1914, whether the Republican party wanted him or not; he KNEW that the voters did, irrespective of party. In the 1914 primary election, Johnson had NO opposition on the Progressive Party ticket that he headed and he swamped the opposition in the general election with almost 50% of the total vote cast. The adoption of cross-filing was a blow to party regularity and party discipline from which it has never recovered, and it contributed immensely to the "cult of personality" that seems dominant in state politics today, as well as on the national scene.

After World War II, cross-filing became a rankling thorn in the side of California's Democrats, who saw their voter registration surpass that of the Republicans, who kept getting elected and re-elected just the same. This led to pious Democratic outcries that cross-filing operated to benefit the incumbent, which was true in the sense that incumbency always is an asset in getting re-elected and most of the incumbents in California then were Republicans, who were rather smug about the whole affair. The political theory behind the Democratic protests was that elimination of cross-filing would enforce party responsibility for adopting and supporting party programs. In any state other than California, a "big wayward girl" politically, this might have been true. When the Democrats finally gained control of the legislature, the primary election of 1958 became the last one in which Johnson's self-serving legacy of cross-filing was employed.

Two matters mentioned earlier — the election of the legislature on a

Senator T. R. Bard waged a vigorous fight to purge corrupt patronage practices from the state, which led him into a bitter fight with the state's other Senator, George C. Perkins, over the removal of Joseph Lynch as collector of internal revenue in San Francisco.   — *Author's Collection*

population basis from 1849 onwards, and the rise of Los Angeles in numbers and economic stature — have great bearing on the next political highlight. Between 1920-1930, the state's population increased by almost 66% but that of Los Angeles, city and county, jumped 136%. As this was going on, San Francisco and the northern rural counties took steps to ensure that Los Angeles would not dominate the legislature when it was re-apportioned following the Census of 1930. This was called the "Federal Plan," to give it the status of the Constitution's provissions by which the two Houses of Congress were elected. It should be noted here, however, that the relationship of county to state is quite different from that of state to federal government.

The San Francisco-rural coalition qualified an initiative measure for the general election of 1926 and it passed by a thumping majority, with support from Southern California counties that feared Los Angeles. This measure called for the Assembly still to be apportioned on a population basis but called for the State Senate to be so distributed that NO county could have more than one Senator and no more than three counties could be combined in a Senatorial District. Under this plan, San Francisco would lose six Senate seats but the northern rural counties would gain, which was infinitely preferable to a gain for Los Angeles. The Angelenos promptly invoked the referendum procedure and, to their dismay, the federal plan was upheld handsomely; again with support from southland counties that feared the all-swallowing sprawl of Los Angeles. The matter then was challenged unsuccessfully in the courts which delayed its effective date until 1932.

In the meantime, the legislature had been re-apportioned following the Census of 1930 and Los Angeles thereby gained eight additional Assembly districts, while the southland as a whole now contained forty-two of the eighty Assembly districts. The barrier to Southern California's domination of the legislature now was in the Senate, thanks to the federal plan, with which was coupled the fact that until Los Angeles came to dominate the southland by its control of Colorado River water through the Metropolitan Water District, it could not count on solid support from its neighboring counties.

The federal plan was attacked three times through the election process over the next thirty years and it was upheld by the voters each time. Then in 1962, the U.S. Supreme Court under Chief Justice Earl Warren, handed down its famous "one man — one vote" decision in a case involving Tennessee, and by 1966 the legislature had been re-apportioned to give Southern California complete control, if its counties and warring political factions could agree on any issue other than more water wherever it could be found. This unity was shown clearly in 1960, when California's voters approved the largest bond issue ever passed by any state to build Oroville Dam and the delivery system to carry its water to Southern California. This was quite a change from the two-to-one vote in Los Angeles against the Central Valley Project with Shasta Dam as its keystone, when the state began it in the

1930s and had to turn it over to the Bureau of Reclamation because the state no longer could finance it due to what properly can be called the Great Depression.

This prolonged period of economic and social collapse can be termed the most traumatic experience in American history. It caused the American attitude towards government to change to the belief that government at all levels had a responsibility for the welfare of each citizen and should regulate the economy to prevent such a disaster from happening again. It ushered in a period of Democratic supremacy in national politics and it changed California to preponderantly Democratic in voter registration, if not in candidate loyalty. California suffered less, perhaps, than other parts of the nation, experiencing far fewer bank failures, for example, but it was bad enough, particularly in Southern California.

This was due to severe cutbacks in the oil, film, and automobile industries there, coupled with the fact that a larger proportion of its population were retired or semi-retired and their sources of income simply dried up. One reaction to this was to station sheriff's deputies at Cajon Pass to turn back refugees from the Dust Bowl, the "Okies" and "Arkies" of John Steinbeck's famous novel, *The Grapes of Wrath*. Another was to repatriate as many of the Mexican population as could be induced to accept free transportation to the border, whence they promptly returned. Over and above these symbolic bandages on a festering problem was the rise of what only can be termed "Pension politics," an array of monetary panaceas that gave rise to the later notion that the United States had been picked up by the eastern seaboard and everything loose had slid into Southern California.

The Townsend plan was a proposal by a retired Long Beach doctor to give $200 a month to every person over sixty, with the provisios that recipients could not perform gainful labor and had to spend this money within thirty days. This was to be financed by a federal sales tax. What became known as "Ham 'n Eggs," or "Thirty Dollars Every Thursday," called for each unemployed Californian over fifty to receive thirty, one-dollar pieces of scrip every Thursday. On the back of each piece were spaces for fifty-two, two-cent stamps, one to be affixed each week by whomever was holding the piece of paper at the time. This was supposed to guarantee rapid circulation of the scrip and provide four cents per piece for the administrative costs at the end of each year when the state was obligated to redeem the scrip at face value. More important politically than these, or any of the almost eighty other "old age welfare schemes" that marked the California scene in the depression years was Upton Sinclair's bold bid for the governorship in 1934 with his End Poverty in California (EPIC) plan.

Sinclair's plan differed from the simple money schemes because it called for a complete restructuring of the economic order in California, and by extension the nation. A longtime Socialist in his political beliefs and a brilliant muckraking journalist and author with *The Jungle* and other novels,

Sinclair changed his registration to Democratic, established a grassroots organization that swept Southern California like wildfire in ripe wheat, started a newspaper that reached almost 1,500,000 circulation, and scared the regular Democrats, to say nothing of the Republicans, out of their wits. Sinclair won the Democratic primary "going away," as they say of a horse that wins by a large margin. This compounded the fears of the state's major parties and was reflected in Washington by President Franklin D. Roosevelt's hands-off attitude towards Sinclair. The problem was aggravated by the fact that Raymond Haight, a former Republican, had won the Progressive and Commonwealth party primaries, which meant a three-way general election in November.

The Republican candidate, Frank F. Merriam, had succeeded to the governorship upon the death of James "Sunny Jim" Rolph, and he hired a young advertising firm to handle his campaign against Sinclair. Composed of Clem Whitaker and Leone Baxter, later husband-and-wife, they were the first and for a long time foremost in the by now numerous field of professional campaign managers. They gave Merriam the first mass media campaign in the state's history and this, plus the gnawing fear that Sinclair was, indeed, a radical revolutionist, brought Merriam the victory in November with 49% of the vote cast. This makes it possible to note that no extremist ever has captured major political office in California since it became a state. This also makes a suitable place to note that despite such measures as unemployment insurance and Social Security, pension politics in California endured into the 1960s, when more state and federal legislation affecting the elderly took away their direct appeal.

Despite both federal and state measures to end the depression, they only alleviated its worst aspects. In common with the rest of the nation, California did not really begin to revive economically until the advent of World War II in Europe stimulated demand for American products, including California foodstuffs and aircraft, and caused a marked upsurge in expenditures for national defense. Direct involvement in the war brought the state such growth that its impact was the equivalent of what the Gold Rush had done almost a century before. It brought the state a period of nonpartisan politics, exemplified by Earl Warren's election in 1942 to the first of his unprecedented three terms as governor and by marked success in the use of the cross-filing technique. A manpower shortage due to military service requirements and the demand for manpower caused by the mushrooming war-related industries brought the state a tremendous increase in both its Negro and Hispanic populations. These increases have continued ever since, augumented by an influx from Southeast Asia after Vietnam, and have caused "ethnic politics" to become an important element of the California political scene.

Wartime wrote a dark chapter in the history of American civil liberties and California was responsible for most of the writing. This was the internment of 113,000 Japanese residents on the mainland United States, of whom almost 94,000 lived in California. Of these, 33,569 were Japanese-born and 60,148 were United States-born, with the latter category being entitled to American citizenship. The unexpected Japanese attack upon Pearl Harbor, the American naval base in the then Territory of Hawaii, triggered an outbreak of hysteria in California which added impetus to demands for Japanese incarceration. Behind it was the deep-rooted California animosity towards Orientals that began with the anti-Chinese actions of Gold Rush years and reached its peak in the anti-Chinese rhetoric and physical persecution of the 1870s. It smoldered beneath the surface thereafter, despite the Chinese Exclusion Act mentioned earlier.

Emigration from Japan did not reach measurable proportions until the period 1901-1910, when 130,000 entered this country, more than one-third the total number of such emigrants between 1861-1969, many of whom settled in California. Hard working, thrifty, and more aggressive in economic advancement than had been the Chinese, particularly in the matter of land acquisition, the Japanese caused the legislature to pass the Alien Land Law in 1913, which was amended and extended by the initiative process in 1920, and by the legislature in 1923 and 1927. California pressure was instrumental in getting federal exclusion of Japanese immigration in 1924, which was a slap in the face to Japan's national honor. Given this California background, and the national reaction to the "sneak attack" upon Pearl Harbor, it is not surprising, as Professor Clarence McIntosh has written, that "hate mongers and patriots by radio and press revived the Japanese issue and that minor politicians sought to make political capital out of the circumstances." In point of fact, any politician who *openly* opposed Japanese internment would have committed political suicide thereby, Governor Culbert Olson succumbed to the pressure for internment and Earl Warren, then the state's Attorney General and a candidate to succeed Olson, upheld its legality.

On February 19, 1942, President Roosevelt issued an executive order authorizing the removal of Japanese without charges or trials from strategic areas on the grounds of military necessity. California's Japanese were sent primarily to internment camps at Tule Lake in the far northeastern part of the state and in the Owens Valley east of the true High Sierra. Japanese property losses from their forced relocation and internment approached $400,000,000 and claims for these losses finally were settled after the war for about 10c on the dollar. Not one Japanese was convicted of espionage activity; the Japanese in Hawaii were not relocated or interned, and the army unit formed from the Japanese in Hawaii became the most decorated American unit in the European theater of the war. Interestingly enough, Mexico, which was not at war with Japan, ordered the relocation of the Japanese on its Pacific Coast on the day after Pearl Harbor, and Canada, although not at war with Japan before Pearl Harbor followed suit forthwith.

California's growth during the war and immediate post-war years is shown dramatically in the growth of the state budget from about $395,000,000 in 1943-44 to well over $1,000,000,000 ten years later. This growth has continued, although at a slower pace, and this has maintained the unstabilizing effects of growth that have been a salient feature of state politics since 1850. It also is a state of multiple economic interests, and of pronounced regional and sectional needs and desires, rural vs. urban and urban vs. urban. It is blessed or cursed as the case may be with numerous social and political philosophies, each with its own passionate adherents, that amount to political pandemonium, and make strong leadership through unification of supporters extremely difficult. The moral crises that racked the nation over civil rights and Vietnam had major support in California and further confused the political picture.

The well-weakened structures of the major political parties have been further fractured by intra-party squabbles between liberals and conservatives, moderates and extremists. These same bickerings have impaired the usefulness of the California Republican Assembly and the California Democratic Council. The emergence of television as the principal weapon in political campaigning has increased its cost, separated the candidates from direct contact with the voters, and contributed immensely to the packaging of candidates and issues like so many boxes of breakfast foods. Television also has diminished the influence of newspapers in the political arena and provided "single interest" groups with a way to dramatize their cause through "confrontation politics," which promote gut reactions rather than rational thought. If the unstable nature of California politics has one redeeming feature it may be that expressed by Houston Flournoy, who lost a close contest for governor to "Jerry" Brown in 1974. "Came to California in 1957 ," he said, "and was elected to the legislature in 1960. Here, nobody controls the system, so anybody can get into it."

This free-for-all nature of post-war politics in California makes it difficult to select its highlights, but three seem important enough to mention here. Such things as the Watts Riot in August 1965 and the so-called Free Speech Movement at Berkeley in 1964, which spread to other California campuses and then nationwide, produced a voter reaction that helped Ronald Reagan gain and hold the governor's office for eight years and made S.I. Hayakawa, then president of San Francisco State College, a U.S. Senator ten years later in his first effort to gain any elective office.

For the past twenty years, the dominant practical issue in California politics has been WATER! Governor Edmund G. Brown regarded passage of the bond act that provided for Oroville Dam and the delivery system for its water as the crowning glory of his long and honorable political career. His son, Edmund G. Brown, Jr., committed himself firmly to but one thing known to this writer — construction of the Peripheral Canal in the Sacramento-San Joaquin Delta as the best means of solving the water shortage problem that confronts both the state's most populous region and its most productive agricultural counties. Defeat of a ballot measure in 1982 authorizing the Canal's construction did not remove some form of trans-Delta water transportation system from the political spectrum.

In the past decade, California has enacted the most stringent measures to protect and preserve the environment of any state in the nation, and probably of any nation in the world. These measures are significant not only for what they purport to do but for what they imply. Taken in conjunction with the "small is beautiful" philosophy once expressed by Governor "Jerry" Brown, they indicate that there is a substantial, extremely vocal and militantly active segment of Californians who want to slow down or halt entirely the "Dance of Growth" that has made California the Mecca of those seeking to better their condition in life since 1841. If they are successful in doing this, the future of California politics will become stable, structured, and stratified, and thus altogether different than it has been since Hiram Johnson and the Progressives destroyed the effectiveness of "boss rule" and political party structure more than seventy years ago.

BIBLIOGRAPHY

REFERENCE

Beck, Warren A., and Ynez D. Haase. *Historical Atlas of California.* Norman: University of Oklahoma Press, 1974.

Donley, Michael W., and others. *Atlas of California.* Culver City, California: Pacific Book Center, 1979.

Geiger, Maynard J. *Franciscan Missionaries in Hispanic California, 1769-1848; a Biographical Dictionary.* San Marine: Huntington Library, 1969.

Gudde, Erwin G. *California Gold Camps: a Geographical and Historical Dictionary of Camps, Towns, and Localities Where Gold Was Found and Mined; Wayside Stations and Trading Centers.* Edited by Elisabeth K. Gudde, Berkeley: University of California Press, 1975.

Gudde, Erwin G. *California Place Names: The Origin and Etymology of Current Geographical Names. Third Edition.* Berkeley: University of California Press, 1969.

Hart, James D. *A Companion to California.* New York: Oxford University Press, 1978.

Hoffman, Abraham. *Vision or Villainy: Origins of the Owens Valley – Los Angeles Water Controversy.* College Station: Texas A & M Press, 1981.

Hoover, Mildred B. and others. *Historic Spots in California* (Third ed. revised by William N. Abeloe) Stanford University Press; 1966.

Kahrl, William L., ed. *The California Water Atlas.* Los Altos, California: William Kaufmann, Inc., 1978, 1979. (The title page states "State of California" but it was printed privately.)

Melendy, H. Brett, and Benjamin F. Gilbert. *The Governors of California; Peter H. Burnett to Edmund G. Brown, Sr.* Georgetown, California: The Talisman Press, 1965.

COLLECTION OR ANTHOLOGY

Caughey, John and Laree. *California Heritage; An Anthology of History and Literature. Revised Edition.* Itasca, Illinois: F.E. Peacock Publishers, 1971.

Caughey, John and LaRee. *Los Angeles; Biography of a City.* Berkeley: University of California Press, 1976.

Haslam, Gerald W., and James D. Houston, editors. *California Heartland; Writings from the Great Central Valley.* Santa Barbara: Capra Press, 1978.

Heizer, R.F., and M.A. Whipple. *The California Indians; A Source Book*. Revised Edition. Berkeley: University of California Press, 1971.

Knoles, George H., editor. *Essays and Assays: California History Reappraised*. San Francisco: California Historical Society, 1973.

Sturtevant, William C., general editor. *Handbook of North American Indians. Volume 8. California*. Volume editor: Robert F. Heizer. Washington: Smithsonian Institution, 1978.

OTHER

Adams, Kramer. *The Redwoods*. New York: Popular Library, 1969.

Cleland, Robert Glass. *This Reckless Breed of Men; The Trappers and Fur Traders of the Southwest*. Albuquerque: University of New Mexico Press, 1976.

Daniels, Roger. *The Politics of Prejudice; the Anti-Japanese Movement in California and the Struggle for Japanese Exclusion*. New York: Atheneum, 1968.

DeVoto, Bernard. *Year of Direction: 1846*. Boston: Little, Brown & Co., 1943.

Egan, Ferol. *Fremont: Explorer for a Restless Nation*. Garden City, New York: Doubleday &Company, Inc., 1977.

Galarza, Ernesto. *Barrio Boy*. Notre Dame: University of Notre Dame Press, 1971.

Geiger, Maynard J. *The Life and Times of Fray Junipero Serra, O.F.M.; or, The Man Who Never Turned Back, 1713-1784, A Biography*. 2 Volumes. Washington: Academy of American Franciscan History, 1959.

Holliday, J.S. *The World Rushed In*. New York, Simon & Schuster, 1981. (The most comprehensive account of individual experiences in the Gold Rush known to this author.)

Hundley, Norris, Jr. *Dividing the Waters: A Century of Controversy Between the United States and Mexico*. Berkeley: University of California Press, 1966.

Hutchinson, W.H. *Oil, Land and Politics: The California Career of Thomas Robert Bard*. 2 Volumes. Norman: University of Oklahoma Press, 1965.

Jackson, Donald Dale. *Gold Dust*. New York: Alfred A. Knopf, 1980.

Jelinek, Laurence J. *Harvest Empire; a History of California Agriculture*. San Francisco: Boyd & Fraser Publishing Company, 1979.

Kirker, Harold. *California's Architectural Frontier; Style and Tradition in the Nineteenth Century*. Santa Barbara and Salt Lake City: Peregrine Smith, Inc., 1973.

Kroeber, Theodora. *The Inland Whale.* Berkeley: University of California Press, 1964.

Lapp, Rudolph. *Afro-Americans in California.* San Francisco: Boyd & Fraser Publishing Company, 1979.

Lewis, Oscar. *The Big Four; the Story of Huntington, Stanford, Hopkins, and Crocker, and the Building of the Central Pacific.* New York: A.A. Knopf, 1938.

Lillard, Richard G. *Eden in Jeopardy; Man's Prodigal Meddling with His Environment: the Southern California Experience.* New York: Knopf, 1966.

Lotchin, Roger W. *San Francisco, 1846-1856: From Hamlet to City.* Lincoln: University of Nebraska Press, 1979. (Paperback edition. Original edition was Oxford University Press.)

McGloin, John B., S.F. *San Francisco: The Story of a City.* San Rafael & London, Presidio Press, 1978.

INDEX